GW00401802

HARDPRESS.NET
HOME OF HARD-TO-FIND BOOKS

A History of the Lives, Sufferings, and
Triumphant Deaths, of the Primitive as Well as
the Protestant Martyrs, from the Commencement
of Christianity to the Latest Periods of Pagan and
Popish Persecution
by John Foxe

Address:
HardPress
8345 NW 66TH ST #2561
MIAMI FL 33166-2626
USA
Email: info@hardpress.net

00, 20, 33

A

HISTORY

OF THE

LIVES, SUFFERINGS,

AND

TRIUMPHANT DEATHS,

OF THE

PRIMITIVE AS WELL AS THE PROTESTANT MARTYRS,

FROM THE

COMMENCEMENT OF CHRISTIANITY

TO THE

LATEST PERIODS OF PAGAN AND POPISH PERSECUTION.

TO WHICH IS ADDED

AN ACCOUNT OF THE INQUISITION: THE BARTHOLOMEW MAS-A
CRE; THE MASSACRE IN FRANCE AND GENERAL PERSECU-
TION UNDER LOUIS XIV.; THE MASSACRES OF THE
IRISH REBELLION IN THE YEAR 1641; AND THE
RECENT PERSECUTIONS OF PROTEST-
ANTS IN THE SOUTH OF FRANCE.

ORIGINALLY COMPOSED BY THE

REV. JOHN FOX, A. M.

ILLUSTRATED EDITION

DETROIT:
KERR, DOUGHTY & LAPHAM.
1853.

HISTORY

OF

CHRISTIAN MARTYRDOM.

PART I.

CHAPTER I.

First Persecution of the Christians and Martyrdom of the Apostles.

No prediction of our Saviour has been more strikingly fulfilled, than that which related to the persecution and sufferings of his people, by reason of their faithfulness and love to him. These things he bequeathed to them, as a portion of their inheritance in this world; and, lest they should become disheartened at the complicated scenes of human misery that awaited them, he not only apprised them, that they should be hated of all men for his name sake, but pronounced a glorious benediction upon all such as should be found worthy to suffer on his account. These gracious promises he often repeated to them, during the days of his public ministry, and renewed them again after his glorious resurrection from the dead, accompanied with assurance of the aid and support of his Holy Spirit, which should dwell with them as a comforter until the end of the world: nor was it long after his ignominious death and glorious ascension to heaven, that they were brought to feel the truth of what he had so often told them. For, notwithstanding the purity of that religion that they professed, which taught them to live peaceably with all men, and to do unto others, as they would that others should do unto them; still, inasmuch as its sublime doctrines and precepts were directly at war with the natural propensities of the human heart, and set forth the one Living and True God as the only object of adoration, through Jesus

1*

Christ his only begotten son; the enmity and rage of both Jews and heathens, was soon aroused against them.

From the time of the crucifixion of our Saviour, to the day of Pentecost, which occurred fifty days after, it appears that the Apostles, together with the other disciples of Jesus, enjoyed a respite from persecution, and were suffered to assemble themselves together for worship unmolested; but when on that memorable day, they spoke boldly in the name of Jesus, and their converts began to be numbered by thousands, the envy and bigotry of their Jewish friends were at once awakened, and a regular system of persecution and opposition to the progress of the gospel was commenced.

This, however, was for a while carried on by gentle means, which proving ineffectual, the increasing enmity of the people at length broke out into open outrage, and more than two thousand Christians perished within the city of Jerusalem.

St. Stephen.

Martyrdom of St. Stephen.

This eminent saint, was the first who suffered death for embracing the religion of Jesus Christ, and therefore was crowned with the immortal honour of being the man who led the van of that glorious band of Christian martyrs that soon followed after.

He was one of the seventy disciples of Jesus, and was chosen, with six others, to officiate as deacon in the church at Jerusalem. Being a very zealous and faithful witness for his Lord and Master; several of the principal persons belonging to five of the Jewish synagogues, entered into an argument with him, on the principles of the religion that he professed, and being unable to withstand the soundness of his doctrines, were greatly irritated; and to gratify their revenge, they suborned false witnesses, who accused him of blaspheming God, and the law of Moses. He was accordingly brought before a council, when he made a noble defence, proving from the scripture of the Old Testament, that Jesus of Nazareth, whom they had crucified and slain, was no other than the true Messiah. At this they were very much enraged, and were about to pass sentence upon him, when he saw a vision from heaven, disclosing to his view, the Lord and Saviour in his glorified state. He exclaimed in rapture, " Behold I see the heavens open, and the Son of Man standing on the right hand of God." Still more enraged at this, they immediately passed sentence upon him, and dragged him out and stoned him to death. He died like his divine Master, imploring mercy for his murderers; saying, " Lord, lay not this sin to their charge." On the place where he was martyred, the Empress Eudocia afterward caused a magnificent church to be erected to his memory. Being put to death, on the 26th day of December, it is consequently observed in commemoration of this event.

St. James the Great.

This disciple was by birth a Galilean, and the son of Zebedee, a fisherman. He was also the elder brother of John, and related to the Lord himself; his mother, Selome, being cousin-german to the Virgin Mary. Being one day engaged with his father, fishing in the sea of Galilee, he was called by the Saviour, with his brother John, to become his disciple. They cheerfully obeyed the mandate, and leaving their father in the vessel, became the followers of Jesus.

It is to be observed, that their Divine Master, placed greater confidence in them together with the apostle Pe-

ter, than in the rest of his disciples; as he always took
them with him, to the exclusion of the rest, when he was
about to make any peculiar disclosure of his power.   He
also surnamed these two brothers, Boanerges, which means,
sons of thunder; by reason of their vigorous minds and
impetuous temper.

When Herod Agrippa was made Governor of Judea, to
ingratiate myself with his Jewish subjects, he raised a
persecution against the christians.   James was accordingly singled out as the first object of his vengeance,
whom he condemned to be beheaded.   But such was his
constancy and serenity of mind, that his accuser was struck
with admiration, and became a convert to Christianity.
This transition so enraged the multitude who had assembled to witness the execution, that, with one voice they
cried out, let him die also: and they were accordingly
both beheaded together.   This event took place, A. D. 44,
and on the 25th day of July; which is observed in commemoration of this saint.   About this time, Timon and
Parmonas, two of the seven deacons, suffered martyrdom;
the former at Corinth, and the latter at Phillipi, in Ma
cedonia.

St. Phillip.

This apostle was born at Bethsaida, in Galilee, and
was the first called by the name of disciple.   He was employed in several important missions by Jesus, and, after
his resurrection, was deputed to preach the Gospel in
Upper Asia.   After labouring for some time in this place,
he travelled into Phrygia, where he found the inhabitants
so sunk in idolatry as to worship a large serpent.   He,
however, succeeded in converting many of them to Christianity, and procured the death of the serpent.   This so
enraged the heathen priests and magistrates, that they first
committed him to prison, after which he was taken out and
severely scourged, and finally crucified.   His friend Bartholomew found an opportunity of taking down his body
and burying it, for which he narrowly escaped the same
fate.   His crucifixion took place May 1, A. D. 52; which
day, together with that of St. James the Less, is observed
in commemoration of the event.

St. Matthew.

This apostle and evangelist was born in Nazareth of Galilee, but resided chiefly in Capernaum ; where he was a collector of toll, or tribute, from such as had occasion to pass the sea of Galilee. On being called as a disciple, he immediately obeyed ; leaving every thing beside, to become a follower of Christ. After the ascension of his master, he continued preaching the gospel in Judea, for nearly nine years. As he was about to leave them, for the purpose of preaching to the Gentiles, he wrote his gospel in Hebrew ; which he left behind, for the use of his Jewish converts. He then travelled into Ethiopia ; where he made many converts and established several churches. He afterwards visited Parthia, and met with the like success ; but, on returning to Ethiopia, he was slain with a halbert, in the city of Madabar, A. D. 60. The 21st day of September is observed in commemoration of his death.

St. Mark.

This Evangelist and martyr was of the tribe of Levi, and is supposed to have been a convert of St. Peter, whom he served as an amanuensis. Being desired by the converts at Rome to commit to writing the admirable discourses they had heard from St. Peter and himself, he composed his gospel, which was first written in the Greek language. He then went to Egypt, and, after establishing the church at Alexandria, travelled into Lybia, where he also made many converts. On returning again to Alexandria, some of the Egyptians, exasperated at his success, determined to put him to death. They therefore tied his feet, and dragged him through the streets till he was nearly dead ; when they cast his mangled body into prison, where he soon after expired. His body was taken out, on the following day, and burned. This occurred on the 25th day of April, which is dedicated to his memory. After the burning of his body, his bones were gathered up by the Christians, and afterward carried to Venice, of which city he is considered the patron saint.

St. James the Less.

This Apostle was so denominated to distinguish him from the other James, who was called the Great. He was the son of Joseph, the reputed father of the Lord, by his first wife, and is therefore called the Lord's brother. After the resurrection and ascension of Christ, he was elected bishop of the church at Jerusalem; and afterwards wrote his general epistle, to counteract a dangerous doctrine that was propagating, viz.: "that Faith in Christ was alone sufficient for salvation without good works." After this the Jews, being greatly exasperated that St. Paul had escaped their fury, by appealing to Rome, determined to wreak their vengeance on James, who was now ninety-four years old. They accordingly cast him down from a pinnacle of the temple, after which they beat out his brains with a fuller's club. His festival, together with that of St. Phillip, is kept on the first day of May.

St. Matthias.

This Apostle was called to that office, by the other Apostles, after the death of Christ to supply the place of Judas the apostate. He had been one of the seventy disciples and his character was eminent for piety. He suffered martyrdom at Jerusalem, being first stoned and then beheaded. The 24th day of February is dedicated to his memory.

St. Andrew.

This Apostle was the brother of St. Peter, and preached the gospel to several of the Asiatic nations. On arriving at Edessa the governor of the country named Egeas, threatened him for preaching against the idols then worshipped. St. Andrew, persisting in the propagation of his doctrines, was ordered to be crucified on a cross, two ends of which were placed transversely in the ground; he boldly told his persecutors that he would not have preached the glory of the cross had he have feared to die upon it. And again, when he came to be crucified, he said that he coveted the cross, and longed to die upon it. He was accordingly fixed upon it, not with nails but with cords, that his death might be more slow. In this manner he continued nearly two days, preaching the greater part of the time, till his strength finally failed him, and he died on the 30th of November, which is commemorated as his festival.

St. Peter.

This apostle was born in Bethsaida in Galilee, being the son of Jonah, a fisherman, which employment he also followed. He was persuaded by his brother Andrew, to become a follower of Christ, who gave him the name of Cephas : which implies, in the Syriac language, a rock. He was called to be an apostle, at the same time with his brother Andrew, and gave uncommon proof of his zeal and faithfulness to Christ, notwithstanding his fears, on one occasion, so far overcame him that he denied him.

After the death of Christ, the Jews, still continuing to persecute his followers, ordered Peter, with several of the other apostles, to be scourged. This they bore with patience, rejoicing that they were found worthy to suffer for the sake of their Redeemer.

When Herod Agrippi had caused James the Great to be put to death, because it pleased the Jews, he proceeded next against Peter, and cast him into prison ; intending, after the festival of Easter, to bring him out to suffer a public execution. And the better to secure him, had appointed sixteen soldiers to keep constant watch at the door of the prison. But an angel appeared to Peter on the evening preceding the day appointed for his execution, and delivered him out of prison ; at which Herod was so much enraged, that he caused the soldiers to be put to death.

St. Peter after various other miracles, retired to Rome, where he defeated all the artifices, and confounded the magic of Simon Magus, a great favourite of the Emperor Nero. He also converted to Christianity one of the favourite concubines of that monarch, which so exasperated him, that he caused both him and Paul to be apprehended. During the time of their confinement, they converted two of the Captains of the guard to Christianity, with forty-seven others. Having been nine months in prison, Peter was brought out from thence and after being severely scourged, was crucified with his head downwards. This position was, however, of his own choice, as he counted himself unworthy to suffer in the same manner as did his master. His festival is observed on the 29th day cf June, on which day he as well as St. Paul suffered. His body was taken down, embalmed, and buried in the Vatican, over which a splendid church was erected. This was, however, destroyed by the Emperor Heliogabalus, and the body removed, till Cornelius, the twentieth Bishop of Rome, had it again returned, and Constantine the Great. erected one of the most magnificent churches in the world over the place. Previous to the death of St. Peter, his wife suffered martyrdom for her faith in Christ, and behaved with great calmness and constancy.

St. Paul.

This apostle was a Jew, of the tribe of Benjamin, born at Tarsus, in Cilicia, and before his conversion, was called Saul. He was at first a great enemy and persecutor of the Christians, and a principal promoter of the death of St. Stephen. Going to Damascus, soon after for the purpose of arresting all such as he should find calling upon the name of the Lord, suddenly a light from heaven shone round about him, accompanied with a voice, saying, " Saul, Saul, why persecutest thou me." At this he was struck to the ground, and smitten with blindness during three days. Immediately after his recovery, he became a professor and an apostle. During his labours in spreading the gospel, he converted to the faith, Sergius Paulus, the proconsul of Cyprus ; on which account he took his name, and, as some suppose, was from thence called Paulus instead of Saulus. After his many labours he took with him Barnabus and went up to Jerusalem, to Peter, James, and John, where he was ordained and sent out to preach to the Gentiles. At Iconium, he and Barnabus were near being stoned to death by the enraged Jews, and fled from thence to Lystra. Here they were stoned, dragged out of the city, and left for dead. They however revived and escaped to Derbe. At Phillip:, they were imprisoned and whipped, and afterward greatly persecuted at Thessalonica. Being afterward taken at Jerusalem,

Paul was sent to Cesarea, but appealing to Cesar, he was sent to Rome. Here he was detained for a while as a prisoner at large, but being at length released, he visited the churches in Rome, and in Greece, and travelled into France and Spain. Returning again to Rome, he was a second time apprehended, and by the order of Nero, was beheaded with a sword. Two days are dedicated to this apostle, one in commemoration of his conversion, and the other of his death; the first being the 25th of January, and the other 29th of June.

St. Jude.

This apostle was the brother of James the Less, and is also called Thaddeus. Being sent to Edessa, he wrought many miracles, and made many converts, which, stirring up the resentment of the people he was crucified, A. D. 72, on the 28th day of October, which is dedicated to his memory.

St. Bartholomew.

This apostle preached in many countries, healed many diseases, and performed other miracles. He finally travelled into India, when he translated the gospel into the Indian language, and made many converts in that country. But the idolaters becoming weary of his preaching, first scourged, then crucified him, and then cut off his head. The anniversary of his martyrdom, is on the 24th of August.

St. Thomas.

This apostle was called, in his native language, Thomas, but in the Syriac, Didymus. He preached in Parthia and India; where, displeasing the Pagan priests, he was thrust through with a spear. His martyrdom is commemorated on the 21st of December.

St. Luke the Evangelist.

This eminent saint was the author of the Gospel that

2

bears his name, as also of the Acts of the Apostles.   He travelled with St. Paul, to Rome, and preached to several barbarous nations.   He was, however, finally hanged, on an olive tree, by order of the heathen priests of Greece. The anniversary of his martyrdom, is on the 18th of October.

St. Simon.

This apostle was distinguished for his zeal, by the name of Zelotes.   He preached with great success in Mauritania, and other parts of Africa, and even in Britain ; where, though he made many converts, he was finally crucified, A. D. 74.   The anniversary of his death, together with that of St. Jude, is commemorated on the 28th day of October.

St. John.

This eminent saint was distinguished for being a prophet, apostle, evangelist, divine, and martyr.   He is called the beloved disciple, and was brother to James the Great.   He was first a disciple of John the Baptist, and was not only afterward one of the twelve apostles, but one of the three to whom Christ communicated the most secret passages of his life.   He founded the churches of Smyrna, Pergamos, Sardia, Philadelphia, Laodicia, and Thyatira, to whom he directed his book of Revelations. Being at Ephesus, he was ordered by the Emperor Domitian, to be sent bound to Rome, where he was condemned to be cast into a caldron of boiling oil.   But here a miracle was wrought in his favour, as he sustained no injury from the oil ; upon which he was sent to the island of Patmos, to work in the mines.   He was afterwards recalled by Nerva who succeeded Domitian, but was deemed a martyr on account of having undergone an execution though it did not take effect.   He wrote his Gospel, Epistle, and Revelations all in a different style, but they are all equally admired.   He was the only apostle who escaped a violent death, and lived the longest of any of them ; being nearly a hundred years old at his death.   The 27th day of December, is kept in commemoration of his death

St. Barnabas.

This saint was a native of the island of Cyprus, but was born of Jewish parents. The time of his death is uncertain; but is supposed to have occurred A. D. 73. His festival is observed on the 11th of June.

CHAPTER II.

The first four Primitive Persecutions under the Roman Emperors.

Persecution under Nero.

THE first persecution in the primitive ages of the church was began by the cruel and tyrannical Nero, the sixth emperor of Rome, in A. D. 67. This emperor reigned for five years with tolerable credit to himself, after which he gave way to the greatest extravagance of temper, and to the most atrocious barbarities. Among many other diabolical outrages, he ordered that the city of Rome should be set on fire; which was done by his officers, guards, and servants. While the city was in flames, he went up to the tower of Mecenas played upon his harp, and sang the song of the burning of Troy; and declared, " That he wished the ruin of all things before his death." Among the noble buildings burned, was the circus, or place appropriated to horse races. It was half a mile in length, of an oval form, with rising seats on either side, and capable of containing upward of one hundred thousand spectators. Many other houses and palaces were consumed, and several thousand of the inhabitants perished in the flames.

This terrible conflagration continued nine days without intermission; and when the tyrant saw that his conduct was greatly blamed by the people, he so managed as to fix the odium upon the Christians; which gave him an opportunity of witnessing new cruelties. A furious persecution was accordingly commenced, and the sufferings of the Christians were such as to excite the compassion of the heathens themselves. Some were sewed up in the skins of wild beasts, and worried to death by dogs; others were dressed in shirts made stiff with wax, then suspended on poles and set on fire, in the gardens of the palace. This persecution was general throughout the whole Roman Empire; but it rather increased than diminished the spirit of Christianity. Beside St. Peter and St. Paul, many of their most distinguished converts, whose names have not been handed down to posterity, were among the sufferers. We shall therefore notice only those whose history is well authenticated.

Erastus, the chamberlain of Corinth, was converted by St. Paul, and determined to follow the fortunes of that apostle. For this purpose he resigned his office, and accompanied him in his voyages and travels, till he was left by the apostle in Macedonia; where he was first made bishop of that province, and afterward suffered martyrdom, being tortured to death by the pagans at Philippi.

Aristarchus, the Macedonian, was born in Thessalonica, and being converted by Paul, became his constant companion. He was with that apostle at Ephesus, during the commotion raised by Demetrius, the silversmith. He also accompanied him into Greece, where they were very successful in propagating the gospel, and bringing over many to Christianity. Having left Greece, they traversed a great portion of Asia Minor and Judea. After this he accompanied St. Paul to Rome, where he suffered the same fate as that apostle, being beheaded with a sword.

Trophinus, an Ephesian by birth, and a Gentile by religion, was converted by St. Paul to christianity, and accompanied him in his travels. On his account, the Jews raised a great disturbance in the temple at Jerusalem, the last time he was in that city, because the apostle introduced him into the temple. But being rescued by the centurion, he accompanied his master to Rome, and afterwards into Gaul; where he was made bishop, and left in the city of Airus. On the following year he visited St. Paul, at Rome, and accompanied him into Asia, but on his return to that city he was beheaded, a few days after the death of his master.

Joseph commonly called Barsabas, was a primitive disciple, and by some is supposed to have been one of the seventy. He was a distant relation of the Redeemer; and was a candidate, together with Matthias, for the apostleship, left vacant by Judas Iscariot. He was, during his life, a very zealous preacher of the gospel, and having suffered many insults from the Jews, was at length put to death by the Pagans in Judea.

Ananias, bishop of Damascus, is celebrated in scripture for being the person who cured St. Paul of his blindness, occasioned by the brightness of the vision at the time of his conversion. He was one of the seventy disciples, and was martyred in the city of Damascus. After his death, a Christian church was erected over the place of his burial, which is now converted into a Turkish Mosque.

Persecution under Domitian.

The Emperor Domitian was naturally cruel, and after having slain his brother, he raised a persecution against the Christians. He commanded all the lineage of David to be slain; hoping, by this means, to stop the progress of Christ's kingdom, which he was taught to consider as a temporal kingdom.

Among the numerous martyrs who suffered during his persecution, was Simon, bishop of Jerusalem, who was crucified. St. John, who was cast into a caldron of oil, and afterward banished to the island of Patmos; and Flavia, the daughter of a Roman Senator, who was banished to Pontus. A law, was also enacted, that no Christians once brought before the tribunal should be exempted from punishment, without renouncing their religion.

During this reign, there were a variety of tales invented, for the purpose of injuring the reputation of the Christians. Among other things they were accused of meeting together for the grossest immorality, of murdering their children, and even of eating them. They were also accused of being rebellious, and opposed to the Roman Government. And when any calamity befel any portion of the Roman Empire, such as earthquakes, pestilence, or famine, it was imputed solely to their impiety.

These persecutions increased the number of informers, who, for the sake of gain, swore away the lives of many eminent persons. When Christians were brought before a magistrate on the charge of being such, they were commanded to take the attest oath, which if they refused, sentence of death was immediately passed on them, and if they confessed themselves to be Christians, the result was the same.

The various kinds of punishment inflicted were imprisonment, confiscation of property, banishment, broiling them upon slow fires, racking, burning, scourging, stoning, hanging, and worrying with dogs and wild beasts. Many were torn piecemeal with red hot pincers, and others were thrown upon the horns of furious bulls.

After having suffered these cruelties, the friends of the deceased were even forbidden to burn or bury their remains. The following are the most remarkable of the numerous martyrs who suffered during this persecution.

Dionysius the Areopagite, was an Athenian by birth, and educated in all the useful and ornamental branches of Grecian literature. He travelled into Egypt, to study astronomy, and made very particular observations on the supernatural eclipse that occurred at the time of our Saviour's crucifixion. On his return to Athens he was highly honoured by the people, and at length promoted to the dignity of senator in that celebrated city. Becoming a convert to the gospel, he changed from a worthy Pagan magistrate to a faithful Christian pastor, for even while involved in the darkness of idolatry, he was highly honoured for his just and benevolent principles. After his conversion, the sanctity of his life was such as recommended him strongly to the love and honour of the Christian brethren, and he was accordingly appointed bishop of Athens. He discharged his duty with the utmost diligence, till the second year of this persecution, viz.: A. D. 69, when he received the crown of martyrdom by being beheaded.

Nicomedea, a Christian of some distinction at Rome, during the reign of Domitian, made great efforts to serve the afflicted, by comforting the poor, visiting those confined, exhorting the wavering, and confirming the faithful. For those and other pious actions, he was seized as a Christian, and being sentenced was scourged to death.

Protasius and Grevasius were martyred at Milan, but the particular circumstances attending their deaths are not recorded.

Timothy the celebrated disciple of St. Paul, and bishop of Ephesus, was born at Lystra, in the province of Lycaonia. His father was a Gentile, and his mother a Jewess, but both his parents and his grandmother embraced Christianity, by which means he was taught from his infancy the precepts of the gospel. When St. Paul arrived at Lycaonia, he ordained Timothy, and made him the companion of his labours. He mentions him with peculiar respect, and declares that he could find no one so truly united to him, both in heart and mind. Timothy attended St. Paul to Macedonia, where, with that apostle and Silas, he laboured in propagating the gospel. St. Paul went from thence to Achaia, but he was left behind to strengthen the faith of those already converted. St. Paul at length sent for him to Athens, and thence despatched him to Thessalonica, to preach to the suffering Christians there, against the terrors of the persecution that then prevailed. Having performed his mission, he returned to Athens, and, there assisted St. Paul and Silas in composing the two Epistles to the Thessalonians. He then accompanied St. Paul to Corinth, Jerusalem, and Ephesus. After performing several other commissions for St. Paul, and attending him on various journeys, the apostle constituted him bishop of Ephesus, though he was only thirty years of age, and in two admirable epistles gave him proper instructions for his conduct. He was so very temperate in his living, that St. Paul blamed him for being too abstemious, and recommended to him the moderate use of wine, to recruit his strength and spirits.

While that great apostle was in his last confinement at Rome, he desired Timothy to come to him. He afterward returned to Ephesus, where he zealously governed the church, till A. D. 97. At this period the Pagans were about to celebrate a feast called Catagogion, the principal ceremonies of which were, that the people should carry sticks in their hands, go masked, and bear about the streets, the images of their Gods. Timothy met the procession, and severely reproved them for their ridiculous idolatry, which so exasperated them, that they fell upon him with their clubs, and beat him in so dreadful a manner, that he expired of the bruises two days after.

Persecution under Trajan.

Between the second and third Roman persecutions was but one year. Upon Nerva succeeding Domitian, he showed respect to the Christians, but reigned only ten months. His successor, Trajan, in the tenth year of his reign, and in the year of our Lord 108, began the third persecution against them. While this persecution raged, Plinius Secundus a heathen philosopher, wrote to the Emperor in favour of the Christians, stating that he found nothing objectionable in their conduct, and that the whole sum of their errors consisted in this, that they were wont at certain times appointed to meet before day, in the morning, to worship one Christ, their God, and to confederate among themselves to abstain from all theft, murder, and adultery, to keep their faith, and to defraud no man, which done, they departed for that time, and having agreed to come together again to commune one with another, and yet without any act of evil. To this epistle, Trajan returned the following indecisive answer: " That Christians ought not to be sought after, but when brought before the magistracy they should be punished." Provoked by this answer, Tertullian exclaimed, " Oh! confused sentence, he would not have them sought for, as innocent men, and yet would have them punished as guilty." The Emperor's incoherent answer, however, occasioned the persecution, in some measure, to abate ; as his officers were uncertain, if they carried it on with severity, how he might choose to explain his own meaning. Trajan, however, soon wrote to Jerusalem, and gave orders to exterminate the stock of David ; in consequence of which, all that could be found of that race were put to death.

About this period, the Emperor Trajan, was succeeded by Adrian, who continued the persecution with the greatest rigour.

Phocas, bishop of Pontus, refusing to sacrifice to Neptune, was, by the immediate order of Trajan, cast first into a hot lime kiln, and being drawn from thence, was thrown into a scalding bath, till he expired.

Trajan likewise commanded the martyrdom of Ignatius, bishop of Antioch. This holy man was the person whom, when an infant, Christ took into his arms, and showed te his disciples, as one that would be a pattern of humility and innocence. He received the gospel afterwards by St. Paul the Evangelist, and was exceedingly zealous in his mission. He boldly vindicated the faith of Christ before the Emperor, for which he was cast into prison, and was tormented in a cruel manner, and after being dreadfully scourged, he was compelled to hold fire in his hands, and at the same time, papers dipped in oil were put to his sides and set on fire. His flesh was then torn with red hot pincers, and at last he was despatched by wild beasts. Ignatius had a timely information or presentiment of his fate; for writing to Polycarp at Smyrna, he says, " Would to God, I were once come to the beasts which are prepared for me, which, also, I wish that they with gaping mouths were ready, whom also I will seek, that they without delay, may devour me. And if they will not, unless they be provoked, I will then enforce them against myself."

Martyrdom of Symphorosa.

Symphorosa, a widow, and her seven sons were commanded by Trajan to sacrifice to the heathen Deities; but on refusing to comply, he ordered her to be hung up by the hair of her head, after which a weight was attached to her neck, and she was cast into the river. Her sons were then put upon the rack, and their limbs dislocated, but as these tortures did not affect their resolution, they were put to death.

About this time Alexander, bishop of Rome, after filling that office for about ten years, was put to death, with two of his deacons, and also Hermes Guirinus, and Zenon, a Roman noblemen, with about ten thousand others.

Many were crucified on Mount Ararat, crowned with thorns in imitation of the crucifixion of the Saviour. Among these was a distinguished military commander, who was commanded to sacrifice, in honour of victories gained by himself, but refusing to comply, he was martyred with his whole family.

During this persecution occurred the martyrdom of Fastines, and Jovita, two brothers of the city of Brescia, their patience was such under their complicated sufferings, that Calconis a Pagan, was struck with admiration, and called out, " great is the God of the Christians," for which, he was immediately apprehended, and put to death with them.

This persecution continued till Guadratus, bishop of Athens, and Aristides, a distinguished philosopher of the same city, addressed each a very learned apology to Adrian in favour of the Christians, who immediately thereafter relaxed his severities, so far as to command that no Christians should be punished merely for their opinions. But the enemies of Christianity, among which were a great many Jews, sought other means of gratifying their malignity, by suborning witnesses, and accusing them of other crimes.

Adrian died A. D. 138 or 139, which was several years after he had discontinued his persecutions against the Christians. He was succeeded by Antoninus Pius. This Emperor possessed by nature so amiable a disposition, that he was termed by his subjects, " the father of virtues." Immediately after ascending the throne, he published an edict with these words, " If any should hereafter vex or accuse the Christians, having no other cause but that they are such, let the accused be released, and the accuser be punished." This put a final stop to the persecution, which until this time was continued in many parts of the Empire, and the Christians enjoyed a respite from their sufferings during this Emperor's reign. Such was the goodness of this Emperor's heart, that he often declared that the preservation of one subject gave him more pleasure than the destruction of a thousand enemies.

Persecution under the Emperors Marcus Aurelius and Commodus.

Primitive Martyrdom.

Antoninus Pius was succeeded by Marcus Aurelius under whom was commenced, what is usually termed the fourth persecution, which raged with the greatest violence in the Asiatic churches, and in France.

Such were the cruelties with which this persecution was characterized, that many of the spectators shuddered at the sight, and were astonished at the intrepidity of the sufferers. Some of the martyrs were compelled to pass with naked feet over thorns and nails, others were scourged till the veins and sinews were laid bare, and after suffering the most excruciating tortures, were finally put to death by the most horrid cruelty.

Germanicus, a young man of Smyrna, who had embraced the Christian faith, was given to be devoured by wild beasts, but behaving with great courage and fortitude, several were struck with admiration, and embraced the Christian faith.

At this, the persecutors were so much enraged, that they determined to extirpate the Christians from that city, and they immediately cried out, " let Polycarp be sought after," who, it will be recollected, was the first bishop of the church, at Smyrna.

Polycarp on hearing that he was sought after, escaped to a small village in the country, but was soon discovered and brought back to Ephesus. Nor did he express any reluctance to return, as he dreamed, about that time, that his bed took fire, and that he was consumed in a moment. From this he concluded it was the will of God that he should suffer martyrdom, and he accordingly awaited his death, with a becoming firmness and resignation.

Those who apprehended him, were so forcibly struck with his venerable appearance and gravity, that they earnestly besought him to save his life by abjuring Christ. He thanked them for the interest which they manifested in his welfare, but declared that he could never forsake a master, who had shown him nothing but kindness. After feasting them, he desired an hour for prayer, which was granted him, and such was his fervour, that they seriously repented having taken any part in his death. He was however, first taken before the proconsul, and condemned to be burnt in the public market place. He was accordingly bound to a stake, and the faggots with which he was surrounded set on fire, but when it became so hot that the soldiers were compelled to retire, he continued praying and singing praises to God for a long time. The flames raged with great violence, but still his body remained unconsumed, and shone like burnished gold. It is also said, that a grateful odour like that of myrrh, arose from the fire, which so much astonished the spectators, that many of them were by that means converted to Christianity. His executioners finding it impossible to put him to death by fire, thrust a spear into his side, from which the blood flowed in such a quantity, as to extinguish the flame. His body was then consumed to ashes, by order of the proconsul lest his followers should make it an object of adoration.

He was nearly a hundred years old when he suffered, having been a disciple of Christ eighty-six years, and seventy years a bishop. He was a convert of St. John the Evangelist, and by him was constituted bishop of Smyrna.

Metrodorus, a minister who preached boldly, and Bronius, who wrote several apologies in behalf of the Christians, were also burnt about the same time. Carpus and Papilus, two worthy Christians, and Agathonica, a pious woman, suffered martyrdom at Pergamapolis in Asia, at about the same period.

Felicitas, an illustrious Roman lady, had seven sons, who together with their mother, had embraced the Christian faith. As various parts of the empire were visited with earthquakes, the cause was imputed to the impiety of the Christians, toward the Gods.

Felicitas and her sons were accordingly apprehended, and great efforts were at first made to induce them to recant, but all to no purpose. They were next threatened with death if they still persisted in their obstinacy, but they treated these threats with as much contempt as they had done the promises. They were accordingly sentenced to death, and all perished together on a scaffold.

Justin, the celebrated philosopher, fell a martyr in this persecution. He was a native of Neapolis, in Samaria, and was born A. D. 103. He was well versed in every branch of literature, and travelled into Egypt for the purpose of gaining a further stock of knowledge. At Alexandria, he was informed of every thing respecting the seventy interpreters of the holy scriptures, and shown the rooms wherein the work was performed. He was a great lover of truth, and investigated most of the systems of philosophy then in use, but was himself rather inclining to that of Plato, when about thirty years of age he became a convert to Christianity. Soon after this, he wrote an elegant epistle to the Gentiles, for the purpose of opening their eyes to the true faith, and so faithfully did he adhere to every virtue, that he was with great propriety termed the Christian Philosopher. He also employed his talents in converting the Jews to Christianity, and travelled for several years, when he finally located himself in the vicinity of Rome, where he taught a very popular school.

As the Christians began to be treated with severity, he wrote his apology in their behalf, addressed to the Emperor Antoninus, two princes whom he had adopted as sons, and to the senate and people of Rome in general. This production displayed great skill and learning, and caused the Emperor to pass an edict in favour of the Christians.

A short time after he entered into frequent contests with Creseus, a person of vicious life, but a celebrated Cynic philosopher, and his arguments appearing so powerful, and

3

still so disgusting to him that he immediately determined on his ruin, which he managed to effect. The second epistle of Justin, was occasioned by the following circumstances. A certain man and his wife living at Rome, the latter became a convert to Christianity, and attempted to bring her husband over to the faith Not succeeding, she then sued for a divorce, which so exasperated him, that he immediately accused her of being a Christian. On her petitioning him, he discontinued his suit against her, and levelled his enmity at Ptolemias, who was the means of converting her. He was consequently condemned to death, and met his fate with fortitude. Justin's remarks on these severities, gave Crescus the advantage he had so ardently desired, and complaining to the Emperor he was immediately apprehended with six of his companions. They were all first severely scourged, and then put to death by beheading.

Among the numerous and valuable productions of this eminent saint and martyr, only seven are now extant.

About this time many others were put to death for refusing to sacrifice to Jupiter, among whom was Concordus, a deacon of the city, who being carried before the image, he not only refused to sacrifice, but spit in its face, upon which he was immediately put to death.

Miraculous interference of the Divine Being.

About this time several of the northern nations having conspired against Rome, the Emperor marched against them with 975,000 men. Having arrived within the country of Germany, they fell unconsciously into an ambuscade of the enemy, where they were in imminent danger of being defeated, and to add still more to their difficulty, they were almost entirely cut off from water. The Emperor in this emergency, commanded his soldiers to call upon their gods for aid, which was accordingly done, but to no purpose. He next called upon that division of his army which was composed of Christians, and commanded them to pray to their God, which was immediately complied with. They prostrated themselves before Heaven and implored relief, when suddenly a heavy shower descended, and the whole army was thus saved, and while it rained upon the Roman army, the hail descended in torrents upon their enemies, which induced a great portion of them to disperse, while many others came over to the Romans. Thus was a great victory gained, and the empire probably saved through the interposition of Heaven.

The Emperor wrote immediately to the Senate on the subject, in which he fully acknowledges the services of the Christians, and gave immediate orders for stopping the persecution against them.

Persecutions in France.

Notwithstanding the above edict of the Emperor tended to stop the persecutions for a time in the immediate vicinity of Rome, in other parts of the empire, particularly in France, it was carried on to an extent which exceeded in cruelty all former examples. In the city of Lyons, all manner of torments were invented, such as banishment, hanging, burning, &c. and many of the servants of opulent Christians, were put upon the rack, to compel them to accuse their masters. The following were the principal of these martyrs, Vetius Agathus, a young man who having professed Christianity being accused before a magistrate, boldly acknowledged himself to be such, and was immediately condemned to death.

Blandinia, a Christian lady of a weak constitution, when put to the torture, received such aid from Heaven, that her tormentors several times became weary in their work of cruelty, and declared that she must have been supported by some invisible power. Sanctus also, a deacon in the city of Vienne, bore his sufferings with equal fortitude, and only exclaimed " I am a Christian." Red hot plates of brass were repeatedly placed upon the most sensitive parts of the body, till the sinews were contracted, still remaining inflexible, he was again consigned to prison. He was brought out again a few days afterward, when his persecutors were greatly astonished to find his wounds healed, and his body perfect. Again they put him to the torture, but being unable to take his life, he was remanded to prison, where he was soon after beheaded.

Attalus a distinguished citizen of Pergamus, suffered about this time, and Pothinus, the venerable bishop of

Lyons, now ninety years of age, being assaulted in the street by an infuriated mob, received such injury that he expired a few days after.

At Lyons, exclusive of those already mentioned, the martyrs were compelled to set upon red hot chains of iron, till their flesh was broiled. This was inflicted with peculiar severity upon Sanctus, already mentioned, and several others. Indeed, so far did the malice of the Pagans proceed that they sat guards over the bodies, while the dogs were devouring them, lest their friends should take them away and bury them.

The whole number of martyrs, at Lyons, was 48, who suffered in the year of Christ 177, and all of them behaved with the greatest fortitude. Besides these, many others suffered soon after, not only in that city, but in various other parts of the Roman empire.

Of these the most celebrated, were Epipodius, and Alexander, the latter a Greek, and the former a citizen of Lyons, distinguished for their friendship and love for each other. Being concealed by a Christian lady, they remained undiscovered for several days. Their hiding place, however, being at length found out, they were apprehended and thrown into prison. When brought out for trial, they avowed themselves Christians, at which the governor was so much enraged, that he exclaimed, " what signify all the former executions, if some yet remain who dare avow themselves Christians."

Through pretended compassion however, the governor attempted to dissuade Epipodius from his belief, by contrasting the sensual enjoyments tolerated by the Pagan religion, with what he was pleased to term, a gloomy life of Christianity. " Do not, said he, ruin yourself, with your obstinacy, our Deities are worshipped by the greater part of the people in the Universe, we adore them with feasting and mirth, while you adore a crucified man. We to honour our Gods, launch into pleasures, you, by your faith are debarred from all enjoyments of a sensual nature. Ours are the joys of licentious blandishments, yours the barren virtue of chastity; can you expect protection from one who could not secure himself from the persecution of a contemptible people. Then quit a profession of such austerity, and enjoy the gratifications which the world affords.

and which your youth demands. Epipodius in his reply, contemned his pretended compassion. "Your kindness said he, is actual cruelty, and the happy life you describe, is replete with everlasting death. Christ suffered for us, that our joys should be immortal, and hath prepared for his followers an eternity of bliss. The frame of man being composed of two parts, a body and soul, the first being mean and perishable, should be brought into subjection to the latter. Your idolatrous feasts may gratify the mortal, but they injure the immortal part. That cannot therefore be called pleasure, which wroks the destruction of the nobler part. Your pleasures lead to eternal death, our pains to eternal pleasure. For this speech, he was first severely beaten, then put upon the rack, and his flesh torn with iron hooks, after which, he was beheaded. Alexander, his companion, was brought before the same judge two days after, and on refusing to abjure Christianity, was first severely scourged, and then beheaded. This was in A. D. 179.

About this time, the following persons also suffered martyrdom, viz. : Valerian, and Marcellus, of Lyons ; Benignus, of Dijon ; Speusippus, and others, at Langres ; Thyrseus, and Felix, at Salieu ; Sympoviani and Florella, at Autun ; Severinus, Felician, and Exuperus, at Vienne ; Cecilia, a virgin, of Sicily; and Thraseus, bishop of Smyrna.

In the year of Christ 180, the Emperor Antoninus died, and was succeeded by his son Commodus, who did not imitate his father in any respect. He had neither his virtues nor his vices, he was without learning or morality ; neither did he possess his prejudice against the Christians. His greatest weakness was a vain and foolish pride, which led him to consider himself as Hercules, and as such he commanded his subjects to worship him. Several of the Christians on refusing to comply with so extravagant a request, were put to death, among whom was Apollonius, a Roman Senator. This eminent man was skilled in all the branches of polite literature, as well as in the sublime truths of the Gospel. He was accused by his slave Severus, and refusing to recant was put to death, by being beheaded on the 18th of April, 186.

About this time also was put to death for the same cause, Anicetus, Soter, and Eleutherius, the latter of whom was
3*

sent to Britain by the request of Lucius, the king, who was
by him converted to Christianity, and on the following year,
Eusebius Vincentius, Potentius, Peregrinus, and the Senator Julius, also suffered martyrdom, for refusing to sacrifice to Commodus.

CHAPTER II.

*The fifth, sixth, seventh, and eighth Persecutions, under
the Roman Emperor.*

The Emperor Commodus dying in the year of Christ,
191, was succeeded by Pertinax, and he by Julianius, both
of whom reigned but a short time.   On the death of the
last, Severus became Emperor in A. D. 172.   Being cured
of a dangerous disease by a Christian physician, he became so friendly toward them, that he even suffered his
son to be nursed by a Christian female.   The Christians
therefore for several years of his reign, enjoyed a respite
from persecutions.   But increasing in numbers very rapidly, the fears of the heathens were excited, lest their religion should become entirely supplanted, and imputing
the various misfortunes which befel the empire to their impiety, a furious persecution was suddenly raised against
them.   Fire, sword, wild beasts, and imprisonments, were
resorted to, and even the dead bodies of Christians were
torn from their graves and subjected to the vilest insults.
The Gospel, notwithstanding, withstood these attacks, and
continued to spread to such a degree, that had its votaries
withdrawn themselves to other countries, the Roman
empire would have been greatly depopulated.   Victor,
bishop of Rome, suffered martyrdom A. D. 201 ; Leonidas,
father of the celebrated Origen, was beheaded about the
same time.   Previous to his death, his son, in order to encourage him, wrote to him in the following words : " Beware sir, that your care for us does not make you change
your resolution."

pitch poured upon her, and then burned, with Marcelia her mother.

Potamiena, the sister of Rhais, was executed in the same manner a short time after, and Basilides the officer who attended her execution, was converted to Christianity by witnessing her fortitude. Being afterward required to take a certain oath, he refused, saying, that he could not swear by the heathen idols, as he was a Christian. The people could not at first believe him serious, but on repeating the assertion, he was dragged before the judge, condemned to death, and suffered martyrdom soon after. Irenæus, bishop of Lyons, was by birth a Greek, and received a Christian education. It is generally supposed that the account of the persecutions at Lyons was written by himself. He succeeded the martyr Pothinus, and ruled his diocess with great propriety. He was a zealous opposer of heresies in general, and wrote a celebrated tract on the subject, about A. D. 187. In consequence of a dispute with Victor, bishop of Rome, on the subject of a particular mode of keeping Easter, he became conspicuous as a champion of Christianity, and was beheaded by order of the Emperor, A. D. 202.

Persecution in Africa.

This persecution extended into Africa, and many were martyred in consequence of their profession, among whom was a very amiable married lady by the name of Perpetua. She was about twenty-six years of age at the time she was apprehended, and had a young infant at her breast. Her father, who loved her tenderly, visited her in prison, and attempted to persuade her to save her life, by renouncing Christianity, and on her refusing, became so exasperated, that he beat her with severity. This however she bore with patience, upon which he left her, and did not visit her again for several days. When he did, however, he was all tenderness, and attempted again to prevail on her to renounce her profession. The consul also before whom she was brought united with the unhappy father, in representing to her the tears of her friends, the helpless condition of her infant, with such other arguments as were most likely to make her recant, but all was to no purpose, as she firmly declared, that she was willing to forsake all for Christ.   Her father finding her immoveable, attempted to carry her off by force, in which attempt he received a severe blow from one of the soldiers.   Irritated at this, Perpetua declared that she felt the blow more severely than if it had fallen on herself.   When remanded to prison she awaited with patience the hour of her execution, when she was put to death with several others, among whom was Felicitas a married Christian lady, who was delivered of a child the day before her execution.

Revocatus, a catechuman and slave of Carthage, with Satur, Saturnius, and Secundulus, accused of being Christians and sentenced to suffer death at the same time.   The first three having the courage to denounce the judgment of Heaven against their persecutors, were compelled to run the gauntlet between two files of soldiers, each of which gave them a severe blow with a lash.   Felicitas and Perpetua were first stripped, and then thrown to a mad bull, when he had tossed them several times, the spectators desired, that for decency's sake, their clothes might be replaced, which was accordingly done.   The bull then made an attack upon them but failing to despatch them, the executioner finished his work with his sword.   Revocatus and Satur were torn in pieces by wild beasts.   Saturnius was beheaded, and Secundulus died in prison.   Their executions took place on the 8th day of March, A. D. 205.

The accusations laid to the charge of the Christians, were sedition and rebellion against the Emperor, sacrilege, murdering of infants, incestuous pollution, eating raw flesh, libidinous commixture, for which many of those called *gnostici* were disgraced.   It was also said of them that they woshipped the head of an ass; which charge was laid against them by the Jews.

They were also charged with worshipping the sun, because they usually assembled early in the morning for the purpose of singing praises to their Redeemer.

Speratus and twelve others were beheaded, as also was Androchus, in France.   Asclepiades bishop of Antioch, suffered many torments about this time, but his life was spared.

Cecilia, a young lady of good family in Rome, was married to a young gentleman by the name of Valerian, and being a Christian herself, she soon persuaded her husband to embrace the same faith. His example was soon after followed by Tiburtius his brother. This drew upon them the vengeance of the laws, and they were immediately condemned to death, which was inflicted in the following manner. The lady was placed naked in a scalding bath, and having continued there a considerable time, her head was struck off with a sword. The others were beheaded, and the officer who led them to execution, becoming a convert to Christianity, suffered with them; this was, A. D. 222.

Two years after, Calistus, bishop of Rome, was martyred, but the particulars of his death are not recorded. Urban, who succeeded him, also suffered the same fate, A. D. 232.

Agapetus, a boy of Prænestc, only fifteen years of age, refusing to sacrifice to idols, was severely scourged, then hung up by his feet and scalding water poured upon him. He was afterward worried to death by wild beasts. During the execution, Antiochus, who ordered it, fell suddenly down from his judicial seat, crying out, " that his bowels burned with the fire of hell," and soon expired.

Persecution under the Emperor Maximus.

This Emperor raised a violent persecution against the Christians in A. D. 235, which extended into Cappadocia, when Semiramus, the president, used great exertions to exterminate the Christians from his kingdom.

A Roman soldier, who refused, on account of being a Christian, to wear a laurel crown bestowed upon him by the Emperor, was scourged, imprisoned, and finally beheaded. Pontianus, bishop of Rome, for preaching against idolatry, was first banished to Sardinia, and afterward executed. Anteros, a Greek, who succeeded to the bishopric of Rome, gave so much offence by collecting an account of the martyrs, that he was deposed from his see forty days after assuming it, and was soon after martyred himself. Pammachius, a Roman senator, with his family, and other Christians, to the number of forty-two, were all beheaded in one day, and their heads placed upon the city gates. Simplicius, another senator, soon after suffered martyrdom in the same way. Calepodius, a Christian minister, after being dragged about the streets in an inhuman manner, was thrown into the Tiber, with a millstone about his neck. Quiritus, a Roman nobleman, with his family and domestics, on account of being Christians, were first severely tortured, and then put to death. Martina, a noble and beautiful virgin, suffered martyrdom, being variously tortured, and then beheaded. Hippolitus, a Christian prelate, was tied to a wild horse and dragged through the streets till he was dead.

During this persecution numerous Christians were slain without a trial, and buried indiscriminately in heaps, sometimes fifty or sixty in a pit together.

But Maximus dying in A. D. 238, and being succeeded by Gordian, the persecution ceased, nor was it revived in the reign of Philip, his successor, which gave the Christian church a respite from suffering, for a term of ten years. But in A. D. 249, a violent persecution broke out in Alexandria. It is, however, worthy of remark, that this was done at the instigation of a Pagan priest, without the knowledge of the Emperor. Such was the fury of the mob, that they broke open and plundered the houses of the Christians without distinction, and murdered those whom they found, without even the ceremony of a trial. Metrus, an aged and venerable Christian, on refusing to blaspheme the name of his Saviour, was beaten with clubs, pricked with thorns, and afterward stoned to death. Quinta, a Christian woman, was carried to a heathen temple, but refusing to sacrifice to idols, was scourged with thongs, and then stoned. Apollonia, an ancient maiden lady, on confessing herself a Christian, had her teeth first beaten out, and was then bound to a stake for the purpose of burning her. She, however, requested to be unbound, which was readily complied with, supposing that it was her intention to recant, but, to their astonishment, she was no sooner at liberty, than she rushed voluntarily into the flames, where she was soon consumed.

Persecution under the Emperor Decius.

Immediately after the succession of Decius to the throne, a violent persecution was raised against the Christians, partly through the hatred that he bore to his predecessor, who was supposed to be a Christian in heart, and partly through a jealousy of the rapid progress of the Christian religion. Christian churches had now became numerous and well filled, while the heathen temples were almost deserted. Decius provoked at this, determined if possible to exterminate the very name of Chris ian from the earth; and, unfortunately for the church, many errors had crept into it, and many of its members were at variance with each other. In this unhappy state of things, the heathens became ambitious to execute the imperial decree, looking upon the murder of Christians, as the most acceptable service they could render to their deities.

Martyrdom of Fabian and others.

Fabian, of Rome, was the first person of eminence who was brought to feel the severity of this persecution. Philip, the former Emperor, had committed his treasures to the care of this good and holy man, but Decius, finding them not as he expected, made it a pretence for wreaking his vengeance upon him. He was accordingly put to death by decapitation. Abdon and Semen, two Persians, were seized on as strangers and Christians, and put to death in the same manner. Moyses, a priest, was beheaded for the same reason. Julian, a native of Cicilia, was seized on for being a Christian, and was several times tortured but still remained inflexible. He was then made to travel for twelve months, together from city to city, for the purpose of exposing himself to the insults of the public. Still refusing to relinquish his faith, he was severely scourged and then sewed up in a leather bag with serpents and scorpions, and in this manner was cast into the sea. Peter, an amiable young man, of Lampsacus, was accused of Christianity before Optimus, the proconsul of Asia, who commanded him to sacrifice to Venus, to which he replied: " I am astonished that you should command me to worship a woman, who, according to your own history was a vile and licentious character, and guilty of such crimes as your own laws now punish with death. No, I shall offer to the one only living and true God, the sacrifice of prayer and praise."   Optimus ordered him to be put upon the rack, which was accordingly done, and most of his bones were broken.   He however smiled on his tormentors as if he would have invited them to a still greater trial of skill.   His head was then struck off, and his body given to the dogs.

Nichomachus, another Christian, being commanded by Optimus to sacrifice to idols, replied, " I cannot render that worship to idols that is due only to God."   Upon this, he was immediately placed upon the rack, and suffered the torments for awhile with great fortitude, but when ready to die with pain, he was weak enough to abjure his faith.   He was thereupon released, when he fell into the most awful horror and distress, and immediately fell down and expired.

Martyrdom of Denisa.

Denisa an amiable young lady of sixteen years of age, when she beheld the signal judgment of heaven upon this apostate young man, exclaimed," O ! miserable wretch, why would you by a moment's ease purchase a miserable eternity ?" upon which she was asked by Optimus whether she were a Christian, to which she replied in the affirmative, when he delivered her over to two libertines, who made several attempts upon her chastity, but without success. They were however alarmed at midnight by a vision from

Heaven, upon which they fell upon their keees before Denisa and implored her forgiveness. This however did not secure her against the rage of Optimus, who caused her to be destroyed by a mad bull.

Andrew and Paul two companions of Nichomachus, confessing themselves Christians, were condemned to die, and delivered to the multitude who stoned them to death. They died like the first Christian martyr, Stephen, calling upon the name of the Lord Jesus.

Alexander and Epimacus of Alexandria, were apprehended for being Christians, and on confessing the accusation, were beat with staves, torn with hooks, and finally burnt; and we are informed by Eusebius, that four female martyrs suffered on the same day by being beheaded.

Lucian and Marcian two Pagan magicians, became converts to Christianity, and to atone for their former lives, became hermits, subsisting only on bread and water. After spending some time in this manner, they reflected that their lives were inefficient, and accordingly left their solitude for the purpose of making converts to Christianity. Becoming zealous preachers, they were seized and carried before the governor of Bithynia, who asked them by what authority they presumed to preach the Christian faith. Lucian answered, " The laws of Christian charity and humanity obliged them to comfort their neighbours." Marcian also said, " That their conversion was by the same grace that was given to St. Paul, who from a zealous persecutor of the church, became a preacher of the gospel." When the proconsul found that he could not prevail on them to renounce their faith, he ordered them to be burnt alive, which was executed accordingly.

Trypho and Respicius, two eminent men, were seized as Christians and imprisoned at Nice. They were soon after put to the rack, which they bore with admirable patience for three hours, uttering the praises of God at the same time. They were then exposed naked in the open air till all their limbs were benumbed, when they were remanded to prison, from which they were afterward taken out, scourged and dragged through the streets, their flesh torn with hooks, and various other torments, which were consumated by beheading them in A. D. 251.

4

Agtha, a Sicilian lady, was remarkable for her beauty, which so enamoured Quintain, the governor, that he made several attempts upon her chastity, which proved unsuccessful. Agtha being a Christian, and knowing him to be both a zealous Pagan and a libertine, removed from the city for the purpose of escaping his power. Her retreat was, however, discovered, and she was brought back to Catana, and delivered to the care of a female of infamous character, who used every means in her power to win her over to prostitution, but without effect. Quintain on being informed of this, determined to wreak his vengeance upon her. She was therefore condemned as a Christian, and, after being severely scourged, was tortured with red hot plates of iron, her flesh torn with hooks, and finally she was laid naked upon hot coals. All these tortures she bore with admirable fortitude, and died on the 1st of February, A. D. 251.

Martyrdom of Cyril.

Cyril, bishop of Gortyna, was seized by order of Lucius, the governor of that place, who first exhorted him to save his valuable life by a recantation, but the venerable prelate, who was eighty-four years old, replied, " I have spent many years in teaching others how to save their souls ; I must not now lose my own for renouncing my only Saviour." He was then sentenced to be burned alive, which was accordingly executed.

Persecution in Crete.

In the island of Crete this persecution raged with great violence, as the governor of the place was very active in putting the decrees of the Emperor into execution. The principal martyrs, whose names have been transmitted to us are the following : Theodulus, Saturnius, and Europus, inhabitants of the city of Gortyna ; Zeticus, Eunicianus, Cleomenes, Agathopas, Bastides and Euaristus, who were brought from different parts of the island on the charge of Christianity. They were all tried at the same time, and were commanded to sacrifice to the gods of the Romans, but to tms they replied, " That they sought no greater enjoyment in the world, than that of suffering for the cause of their Redeemer." Enraged at this, the governor first put them to the rack, and then beheaded them.

Martyrdom of Babylas, bishop of Antioch, and others.

Babylas was a native of the city of Antioch, and a man of superior firmness, and endowed with a liberal education. He succeeded to that see at the death of Zebinus, in A.D. 237. He governed the church during those troublesome times with great prudence. On Gordian's death, in the reign of Decius, that Emperor came to Antioch, and on expressing a desire to visit the congregation of Christians in that city, was opposed by Babylas. He dissembled his anger for the present, but soon after sending for the bishop reproved him with severity, and commanded him to worship the heathen deities. To do this he refused, upon which he was sent to prison and loaded with chains. In a short time after he was brought out to be beheaded with three young men who had been his pupils. On going to the place of execution, the bishop exclaimed, " Behold me and the children that the Lord hath given me." They were martyred in A. D. 251, and the chains worn by the bishop were buried with him. Alexander, bishop of Jerusalem, was cast into prison about this time, on account of his religion, where he died soon after, in consequence of the severity of his treatment.

Serapion, of Alexandria, suffered martyrdom about this time, by having his bones broken, and being thrown from a loft. Julianus and Cronion two aged Christians of the same place, were bound upon the backs of camels, severely scourged, and then consumed with fire. A spectator who seemed to commiserate them was ordered to be beheaded, as a reward for his sentiments of tenderness. Macar, a Lybian Christian, was burnt. Horon-Ater, Isodorus, and Dioschorus, a boy of fifteen, were burnt in Egypt, and forty virgins suffered martyrdom at Antioch.

Theodora, a young lady of Antioch, who is represented as exceedingly beautiful, refusing to sacrifice to idols, was condemned to a brothel, that her virtue might be sacrificed.

Didymus, a Christian, being informed of her situation, disguised himself as a Roman, went to the house, and informed Theodora who he was. He prevailed on her to escape in his dress, which she accordingly did, while he continued in her stead. Her escape becoming known, Didymus was immediately condemned to death. In the mean time Theodora, hearing that her deliverer was likely to suffer, came to the judge, threw herself at his feet, and begged to die in his stead. But the ruthless monster ordered them both to be beheaded.

Account of Origen.

Origen, the celebrated presbyter and catechist of Alexandria, at the age of sixty-four years, was seized and thrown into a loathsome prison, his feet placed in the stocks, and his legs extended to the utmost for several days. He was threatened with fire, and every other torment that the malignity of his persecutors could invent, but his Christian fortitude bore him through all. Notwithstanding, the executioners were commanded to extend his sufferings as long as possible, that death might not too soon release him, he bore all without a murmur, and his faith seemed rather to increase with his pains. During his protracted scenes of suffering, the Emperor Decius died, and was succeeded by Gallus, who being engaged in a war with the Goths, the Christian church enjoyed a respite from persecution for a season. During the interval, Origen obtained his liberty and removed to Tyre, where he remained till his death, which occurred in the sixty-ninth year of his age. Among those who are distinguished by the title of fathers of the church, few deserved it more than Origen, for faithfulness, zeal, and piety. Besides performing his other duties, it is said that he wrote the incredible number of seven thousand volumes on different subjects.

Numerous Martyrs in the reign of Decius.

Besides those martyrs already mentioned, great numbers suffered in Phrygia, Cappadocia, Asia Minor, and other parts of the Roman empire, the particulars of whose martyrdom are not handed down to us.

The Emperor Gallus, having finished his warfare with the Goths, a pestilence broke out in the empire, when the Christians, refusing to supplicate the gods of the heathens to stay the plague, were charged with being the cause of it, and a general persecution was again revived against them. Cornelius, the bishop of Rome, was among the most distinguished persons who were martyred during this persecution. He was first banished to Centum-Cellæ, and, after being cruelly scourged, was beheaded the 14th day of September, A. D. 252, having officiated as bishop only fifteen months. He was succeeded by Lucius, who soon after shared the same fate. The successor of Lucius was Stephanus, who continued in that office for several years, during which time the church enjoyed a respite from persecution.

Persecution under Valerian.

After the death of Gallus, Valerian was elected Emperor; for four years he governed with moderation, and showed much favour to the Christians; but a certain Egyptian, gaining great ascendency over him, persuaded him to raise a persecution against them. Edicts were accordingly published, and the persecution, which commenced in the month of April, continued three years and six months. The martyrs who fell in this persecution were numerous, and their sufferings as various as the malignity of the human heart could devise. The most distinguished personages were the following:

Rufina and Secunda were the daughters of a distinguished Roman, and were both engaged in marriage to gentlemen of high distinction, who like their intended brides were professed Christians before the persecution commenced, but fearing for their persons and fortunes, they relinquished their faith when danger assailed them, and strove to persuade the young ladies to do the same. But remaining steadfast, they finally concluded to leave the province, which they accordingly did. Armentarius and Verinus, the young men before mentioned, through a revengeful motive, informed against them as Christians, in conse-

4*

quence of which, they were brought back to Rome, and after suffering a variety of tortures, were finally put to death by beheading.

In the same year Stephanus, bishop of Rome, was beheaded, and Saturnius, bishop of Thoulouse, was tied to the tail of a bull, which was driven down the steps of a heathen temple, by which means his brains were dashed out. Sextus succeeded Stephanus as bishop of Rome, and is represented as a man of extraordinary prudence, learning, and piety. When an edict was signed by Valerian, for putting to death all the Christian clergy at Rome, Sextus is said to have been one of the first who felt its severity. He was beheaded, according to Cyprian, August 6th, A. D. 258.

Martyrdom of St. Laurence.

Laurentius, generally called St. Laurence, was a deacon under Sextus, and followed him to the place of execution. Just before he suffered, Sextus predicted that Laurentius would meet him in heaven within three days. Considering this as a certain indication of his fate, Laurentius went home, called the poor people of the church together, and distributed among them all the moneys committed to his care, thinking, in the present crisis, that it could not be better disposed of. His conduct alarming the persecutors, they immediately seized him, and commanded him in the name of the Emperor to give an account of the church treasures entrusted to his charge. This he promised to do if they would give him time to put things in their proper order. Three days were allowed him, during which time he collected a great number of aged, infirm, and impotent poor, and taking them before the magistrate said : " These are the true treasures of the church."

Provoked and disappointed, the governor in a great rage ordered him to be severely scourged, then binding him upon a wooden horse, and tying weights to his hands and feet, they dragged him about the streets till several of his joints were dislocated. He was then placed upon a large gridiron over a slow fire for a long time, and notwithstanding that he was actually roasted alive, he remained calm and collected, even to the last moment, exhorting the spec tators to embrace the religion of Jesus Christ. It is also said of him, that after having been awhile on the gridiron, he called out jocosely to the Emperor, who was present, in a Latin distich, which may be translated thus :

> This side enough is toasted,
> Then turn me tyrant, and eat ;
> And see whether raw or roasted,
> I am the better meat.

On this the executioner turned him over, and having laid awhile longer on the other side, he again called out to the Emperor, saying that he was now sufficiently roasted and was ready to be served up. He then cheerfully lifted up his eyes to heaven and with calmness yielded up his breath. This occurred on the 10th day of August, A. D. 258.

Romanus, a soldier who attended the execution of Laurentius, was so struck with his firmness, that he became a convert and was immediately beheaded

Persecution in Africa.

About this time the persecution raged in Africa with peculiar violence, and many thousands received the crown of martyrdom, among whom the following were the most distinguished.

Cyprian, bishop of Carthage, was an eminent prelate, and a pious ornament to the church. His doctrines were orthodox and pure, his language easy and elegant, and his manners graceful. He was said to have been so perfect in the practice of elocution and the principles of philosophy, that he was made a professor of these branches in his native city of Carthage. He was bred up in the religion of the Gentiles, and possessing a large fortune, lived in great pomp and splendour. In this manner he spent the former part of his life, indulging in every sensual gratification, till about A. D. 246, when becoming acquainted with the principles of the Christian religion through the preaching of Coecilius, he immediately became a convert of Christianity, and disposed of the greater portion of his estate, distributed the whole of it among the poor, dressed himself in plain attire, and commenced a life of austerity and solitude. Soon after this he was made a presbyter, and

being greatly admired for his virtues, was elected bishop
of Carthage in A. D. 248. In the year 250 he was publicly proscribed by the emperor Decius, and was in great
danger of suffering martyrdom from the rage and fury of
the pagans. He however withdrew from the rage of the
populace, upon which his effects were immediately confiscated. During his retirement he wrote often to his
flock for the purpose of warning them against many evils
that were now beginning to creep into the church, and
which gave him great uneasiness. But all his efforts
were ineffectual; and when the rigour of the persecution
was a little abated, he returned again to Carthage for the
purpose of expunging these errors from the church. But
a terrible plague soon breaking out in the city, as usual it
was imputed to the impiety of the Christians, and the persecution was again revived against them with greater
vigour than before.

Cyprian was brought before the proconsul, and commanded to conform to the religion of the empire, but he
boldly refused, and made an open avowal of his faith.
This, however, did not occasion his death, but he was banished to a small city on the Libyan sea. After the death
of the proconsul, he returned again to Carthage, where he
was seized by the governor, who ordered him to be beheaded; which was accordingly done on the 14th day of
September, A. D. 258. Several of his disciples were
also martyred at the same time.

Martyrdom of three hundred Christians.

Perhaps there is not a more striking instance recorded
in church history of Christian fortitude on the one hand,
and cruelty on the other, than that which transpired in
the city of Utica, during the persecution before mentioned. Three hundred Christians, of both sexes, were
placed around the orifice of a burning limekiln, and a pan
of coals and incense being prepared, they were commanded either to sacrifice to Jupiter, or be thrown into the
flame. They all with one accord refused to sacrifice, and
jumped into the pit themselves, where they were suffocated
immediately.

Singular Account of a Christian Lady.

Philippus, governor of Alexandria, had a beautiful daughter, who had received a liberal education and every other accomplishment that the age admitted. Having been much in the company of Christians, she at length became a convert, and to escape the persecution that was then raging, she escaped from her father's house, clothed herself in male attire, and calling her name Eugenius, was admitted into a convent of Christians, of which, at length, by reason of her virtue and learning, she was made the head. Here, it is said, she performed many miracles, and among others who were cured by her, was a matron of Alexandria, by the name of Melancia, who, supposing her to be a man, conceived a criminal passion for her, and besought her to gratify her desires. Eugenius exhorted her to continue in the path of virtue, but Melancia, enraged at the refusal, and fearful of an exposure, determined to anticipate the accusation. She accordingly accused Eugenius and her companions of an attempt to debauch her, upon which they were immediately apprehended and brought before Philippus, the governor. Eugenius, thinking it now no time for dissimulation, disclosed herself to Philippus as his daughter, and her two companions, Protheus and Hiacinthus, as two pious eunuchs, and revealed to him the cause of her departure. By this the judges were fully satisfied as to her innocence, and her accuser was utterly confounded. Philippus was soon after converted to Christianity and suffered martyrdom, but Eugenius, going to Rome, was apprehended as a Christian, and assailed with various kinds of torment, from all of which she was miraculously delivered. She was first cast into the Tiber with a stone about her neck, but was nevertheless saved from drowning. She was next put into a scalding bath, but escaped uninjured; and lastly, being cast into prison to die of hunger, was fed in a supernatural manner.

Fate of the Emperor Valerian.

This tyrant, who so long and so cruelly persecuted the Christian church, was finally taken prisoner by Saphores, king of Persia, who treated him with the most unexampled indignity, making him to kneel down, and placing his foot upon his neck when he mounted his horse. Having kept him in this manner for seven years, he first caused his eyes to be put out, and then ordered him to be flayed alive, and to have his body rubbed with salt. Under this operation he died.

Valerian was succeeded by Gallienus, his son, in A. D. 260, during whose reign the church was mostly free from persecution.

CHAPTER IV.

The ninth and tenth persecutions under the Roman Emperors.

Gallienus was succeeded by Aurelian, who, in A. D. 274, commenced a persecution against the Christians and caused many to be put to death, among whom was Felix, bishop of Rome, who was beheaded the 22d day of December, 274. But the emperor being murdered soon after, by his own domestics, he was succeeded by Tacitus. He being soon after slain, was succeeded by Probus, and he again by Carus. This Emperor, being killed by lightning, was succeeded by his sons, Carinus and Numerian, during the reign of all which the church enjoyed a state of rest.

Diocletian next succeeded to the throne, in A. D. 284, and at first showed great favour to the Christians, but in the year 286, he associated with him in the empire Maximian, and the following Christians were put to death before any general persecution commenced. Felician and Primus, two brothers, were seized by an order from the emperor, and confessing themselves Christians, were first tortured and then beheaded.

Marcus and Marcelianus were two twin brothers of noble descent. Their parents were heathen, but they, having been brought up under the care of Christian tutors, had embraced the Christian faith. They were sentenced to death on account of their faith, but a respite of a month was allowed them, during which time their parents and friends used every means in their power to win them over to paganism, but all to no purpose. Their constancy finally won over their persuaders to Christianity, and the whole family became converts just before the sentence was executed on the two young men.

Tranquillinus, the father of the two young men, being sent for by the prefect, to give an account of the success of his endeavours, he replied, that instead of prevailing on his sons to renounce their religion, he had himself become a convert to Christianity. He then stopped till the magistrate had recovered from his surprise, and resuming his discourse, used such arguments as prevailed upon the magistrate himself to become a convert, who immediately thereupon resigned his office, and spent the remainder of his days in pious retirement. His successor in office was a man of a very morose and cruel temper, whose first official act was to compel this newly converted family to suffer a variety of torture, after which they were all beheaded. These, with several other persons of distinction, suffered martyrdom before a general persecution was commenced.

Massacre of a whole Legion of Christian Soldiers.

A very remarkable event occurred in A. D. 286. A legion of soldiers, consisting of 6666 men, contained none but Christians. This was called the Theban Legion, because the men had been raised in Thebes. They had been quartered in the east, till the emperor Maximian commanded them to march to Gaul, to assist in quelling a rebellion in Burgundy. Having passed the Alps, the emperor ordered a general sacrifice, at which the whole army were to assist; after which they were to take the oath of allegiance, and swear at the same time, to assist him in the extirpation of Christianity from Gaul.

To this measure the whole legion absolutely refused obedience, professing to the emperor, that they were ready to serve him when his laws did not interfere with the commands of their Divine Master, but when the opposite was the case, they should on all occasions hazard the consequences of obeying God rather than man. Maximian, instead of being softened at this reply, ordered the whole legion to be put to the sword, which was accordingly done, on the 26th day of September, A. D. 286.

Alban, the First British Martyr.

Alban, from whom St. Albans in Hertfordshire received its name, was the first British martyr.   He was originally a pagan, and being naturally of a humane disposition, he sheltered a Christian missionary named Amphibalus, who was pursued on account of his religion.   The pious example and edifying conversation of the fugitive, led Alban to inquire into the principles of a religion that produced such fruits, and the consequence was, he soon became a convert to christianity.   The enemies of Amphibalus, learning at length where he had taken shelter, came in pursuit of him, upon which Alban prevailed on him to exchange dresses with him, and make his escape in disguise.   When the pursuers came to the house of Alban, he offered himself to them, who took him immediately before a magistrate, when the deception was discovered.   The magistrate, enraged at the escape of Amphibalus, determined to wreak his revenge on Alban.   He accordingly commanded him to sacrifice to the pagan deities, which Alban refusing to do, and confessing himself a christian, was first cruelly scourged, and then beheaded.   This happened on the 22d day of June, A. D. 287, at Verulam, now St. Albans, in Hertfordshire.   A magnificent church was erected on the spot about the time of Constantine, which was destroyed during the Saxon wars.   Another church and monastery was afterward erected on the same spot, some remains of which are still visible.

Second Persecution, under Diocletian.

Notwithstanding the repeated efforts of the heathen to exterminate the Christians, they increased so fast that they had now become formidable by their numbers.   Forgetting, however, the precepts of their religion, which taught them humility and meekness, they became gaudy in their apparel, and extravagant in their manner of living, insomuch that they excited the envy of the heathen, who were preparing to commence against them another persecution.

Galerius, an adopted son of Diocletian, was an inveterate enemy of the Christians, and used every means in his power to persuade him to raise a persecution against them. It accordingly began on the 23d day of February, A. D. 303, that being the day on which the Terminalia were celebrated, and on which, as the pagans boasted, they hoped to put an end to Christianity. The persecution was begun in Nicomedia; the prefect of that city repaired, with a great number of officers and soldiers, to the churches of the Christians, which were first robbed of their treasures, and then razed to the ground. This was followed by an edict pronouncing Christians of every denomination outlaws, confiscating their property, and denying to them the protection of the laws of the realm. This was also followed by a general sacrifice, which occasioned a great number of martyrdoms, in which almost every means of cruelty was adopted that the malignity of the human heart could devise. Many houses were set on fire, and whole families perished in the flames. Others had stones fastened about their necks, and were cast into the sea. The persecution extended into all the Roman governments, but more particularly in the eastern provinces, and as it lasted ten years, it is impossible to ascertain the number martyred, or to enumerate the various modes by which they were made to suffer. Many were beheaded in Arabia; many devoured by wild beasts in Phœnicia; great numbers were broiled on gridirons in Syria; others had their bones broken, and in that manner were left to expire; in Cappadocia, and in Mesopotamia, several were hung with their heads downward over a slow fire. In Pontus a variety of tortures were used; in particular, pins were thrust under the nails, melted lead was poured upon them, but all these torments were to no effect. In Egypt some Christians were drowned in the Nile, others were hung in the air till they perished, and great numbers were consumed with fire. Scourges, racks, swords, daggers, poison, crosses, and famine were used in various places to despatch the Christians. Phrygia, a town consisting wholly of Christians, was surrounded by soldiers, to prevent any from escaping, and then set on fire, and all the inhabitants perished in the flames.

After this persecution had continued for several years,

5

many of the provincial governors, weary of the repeated scenes of suffering that they had been compelled to witness, addressed the emperor, beseeching him to withdraw his edict, and stop the effusion of blood. With these requests he complied, and this long and cruel persecution was at length brought to a close.

It would exceed the bounds of the present work to enumerate the many eminent persons, of both sexes, who perished during this long scene of affliction, nor have we room to detail the many instances of Christian fortitude that were exhibited by those who were martyred. A few examples shall suffice.

Sebastian, a celebrated and holy man, who was an officer of the emperor's guard, continued steadfast in the faith during this bloody persecution, and was highly esteemed both by Christians and heathen. He was, however, informed against by a pretended Christian, and brought before the emperor, who reproached him with ingratitude, for daring to profess a religion that he himself discountenanced. To which Sebastian replied, that his religion was of good and not of evil tendency, and taught him to do nothing contrary to the interest of his master, and that the greatest proof he could give of his fidelity, was the praying to the only true God for his health and prosperity. Incensed at this reply, the emperor ordered him to be taken to a field near the city, called the Campus Martius, and there be shot with arrows. This was accordingly done, but some Christians, on taking up his body for interment, discovered signs of life; and by using proper means, he was soon restored again to health; but this was only preparatory to a second martyrdom, for, placing himself near a heathen temple, he waited till the emperor approached, who was not a little astonished in finding him still alive. Nor was he less surprised when Sebastian, with great boldness, began to rebuke him for his many acts of cruelty. When the emperor's surprise was a little subsided, he ordered him to be beaten to death with clubs, which was accordingly done, and his body was thrown into a sewer, from which it was recovered by a female member of the church, and interred with the rights of Christian burial.

Noble conduct of three Christian Friends.

While Maximus, governor of Cilicia, was at Tarsus, three Christians were brought before him, by Demetrius, a military officer. Tarachus, the eldest of the three, was asked by Maximus, what he was? The prisoner replied, a Christian. The governor, offended at this answer, commanded him to sacrifice to the gods, adding, at the same time, that by so doing he would gain his favour. To this Tarachus replied, that to be a follower of Christ was the only honour that he desired in this world, and so far from coveting the condition of such as he, he considered him rather an object of pity, inasmuch as he was a worshipper of dumb idols, and deceived and led astray by the devil. For this boldness of speech his jaws were commanded to be broken, and he was thrown into prison to await the trial of the other prisoners.

Probus was next brought before Maximus, who, as usual, asked his name. To this he replied, " The most noble name that I can boast of is that of Christian." " That name will be of little service to you," said Maximus ; " be therefore guided by me. Sacrifice to the gods ; engage my friendship, and the favour of the emperor." Probus nobly answered, " As he had already sacrificed much for the name of Christian, it might appear evident that he neither cared for his friendship, or the favour of the emperor." He was then severely scourged, and Demetrius observing how the blood flowed, exhorted him to relinquish his profession of Christ ; but Probus answered that nothing gave him greater pleasure than to be found worthy to suffer for Christ's sake. " What," said Maximus, " does the madman still persist in his resolution ?" To this he answered, " The term madman is ill applied to a disciple of Jesus." He was then again scourged, loaded with chains, and consigned to prison.

Andronicus was next brought forth, and being asked who he was, replied, " I am a Christian ; a native of Ephesus, and descended from one of the noblest families in that city." He was ordered to undergo a similar punishment to that of Tarachus and Probus, and was then remanded to prison.

Having been confined for some days, they were brought

again before Maximus, who at first began to reason with them, but finding them still steadfast, he caused them to be tortured in various ways, after which he again inquired of them whether they would not relinquish their faith and sacrifice to the gods. " I come better prepared," replied Probus, " than before ; for what I have suffered has only strengthened me in my resolution. Employ your whole power upon me ; and you shall find that neither you, nor your master the emperor, or the gods whom ye serve, nor even the Devil, who is your father, shall compel me to worship idols." The governor, however, attempted again to reason with him ; extolled, in the most extravagant manner, the gods whom they served ; to whom Probus replied " Shall I pay divine honours to Jupiter, to one who married his own sister ; to an infamous debauchee, as he is acknowledged to have been even by your own poets." Provoked at this, the governor ordered him to be struck upon the mouth for uttering what he considered to be blasphemy. He was then tortured in various ways and consigned again to prison.

Andronicus was next brought forward, whom Maximus attempted to deceive, by telling him that his companions had repented of their obstinacy, and owned the gods of the empire. " I will never believe it," said Andronicus, " I know them too well to believe they will ever, under any circumstances, forsake the worship of the true God to pay their adoration to devils ; so seek not to deceive me, but do your worst: I am a Christian ; Christ is my help and supporter, and thus armed I will neither serve your gods, nor do I fear your authority, or that of your master, the emperor : commence your torments as soon as you please, and make use of every means that your malignity can invent, and you shall find in the end, that I am not to be shaken from my resolution." For this answer he was most cruelly scourged, and his wounds rubbed with salt, after which he was again consigned to prison. A few days after, they were brought out for a third examination, and finding that they still retained their constancy, they were first severely tortured, and then consigned to the amphitheatre, to be torn in pieces by wild animals. Several beasts were accordingly let loose upon them, but neither of them, though hungry, would touch them. A large bear was next brought out that had torn three persons the same day. but this creature and a fierce lioness also refused to touch them. Finding this means of destroying them ineffectual, Maximus ordered them to be slain with a sword, which was accordingly done on the 11th day of October, A. D. 303.

Horrid Martyrdom of Romanus.

Romanus was a native of Palestine, and a deacon in the church of Cesarea, at the time of Diocletian's persecution. He was at Antioch at the time the imperial edict came for sacrificing to idols, and was much grieved to see many Christians, through fear, submit to the idolatrous mandate, and deny their faith to preserve their lives. While censuring some of them for their conduct, he was informed against, and soon after apprehended. Being brought before the tribunal, he confessed himself a Christian, and declared that he was willing to suffer any thing they might see fit to inflict upon him, for the sake of Christ. When condemned, he was scourged, put to the rack, his body torn with hooks, his flesh cut with knives, his face scarified, his teeth knocked out, and his hair plucked out by the roots. Thus cruelly mangled, he turned to the governor, and very calmly thanked him for what he had done, and for having opened for him so many mouths with which to preach the gospel of Christ. He was then ordered to be strangled, which was accordingly done on the 17th day of November, A. D. 303.

Conversion and Death of Cyprian.

Cyprian, known by the name of the magician, to distinguish him from Cyprian, bishop of Carthage, before mentioned, was a native of Antioch, and after receiving a liberal education, travelled in other countries, in search of knowledge, and finally settled near Babylon; being skilled in the Chaldean mysteries, he employed his talents in attempting to seduce virtuous women from their chastity, and in persecuting the Christians. He became acquainted with Justina, a young lady of Antioch, of high birth, beauty, and accomplishments, who had been brought up in

5*

idolatry, but had now become a Christian, and persuaded both of her parents to embrace the same faith.

A pagan gentleman, falling in love with her, and being unable to obtain a favourable return of his affection on account of his religion, he employed Cyprian to win her over to his wishes, who undertook to do so, but with the treacherous plan of possessing her himself. To effect this he employed all his skill, but to no purpose, which led him to suppose that she must be protected by some superior power. He accordingly applied himself to the study of the principles of Christianity, with such beneficial effects to himself, that he soon became a convert to the faith, and his repentance was as sincere as his iniquities had been great. He immediately burned his books, and did every thing in his power to atone for his former errors.

His conversion had such an effect upon the lover of the young lady, that he himself became a convert, and soon after married the beautiful Justina.

During the persecution of Diocletian, Justina and Cyprian were seized upon as Christians, when, after being variously tortured, they were both put to death by being beheaded.

Martyrdom of Three Sisters.

Three sisters, whose names were Chionia, Agape, and Irene, who had been educated in the Christian faith, were seized upon as Christians, in Thessalonica, during the before mentioned persecution. Being desirous of continuing unknown, they had retired to a solitary place, and spent their leisure hours in performing religious duties. Being, however discovered and seized, they renounced their former timidity, blamed themselves for being thus fearful, and begged of God to strengthen them for the trials that awaited them. When Agape was examined before Dalcatius, the governor, she was asked whether she felt disposed to comply with the laws of the empire? she answered, "That being a Christian, she would not obey any laws that commanded the worship of idols and devils, that her resolutions were taken, and that nothing should deter her from continuing in them."

Her sister Chionia replied in the same manner, and the governor finding himself unable to draw them from their faith, passed sentence of death upon them, and they were accordingly burnt, March 25, A. D. 304.

Irene was then brought before the judge, who fancied that the death of her sisters would have an effect upon her fears, and that the dread of a similar fate would induce her to comply with his offers of mercy. He therefore exhorted her to acknowledge the heathen deities, to sacrifice to them, and to give up her books on Christianity. But she positively refused, and told him firmly, that no punishment that he had the power to inflict, should ever shake her resolution in the least; that that God who had commanded her to love Him to the last, would give her strength to endure her sufferings; and that she was in readiness to follow the example of her faithful sisters, but not to abjure her religion.

The governor finding that he could not prevail on her to relinquish her faith, commanded her first to be exposed naked in the streets, and when this shameful order was complied with, she was burned, April 1, A. D. 204, on the same spot where her sisters had suffered.

Conduct of Philip, Bishop of Heraclea.

This venerable bishop had ever proved himself to be a true Christian, by every work of virtue and charity. He was advised by his friends to shut himself up, or to leave the city during the persecution, but instead of complying, he reproved those with severity who offered this advice, and continued in the open performance of his duties, till apprehended by order of the governor, who addressed him in the following manner, " Bring all the vessels used in your worship, and also the scriptures which you read and teach; and see that you surrender them, before compelled so to do by the tortures that will be inflicted upon you in case of a refusal."

" If," replied the bishop, " you take any pleasure in seeing us suffer, my old and infirm body is in your power, do with it as you choose. The vessels you demand shall be given up, for our God is not honoured by gold and silver, but by the fear of his power. But as to the Sacred volumes, it is neither proper for me to part with them, nor for you to receive them." This answer so much incensed the governor, that he ordered him to the torture. Hermes, one of Philip's disciples, and a deacon of the church, remonstrated with the judge on such an arbitrary act of cruelty, for which he was ordered to be scourged at the same time. The pagans, having proceeded to the place where the scriptures and church plate were kept, embezzled the treasure, burned the scriptures, and then demolished the church. Philip was then taken to the market-place, and commanded to sacrifice to the Roman deities in general, and Hercules in particular. In answer to which command he made an animated address on the real nature of the true Deity, and concluded, with saying that the heathen worshipped what might lawfully be trodden upon, and made gods of things only destined for their own service. At this animated address the governor was highly incensed, and ordered Phillip to be dragged through the streets by his feet, till he was bruised in a most shocking manner. He was then brought again before the governor, who charged him with obstinacy and rashness, and besought him to save his life by acknowledging the Roman deities. Philip, however, replied " that he preferred heaven to earth, and that his faith commanded him to obey God rather than man." Immediately upon this he was sentenced to be burnt, which was executed accordingly, and he died praising God in the midst of the flames. Hermes and Severus, for similar conduct, was shortly after condemned to the stake.

Not long after this Diocletian and Maximian, weary of the toils of government, resigned the imperial diadem, which checked for a time a persecution more cruel and extensive than the church had ever before suffered. Our limits prohibit from even naming the numerous persons of the highest distinction, as well as thousands of others, in every part of the Roman empire, who suffered the most cruel tortures, and displayed the utmost fortitude, by occasion of their faith as Christians.

This resignation took place in A. D. 304, and Constantius and Galerius succeeded to the government of the empire.

Constantius was a prince of a mild, humane, and amiable disposition, while Galerius was equally remarkable for tyranny and cruelty. These two princes divided the empire into two equal parts, the former governing the west, and the latter the east. According to the disposition of these two sovereigns, such was the condition of the church in their respective dominions during their reigns. While those in the west enjoyed a state of rest and quietness, those in the east were made to feel the utmost rigour of their cruel and tyrannical master.

Martyrdom of St. George.

This eminent saint was born of Christian parents, in Cappadocia, by whom he was instructed in the principles of Christianity. His father dying when he was young, he travelled with his mother into Palestine, which was her native country, and where she inherited a large estate, that afterward descended to her son.

George, being ambitious and spirited, became a soldier, and was made a tribune, or colonel. In this station he exhibited great courage, and was promoted in the army by Diocletian. During the persecution he resigned his command, went boldly to the senate house and declared himself a Christian, remonstrating at the same time against the gods of the heathen. This conduct so incensed the senate that they ordered him to be put to the torture, which he endured with a fortitude becoming his character. He was afterward, by order of the emperor, dragged through the streets by his feet and afterward beheaded.

The calendar commemorates his martyrdom on the 23d of April, and he is considered as the tutelar saint of England.

Account of Constantine the Great.

Constantius was succeeded by his son, Constantine, who is, with much justice, called the Great, as he possessed every virtue becoming the character of a prince in an eminent degree. Not long after the death of his father he determined to redress the grievances of the Christians, and for this purpose raised an army of 30,000 foot and 8000 horse, with which he marched toward Rome against the

emperor Maxentius.   But remembering the fatal miscar-
riages of his predecessors who had maintained a multiplicity
of gods, and reflecting that while his father adored only one
God he continually prospered, he rejected the worship of
idols and implored the aid of the Almighty ; and such
weer the miraculous interpositions of heaven in his favour,
says Eusebius, that they would have appeared to him incredible had he not received them from the emperor's
own mouth, who solemnly ratified them with an oath.

Vision of Constantine.

  " The army having advanced within three miles of
Rome, the emperor, employed in his devout ejaculations,
on the 27th of October, about three o'clock in the afternoon,
when the sun was declining, there suddenly appeared to
him, a pillar of light in the heavens in the form of a cross
with this plain inscription, on or about it, ΤΟΥΤΩ ΝΙΚΑ.
" In this overcome."   Constantine was greatly surprised
at this strange sight which was equally visible to the whole
army, who equally wondered at it with himself.   The
officers and commanders prompted by the soothsayers considered it an inauspicious omen, portending an unfortunate
expedition, nor did the emperor himself understand it till
the Saviour appeared to him in a vision. holding a cross

in his hand, and commanding him to make a royal standard, like that he had seen in the heavens, and cause it to be continually carried before his army, as an ensign both of victory and safety.   Early the next morning, Constantine informed his friends and officers of what he had seen in the night, and sending for proper workmen, described to them the form of the standard, which was accordingly made with the greatest art and magnificence.   The form of it was thus: A long spear plated with gold, with a transverse piece at the top, in the form of a cross, to which was fastened a foursquare banner of purple, embroidered with gold and beset with precious stones.   Toward the top was depicted the emperor between his two sons ; on the top of the shaft, above the cross, stood a crown overlaid with gold and precious stones, within which was placed the sacred symbol, viz. : the two first letters of Christ in Greek, X and P, stuck one through the other.   This device he afterward bore upon his shield, and upon his coins, many of which are now extant.

Not long after this he engaged Maxentius, and defeated him, entering Rome in triumph.   Immediately after this, a law was passed giving free toleration to Christianity throughout the empire, and thus ended the bloody trials of the church, at least for a season.

PART II.

CHAPTER I.

Miscellaneous Persecutions during the Fourth Century.

AFTER Constantine had subdued Maxentius, the persecution of the Christians was not only forbidden, but becoming himself a faithful follower of Christ, the Christian religion was soon established throughout the empire.

A law was now published in favour of the Christians, in which Licinius joined with Constantine, and a copy served upon Maximus, Constantine's associate in the empire.   Maximus was a bigotted pagan, and greatly disliked this edict, but suppressed his disapprobation, for fear of Constantine's anger.   At length he invaded the do-

minions of Licinius, but being defeated he put an end to
his life by poison. Licinius, however, who at first joined
with Constantine, caused many eminent bishops and priests
to be put to death within his own dominions. This hypocrisy and cruelty so incensed Constantine that he marched against and defeated him, after which he was slain by
his own soldiers.

But notwithstanding the church, in general, enjoyed
rest and prosperity ; the gospel having spread beyond the
bounds of the Roman empire, its votaries still continued
to feel the effects of heathen cruelty, when the power of
Constantine did not extend for their protection.

Persecution of the Christians in Persia.

In consequence of the gospel having spread into this
country, the pagan priests became alarmed lest their religion should finally become extinct. They, therefore, complained to their sovereign, that the Christians were enemies to the state, and held treasonable correspondence
with the Romans, the great enemies of Persia. The emperor, being himself averse to Christianity, gave orders for
a general persecution of the Christians throughout his dominions.

In consequence of this mandate, Simeon, archbishop of
Selucia, with other ecclesiastics, to the number of one
hundred and twenty-eight, were apprehended, and accused
of having betrayed the empire to the Romans. Being
brought before the emperor, Simeon boldly avowed his
faith.   Offended at his freedom, the monarch ordered him
to kneel before him, as he had heretofore done.   To this
Simeon answered, that being brought before him as a prisoner on account of his religion, it was not lawful for him
to kneel, lest he should be thought to worship a man, and
betray his faith to his God.   The emperor, still more enraged, told him if he did not knee , he and all the Christians in the empire should be put to death.   But he still
rejected the command with disdain, and was ordered to be
sent to prison.

A short time after, Simeon and his companions were
again brought before the emperor for examination, who
commanded them to worship the sun, agreeably to the

Persian custom, but this they unanimously refused. They were then sentenced to be beheaded, which was accordingly executed upon them.

When Simeon was led to execution, he was saluted by Usthazares, who had been the tutor of the emperor, and was held in high estimation at court, but Simeon refused to return the salutation, on account of Usthazares, who having been once a Christian, had apostatized to please his master. When thus reproved by Simeon, he could not refrain from exclaiming, " Ah! how shall I hereafter look upon my God, whom I have denied, when Simeon, my old companion and familiar acquaintance, disdains to give me a gentle word, or to return my salute !"

The emperor, on being informed of this, called for his tutor, and asked him the cause of his unhappiness ; telling him, at the same time, that if there were any thing that could be done to make him happy, it should not be withheld. To this he replied, " That there was nothing that this world could afford that he desired, but that the cause of his sorrow was the having denied his God against the dictates of his conscience ; for which," continued he, " I am deserving a double death : first, for denying of Christ, and secondly, for dissembling with my king."

The emperor, greatly offended at this speech, ordered him to be beheaded ; at which, Usthazares requested that it might be publicly proclaimed, that he died for no crime against the emperor or the state, but only that, being a Christian, he would not deny his God. This petition was granted, and he died with great composure.

A short time after this an edict was published, ordering that all who confessed themselves Christians should be put to death ; in consequence of which, great multitudes suffered death ; and the persecution continued till Constantine the Great wrote to the emperor of Persia, requesting him in a very friendly manner to desist from persecuting the Christians. He enforced his request by declaring that it was only through faith in Christ that he had been enabled to subdue his enemies and enlarge the borders of the Roman empire. He also alluded to the troubles of his predecessors who had persecuted the Christian church, and the prosperity of those who had favoured it ; and concluded by expressing his desire that he would show favour

6

to the Christians that resided in Persia; and this he would consider as the strongest evidence of his friendship toward himself.

With this request the Persian monarch immediately complied, and a stop was put to the persecution, after 16,000 had either suffered death or banishment.

Persecution by the Arians.

The sect denominated Arians took their rise from Arius, a priest of Lybia, who first began to propagate his sentiments in Alexandria, A. D. 318. He was condemned by a council of Lybian and Egyptian bishops, and the sentence was sanctioned by the council of Nice, A. D. 325. After the death of Constantine, they found means to ingratiate themselves with his son and successor, and soon raised a persecution against the orthodox bishops and clergy. The celebrated Athanasius and other bishops were banished, and their sees were filled with Arians.

In Egypt and Lybia, thirty bishops were martyred, and a great many other Christians were cruelly tortured. In A. D. 336, George the Arian, bishop of Alexandria, under the authority of the emperor, began a persecution in that city and its environs, in which he was assisted by the governor and several of the emperor's officers. The cruelty of these heretics fell but little short of that practised by the pagans. They commenced by shutting up the churches of the orthodox party, by banishing them, and plundering their effects, but soon proceeded to greater deeds of violence. As the orthodox Christians were prohibited from worshipping in the city, they used often to retire to the desert for the purpose, and for a while were permitted to do so without molestation; but on a Trinity Sunday, while thus engaged, George, the Arian bishop engaged Sebastian, a Roman general, to fall upon them with his soldiers, while they were at their prayers, and great numbers were sacrificed to the fury of his troops. This outrage was followed by others of similar nature, and for several years the whole Roman empire was a scene of contention, rapine, and slaughter.

The western half of the empire, however, was more free from Arian influence and persecution, as Constans, its emperor, favoured the orthodox party, while his brother Constantius favoured those of the Arians.

Persecution under Julian.

Julian the apostate, as he is usually called, who succeeded Constans in the imperial government, was the son of Julius Constantius, and nephew of Constantine the Great.

He studied the rudiments of grammar under the inspection of Mardonius, a eunuch and a heathen. His father sent him afterward to Nicomedia to be instructed in the christian religion by Eusebius, his kinsman, but his principles were corrupted by Maximus the magician and Eubalius, a professor of rhetoric.

Constans died in A. D. 361, when Julian succeeded him, but he had no sooner ascended the imperial throne than he renounced Christianity, and embraced heathenism. He again instituted idolatrous worship, by opening several heathen temples that had been shut up, rebuilding such as had been destroyed, and ordering the magistrates and people generally to follow his example. He did not, however, issue any edict against the Christians, but gave free toleration to the exercise of every religion, though he deprived the Christians of all offices, civil or military, and the clergy of the privileges that had been granted to them by Constantine.

Nor did he follow the profligate course of his predecessors, but was reserved, temperate, laborious, and apparently pious, which rendered him a more dangerous enemy to the Christians than any that had gone before him. He at first attempted to win them over to idolatry by lavishing gifts and honours upon such as followed his example of apostacy ; and then, by prohibiting Christian schools, he compelled the children either to become idolaters or to remain illiterate.

He also ordered that the Christians might be treated coldly upon all occasions, and in all parts of the empire ; and employed witty persons to turn them and their principles into ridicule. Many also were martyred in his reign, for though he did not publicly persecute them himself, he connived at their being murdered by his governors and other officers; though he affected never to reward them for those cruelties, neither did he ever punish them.

Among the most distinguished personages who suffered martyrdom during his reign, was Basil, who rendered himself conspicuous by his opposition to the Arian heresy. He was an eminent preacher in the city of Ancyra, the capital of Galatia, and notwithstanding he was violently opposed by the Arian bishops of Constantinople, he continued in the faithful performance of his duty till he was apprehended on the charge of being an incendiary and disturber of the public peace. But Julian, being engaged in an expedition against Persia, paid but little attention to the subject for the present, during which interval Basil improved his time in preaching against idolatry on the one hand, and Arianism on the other.

One day, meeting with a number of pagans going in procession to sacrifice, he boldly expostulated with them on the wickedness and folly of such worship, and was seized by the multitude and carried before Saturninus, the governor, to whom he was accused of reviling the gods and the emperor, and disturbing the peace of the city. Having heard these accusations, the governor desired to know his sentiments from his own mouth, when finding him to be a strenuous Christian, he ordered him to be put, first to the rack, and then to be cast into prison. He then wrote an account of his proceedings to the emperor, who not only confirmed what had been done, but sent two apostate Christians to the place where Basil was confined, to endeavour to win him over to paganism. Finding their efforts vain they gave over their object ; and immediately on the return of the emperor, gave him an account of the failure of their exertions.

Julian then ordered Basil before himself, and by threats and promises strove to make him forsake the Christian faith and embrace idolatry, but he not only obstinately refused, but, with a prophetical spirit, foretold the death of the emperor, and that he should be tormented in the other world. At the boldness of this conduct the emperor was very much enraged, and commanded that he should be put to death, by having a part of his flesh torn off daily in seven different places, till his body was completely mangled. This cruel sentence was accordingly executed, and Basil died under the operation, on the 28th day of June, A. D. 362.

About this time also, Donatus, bishop of Arezzo, and Hilarinus, a hermit, suffered martyrdom, the first being beheaded, and the latter scourged to death. Beside these, many other persons of distinction, among whom was Artemius, commander of the Roman forces in Egypt, Maximilian and Bonosus, two officers of the Herculean Guards, and Marcus, bishop of Arethusa, suffered martyrdom in different ways.

Persecution of the Christians by the Goths.

During the reign of Constantine the Great, several Scythian Goths embraced Christianity, notwithstanding, the greater part of that people continued pagans. Fritegern, king of the western Goths, was an ally of the Romans. But Athanaric, king of the eastern Goths, was at war with them. The Christians, in the dominions of the former, lived unmolested; but the latter, having been defeated by the Romans, wreaked his vengeance on his Christian subjects. Sabas, a Christian, was the first who felt his king's resentment; he was humble and modest, though zealous and fervent in the advancement of the gospel.

In A. D. 370, Athanaric gave orders for a general sacrifice, and commanded that all who refused to partake of that which had been offered to the heathen deities, should be put to death. Many of the more humane pagans, who assisted at the sacrifice, in order to spare the Christians, gave them to eat of that which had not been offered; though they managed in such a manner as to make the magistrates suppose it had; but Sabas, too well understood the sentiments of St. Paul, to suppose that the sin lay in eating; but knew that giving the enemies of Christ an advantage over the weak, was all that made the action criminal to Christians. He, therefore, not only refused to eat of the meat himself, but openly declared, " That those who sheltered themselves under this artifice were not good Christians."

Sabas was soon after apprehended and conveyed before a magistrate, who, finding that he was a person of obscure birth, and small fortune, dismissed him as unworthy of no-

6*

tice. He accordingly went to spend the ensuing Easter with Sansala, a Christian priest of great sanctity, but on the third night after his arrival, they were both seized by a company of soldiers. Sansala was permitted to dress himself, but Sabas was taken from his bed naked, and compelled to walk a considerable distance, during which time they drove him through thorns and briars. This cruelty he bore without a murmur, and when they stopped for the night, they extended him between two beams tying his feet to one end, and his hands to the other. The woman of the house, however, went and released him, but though he was now at liberty, he did not attempt to escape.

On the following morning his persecutors began to tamper with him and his fellow prisoner to renounce their religion, but finding them both steadfast, they released Sansala, but put Sabas to death by drowning. This happened on the 12th day of April, A. D. 372.

Account of Eusebius.

Eusebius, bishop of Samasata, made a distinguished figure in ecclesiastical history, and was one of the most eminent champions of Christ against the Arian heresy. The Arians having advanced Miletus to the see of Antioch, thinking him of their party, the document of his advancement was placed in the care of Eusebius. When Miletus preached his first sermon, the Arians, to their great surprise, found that they had been mistaken in him, for his doctrine was pure. They therefore persuaded the emperor to displace him, and likewise to get the instrument out of the hands of Eusebius. Miletus was accordingly deposed, and Eusebius commanded to give up the article, but he refused, saying that he could not part with it without the consent of all parties concerned. The emperor, incensed at this reply, wrote to him that he had given the messenger orders to cut off his right hand in case he refused a second time to give up the instrument. Eusebius, without the least emotion, offered his hands, and declared that he would lose them both rather than betray his trust. The emperor, when he was informed of this, applauded his resolution, and professed a high esteem for him ever after.

The Arians now looked upon Eusebius as a powerful and dangerous enemy, and as he was very active and successful in opposing the progress of their heresy, they at length procured from the emperor an order for his banishment from the see of Samasata.

When the messenger came with his commission, it was late in the evening, and Eusebius, who was beloved of the people, begged of him to conceal his business; "For," says he, "if it becomes known, the people will fall on you, throw you into the river, and I shall be charged with your death." He then went through with his usual devotions, and late at night set off upon his journey, attended only by a faithful servant.

When, on the following day, his people discovered that he was absent, and learning what course he had taken, by great numbers pursued him, and when they had overtaken him, with tears they besought him not to forsake them; but finding that they could not prevail, they furnished him with every necessary for his journey, and returned.

Thrace, the country to which he was banished, was at the time the seat of war between the Goths and Romans; and in these contests the life of Eusebius was in great danger. At length the emperor, in order to put an end to the war, determined to march against the Goths in person, but first, to secure the prayers of the Christians, he gave peace to the church, and allowed the banished prelates to return to their churches. Eusebius was therefore restored to his see, but did not enjoy it long, for an Arian woman threw a tile at him from the top of a house, which fractured his skull, and terminated his life. This happened in A. D. 380.

Persecution of the Christians by the Arian Vandals.

The Arian Vandals proceeding from Spain to Africa in the fifth century, under Genseric, their leader, committed many horrid cruelties. They persecuted the Christians wherever they came, laying waste the country, that famine might destroy what the sword had spared. They plunder ed the churches, and massacred the bishops and ministers by a variety of tortures; in particular, they poured fetid oil and vinegar down the throats of some till they expired. They suffocated some by filling their mouths with mud, and murdered others by stretching their limbs with cords and screws till the veins bursted. They compelled some of the nobility to carry their baggage, and if they did not travel fast enough they pricked them onward by sharp goads, insomuch that many of them died under their burdens. Old men found no mercy, and even guiltless infants felt the rage of their barbarity; stately buildings were destroyed, and the principal cathedrals in Carthage were employed in their heretical worship or put to profane uses. Where any castle held out against them, they brought great numbers of captive Christians and slew them, leaving their bodies under the walls, that the beseiged might be forced to surrender, on account of the offensive stench that arose from them.

When they had seized and plundered the city of Carthage they put the bishops and all the clergy into a leaky ship and committed them to the mercy of the waves, thinking that they all must perish; but the vessel, through Divine Providence, arrived safe at Naples. Several Christians were scourged, beaten, and banished to Capsur, where it pleased God to make them instrumental in converting many of the Moors to Christianity. But this coming to the knowledge of Genseric he sent orders that they and their converts should be tied by their feet to chariots and dragged till they were dashed to pieces.

Pampinian, bishop of Mansuetis, was burnt to death with plates of hot iron; the bishop of Urice was burnt; the bishop of Habensa was banished, for refusing to give up the sacred books which were in his possession; and a whole congregation who were assembled in a church at their devotions, together with the clergyman who was preaching to them, were murdered by these barbarians, who broke in upon them.

Archinimus was a devout Christian upon whom many artifices were empl____ ___ in vain to make him renounce his faith. At le· _____ _____ ____ndertook to persuade _·   ____   · he ordered him to be beheaded. He however ordered the executioner to perform his office only in case the prisoner seemed intimidated and afraid; " for then," said he, " the crown of martyrdom will be lost to him ; but if he appears courageous and willing to die, strike not, for I do not intend that he shall have the honour of being deemed a martyr." The executioner finding Archinimus happy in the thoughts of dying for the sake of Christ, brought him back again. He was soon after banished and never heard of more, though it is conjectured that he was murdered privately by the king's orders.

About this time, five thousand Christians of Carthage were banished by king Huneric into a desert, where a great proportion of them perished with famine.

Persecutions from the Fifth to the Seventh Century.

From the time of the persecution under Genseric, the church, in general, enjoyed a tolerable state of tranquility, excepting an occasional tumult between the orthodox and Arian, or some other heterodox party.

The most distinguished of these, is that which occurred at Alexandria, about the year 457.

A new heresy having arisen at about this period, which being first propagated by Eutyches, was called by his name. He gained many proselytes, especially among the Arian party. Among these was Diascorus, bishop of Alexandria. For the embracing of this faith he was tried by a council, and condemned to be removed from his see, and Proterius appointed his successor, of which choice the emperor approved. After the removal of Diascorus, his adherants, who were numerous, determined to resist not only the decree of the council, but also the will of the emperor, by physical force, and for this purpose armed themselves for the contest. The governor of Thebais, to quell this insurrection, marched against them with a body of troops, but they, being in a kind of phrensy, attacked and defeated him. The intelligence of this affair so exasperated the emperor, that he sent a detachment of 2000 men against them, the sight of whom, together with the prudent conduct of the governor, soon restored peace to the city. The disaffected party, nevertheless, continued to view Proterius with resentment, insomuch that he was compelled tc excommunicate some of them, and procure their banishment from Alexandria.

In about two years after the emperor Marcian died, and the banished persons returned again to the city, where they commenced anew their opposition to Proterius, whom at last they murdered, A. D. 457, at the altar of his church. After which they dragged his body through the streets, and then burned it and dispersed the ashes.

Account of Anastasius.

Anastasius was by birth a Persian, and instructed during his childhood in the pagan religion. He bore arms as a soldier under Cosroes, king of Persia, at the time that that monarch plundered Jerusalem, and carried off the true cross, on which our Lord was crucified. Anastasius could not imagine why the Christians had such a veneration for a person who had died so mean a death as that of being crucified—for that mode of death, by the Persians, is held in the greatest contempt. At length some Christian captives instructed him in the mysteries of the Christian religion, when he left the army, retired to Syria, and studied the Greek language, in order to become better acquainted with the Scriptures. After this he went to Cesarea, which was at that time in the hands of the Persians. Here he was apprehended as a spy, and on confessing himself a Christian, he was cast into prison, and many efforts were used to prevail on him to relinquish his faith. These efforts proving ineffectual, he was put to death in the following manner: he was laid upon his back, with a heavy piece of wood across his body, and pressed down with the weight of two strong men. He was then severely beaten, and hung up by one hand, with a weight fastened to his feet. After remaining in this condition for several hours, he was finally strangled, after which his head was cut off and sent to the king.

CHAPTER III.

Account of Bishop Martin.

Martin, bishop of Rome, was born in Lodi. He was naturally virtuous, and his parents bestowed on him a liberal education. He took orders on the death of Theodore, bishop of Rome, and was advanced to that important see by a unanimous vote of all parties.

Not long after his elevation to this important station he was called to contend with a body of heretics called Monothelites; who after the decision of the council of Chalcedon dared not to maintain the unity of nature in Christ, asserted artfully that he had but one will and operation of mind. This sect was patronised by the emperor Heraclius; and the first who attempted to stop the progress of these errors was Sophronius, bishop of Jerusalem. Martin, whose sentiments corresponded with those of Sophronius united with him in calling a council of one hundred and five bishops, who unanimously condemned the errors in question.

The emperor, provoked at these proceedings, commanded Olympius, his lieutenant, to repair to Rome and apprehend Martin; but on arriving at the city, he found him so much in favour with the people that he dared not attempt it, and therefore putting himself at the head of his troops marched against the Saracens.

Another officer was sent soon after to apprehend the bishop, who succeeded in so doing only by the aid of a large number of soldiers, and brought him before the imperial court at Constantinople. Here he was accused of holding a treasonable correspondence with the Saracen army. This, however, he denied, though he confessed that he had sent money for the relief of the Christian prisoners among them. He was nevertheless stripped of all his ecclesiastical dignities and cast into prison. After remaining in confinement for several months, he was banished to an island at some distance, and there cut in pieces, a. d. 655.

Several other persons of distinction suffered martyrdom from the Arian party during this century, among whom was John, bishop of Bergamo, who was assassinated on the 11th of July, A. D. 683, and Kilien, a distinguished Irish ecclesiastic.

CHAPTER IV.

Persecutions from the eighth to the tenth century.

Account of Boniface.

Boniface, archbishop of Mentz, and father of the German church was an Englishman by birth, and is considered as one of the brightest ornaments of his country. His name was originally Winfrith, and he was born at Kirton, in Devonshire, then part of the West Saxon kingdom. When only six years old he showed a propensity for reflection, and seemed anxious to gain information on religious subjects. Some missionaries coming into Kirton at about this time, stopped at his father's house, which determined him to devote himself to a religious life.

When he informed his father of his resolution, he would have dissuaded him from it, but finding him fully resolved upon it, permitted him to go and reside at the monastery in Exeter. Walfred, the abbot, finding that he possessed a bright genius, had him removed to Nutscelle, a seminary of learning in the diocese of Winchester. The abbot of Nutscelle, who was a man of great learning, took extraordinary pains with his young pupil, who soon became such a prodigy in the science of theology, that he became one of the principal teachers.

We are informed by the ancient Saxon historians, that those who studied under him had no need to remove to any other place to finish what they had began, for there was scarcely any branch of science that he was not furnished with. His mode of life was exemplary, his manners amiable, and his character generally such as endeared him to all with whom he was acquainted.

When about thirty years of age he received holy orders, and commenced the noble work of preaching the gospel, which was the means of bringing so many savages and barbarians from heathenish darkness to the glorious light of Christianity. There being an important occasion for calling a council in the kingdom of West Saxony. Boniface was unanimously chosen to wait upon the archbishop of Canterbury, and make known to him the exigences of the case.

Boniface discharged this trust with great prudence and discretion, insomuch that he obtained the applause of every member of the Synod, but far from being vain of the reputation he had acquired, he asked permission to leave his native country, that he might be instrumental in disseminating the truths of Christianity upon the continent. Having obtained permission, he set out on his mission in A. D. 716, and on arriving at Friesland, the place of his destination, found the country in the utmost disorder and confusion, and under the governmant of a pagan prince, who refused to receive the gospel; he concluded that the time had not yet come for converting the country to Christianity, and returned to his own convent in England.

Soon after this, the Abbot dying, Boniface was invited to become his successor, but either did not accept at all of the office, or else did not long continue invested with his new dignity, for about this time he obtained letters from the bishop of Winchester, his diocesian, which recommended him to the pope, and all the bishops, abbots, and friars in his way to Rome, when he arrived in the beginning of the year 719.

Gregory II., who then filled the papal seat, treated him with the greatest respect, and after holding several conferences with him, gave him an unlimited commission to preach the gospel to all pagans, wherever he might find them. With this authority he travelled through Lombardy, and Bavaria, and came to Thuringia, which country had before received the gospel, though it had, as yet, made but little progress. His first effort was to bring back the corrupted Christians to the purity of the gospel, and having completed this pious work, travelled into other parts of Germany, and was the means of converting several thousand souls to the Christian faith. He then proceeded to Saxony, where he was more than ordinarily successful in inculcating the principles of true religion. After labouring in this field for about a year, he despatched one of his companions to Rome with an account of the result of his exertions; upon the reception of his message, Gregory sent him a letter, desiring his presence in Rome. Boniface accordingly set out for that city, and upon his arrival, he received from the pope every mark of esteem and affection, and was not permitted to return to his labours until he had been invested with the episcopal character, in order that he might pursue them with more authority, and to greater advantage. It was on this occasion that he relinquished his name of Winfrith, and assumed that of Boniface.

Gregory having then given him recommendatory letters to all the prelates and princes of Christendom, Boniface hastened to resume his labours. After preaching with his usual success, not only in Germany, but also in several of the neighbouring kingdoms, for the term of nine years, he was again recalled to Rome by Gregory III., in 731. He was now constituted an archbishop, and authorised to erect new bishoprics throughout Germany. Here he continued to labour with unabated zeal till 752, when, by reason of his great age, he consecrated Lallus, his fellow country-man and faithful disciple, as his assistant.

After this he travelled into Friesland, where he converted and baptized several thousand of the natives, demolished their temples, and raised churches in their stead. Having appointed a day for administering the rite of confirmation, he ordered them to assemble on an open plain near the river Bourde, whither he repaired the day before, to be in readiness on the following morning.

The pagans having knowledge of this, rushed upon him and his associates with great violence, and meeting with no resistance, Boniface, with fifty others, was slain. This happened on June 5th, A. D. 755. Thus fell the great ther of the Germanic church, the honour of England, the glory of his barbarous age.

CHAPTER V.

Other Martyrdoms between the Sixth and Tenth Centuries.

Massacre by the Saracens.

Forty-two persons of Upper Phrygia, were martyred, A. D. 845, by the Saracens, the circumstances of which are thus related :

In the reign of Theophilus, the Saracens ravaged many parts of the eastern empire, gained many advantages over the Christians, and finally laid siege to the city of Armorian, in Upper Phrygia. The garrison bravely defended the place for a considerable time, but being betrayed by a renegado, the town was taken, many put to the sword, and two general officers, with a number of persons of distinction, were made prisoners and carried to Bagdat.

They were here loaded with chains and cast into prison, where they remained for a long time, without seeing any person but their gaoler. At length they were informed that nothing would preserve their lives but the embracing of the Mahometan faith. For the purpose of winning them over, the caliph professed great anxiety for their welfare, and sent priests to instruct them in the mysteries of the Mahometan creed. But notwithstanding they were all aware of the consequence, they continued steadfast in their faith, rejecting the religion of the imposter with horror and contempt. They were accordingly commanded by the caliph to be beheaded ; and they were subsequently executed, after having been kept in confinement for the space of seven years.

Theodore, one of their number, had formerly received orders, and officiated as a priest, but afterward resigning his profession, he followed the military life, and at length became a commander of distinction. The officer who attended the execution, being apprized of these circumstances, said to Theodore, " You might, indeed, pretend to rank among the Christians while you served as a priest in the church, but the employment you have since taken up

is so contrary to your former profession, that you should
not think of passing among us for one of that religion.
When you quitted the altar for the camp you renounced
Christ. Why then will you dissemble any longer? Would
you not act more conformably with your own principles, and
make your conduct all of a piece, if you come to a resolution of saving your life by acknowledging the great prophet?" Theodore, overcome with a virtuous confusion,
replied, " It is true I did in some measure abandon my
God when I engaged in the army, and scarce deserve the
name of a Christian ; but the Almighty has given me grace
to see my character in its true light, and made me sensible
of my fault, and I hope he will be pleased to accept of my
life as the only atonement I can make for guilt." This
pious answer confounded the officer, who only replied that
he should soon have an opportunity of giving a proof of his
fidelity to his Master ; and he was accordingly beheaded
with his companions.

Account of Perfectus.

Perfectus was born at Corduba, and brought up in the
Christian faith. He made himself master of the useful and
polite literature of the age, and at length took priest's
orders, and performed his duty with great zeal and assiduity. One day, while walking in the streets of Corduba,
some Arabians entered into conversation with him, in
which they asked his opinion as to Mahomet and Jesus.
Perfectus gave them an exact account of the Christian
faith respecting the Divinity of Jesus Christ, and the re-
demption of mankind ; but would not deliver his sentiments
respecting Mahomet. The Arabians pressed him to speak
freely, but he refused, saying, that what he should utter
would probably be disagreeable to them, and therefore he
would be silent, as he did not wish to offend any one.
They nevertheless entreated him to speak his thoughts
freely, saying, they would not be offended at any thing he
might say. Hence believing them sincere, and hoping
that this might be the favourable time allotted for their
conversion, Perfectus told them that the Christian looked
upon Mahomet as one of the false prophets spoken of in
the Gospel, who were to deceive and seduce great num-

bers to their destruction. To illustrate this he descanted on some of the absurd doctrines of the Alcoran, and exhorted them in very strong terms to quit the miserable state in which they then were, and which would certainly be followed by eternal misery.

The infidels could not listen to such a discourse without conceiving an indignation against the speaker; they thought proper, however, to disguise their resentment, but were resolved not to let him escape. At first they were unwilling to use any violence toward him, because they had given him a solemn assurance that he should come to no harm; but they were soon eased of that scruple, and watching a favourable opportunity, seized him, hurried him away to one of their chief magistrates, and accused him of blaspheming their great prophet. The judge ordered him to be put in chains and confined in prison till the fast of Ramadan, when he should be made a victim to Mahomet. He heard the determination with joy, and prepared for his martyrdom with great fervency. At the time appointed he was led to the place of execution, where he made another declaration of his faith, declared that Mahomet was an imposter, and that the Alcoran was filled with absurdities and blasphemies. He was beheaded A. D. 850, and his body was interred by the Christians.

Martyrdom of two Ladies at Corduba.

Two ladies, named Mary and Flora, suffered martyrdom at the same period as the forty-two before recorded. Flora was the daughter of an eminent Mahometan of Seville, from whence he removed to Corduba, where the Saracen king kept his court. Her father dying when she was young, Flora was left to the care of her mother, who, being a Christian, brought her up in the true faith, and inspired her with sentiments of virtue and religion. Her brother being an enemy of Christianity, and of a savage and barbarous temper, she was obliged for some time to use great caution in the practice of such virtues as must have exposed her to a persecution. She was too zealous to be under this restraint long; for which reason she left Corduba in company with her sister. Her departure soon alarmed her brother, who guessed her motives, and in revenge informed against

7*

several Christians in Corduba; for as he did not know whither his sister was gone, he determined to wreak his vengeance on such Christians as were present. When Flora was informed of these things, she considered herself as the cause of what the Christians had suffered, she returned to Corduba, and presented herself before the persecutors, among whom she found her brother. "It," said she, "I am the object of your inquiry, if the servants of God are tormented on my account, I declare that I believe in Jesus Christ, glory in his cross, and profess the doctrines which he taught." None of the company seemed so much enraged at these words as her brother; who, after some threats, struck her, but afterward endeavoured to gain her by expressions of pretended kindness. Finding her unmoved by all he could say, he insinuated that she had been educated in the religion of Mahomet, but had renounced it at the suggestion of some Christians, who had inspired her with contempt for the great prophet. When she was called on to answer to the charge, she declared that she had never owned Mahomet, but sucked in the Christian religion with her milk, and was entirely devoted to the Redeemer of mankind.

The magistrate, finding her resolute delivered her to her brother, and gave him orders to use his utmost endeavours to make her a Mahometan. She however soon found an opportunity of escaping over a wall in the night, and of secreting herself in the house of a Christian. She then withdrew to Tucci, a village of Andalusia, where she met with her sister, and they never separated again till her martyrdom.

Mary, who suffered at the same time, was the daughter of a Christian tradesman at Estremadura, who afterward removed to a town near Corduba. When the persecution commenced under Abderrama, king of the Saracens, in Spain, Mary's younger brother was one who fell a victim to the rage of the infidels on that occasion. Mary hearing of his martyrdom, and filled with confusion at being left behind by one so much younger than herself, went to Corduba, where, going into a church, she found Flora, who had left her retreat on the same motive. On conversing together, and finding that they acted upon the same principles, and proposed the same end to their labours, they agreed to go together, and declare their faith before the judge. Accordingly, they proceeded to the magistrate, when Flora boldly told him that she looked upon Mahomet as no better than a false prophet, an adulterer, and a magician. Mary also told the magistrate that she possessed the same faith, and entertained the same sentiments as Flora, and that she was sister to Walabonzas, who had already suffered for being a Christian. This behaviour so much enraged the magistrate, that he ordered them to be committed to prison for some time, and then to be beheaded, which sentence was executed on the fourth of November, A. D. 850.

Female Martyrdom.

Besides the instances already mentioned, many other martyrdoms occurred in different countries that our limits will not permit us to mention.

CHAPTER V.

Miscellaneous Martyrdoms during the Seventh Century.

Account of Archbishop Alphage.

ALPHAGE, archbishop of Canterbury, came from a considerable family in Gloucestershire, who being devoted Christians, gave him an education becoming his station, and as he early showed a strong predilection for theological acquirements, he not only prepared himself for taking holy orders, but to pursue his study and pious contemplations, he retired to a secluded spot, and assumed habits of the most rigid austerity.   But, notwithstanding his solitary habits, his talents and virtues soon became known in the neighbourhood of his retreat, and many persons were anxious to place themselves under his pastoral care.   The place of his retirement was a cave near to Bath, and having early taken the habit of a Benedictine monk, he was at length induced to raise a monastery near his cell, and having prescribed rules, and placed an abbot over them, again returned to his former retreat.

Shortly after this the see of Winchester becoming vacant, by the death of Ethelwold, a violent dispute arose between the clergy of the diocese, as to the choice of a successor.   When this contest had continued for a considerable time, the archbishop of Canterbury, who was then primate of all England, put a stop to the contest by appointing, with the approbation of both parties, Alphage to the vacant see.

The effects of this judicious choice was very soon visible throughout the diocese, as piety flourished, unity was established among the clergy, and the conduct of the church of Winchester made its bishop an object of admiration throughout the kingdom.

Dunstan the archbishop had such a veneration for Alphage, that when upon his deathbed he prayed that the Lord would cause him to become his successor.   This prayer was answered, though not till eighteen years after the death of Dunstan. Soon after Alphage was raised to this dignity, he went to Rome, which was in 1006, and received the pall from pope John XVIII.

When Alphage had governed the see of Canterbury with great honour to himself, the Danes made an incursion into England. Ethelred, who was then king, was a man of a weak mind, without courage sufficient to face the enemy himself, or energy enough to furnish others the means of doing so. In consequence of this weakness, a great portion of the country was plundered and laid waste by the enemy. During this crisis, Alphage acted with great decision and courage. He went boldly to the Danes, purchased the freedom of many of the captives, and provided food and clothing for others that he was unable to ransom. He also **converted many of the pagans to Christianity, which gave great offence to the remainder, and they were determined to be revenged on him.**

Edric, a British malecontent and traitor, gave the Danes every encouragement, and assisted them in laying siege to the town of Canterbury, which was soon after taken by storm. Having but little mercy to expect from their captors, the monks fled to the church, and endeavoured to detain Alphage while a general massacre was going on without. But in spite of their remonstrances, he hastened into the midst of the danger, and begged the enemy to spare the people, and accept of himself as a victim. The barbarians seized him, tied his hands and feet, and abused him in the most shameful manner, while they burned down his church before him. They then decimated the inhabitants, both ecclesiastics and laymen, leaving every tenth person alive, so that out of 8040 persons, only eight hundred laymen and four monks remained.

Alphage was then cast into prison, where, after remaining for several months, they proposed to ransom him for £3000; but not having the means, they put him to the torture for the purpose either of extorting it from him, or to force him to discover the treasures of the church. But as he proved inflexible, he was again remanded to prison; and after six days was brought to Greenwich for trial. Here he exhorted them to forsake idolatry and embrace Christianity, at which they were so much enraged that they dragged him out of the camp, and beat him most unmercifully. This he bore with patience, and even prayed for his persecutors, till one of the soldiers, who had been converted to Christianity by him, to put an end to his sufferings, cut off his head.

This event happened April 19, A. D. 1012, on the very spot where the church of Greenwich, which was dedicated to him, now stands. His body was thrown into the water, but being found on the following day, was buried in St. Paul's church and was removed to Canterbury, in A. D. 1023.

Account of Gerard.

Gerard, a Venetian, having devoted himself to the service of God from a youth, entered into a religious house for some time, and then determined to visit the Holy Land. On arriving in Hungary, he became acquainted with Stephen, the king of that country, who acted the parts of prince and preacher, and not only regulated his subjects by wholesome laws, but taught them religious duties. Finding Gerard qualified to instruct his people, he tried to detain him in his kingdom ; and, at length, founding several churches, he made Gerard bishop of that of Chonad. Here the new bishop had a very difficult task to perform, the people of his diocese being accustomed to idolatry. The bishop, however, assiduous in his zeal for the salvation of his flock, laboured to bring them to a sense of their duty, and soon had the pleasure to find that his endeavours were not unsuccessful, for his sweetness of disposition won greatly upon the people. During the life of Stephen he received every assistance, but after the death of this prince, the throne was filled by Peter, a man of so morose and tyrannical a disposition that he was deposed by his subjects before he had reigned two years. He was succeeded by Ouvo, who proved still more cruel than Peter, insomuch that he was shortly after beheaded and Peter again recalled. The people soon found that retirement had produced no change in his disposition, and he was a second time deposed, and Andrew, cousin german to Stephen. was called to the throne by the nobility, and the crown was offered him on condition that he would employ his authority in exterminating Christianity from his dominions.

This he promised to do; upon which Stephen, with three other prelates, set out to visit him for the purpose of persuading him to recall his promise, but on the way they were met by a company of soldiers who murdered them. This was in A. D. 1045.

Account of Stanislaus.

Stanislaus, bishop of Cracow, was of an illustrious family. The piety of his parents was equal to their opulence, and they rendered their wealth subservient to all the purposes of benevolence. Stanislaus was their only child; he possessed a penetrating genius, retentive memory, and solid understanding; hence study became his amusement. His disposition was not inferior to his abilities, and he early gave himself to such austerities as might have acquired for him the reputation of a hermit.

He was first sent to a seminary in Poland, and afterward to the university at Paris. After remaining there for several years he returned home, and on the death of his parents he became possessed of a large estate, which he principally devoted to deeds of charity. His views were now solely directed to the ministry; but he remained for some time undetermined whether he should embrace a monastic life, or become a secular clergyman.

He was at length persuaded to the latter by Zula, bishop of Cracow, who invested him with holy orders, and made him a canon in his cathedral. Here he remained for several years in the faithful performance of every Christian virtue, insomuch that, at the age of thirty-six years he was appointed bishop of the see of Cracow, which had become vacant on the death of Zula. Bolislaus II., king of Poland, who reigned at this time, possessed many good qualities, but giving way too much to his passions, committed many errors, and acquired the name of CRUEL. The nobility and clergy beheld his conduct with disapprobation; but Stanislaus alone had the courage to tell him of his faults. The king was greatly exasperated at this freedom, but dissembled his resentment, and even promised to reform his errors.

Not long after this, however, he attempted the chastity of a married lady, who rejecting his offers with disdain, he

violated her by force. This iniquitous act greatly incensed the nobility, who calling a council of their col-
leagues and bishops, remonstrated with the king on the
impropriety of his conduct. The archbishop of Gresne
was appointed to bear the remonstrance ; but being naturally timid, he declined ; and when many others had followed his example, Stanislaus volunteered his service,
and boldly reproved the king for the heinousness of his
crime.

Bolislaus, violently enraged, threatened the prelate with
his severest vengeance ; but Stanislaus, unintimidated by his
menaces, visited him twice more, and remonstrated with
him in a familiar manner, which increased his wrath.

The nobility and clergy, finding that the admonitions of
the bishop had not the desired effect upon the king, advised
him to desist, and also endeavoured to turn the anger of
the monarch from Stanislaus, for his charitable remonstrances. But the haughty king, determined to rid him-
himself of so daring and faithful a monitor, hearing that
he was alone in the chapel of St. Michael, sent some soldiers to murder him. These men coming into his presence,
were so overawed by the venerable aspect of the prelate,
that they dared not to raise their hands against him.
When they returned without having obeyed their orders,
Bolislaus seized a dagger, hastened to the chapel, where,
finding Stanislaus at the altar, he plunged the weapon into
his heart. This occurred on the 8th May, A. D. 1079

PART III.

CHAPTER I.

Persecutions of the Waldenses in France.

BEFORE this time the church of Christ was tainted with
many of the errors of popery, and superstition began to
predominate ; but a few, who perceived the pernicious
tendency of such errors, determined to show the light of

the gospel in its real purity, and to disperse those clouds which artful priests had raised about it, in order to delude the people. The principal of these worthies was Berengarius, who, about the year 1000, boldly preached gospel truths according to their primitive purity. Many, from conviction, went over to his doctrine, and were on that account called Berengarians. Berengarius was succeeded by Peter Bruis, who preached at Toulouse, under the protection of an earl, named Hildephonsus; and the whole tenets of the reformers, with the reasons of their separation from the church of Rome, were published in a book written by Bruis, under the title of ANTICHRIST.

In the year 1140, the number of the reformed was very great, and the probability of their increasing alarmed the pope, who wrote to several princes to banish them their dominions, and employed many learned men to write against them.

In 1147, Henry of Toulouse, being deemed their most eminent preacher, they were called Henricians; and as they would not admit of any proofs relative to religion, but what could be deduced from the scriptures themselves, the popish party gave them the name of Apostolics. Peter Waldo, or Valdo, a native of Lyons, at this time became a strenuous opposer of popery: and from him the reformed received the appellation of Waldoys, or Waldenses. Waldo was a man eminent for his learning and benevolence; and his doctrines were adopted by multitudes. The bishop of Lyons taking umbrage at the freedom with which he treated the pope and the Romish clergy, sent to admonish him to refrain in future from such discourses; but Waldo answered, " That he could not be silent in a cause of such importance as the salvation of men's souls ; wherein he must obey God rather than man."

Accusations of Peter Waldo against Popery.

His principal accusations against the Roman Catholics were, that they affirm the church of Rome to be the only infallible church of Christ upon earth ; and that the pope is its head, and the vicar of Christ ; that they hold the absurd doctrine of transubstantiation, insisting that the bread and wine given in the sacrament are the very identi-

8

cal body and blood of Christ which were nailed to the cross ; that they believe there is a place called purgatory, where the souls of persons, after this life, are purged from the sins of mortality, and that the pains and penalties here inflicted may be abated according to the masses said by, and the money paid to the priests ; that they teach, the communion of one kind, or the receiving the wafer only, is sufficient for the lay people, though the clergy must be indulged with both bread and wine ; that they pray to the Virgin Mary and saints, though their prayers ought to be immediately to God ; that they pray for souls departed, though God decides their fate immediately on the decease of the person ; that they will not perform the service of the church in a language understood by the people in general ; that they place their devotion in the number of prayers, and not in the intent of the heart ; that they forbid marriage to the clergy, though God allowed it ; and that they use many things in baptism, though Christ used only water. When pope Alexander the Third was informed of these transactions, he excommunicated Waldo and his adherents, and commanded the bishop of Lyons to exterminate them : thus began the papal persecutions against the Waldenses.

Tenets of the Waldenses.

1. That holy oil is not to be mingled in baptism.
2. That prayers used over things inanimate are superstitious.
3. Flesh may be eaten in Lent ; the clergy may marry ; and auricular confession is unnecessary.
4. Confirmation is no sacrament ; we are not bound to pay obedience to the pope ; ministers should live upon tithes ; no dignity sets one clegyman above another, for their superiority can only be drawn from real worth.
5. Images in churches are absurd ; image-worship is idolatry ; the pope's indulgences ridiculous ; and the miracles pretended to be done by the church of Rome are false.
6. Fornication and public stews ought not to be allowed ; purgatory is a fiction ; and deceased persons, called saints, ought not to be prayed to.

7. Extreme unction is not a sacrament; and masses, indulgences, and prayers, are of no service to the dead.

8. The Lord's prayer ought to be the rule of all other prayers.

Waldo remained three years undiscovered in Lyons, though the utmost diligence was used to apprehend him but at length he found an opportunity of escaping from the place of his concealment to the mountains of Dauphiny. He soon after found means to propagate his doctrines in Dauphiny and Picardy, which so exasperated Philip, king of France, that he put the latter province, which contained most of the sectaries, under military execution; destroying above three hundred gentlemen's seats, razing some walled towns, burning many of the reformed, and driving others into Flanders and Germany.

Notwithstanding these persecutions, the reformed religion seemed to flourish; and the Waldenses, in various parts, became more numerous than ever. At length the pope accused them of heresy, and the monks of immorality. These slanders they, however, refuted; but the pope, incensed at their increase, used all means for their extirpation; such as excommunications, anathemas, canons, constitutions, decrees, &c. by which they were rendered incapable of holding places of trust, honour, or profit; their lands were seized, their goods confiscated, and they were not permitted to be buried in consecrated ground. Some of the Waldenses having taken refuge in Spain, Aldephonsus, king of Arragon, at the instigation of the pope, published an edict, strictly ordering all Roman catholics to persecute them wherever they could be found; and decreeing that all who gave them the least assistance should be deemed traitors.

The year after this edict, Aldephonsus was severely punished by the hand of Providence; for his son was defeated in a great battle, and 50,000 of his men slain, by which a considerable portion of his kingdom fell into the hands of the Moors.

The reformed ministers continued to preach boldly against the Romish church; and Peter Waldo, in particular, wherever he went, asserted, that the pope was antichrist, that mass was an abomination, that the host was an idol, and that purgatory was a fable

Origin of the Inquisition.

These proceedings of Waldo and his reformed com panions, occasioned the origin of inquisitors; for pope Innocent III. authorized certain monks inquisitors to find and deliver over the reformed to the secular power.   The monks, upon the least surmise or information, gave up the reformed to the magistrate, who delivered them to the executioner ; for the process was short, as accusation supplied the place of evidence, and a fair trial was never granted to the accused.

Cruelties of the Pope, and artifices of Dominic.

When the pope found that these cruel means had not the desired effect, he determined to try others of a milder nature ; he therefore sent several learned monks to preach among the Waldenses, and induce them to change their opinions.   Among these monks was one Dominic, who appeared extremely zealous in the cause of popery.   He instituted an order, which, from him, was called the order of Dominican friars ; and the members of this order have ever since been the principal inquisitors in every country into which that horrible tribunal has been introduced. Their power was unlimited ; they proceeded against whom they pleased, without any consideration of age, sex, or rank.   However infamous the accusers, the accusation was deemed valid ;   and even anonymous informations were thought sufficient evidence.   The dearest friends or kindred could not, without danger, serve any one who was imprisoned on account of religion ; to convey to those who were confined a little straw, or give them a cup of water, was called favouring the heretics ; no lawyer dared to plead even for his own brother, or notary register any thing in favour of the reformed.   The malice of the papists, indeed, went beyond the grave, and the bones of many Waldenses, who had been long dead, were dug up and burnt.   If a man on his death bed were accused of being a follower of Waldo, his estates were confiscated, and the heir defrauded of his inheritance ; and some were even obliged to make pilgrimages to the Holy Land, while the Dominicans took possession of their houses and property, which they refused to surrender to the owners upon their return.

Persecutions in Calabria.

Waldenses in Calabria.

About the fourteenth century, a great many Waldenses of Pragela and Dauphiny emigrated to Calabria, where, having received permission to settle in some waste lands, they soon, by the most industrious cultivation, converted those wild and barren spots into regions of beauty and fertility.

The nobles of Calabria were highly pleased with their new subjects and tenants, finding them honest, quiet, and industrious; but the priests, filled with jealousy, soon exhibited complaints against them, charging them with not being Roman Catholics, not making any of their boys priests, not making any of their girls nuns, not going to mass, not giving wax tapers to their priests, as offerings, not going on pilgrimages, and not bowing to images.

To these the Calabrian lords replied, that these people were extremely harmless, giving no offence to the Roman Catholics, but cheerfully paying the tithes to the priests.

8*

whose revenues were considerably increased by their coming into the country, and who, consequently, ought to be the last persons to make a complaint.

Those enemies to truth being thus silenced, things went on in peace for a few years, during which the Waldenses formed themselves into two corporate towns, annexing several villages to their jurisdiction. At length they sent to Geneva for two clergyman, one to preach in each town. This being known, intelligence was conveyed to pope Pius the Fourth, who determined to exterminate them from Calabria without further delay. To this end cardinal Alexandrino, a man of a violent temper, and a furious bigot, was sent, together with two monks, to Calabria, where they were to act as inquisitors. These authorized persons came to St. Xist, one of the towns built by the Waldenses, where, having assembled the people, they told them, that they should receive no injury if they would accept of preachers appointed by the pope; but if they refused, they should be deprived both of their properties and lives; and that to prove them, mass should be publicly said that afternoon, at which they must attend.

But the people of St. Xist, instead of obeying this, fled with their families into the woods, and thus disappointed the cardinal and his coadjutors. Then they proceeded to La Garde, the other town belonging to the Waldenses, where, to avoid the like disappointment, they ordered the gates to be locked, and all avenues guarded. The same proposals were then made to the inhabitants as had been made to those of St. Xist, but with this artifice: the cardinal assured them that the inhabitants of St. Xist had immediately come into his proposals, and agreed that the pope should appoint them preachers. This falsehood succeeded; for the people of La Garde, thinking what the cardinal had told them to be truth, said they would exactly follow the example of their brethren at St. Xist.

Having thus gained this point by a lie, he sent for two troops of soldiers with a view to massacre the people of St. Xist. He accordingly commanded them into the woods, to hunt them down like wild beasts, and gave them strict orders to spare neither age nor sex, but to kill all they came near. The troops accordingly entered the woods, and many fell a prey to their ferocity, before the

Waldenses were apprised of their design. At length, however, they determined to sell their lives as dear as possible, when several conflicts happened, in which the half-armed Waldenses performed prodigies of valour, and many were slain on both sides. At length, the greater part of the troops being killed in the different rencounters, the remainder were compelled to retreat; which so enraged the cardinal, that he wrote to the viceroy of Naples for reinforcements.

The viceroy, in obedience to this, proclaimed throughout the Neapolitan territories, that all outlaws, deserters, and other proscribed persons, should be freely pardoned for their several offences, on condition of making a campaign against the inhabitants of St. Xist, and of continuing under arms till those people were destroyed. On this several persons of desperate fortune came in, and being formed into light companies, were sent to scour the woods, and put to death all they could meet with of the reformed religion. The viceroy himself also joined the cardinal, at the head of a body of regular forces; and, in conjunction, they strove to accomplish their bloody purpose. Some they caught, and. suspending them upon trees, cut down boughs and burnt them, or ripped them open and left their bodies to be devoured by wild beasts. or birds of prey. Many they shot at a distance; but the greatest number they hunted down by way of *sport*. A few escaped into caves; but famine destroyed them in their retreat: and the inhuman chase was continued till all these poor people perished.

The inhabitants of St. Xist being exterminated, those of La Garde engaged the attention of the cardinal and viceroy. The fullest protection was offered to themselves, their families, and their children, if they would embrace the Roman Catholic persuasion; but, on the contrary, if they refused this *mercy*, as it was insolently termed, the most cruel deaths would be the certain consequence. In spite of the promises on one side, and menaces on the other, the Waldenses unanimously refused to renounce their religion, or embrace the errors of popery. The cardinal and viceroy were so enraged at this, that they ordered thirty of them to be put immediately to the rack, as a terror to the others. Several of these died under the torture: one Charlin, in particular, was so cruelly used that his belly burst, his bowels came out, and he expired in the greatest agonies. These barbarities, however, did not answer the end for which they were intended; for those who survived the torments of the rack, and those who had not felt it, remained equally constant in their faith, and boldly declared, that nothing, either of pain or fear, should ever induce them to renounce their God, or bow down to idols. The inhuman cardinal then ordered several of them to be stripped naked, and whipped to death with iron rods: some were hacked to pieces with large knives; others were thrown from the top of a high tower; and many were cased over with pitch and burnt alive.

One of the monks who attended the cardinal, discovered a most inhuman and diabolical nature. He requested that he might shed some of the blood of these poor people with his own hands; his request being granted, the monster took a large sharp knife, and cut the throats of fourscore men, women, and children. Their bodies were then quartered, the quarters placed upon stakes, and fixed in different parts of the country.

The four principal men of La Garde were hanged, and the clergyman was thrown from the top of his church steeple. He was dreadfully crushed, but not quite killed by the fall. The viceroy being present, said, "Is the dog yet living? Take him up, and cast him to the hogs:" which brutal sentence was actually put in execution.

The monsters, in their hellish thirst of cruelty, racked sixty of the women with such severity, that the cords pierced their limbs quite to the bone. They were after this remanded to prison, where their wounds mortified, and they died in the most miserable manner. Many others were put to death by various means; and so jealous and arbitrary were those monsters, that if any Roman Catholic, more compassionate than the rest, interceded for any of the reformed, he was immediately apprehended, and sacrificed as a favourer of heretics.

The viceroy being obliged to return to Naples, and the cardinal having been recalled to Rome, the marquis of Butiane was commissioned to complete what they had began; which he at length effected by acting with such barbarous rigour, that there was not a single person of the reformed religion left in all Calabria. Thus were a great number of inoffensive and harmless people deprived of their possessions, robbed of their property, driven from their homes, and, at length, murdered, only because they would not sacrifice their consciences to the superstitions of others, embrace doctrines which they abhorred, and attend to teachers they could not believe.

CHAPTER II.

Persecutions in Dauphiny.

In 1400, the Waldenses who resided in the valley of Pragela, were, at the instigation of some priests, suddenly attacked by a body of troops, who plundered their houses, murdered many, and drove others into the Alps, where great numbers were frozen to death, it being in the depth of winter. In 1460, a persecution was carried on in Dauphiny against the Waldenses, by the archbishop of Ambrune, who employed a monk, named John Vayleti, who proceeded with such violence, that not only the Waldenses, but even many papists, were sufferers : for if any of them expressed compassion or pity for the inoffensive people who were so cruelly treated, they were accused of favouring the Waldenses, and punished. At length Vayleti's proceedings became so intolerable, that a great number of the papists themselves addressed a petition against him to Louis XI., king of France, who granted the request of the petitioners, and sent an order to the governor of Dauphiny to stop the persecution. Vayleti, however, by order of the archbishop, still continued it ; for, taking advantage of the last clause of the edict, he pretended that he did nothing contrary to the king's precept, who had ordered punishment to such as affirmed any thing against the holy catholic faith. This persecution at length concluded with the death of the archbishop, which happened in 1487.

Attempts of the Pope to Exterminate the Waldenses.

Pope Innocent VIII., in 1488, determined to persecute the Waldenses. To this end he sent Albert de Capitaneis, archdeacon of Cremona, to France; who, on arriving in Dauphiny, craved the assistance of the king's lieutenant to exterminate the Waldenses from the valley of Loyse: the lieutenant readily granted his assistance, and marched a body of troops to the place; but when they arrived at the valley, they found that it had been deserted by the inhabitants, who had retired to the mountains, and hid themselves in caverns, &c. The archdeacon and lieutenant immediately followed them with the troops, and apprehending many, they cast them headlong from the precipices, by which they were dashed to pieces. Several, however, retired to the innermost parts of the caverns, and knowing the intricacies, were able to conceal themselves. The archdeacon and lieutenant, not being able to come at them, ordered the mouths of the caves to be filled with fagots, which being lighted, those within were suffocated. On searching the caves, 400 infants were found smothered, either in their cradles or in their mother's arms; and, upon the whole, about 3000 men, women, and children, were destroyed in this persecution.

After this tragical work, the lieutenant and archdeacon proceeded with the troops to Pragela and Frassanier, in order to persecute the Waldenses in those parts. But these having heard the fate of their brethren in the valley of Loyse, thought proper to arm themselves: and by fortifying the different passes, and bravely disputing the passages through them, they so harassed the troops, that the lieutenant was compelled to retire without effecting his purpose.

The King of France favours the Waldenses.

In 1494, Anthony Fabri and Christopher de Salience, having a commission to persecute the Waldenses of Dauphiny, put some to death, sequestered the estates of others, and confiscated the goods of many; but Louis XII. coming to the crown in 1498, the Waldenses petitioned him for a restitution of their property. The king determined to have the affair impartially canvassed, and sent a commissioner of his own, together with a commissary from the pope, to make the proper inquiries. The witnesses against the Waldenses having been examined, the innocence of those poor people evidently appeared, and the king's commissioner declared, "That he only desired to be as good a Christian as the worst of them." When this favourable report was made to the king, he immediately gave orders that the Waldenses should have their property restored to them. The archbishop of Ambrune, having the greatest quantity of these poor people's goods, it was generally imagined that he would set a laudable example to others, by being the first to restore them. The archbishop, however, declared, that he would not restore any of the property, for it was incorporated with, and become part of his archbishopric. He, however, with an affectation of candour, offered to relinquish several vineyards, of which he had dispossessed the Waldenses, provided the lords of Dauphiny would restore all they had taken from those poor people: but this the lords absolutely refused, being as desirous of keeping their plunder as the archbishop himself.

The Waldenses finding that they were not likely to recover any of their property, again appealed to the king; and the monarch having attended to their complaints, wrote to the archbishop; but that artful and avaricious prelate replied, "That at the commencement of the persecution the Waldenses had been excommunicated by the pope, in consequence of which their goods were distrained; therefore, till the sentence of excommunication was taken off, which had occasioned them to be seized, they could not be restored with propriety." This plea was allowed to be reasonable; and application was ineffectually made to the pope to remove the sentence of excommunication; for the archbishop, supposing this would be the case, had used all his interest at Rome to prevent the application from succeeding.

Progress of the Waldenses.

At length this sect having spread from Dauphiny into several other provinces, became very numerous in Provence. At their first arrival, Provence was almost a desert, but by their great industry it soon abounded with corn, wine, oil, fruit, &c.   The pope, by being often near them at his seat at Avignon, heard occasionally many things concerning their differing from the church of Rome, which greatly exasperated him, and he determined to persecute them. Proceeding to some extremities, under the sanction of his ecclesiastical authority only, without consulting the king of France, the latter became alarmed, and sent his master of requests, and his confessor, to examine into the affair.   On their return they reported that the Waldenses were not such dangerous or bad people as they had been represented ; that they lived with perfect honesty, were friendly to all, caused their children to be baptized, had them taught the Lord's prayer, creed, and ten command-ments ; expounded the scriptures with purity, kept the Lord's day sacred, feared God, honoured the king, and wished well to the state.   "Then," said the king, "they are much better Christians than myself, or my catholic subjects, and therefore they shall not be persecuted."   He was as good as his word, and sent orders to stop the per-secution.

Persecutions in the Valley of Piedmont.

The Waldenses, in consequence of the continued perse-cutions they met with in France, fled for refuge to various parts of the world; among other places, many of them sought an asylum in the valleys of Piedmont, where they increased and flourished exceedingly for a considerable time.

Notwithstanding their harmless behaviour, inoffensive conversation, and their paying tithes to the Romish clergy, the latter could not be contented, but sought to give them disturbance, and accordingly complained to the archbishop of Turin that the Waldenses were heretics; upon which he ordered a persecution to be commenced, in consequence of which many fell martyrs to the superstitious rage of the monks and priests.

At Turin, one of the reformed had his bowels torn out and put into a basin before his face, where they remained, in his view, till he expired. At Revel, Catelin Girard being at the stake, desired the executioner to give him up a stone, which he refused, thinking that he meant to throw it at somebody; but Girard assuring him that he had no such design, the executioner complied; when Girard, looking earnestly at the stone, said, "When it is in the power of a man to eat and digest this stone, the religion for which I am about to suffer shall have an end, and not before." He then threw the stone on the ground, and submitted cheerfully to the flames. A great many more were oppressed or put to death, till, wearied with their sufferings, the Waldenses flew to arms in their defence, and formed themselves into regular bodies. Full of revenge at this, the archbishop of Turin sent troops against them; but in most of the skirmishes the Waldenses were victorious; for they knew, if they were taken, they should not be considered as prisoners of war, but be tortured to death as heretics.

Noble conduct of the Duke of Savoy.

Philip the Seventh, who was at this time duke of Savoy, and supreme lord of Piedmont, determined to interpose his authority, and stop these bloody wars, which so disturbed his dominions. Nevertheless, unwilling to offend the pope or the archbishop of Turin, he sent them both messages, importing, that he could not any longer tamely see his dominions overrun with troops, who were commanded by prelates in the place of generals; nor would
9

he suffer his country to be depopulated, while he himself had not been consulted upon the occasion.

The priests, perceiving the determination of the duke, had recourse to their usual artifice, and endeavoured to prejudice his mind against the Waldenses; but he told them, that although he was unacquainted with the religious tenets of these people, yet he had always found them quiet, faithful, and obedient, and was therefore determined they should be persecuted no longer. The priests then vented the most palpable and absurd falsehoods: they assured the duke that he was mistaken in the Waldenses, for they were a wicked set of people, and highly addicted to intemperance, uncleanness, blasphemy, adultery, incest, and many other abominable crimes; and that they were even monsters in nature, for their children were born with black throats, with four rows of teeth, and bodies covered with hair. But the duke was not so to be imposed upon, nothwithstanding the solemn affirmations of the priests. In order to come at the truth, he sent twelve gentlemen into the Piedmontese valleys, to examine into the real character of the people.

These gentlemen, after travelling through all their towns and villages, and conversing with the Waldenses of every rank, returned to the duke, and gave him the most favourable account of them, affirming in contradiction to the priests, that they were harmless, inoffensive, loyal, friendly, industrious, and pious; that they abhorred the crimes of which they were accused; and that, should an individual, through his depravity, fall into any of those crimes, he would, by their laws, be punished in the most exemplary manner. With respect to the children, of whom the priests had told the most gross and ridiculous falsehoods, they were neither born with black throats, teeth in their mouths, nor hair on their bodies, but were as fine children as could be seen. "And to convince your highness of what we have said," continued one of the gentlemen, "we have brought twelve of the principal male inhabitants, who are come to ask pardon in the name of the rest, for having taken up arms without your leave, though even in their own defence, and to preserve their lives from their merciless enemies. We have likewise brought several women, with children of various ages, that your highness may have an opportunity of judging for yourself." His highness then accepted the apology of the twelve delegates, conversed with the women, examined the children, and afterward graciously dismissed them. He then commanded the priests, who had attempted to mislead him, immediately to leave the court; and gave strict orders that the persecution should cease throughout his dominions.

During the remainder of the reign of this virtuous prince, the Waldenses enjoyed repose in their retreats; but, on his death, this happy scene changed, for his successor was a bigoted papist. About the same time, some of the principal Waldenses proposed that their clergy should preach in public, that every one might know the purity of their doctrines; for hitherto they had preached only in private, and to such congregations as they well knew to consist of none but persons of the reformed religion.

When this reached the ears of the new duke, he was greatly exasperated, and sent a considerable body of troops into the valleys, swearing that if the people would not conform to the Romish faith, he would have them flayed alive. The commander of the troops soon found the impracticability of conquering them with the number of men then under him: he, therefore, sent word to the duke that the idea of subjugating the Waldenses with so small a force was ridiculous; that they were better acquainted with the country than any that were with him; that they had secured all the passes, were well armed, and determined to defend themselves. Alarmed at this, the duke commanded the troops to return, determining to act by stratagem. He, therefore, ordered rewards for taking any of the Waldenses, who might be found straying from their places of security; and these, when taken, were either flayed alive or burnt.

Pope Paul the Third, a furious bigot, ascending the pontifical chair, immediately solicited the parliament of Turin to persecute the Waldenses, as the most pernicious of all heretics. To this the parliament readily assented, when several were suddenly seized and burnt by their order. Among these was Bartholomew Hector, a bookseller of Turin. He had been brought up a Roman Catholic, but some treatises written by the reformed clergy having fallen into his hands, he was fully convinced of their truth, and of the errors of the church of Rome ; yet his mind was, for some time, wavering between fear and duty, when, after serious consideration, he fully embraced the reformed religion, and was apprehended, as we have already mentioned, and burnt.

A consultation was again held by the parliament of Turin, in which it was agreed that deputies should be sent to the valleys of Piedmont with the following propositions; 1. That if the Waldenses would return to the bosom of the church of Rome, they should enjoy their houses, properties, and lands, and live with their families, without the least molestation. 2. That to prove their obedience, they should send twelve of their principal persons, with all their ministers and schoolmasters, to Turin, to be dealt with at discretion. 3. That the pope, the king of France, and the duke of Savoy, approved of and authorized the proceedings of the parliament of Turin, upon this occasion. 4. That if the Waldenses of Piedmont rejected these propositions, persecution and death should be their reward.

In answer to these hostile articles, the Waldenses made the following noble replies : 1. That no consideration whatever should make them renounce their religion. 2. That they would never consent to intrust their best friends to the custody and discretion of their worst enemies. 3. That they valued the approbation of the King of Kings, who reigns in heaven, more than any temporal authority. 4. That their souls were more precious than their bodies.

As may be conjectured, these spirited and pointed answers greatly exasperated the parliament of Turin ; in consequence of which they continued with more avidity than ever to seize such Waldenses as unfortunately had strayed from their hiding-places, and put them to the most cruel deaths.

They soon after solicited from the king of France a considerable body of troops, in order to exterminate the reformed from Piedmont ; but just as the troops were about to march, the protestant princes of Germany interposed, and threatened to send troops to assist the Waldenses. On this, the king of France, not wishing to enter into a war, remanded the troops. This greatly disappointed the sanguinary members of the parliament, and for want of power the persecution gradually ceased, and they could only put to death such as they caught by chance, which, owing to the caution of the Waldenses, were very few.

After a few years' tranquillity, they were again disturbed in the following manner : the pope's nuncio, coming to Turin, told the duke he was astonished that he had not yet either rooted out the Waldenses from Piedmont entirely, or compelled them to return to the church of Rome. That such conduct in him awakened suspicion, and that he really thought him a favourer of those heretics, and should accordingly report the affair to the pope. Roused by this reflection, and fearful of being misrepresented to the pope, the duke determined to banish those suspicions; and, to prove his zeal, resolved to persecute the unoffending Waldenses. He accordingly issued express orders for all to attend mass regularly, on pain of death. This they absolutely refused to do, on which he entered Piedmont with a great body of troops, and began a most furious persecution, in which great numbers were hanged, drowned, ripped open, tied to trees, pierced with prongs, thrown from precipices, burnt, stabbed, racked to death, worried by dogs, and crucified with their heads downward. Those who fled had their goods plundered and their houses burned. When they caught a minister or a schoolmaster, they put him to such exquisite tortures as are scarcely credible. If any whom they took seemed wavering in their faith, they did not put them to death, but sent them to the galleys, to be made converts by dint of hardships.

In this expedition the duke was accompanied by three men who resembled devils, viz.: 1. Thomas Incomel, an apostate, brought up in the reformed religion, but who had renounced his faith, embraced the errors of popery, and turned monk. He was a great libertine, given to unnatural crimes, and most particularly solicitious for the plunder of the Waldenses. 2. Corbis, a man of a very ferocious and cruel nature, whose business was to examine the prisoners. 3. The provost of justice, an avaricious wretch, anxious for the execution of the Waldenses, as every execution added to his hoards.

These three monsters were unmerciful to the last degree ; wherever they came, the blood of the innocent was shed. But, besides the cruelties exercised by the duke with these three persons and the army, in their differen

9*

marches many local barbarities took place. At Pignero!
was a monastery, the monks of which finding they might
injure the reformed with impunity, began to plunder their
houses, and pull down their churches; and not meeting
with opposition, they next seized upon the persons of those
unhappy people, murdering the men, confining the women,
and putting the children to Roman Catholic nurses.

In the same manner the Roman Catholic inhabitants of
the valley of St. Martin did all they could to torment the
neighbouring Waldenses; they destroyed their churches,
burnt their houses, seized their property, carried away
their cattle, converted their lands to their own use, committed their ministers to the flames, and drove the people
to the woods, where they had nothing to subsist on but
wild fruits, the bark of trees, roots, &c, &c.

Some Roman Catholic ruffians having seized a minister,
as he was going to preach, determined to take him to a
convenient place and burn him. His parishioners hearing
of this, armed themselves, pursued and attacked the vil-
lians; who, finding they could not execute their first intent,
stabbed the poor gentlemen, and leaving him weltering in
his blood, made a precipitate retreat. His parishoners did
all they could to recover him, but in vain; for he expired
as they were carrying him home.

The monks of Pignerol having a great desire to get into
their possession a minister of the town of St. Germain,
hired a band of ruffians for the purpose of seizing him.
These fellows were conducted by a treacherous servant to
the clergy man, who knew a secret way to the house, by
which he could lead them without alarming the neighbourhood. The guide knocked at the door, and being asked
who was there, answered in his own name. The clergyman, expecting no injury from a person on whom he had
heaped favours, immediately opened the door; perceiving
the ruffians, he fled, but they rushed in and seized him.
They then murdered all his family; after which they proceeded with their captive toward Pignerol, goading him
all the way. He was confined a considerable time in prison, and then burnt.

The murderers continuing their assaults about the town
of St. Germain, murdering and plundering many of the
inhabitants, the reformed of Lucerne and Angrone sent

some armed men to the assistance of their brethren. These men frequently attacked and routed the ruffians, which so alarmed the monks, that they left their monastery of Pig nerol, till they could procure regular troops for their protection.

The duke of Savoy, not finding himself so successful as he at first imagined he should be, augmented his forces, joined to them the ruffians, and commanded that a general delivery should take place in the prisons, provided the persons released would bear arms, and assist in the exter-mination of the Waldenses.

No sooner were the Waldenses informed of these pro-ceedings than they secured as much of their property as they could, and quitting the valleys, retired to the rocks and caves among the Alps.

The army no sooner reached their destination than they began to plunder and burn the towns and villages; but they could not force the passages of the Alps, gallantly defended by the Waldenses, who in those attempts always repulsed their enemies; but if any fell into the hands of the troops, they were treated in the most barbarous manner. A soldier having caught one of them, bit his right ear off, saying, " I will carry this member of that wicked heretic with me into my own country, and preserve it as a rarity." He then stabbed the man, and threw him into a ditch.

At one time, a party of troops found a venerable man upwards of a hundred years of age, accompanied by his grand-daughter, a maiden of about eighteen, in a cave. They murdered the poor old man in a most inhuman man-ner, and then attempted to ravish the girl, when she started away, and being pursued, threw herself from a precipice and was dashed to pieces.

Determined, if possible, to expel the invaders, the Wal-denses entered into a league with the protestant powers in Germany, and with the reformed of Dauphiny and Pragela. These were respectively to furnish bodies of troops; and the Waldenses resolved, when thus reinforced, to quit the mountains of the Alps, where they soon must have perished, as the winter was coming on, and to force the duke's army to evacuate their native valleys.

But the duke of Savoy himself was tired of the war; it having cost him great fatigue and anxiety of mind, a vast number of men, and very considerable sums of money. It had been much more tedious and bloody than he expected, as well as more expensive than he at first imagined, for he thought the plunder would have discharged the expenses of the expedition : in this, however he was mistaken ; for the pope's nuncio, the bishops, monks, and other ecclesiastics, who attended the army and encouraged the war, sunk the greatest part of the wealth that was taken, under various pretences. For these reasons, and the death of his dutchess, of which he had just received intelligence, and fearing that the Waldenses, by the treaties they had entered into, would become too powerful for him, he determined to return to Turin with his army, and to make peace with them.

This resolution he put in practice, greatly against the wish of the ecclesiastics, who by the war gratified both their avarice and their revenge. Before the articles of peace could be ratified, the duke himself died ; but on his deathbed he strictly enjoined his son to perform what he had intended, and to be as favourable as possible to the Waldenses.

Charles Emanuel, the duke's son, succeeded to the dominions of Savoy, and fully ratified the peace with the Waldenses, according to the last injunctions of his father, though the priests used all their arts to dissuade him from his purpose.

CHAPTER III.

Persecutions of the Albigenses.

THE Albigenses were people of the reformed religion, who inhabited the country of Albi. They were condemned on account of religion, in the council of Lateran, by order of pope Alexander III. ; but they increased so prodigiously, that many cities were inhabited by persons only of their persuasion, and several eminent noblemen embraced their doctrines. Among the latter were Raymond, earl of Toulouse, Raymond, earl of Foix, the earl of Bezieres, &c. The pope, at length, pretended that he wished to draw them to the Romish faith by sound argument and clear reasoning, and for this end ordered a general disputation; in which, however, the popish doctors were entirely overcome by the arguments of Arnold, a reformed clergyman, whose reasonings were so strong, that they were compelled to confess their force.

Persecution of the Earl of Toulouse.

A friar, named Peter, having been murdered in the dominions of the earl of Toulouse, the pope made the murder a pretence to persecute that nobleman and his subjects. He sent persons throughout all Europe, in order to raise forces to act coercively against the Albigenses, and promised paradise to all who would assist in this war, (which he termed holy,) and bear arms for forty days. The same indulgences were held out to all who entered for this purpose, as to such as engaged in crusades to the Holy Land. The pope likewise sent orders to all archbishops, bishops, &c. to excommunicate the earl of Toulouse every Sabbath and festival; at the same time absolving all his subjects from their oaths of allegiance to him, and commanding them to pursue his person, possess his lands, destroy his property, and murder such of his subjects as continued faithful to him. The earl of Toulouse, hearing of these mighty preparations against him, wrote to the pope in a very candid manner, desiring not to be condemned unheard, and assuring him that he had not the least hand in Peter's death; for that friar was killed by a gentleman, who, immediately after the murder, fled out of his territories. But the pope being determined on his destruction, was resolved not to hear his defence: and a formidable army, with several noblemen and prelates at the head of it, began its march against the Albigenses. The earl had only the alternative to oppose force by force, or submit: and as he despaired of success in attempting the former, he determined on the latter. The pope's legate being at Valence, the earl repaired thither, and said, " He was surprised that such a number of armed men should be sent against him, before the least proof of his guilt had been deduced. He therefore came voluntarily to surrender himself, armed only with the testimony of a good conscience, and hoped that

the troops would be prevented from plundering his innocent subjects, as he thought himself a sufficient pledge for
any vengeance they chose to take on account of the death
of the friar." The legate replied, that he was very glad
the earl had voluntarily surrendered ; but with respect to
the proposal, he could not pretend to countermand the
orders to the troops, unless he would consent to deliver up
seven of his best fortified castles as securities for his future
behaviour. At this demand the earl perceived his error
in submitting, but it was too late ; he knew himself to be
a prisoner, and therefore sent an order for the delivery of
the castles. The pope's legate had no sooner garrisoned
these places, than he ordered the respective governors to
appear before him. When they came, he said, " That
the earl of Toulouse having delivered up his castles to the
pope, they must consider that they were now the pope's
subjects, and not the earl's ; and that they must therefore
act conformably to their new allegiance." The governors
were greatly astonished to see their lord thus in chains,
and themselves compelled to act in a manner so contrary
to their inclinations and consciences. But the subsequent
treatment of the earl afflicted them still more ; for he was
stripped nearly naked, led nine times round the grave of
friar Peter, and severely scourged before all the people.
Not contented with this, the legate obliged him to swear
that he would be obedient to the pope during the remainder
of his life, conform to the church of Rome, and make ir-
reconcilable war against the Albigenses ; and even ordered him, by the oaths he had newly taken, to join the
troops, and inspect the siege of Bezieres. But thinking
this too hard an injunction, he took an opportunity privately to quit the army, and determined to go to the pope
and relate the ill usage he had received.

Siege of Bezieres.

The army, however, proceeded to besiege Bezieres, and
the earl of Bezieres, who was governor of that city, thinking it impossible to defend the place, came out, and presenting himself before the legate, implored mercy for the
inhabitants ; intimating, that there were as many Roman
catholics as Albigenses in the city. The legate replied,

that all excuses were useless; the place must be delivered up at discretion, or the most dreadful consequences would ensue.

The earl of Bezieres returning into the city, told the inhabitants he could obtain no mercy, unless the Albigenses would abjure their religion, and conform to the worship of the church of Rome. The Roman catholics pressed the Albigenses to comply with this request; but the Albigenses nobly answered, that they would not forsake their religion for the base price of their frail life: that God was able, if he pleased, to defend them; but if he would be glorified by the confession of their faith, it would be a great honour to them to die for his sake. They added, that they had rather displease the pope, who could but kill their bodies, than God, who could cast both body and soul into hell. On this the popish party, finding their importunities ineffectual, sent their bishop to the legate, beseeching him not to include them in the chastisement of the Albigenses; and representing, that the best means to win the latter over to the Roman catholic persuasion, was by gentleness, and not by rigour. The legate, upon hearing this, flew into a violent passion with the bishop, and declared that, " If all the city did not acknowledge their fault, they should taste of one curse without distinction of religion, sex, or age."

The inhabitants refusing to yield upon such terms, a general assault was made, and the place taken by storm, when every cruelty that barbarous superstition could devise was practised; nothing was to be heard but the groans of men who lay weltering in their blood; the lamentations of mothers, who, after being violated by the soldiery, had their children taken from them, and dashed to pieces before their faces. The city being fired in various parts, new scenes of confusion arose; in several places the streets were streaming with blood. Those who hid themselves in their dwellings, had only the dreadful alternative to remain and perish in the flames, or rush out and fall by the swords of the soldiers. The bloody legate, during these infernal proceedings, enjoyed the carnage, and even cried out to the troops, " Kill them, kill them all; kill man, woman, and child; kill Roman catholics as well as Albigenses, for when they are dead the Lord knows how to pick out

his own." Thus the beautiful city of Bezieres was re
duced to a heap of ruins; and 60,000 persons were mur
dered.

Courage of the Earl of Bezieres.

The earl of Bezieres and a few others made their escape, and went to Carcasson, which they endeavoured to
put into the best posture of defence. The legate, not
willing to lose an opportunity of spilling blood during the
forty days which the troops were to serve, led them immediately against Carcasson. As soon as the place was invested, a furious assault was given, but the besiegers were
repulsed with great slaughter; and upon this occasion the
earl of Bezieres gave the most distinguished proofs of his
courage, saying, to encourage the besieged, "We had
better die fighting than fall into the hands of such bigoted
and bloody enemies."

Two miles from the city of Carcasson there was a small
town of the same name, which the Albigenses had likewise fortified. The legate, being enraged at the repulse
he had received from the city of Carcasson, determined to
wreak his vengeance upon the town: the next morning he
made a general assault: and, though the place was bravely
defended, he took it by storm, put all within it to the
sword, and then burnt the town.

During these transactions the king of Arragon arrived
at the camp, and after paying his obedience to the legate,
told him he understood the earl of Bezieres, his kinsman,
was in the city of Carcasson, and that, if he would grant
him permission, he would go thither, and endeavour to
make him sensible of the duty he owed to the pope and
church: the legate acquiescing, the king repaired to the
earl, and asked him from what motives he shut himself up
in that city against so great an army. The earl answered,
it was to defend his life, goods, and subjects; that he knew
the pope, under pretence of religion, resolved to destroy
his uncle, the earl of Toulouse, and himself; that he saw
the cruelty which they had used at Bezieres, even against
the priests, and at the town of Carcasson; and that they
must look for no mercy from the legate or his army; he,
therefore, rather chose to die, defending himself and his

subjects, than fall into the hands of so inexorable an enemy as the legate ; that though he had in his city some that were of another religion, yet they were such as had not wronged any, were come to his succour in his greatest extremity, and for their good service he was resolved not to abandon them ; that his trust was in God, the defender of the oppressed ; and that he would assist them against those ill-advised men who forsook their own houses, to burn, ravage, and murder without reason, judgment, or mercy.

Infamous Treachery of the Legate.

The king reported to the legate what the earl had said : the legate, after considering for some time, replied, " For your sake, sir, I will receive the earl of Bezieres to mercy, and with him twelve others shall be safe, and be permitted to retire with their property : but as for the rest, I am determined to have them at my discretion." This answer displeased the king ; and when the earl heard it, he absolutely refused to comply with such terms. The legate then commanded another assault, but his troops were again repulsed with great slaughter, and the dead bodies occasioned a stench that was exceedingly offensive both to the besieged and besiegers. The legate, vexed and alarmed at this second disappointment, determined to act by stratagem. He therefore sent a person, well skilled in dissimulation and artifice, to the earl of Bezieres with a seeming friendly message. The design was, by any means, to induce the earl to leave the city, in order to have an interview with the legate ; and to this end the messenger was to promise or swear whatever he thought proper ; " For," said the legate, " swear to what falsehoods you will in such a cause, I will give you absolution."

This infamous plot succeeded : for the earl, believing the promises made him of personal security, and crediting the solemn oaths that the perjured agent swore upon the occasion, left the city and went with him. The legate no sooner saw him, than he told him that he was a prisoner, and must remain so till Carcasson was surrendered, and the inhabitants taught their duty to the pope. The earl, on hearing this, cried out that he was betrayed, and exclaimed against the treachery of the legate, and the per

10

jury of the person he had employed.   But he was ordered into close confinement, and the place summoned to surrender immediately.

The people, on hearing of the captivity of the earl, were thrown into the utmost consternation, when one of the citizens informed the rest, that he had been formerly told by some old men that there was a very capacious subterraneous passage, which led from thence to the castle of Camaret, at three leagues distance.   "If," continued he, "we can find this passage, we may all escape before the legate can be apprized of our flight."   This information was joyfully received; all were employed to search for the passage; and, at length, it was discovered.   Early in the evening the inhabitants began their flight, taking with them their wives, children, a few days' provisions, and such property as was most valuable and portable.   They reached the castle by the morning, and escaped to Arragon, Catalonia, and such other places as they thought would secure them from the power of the sanguinary legate.

Next morning the troops were astonished, not hearing any noise nor seeing any man stir in the city; yet they approached the walls with much fear, lest it should be but a stratagem to endanger them; but finding no opposition, they mounted the walls, crying out that the Albigenses were fled; and thus was the city, with all the spoils, taken, and the earl of Bezieres committed to prison in one of the strongest towers of the castle, where he soon after died.

The legate now called all the prelates and great lords of his army together, telling them, that though it was requisite there should be always a legate in the army, yet it was likewise necessary that there should be a secular general, wise and valiant, to command in all their affairs, &c. This charge was first offered to the duke of Burgogne, then to the earl of Ennevers, and, thirdly, to the earl of St. Paul; but they all refused it.   At length it was offered to Simon, earl of Montfort, who, after some excuses, accepted of it.   Four thousand men were left to garrison Carcasson, and the deceased earl of Bezieres was succeeded in title and dignity by earl Simon, a bigoted Roman Catholic, who threatened vengeance on the Albigenses unless they conformed to the worship of the church of Rome. But the king of Arragon, who was in his heart of the reformed persuasion, secretly encouraged the Albigenses, and gave them hopes that if they acted with prudence they might cast off the yoke of the tyrannical earl Simon. They took his advice, and while Simon was gone to Montpelier, they surprised some of his fortresses, and were successful in several expeditions against his officers.

Conduct of Simon.

These proceedings so enraged Simon, that returning from Montpelier, he collected together some forces, marched against the Albigenses, and ordered every prisoner he took to be immediately burnt. But not succeeding in some of his enterprises, he grew disheartened, and wrote to every Roman Catholic power in Europe to send him assistance, otherwise he should not be able to hold out against the Albigenses. He soon received some succours, with which he attacked the Castle of Beron, and making himself master of it, ordered the eyes to be put out and the noses to be cut off of all the garrison, one person alone accepted, who was deprived of one eye only, that he might conduct the rest to Cabaret. He then undertook the siege of Menerbe, which, on account of the want of water, was obliged to yield to him. The lord of Termes, the governor, was put in prison, where he died; his wife, sister, daughter, and one hundred and eighty others, were committed to the flames. Many other castles surrendered to the forces of this monster, and the inhabitants were butchered in a manner equally barbarous.

In the mean time the earl of Toulouse, by means of letters of recommendation from the king of France, was reconciled to the pope: at least the pope pretended to give him remission for the death of friar Peter, and to absolve him from all other crimes he had committed. But the legate, by the connivance of the pope, did all he could to ruin the earl. Some altercations having passed between them, the legate excommunicated the earl; and the bishop of Toulouse, upon this encouragement, sent this impudent message to the earl, " That as he was an excommunicated person, he commanded him to depart the city; for an ecclesiastic could not say mass with propriety, while a per son of such a description was so near him."

Being greatly exasperated at the bishop's insolence, the earl sent him an order immediately to depart from the place on pain of death. This order was all the prelate wanted, as it would give him some reason to complain of his lord. The bishop, with the canons of the cathedral church, marched out of the city in solemn procession, barefooted, and bareheaded, taking with them the cross, banner, host, &c., and proceeded in that manner to the legate's army, where they were received with great respect as persecuted saints, and the legate thought this a sufficient excuse to proceed against the earl of Toulouse for having, as he termed it, relapsed from the truth. He attempted to get the earl into his power by stratagem, but the latter being apprized of the design, escaped. The legate, enraged at this disappointment, laid siege to the castle of Montferrand, which belonged to the earl, and was governed by Baldwin his brother. On the first summons Baldwin not only surrendered, but abjured his religion, and turned papist. This event, which severely afflicted the earl, was followed by another that gave him still greater mortification; for his old friend the king of Arragon forsook his interest; and agreed to give his daughter in marriage to earl Simon's eldest son : the legate's troops were then joined by the forces of Arragon and those belonging to earl Simon, on which they jointly laid siege to Toulouse.

Success of the Albigenses.

Nevertheless, the Earl determined to interrupt the besiegers by frequent sallies. In the first attempt he met with a severe repulse; but in the second he took Simon's son prisoner, and in the third he unhorsed Simon himself. After several furious assaults given by the popish army, and some successful sallies of the Albigenses, the earl of Toulouse compelled his enemies to raise the siege. In their retreat they did much mischief in the countries through which they passed, and put many defenceless Albigenses to death.

The Earl of Toulouse now did all he could to recover

the friendship of the king of Arragon; and as the marriage ceremony between that monarch's daughter and Simon's son had not been performed, he entreated him to break off that match, and proposed another more proper, viz.: that his own eldest son and heir should wed the princess of Arragon, and that by this match their friendship should be again united and more firmly cemented. His majesty was easily persuaded not only to agree to this proposal, but to form a league with the principal Albigenses, and to put himself as captain-general at the head of their united forces, consisting of his own people, and of the troops of the earls of Toulouse, Foix, and Comminges. The papists were greatly alarmed at those proceedings; Simon sent to all parts of Europe, to engage the assistance of the Roman Catholic powers, and the pope's legate began hostilities by entering the dominions of the Earl of Foix, and committing the most cruel depredations.

As soon as the army of Albigenses was ready, the king of Arragon began his operations by laying siege to Murat, a strongly fortified town near Toulouse, belonging to the Roman Catholics. Earl Simon, by forced marches, came to the assistance of the place, at a time when the king of Arragon, who kept very little discipline in his army, was feasting and revelling. Simon suddenly attacked the Albigenses, while they were in confusion, when the united forces of the reformed were defeated, and the king of Arragon was killed. The loss of this battle was imputed to the negligence of the king, who would have as much entertainment in a camp as if he had been securely at peace in his capital. This victory made the popish commanders declare they would entirely extirpate the whole race of the Albigenses; and Simon sent an insolent message to the earls of Toulouse, Foix, and Comminges, to deliver to him all the castles and fortresses of which they were possessed. Those noblemen, instead of answering the demand, retired to their respective territories, to put them into the best posture of resistance.

Surrender of Toulouse.

Soon after, Simon marched towards the city of Toulouse, when the earl of Toulouse, who had retired to Mon-
10*

talban, sent word to the citizens to make the best terms they could with the Roman Catholics, as he was confident they could not hold out a siege; but he recommended them to preserve their hearts for him, though they surrendered their persons to one another. The citizens of Toulouse, upon receiving this intimation, sent deputies to Simon, with offers of immediate surrender, provided the city itself, and the persons and properties of its inhabitants, should be protected from devastation. These conditions were agreed to, and Simon, in order to ingratiate himself at court, wrote a letter to Prince Louis, the son of Philip, king of France, informing him that the city of Toulouse had offered to surrender to him; but being willing that the prince should have the honour of receiving the keys and the homage of the people, he begged that he would repair to the camp for that purpose. The prince, pleased with the invitation, went directly to the army, and had the city of Toulouse surrendered to him in form. The pope's legate, however, was greatly displeased at the mild conditions granted to the people, and insisted, that though the prince might take upon him the sovereignity of the place and receive the homage of the people, yet the plunder belonged to the *holy pilgrims*, (for so the popish soldiers employed in these expeditions were called;) and that the place, as a receptacle of heretics, ought to be dismantled. The prince and earl Simon in vain remonstrated against proceedings so contrary to the conditions granted at the surrender : the legate was peremptory, when earl Simon and the Prince, unwilling to come to an open rupture with him gave up the point. The legate immediately set his holy pilgrims to work, when they presently dismantled the city, and plundered the inhabitants of all their property, in defiance of the security granted to them by the articles of the surrender.

Dispute between the Legate and Prince.

Now the legate finding that among the Albigenses were many lucrative places which would fall to the disposal of the prince, determined, by an artifice, to deprive him of any advantage which might accrue from them ; to this end he gave absolution to the Albigenses, which, though they had not in the least changed their religious opinions, he called reconciling them to the church. The prince, not apprized of this stratagem, was about to give his officers possession of some places of profit; when, to his great astonishment, the legate informed him, that he had no power to dispose of those places. The prince demanded an explanation of his meaning. "My meaning," replied the legate, " is, that the people have received absolution, and being reconciled to, are consequently under the protection of the church; therefore, all places among or connected with them, are in the disposal of the church only."

The prince, offended at this mode of reasoning, and highly displeased at the meanness of the subterfuge, nevertheless thought proper to dissemble his resentment. But being determined to quit the legate, he put the troops that were under his command in motion, and marched to attack some other fortresses; but he found, wherever he came, that the legate had played the same trick, and plainly perceived, if he continued his military operations, that when unsuccessful, he should bear all the blame, and when successful, the legate would steal all the profit; he therefore left the army in disgust, and returned to court.

Defeat of Earl Simon.

On this, earl Simon, with his own forces, those the prince had just quitted, and some other auxiliaries, undertook the siege of Foix, being chiefly provoked to it by the death of his brother, who was slain by the earl of Foix He lay before the castle of Foix for ten days, during which time he frequently assaulted it, but was as often repulsed. Hearing that an army of Arragonese were in full march toward him, in order to revenge the death of their king he raised the siege and went to meet them. The earl of Foix immediately sallied out and harassed his rear, and the Arragonese attacking his front, gave him a total defeat, which compelled him to shut himself up in Carcasson.

Soon afterward the pope's legate called a council at Montpelier, for renewing the military operations against the Albigenses, and for doing proper honour to earl Simon, who was present; for the Arragonese, not taking advantage of their victory, had neglected to block up Carcasson, by which omission Simon had an opportunity of repairing to Montpelier.   On meeting the council, the legate, in the pope's name, paid many compliments to Simon, and declared that he should be prince of all the countries that might in future be taken from the Albigenses : at the same time, by order of the pontiff, he styled him " the active and dexterous soldier of Jesus Christ, and the invincible defender of the catholic faith."   But just as the earl was about to return thanks for these great honours and fine encomiums, a messenger brought word that the people, having heard earl Simon was in the council, had taken up arms, and were coming thither to destroy him as a common disturber.   This intelligence threw the whole council into great confusion : and earl Simon, though a minute before styled an *invincible* defender of the faith, jumped out of a window, and stole away from the city.

Council of Lateran.

The disputes becoming serious, according to the opinion of the papists, the pope himself soon after called a council, to be held at Lateran, in which great powers were granted to Roman catholic inquisitors, and many Albigenses were immediately put to death.   This council of Lateran likewise confirmed to earl Simon all the honours intended him by the council of Montpelier, and empowered him to raise another army against the Albigenses.   Earl Simon immediately repaired to court, received his investiture from the French king, and began to levy forces.   Having now a considerable number of troops, he determined, if possible, to exterminate the Albigenses, when he received advice, that his countess was besieged in Narbonne by the earl of Toulouse.   He proceeded to the relief of his wife, when the Albigenses met him, gave him battle, and defeated him ; but he found means to escape and get into the castle of Narbonne.

Recovery of Toulouse by the Albigenses.

After this, Toulouse was recovered by the Albigenses , but the pope espousing earl Simon's cause, raised forces for him, and enabled him once more to undertake the siege of that city. The earl assaulted the place furiously, but being repulsed with great loss, he seemed sunk in affliction: when the pope's legate said to comfort him, "Fear nothing, my lord, make another vigorous attack; let us by any means recover the city and destroy the inhabitants; and those of our men who are slain in the fight, I will assure you shall immediately pass into paradise." One of the earl's principal officers, on hearing this, said with a sneer, "Monsieur cardinal, you talk with great assurance; but if the earl believes you, he will, as heretofore, pay dearly for his confidence." Earl Simon, however, took the legate's advice, made another assault, and was again repulsed. To complete his misfortune, before the troops could recover from their confusion, the earl of Foix made his appearance, at the head of a formidable body of forces, and attacking the already dispirited army of earl Simon, easily put them to the rout; when the earl himself narrowly escaped drowning in the Garonne, into which he had hastily plunged, in order to avoid being captured. This miscarriage almost broke his heart; but the people's legate continued to encourage him, and offered to raise another army; which promise, with some difficulty, and three years delay, he at length performed, and that bigoted nobleman was once more enabled to take the field. On this occasion he turned his whole force against Toulouse, which he besieged for the space of nine months, when in one of the sallies made by the besieged, his horse was wounded. The animal being in great anguish, ran away with him, and bore him directly under the ramparts of the city, when an archer shot him in the thigh with an arrow; and a woman immediately after throwing a large stone from the wall, it struck him upon the head, and killed him; thus were the Albigenses, like the Israelites, delivered by the hand of a woman; and thus this atrocious monster, who had so long persecuted the people of God, was at length himself slain by one of those whom he had intended to have slaughtered if he had been successful. The siege was raised; but the legate, enraged to be disappointed of his vengeance on the inhabitants, engaged the king of France in the cause, who sent his son to besiege it. The French prince, with some chosen troops, furiously assaulted Toulouse; but meeting with a severe repulse, he

abandoned that city to besiege Miromand.   This place he
soon took by storm, and put to the sword all the inhabitants, consisting of 5000 men, women, and children.

Guido, earl of Montfort, the son of earl Simon, undertook the command of the troops, and laid siege to Toulouse, before the walls of which he was killed.   His brother
Almeric succeeded to the command, but was soon obliged
to raise the siege.   On this the legate prevailed upon the
king of France to undertake the siege of Toulouse in person.   The earl of Toulouse sent the women, children, cattle, &c., into secure places in the mountains, ploughed up
the land, that the king's forces should not obtain forage,
and did all that a skilful general could perform to distress
the enemy.   By these wise regulations the French army
suffered all the extremities of famine, which obliged the
troops to feed on the carcasses of dogs, cats, &c. which
diet produced the plague.   The king died of grief; but
his son, who succeeded him, determined to carry on the
war : he was, however, defeated in three engagements by
the earl of Toulouse.   The king, the queen-mother, and
three archbishops again raised an army, and had the art to
persuade the earl of Toulouse to come to a conference,
when he was made a prisoner, and forced to appear barefooted and bareheaded before his enemies, and to subscribe
to the following ignominious conditions : 1. That he should
abjure the faith that he had hitherto defended.   2. That
he should be subject to the church of Rome.   3. That he
should give his daughter Joan in marriage to one of the
brothers of the king of France.   4. That he should maintain in Toulouse six popish professors of the liberal arts,
and two grammarians.   5. That he should take upon him
the cross, and serve five years against the Saracens.   6.
That he should level the walls of Toulouse with the ground.
7. That he should destroy thirty of his other cities and castles, as the legate should direct.   8. That he should remain prisoner at Paris till his daughter was delivered to the
king's commissioners.   After these cruel conditions a severe persecution took place against the Albigenses, many
of whom suffered for the faith ; and express orders were
issued that the *laity should not be permitted to read the
sacred writings !*

From this period we find no further account of the Albigenses till the commencement of the seventeenth century: but although they are not distinctly mentioned, they suffered cruel persecutions at various times.

CHAPTER IV.

Martyrdom of Marcus, bishop of Arethusa.

Persecutions in France.

DURING the internal commotions of this country, which lasted from about the middle of the sixteenth century to the time of the general massacre of the protestants in 1572, a constant persecution had been carried on against the protestants, during which several thousand suffered martyrdom by the most horrid cruelty.

Horrible Massacre of A. D. 1572.

After a long series of troubles, the papists seeing nothing could be done against the protestants by open force, began to devise how they could entrap them by subtlety, and that by two ways : first, by pretending that an army was to be sent into the lower country, under the command of the admiral, prince of Navarre and Conde ; not that the king had any intention of so doing, but only with a view to ascertain what force the admiral had under him, who they were, and what were their names.   The second was, a marriage suborned between the prince of Navarre and the sister of the king of France; to which were to be invited all the chief protestants.   Accordingly they first began with the queen of Navarre; she consented to come to Paris, where she was at length won over to the king's mind.   Shortly after she fell sick, and died within five days, not without suspicion of poison; but her body being opened, no sign thereof appeared.   A certain apothecary, however, made his boast, that he had killed the queen by venomous odours and smells, prepared by himself.

Notwithstanding this, the marriage still proceeded. The admiral prince of Navarre and Conde, with divers other chief states of the protestants, induced by the king's letters and many fair promises, came to Paris, and were received with great solemnity.   The marriage at length took place on the 18th of August, 1572, and was solemnized by the cardinal of Bourbon, upon a high stage set up on purpose without the church walls; the prince of Navarre and Conde came down, waiting for the king's sister, who was then at mass.   This done, the company all went to the bishop's palace to dinner.   In the evening they were conducted to the king's palace to supper.   Four days after this, the admiral coming from the council table, on his way was shot at with a pistol, charged with three bullets, and wounded in both his arms.   Notwithstanding which, he still remained in Paris, although the Vidam advised him to flee.

Soldiers were appointed in various parts of the city to be ready at a watch-word, upon which they rushed out to the slaughter of the protestants, beginning with the admiral, who being dreadfully wounded, was cast out of the window into the street, where his head being struck off, was embalmed with spices to be sent to the pope.   The savage people then cut off his arms and privy members, and drew him in that state through the streets of Paris, after which they took him to the place of execution, out of the city, and there hanged him up by the heels, exposing his mutilated body to the scorn of the populace.

The martyrdom of this virtuous man had no sooner

aken place than the armed soldiers ran about slaying all the protestants they could find within the city. This continued many days, but the greatest slaughter was in the three first days, in which were said to be murdered above 10,000 men and women, old and young, of all sorts and conditions. The bodies of the dead were carried in carts and thrown into the river, which was all stained therewith; also whole streams in various parts of the city ran with the blood of the slain. In the number that were slain of the more learned sort, were Petrus Ramus, Lambinus, Plateanus, Lomenius, Chapesius, and others.

These brutal deeds were not confined within the walls of Paris, but extended into other cities and quarters of the realm, especially to Lyons, Orleans, Toulouse, and Rouen, where the cruelties were unparalleled. Within the space of one month thirty thousand protestants, at least, are said to have been slain, as is credibly reported by them who testify of the matter.

When intelligence of the massacre was received at Rome, the greatest rejoicings were made. The pope and cardinals went in solemn procession to the church of St Mark to give thanks to God. A jubilee was also published, and the ordnance fired from the castle of St. Angelo. To the person who brought the news the cardinal of Lorraine gave one thousand crowns. Like rejoicings were also made all over France for this imagined overthrow of the faithful.

The following are among the particulars recorded of the above enormities:

The admiral, on being wounded in both his arms, said to Maure, preacher to the queen of Navarre, "O my brother, I now perceive that I am beloved of my God, **seeing that for his most holy name's sake I do suffer these wounds."** He was slain by Bemjus, who afterward reported that he never saw man so constantly and confidently suffer death.

Many honourable men and great personages were at the same time murdered, namely, Count Rochefoucault, Telinius, the admiral's son-in-law, Antonius Claromontus, marquis of Ravely, Lewis Bussius, Bandineus, Pleuvialius, Bernius, &c.

11

The Massacre at Vassy, in Champaigne.

The duke of Guise, on his arrival at Joinville, asked whether the people of Vassy used to have sermons preached constantly by their minister? It was answered, they had, and that they increased daily. At the hearing of which report, he fell into a violent passion; and upon Saturday, the last day of February, 1562, that he might the more covertly execute his conceived wrath against the protestants of Vassy, he departed from Joinville, accompanied with the cardinal of Guise, his brother, and those of their train, and lodged in the village of Dammartin, distant about two miles and a half.

The next day, after he had heard mass very early in the morning, he left Dammartin, with about two hundred armed men, passing along to Vassy. As he went by the village of Bronzeval, which is distant from Vassy a quarter of a mile, the bell (after the usual manner) rang for sermon. The duke hearing it, asked those he met, why the bell rang so loud. A person named La Montague told him, it was for the assembling of the Hugonots; adding, that there were many in the said Bronzeval who frequented the sermons preached at Vassy; therefore, that the duke would do well to begin there, and offer them violence. But the duke answered, " March on, march on, we shall take them among the rest of the assembly."

Now, there were certain soldiers and archers accompanying the duke, who compassed about Vassy; most of them being lodged in the houses of papists. The Saturday before the slaughter, they were seen to make ready their weapons, arquebuses, and pistols; but the faithful not dreaming of such a conspiracy, thought the duke would offer them no violence, being the king's subjects; also, that not above two months before, the duke and his brethren passing by the said Vassy, gave no sign of their displeasure.

The duke of Guise being arrived at Vassy with all his troops, they went directly toward the common-hall or market-house, and then entered into the monastery; where, having called to him one Dessales, the prior of Vassy, and another whose name was Claude le Sain, provost of Vassy, he talked awhile with them, and issued hastily out of the monastery, attended by many of his followers. Then command was given to the papists, to retire into the monastery, and not to be seen in the streets, unless they would venture the loss of their lives. The duke perceiving others of his retinue to be walking to and fro under the town-hall, and about the churchyard, commanded them to march on toward the place where the sermon was, being in a barn, about a hundred paces distant from the monastery. This command was put in execution by such of the company as went on foot. He that marched foremost of this rabble, was *La Brosse*, and on the side of these marched the horsemen, after whom followed the duke with another company of his own followers, likewise those of the cardinal of Guise, his brother. By this time, Mr. Leonard Morel, the minister, after the first prayer, had begun his sermon before his auditors, who might amount to about 1200 men, women, and children. The horsemen first approaching to the barn within about twenty-five paces, shot off two arquebuses right upon those who were placed in the galleries joining to the windows. The people within, perceiving this, endeavoured to shut the door, but were prevented by the ruffians rushing in upon them, who drawing their swords, furiously cried out, " Death of God, kill, kill these Huguenots."

Three persons were slain at the door; and the duke of Guise with his company rushed in among the congregation, striking the poor people down with their swords, daggers and cutlasses, not sparing any age or sex: besides, they within were so astonished that they knew not which way to turn them, but running hither and thither fell one upon another, flying as poor sheep before a company of ravening wolves entering in among the flock. Some of the murderers shot off their pieces against them that were in the galleries; others cut in pieces such as they lighted upon; some had their heads cleft in twain, their arms and hands cut off; so that many of them gave up the ghost even in the place. The walls and galleries of the place were dyed with the blood of those who were everywhere murdered: yea, so great was the fury of the murderers, that part of the people within were forced to break open the roof of the house, in hopes to save themselves upon the top thereof. Being got thither and then fearing to fall again into the hands of these cruel tigers, some of them eaped over the walls of the city, which were very high, flying into the woods and among the vines, which with most expedition they could soonest attain unto ; some hurt in their arms, others in their heads, and other parts of their bodies. The duke presented himself in the house with his sword drawn in his hand, charging his men to kill especially the young men. Only, in the end, women with child were spared. And pursuing those who went upon the house tops, they cried, " Come down, ye dogs, come down !" using many cruel threatening speeches to them. The cause why women with child escaped, was, as the report went, for the dutchess's sake, his wife, who, passing along by the walls of the city, and hearing so hideous outcries among these poor creatures, with the noise of the pieces and pistols continually discharging, sent in all haste to the duke her husband with much entreaties to cease his persecution, for frighting women with child.

During this slaughter, the cardinal of Guise remained before the church of Vassy, leaning upon the walls of the church yard, looking toward the place where his followers were busied in killing and slaying all they could. Many of this assembly being thus hotly pursued, did in the first brunt save themselves upon the roof of the house, not being discerned by those who stood without : but at length, some of this bloody crew espying where they lay hid, shot at them with long pieces, wherewith many of them were hurt and slain. The household servants of Dessalles, prior of Vassy, shooting at the people on the roof, one of that wretched company was not ashamed to boast, after the massacre was ended, that he for his part had caused six at least to tumble down in that pitiful plight, saying, that if others had done the like, not many of them could possibly have escaped.

The minister, in the beginning of the massacre, ceased not to preach, till one discharged his piece against the pulpit where he stood, after which, falling down upon his knees, he entreated the Lord not only to have mercy upon himself, but also upon his poor persecuted flock. Having ended his prayer, he left his gown behind him, thinking thereby to keep himself unknown : but while he approached toward the door, in his fear he stumbled over a dead body, where he received a blow with a sword upon his right shoulder. Getting up again, and then thinking to get forth, he was immediately laid hold of, and grievously hurt on the head with a sword, whereupon being felled to the ground, and thinking himself mortally wounded, he cried, "Lord, into thy hands I commend my spirit, for thou hast redeemed me, thou God of truth." While he thus prayed, one of this bloody crew ran upon him, with an intent to have hamstringed him; but it pleased God his sword broke in the hilt. Two gentlemen knowing him, said, "He is the minister, let him be conveyed to my lord duke." These leading him away by both the arms, they brought him before the gate of the monastery, from whence the duke and the cardinal his brother coming forth, said, "Come hither;" and asked him, saying, "Art thou the minister of this place? Who made thee so bold to seduce this people thus?" "Sir," said the minister, "I am no seducer, for I have preached to them the gospel of Jesus Christ." The duke perceiving that this answer condemned his cruel outrages, began to curse and swear, saying, "Death of God, doth the gospel preach sedition? Provost, go and let a gibbet be set up, and hang this fellow." At which words the minister was delivered into the hands of two pages, who misused him vilely. The women of the city, being ignorant papists, caught up dirt to throw in his face, and with great outcries, said, "Kill him, kill this varlet, who hath been the cause of the death of so many." In the meantime, the duke went into the barn, to whom they presented a great Bible, which they used for the service of God. The duke taking it into his hands, calling his brother the cardinal, said, "Lo, here is one of the Huguenot books." The cardinal viewing it, said, "There is nothing but good in this book, for it is the Bible, to wit, the holy scriptures." The duke being offended, that his brother suited not to his humour, grew into a greater rage than before, saying, "Blood of God, how now? What! the holy scripture? It is one thousand five hundred years ago since Jesus Christ suffered his death and passion, and it is but a year since these books were printed, how then say you that it is the gospel? You say you know not what." The unbridled fury of the duke displeased the cardinal, so that he was heard secretly to mutter, "An unworthy brother!"

I*

This massacre continued a full hour, the duke's trum peters sounding the while two several times. When any of these desired to have mercy showed them for the love of Jesus Christ, the murderers in scorn would say unto them, "You use the name of Christ, but where is your Christ now?"

There died in this massacre, within a few days, three-score persons; besides these, there were about two hundred and fifty, as well men as women, that were wounded, whereof many died. The poor's box, which was fastened to the door of the church with two iron hooks, containing twelve pounds, was wrested thence, and never restored.

The minister was closely confined and frequently threatened to be sewed up in a sack and drowned. He was, however, on the 8th of May, 1563, liberated at the earnest suit of the prince of Portien.

Massacre at Angers.

As soon as the massacre commenced at Paris, a gentleman named Monsoreau obtained a passport with letters to massacre the protestants at Angers. Being disappointed of his prey in one place, he came to the lodging of a reverend and learned minister, Mr. John Mason. Meeting his wife at the entrance of the house, he saluted her, and asked her, "Where her husband was?" She answered him, "That he was walking in his garden."

He immediately went in search of him; and meeting him, embraced him, and said, "Do you know wherefore I am come? The king hath commanded me to kill you forthwith, and hath given me express charge to do it, as you shall see by his letters." Upon which he showed him a pistol ready charged. Mason replied, "That he knew not wherein he had offended the king; but seeing," said he, "you seek my life, give me a little time to recommend my spirit into the hands of God."

Having made a short prayer, he presented his body to the murderer, who shot him immediately. His wife was soon after drowned, with nine others; and six thousand were murdered at Rouen in much the same manner.

The king of France proposed three things to the prince of Conde: "Either to go to mass, to die, or else to be perpetually imprisoned; and therefore to weigh well with himself which he liked best." The prince answered, "That by God's grace he would never choose the first; as for the latter, he referred himself to the king's pleasure."

About three hundred were barbarously murdered at Toulouse, and after taking all their goods, their bodies were stripped naked, and exposed to public view for two days, and then thrown in heaps into great pits. Certain counsellors after they were massacred were hung up in their long gowns, upon a great elm which was in the court of the palace.

Siege of Sancerre.

In 1573, Sancerre, a city inhabited chiefly by protestants, and to which many fled from other places for refuge, was besieged by the Catholic army. The want of provisions was soon felt by the inhabitants, and they were compelled to feed on the flesh of horses, asses, &c. At length even this failed; and they were then reduced to devour offal and excrements; and some, less capable of resisting the calls of hunger, even had recourse to the horrible expedient of cannibalism. This outrage on humanity it was necessary to punish, and accordingly we find that on the 29th of July, a man and his wife were executed for having eaten the head, brains, and entrails of a child, three years old, which died of hunger; having preserved the other parts to eat at another meal. An old woman, who lodged in their house, and had eaten a part, died a few hours after her imprisonment. The greater part of the children died of famine; and many affecting accounts are given of their patience and fortitude, among which the following is worthy of record:

A boy of ten years old, being ready to yield up the ghost, seeing his father and mother weeping over him, said unto them, "Wherefore weep ye thus, in seeing me famished to death? Mother, I ask you no bread, I know you have none: but seeing it is God's will I must die this death, let us be thankful for it. Did not the holy man Lazarus die of famine? have I not read it in my Bible?" In uttering these, with the like speeches, he expired the 30th of July.

Not more than eighty-four persons died by the hand of he enemy, but of the famine more than five hundred. Many soldiers, in order to avoid the lingering death of hunger, fled from the city, and chose rather to die by the sword of the enemy; whereof some were imprisoned, and others put to death.

Every hope seemed cut off from them, and death appeared both within and without their walls; and so far was the king of France from relenting at their hapless state, that, enraged at their courage, he swore they should eat up one another. But the King of kings had ordained it otherwise; for the election of the duke of Anjou to the throne of Poland, caused a general pacification, and the protestants once more enjoyed liberty of conscience and freedom from persecution.

CHAPTER V.

Persecutions in France, continued.

It was observed in the preceding chapter, that the persecution of the protestants was arrested by the election of the duke of Anjou to the throne of Poland; one of the conditions of that election being, that the king of France should cease to molest his protestant subjects on account of their faith. But this state of peace did not continue long; the wars were renewed during the succeeding reigns, with various success; and the history of this period is filled with the most horrible relations of battles, sieges, assassinations, massacres, and treasons. At length, Henry III. favouring the protestants, although more from political than religious motives, was assassinated by Clement, a friar; and was succeeded by the king of Navarre, under the title of Henry IV.

This prince, after struggling with his numerous enemies during several years, found it expedient to declare himself a Roman Catholic, and thus to obtain the suffrages of the majority of his subjects. This apostacy was a severe affliction to the faithful; but, although he abandoned his religion, and sacrificed a heavenly for an earthly crown, he did not, like many apostates, persecute the members of the church which he had quitted. He was, in all other respects, truly worthy of the appellation of *Great*; a title so frequently and so unjustly bestowed on men who sacrifice the lives and happiness of their fellow-creatures at the shrine of their own vanity and cruelty, and deserve rather to be execrated than admired, and regarded as demons than as demi-gods.

Upon the restoration of tranquillity in his dominions, Henry applied himself to the cultivation of the arts of peace, and by encouraging agriculture, manufactures, and trade, laboured successfully to recover France from the desolation and misery which thirty years of civil war and religious persecution had brought upon her. Nor was he unmindful of his ancient friends the protestants. By the Edict of Nantes, issued in 1598, he granted them a full toleration and protection in the exercise of their religious opinions. In consequence of this the true church of Christ abode in peace during many years, and flourished exceedingly.

Henry was at length assassinated, 1610, by Ravaillac, a Jesuit, filled with that frantic bigotry which the Roman Catholic religion has so peculiar a tendency to inspire and to cherish.

Louis XIII. being a minor at the death of his father, the kingdom was nominally governed by the queen mother, but really by her minion, cardinal Richelieu, a man of great abilities, which were unhappily perverted to the worst purposes. He was cruel, bigoted, tyrannical, rapacious, and sensual; he trampled on the civil and religious liberties of France: and hesitated not to accomplish his intentions by the most barbarous and infamous methods.

The protestants, at length, unable longer to endure the injuries daily heaped upon them, resolved to take arms in defence of their religion and their liberty. But the vigour of the cardinal defeated all their enterprises, and Rochelle, the last fortress which remained in their possession, was, in 1628, after a long siege, in which the defenders were reduced to the most horrible extremities of famine and suffering, surrendered to his victorious arms. He immediately caused the walls and fortifications to be destroyed; and those of the garrison who survived, were either put to death by the infuriated soldiery, or condemned to the galleys for life.

After this unhappy event, although the power of the protestants was too much broken to permit them to assert their rights in the field, and they therefore appeared to their enemies as if crushed and extinguished, there yet remained many thousands who " refused to bow the knee to Baal ;" their God upheld them by his gracious promises ; they knew that He without whose orders, " not even a sparrow shall perish," would not allow his faithful servants to fall unregarded ; and they consoled themselves with the reflection, that however they might be despised, contemned, and persecuted on earth, they would in the end arrive at those heavenly mansions prepared for them by their Father, where " all tears shall be wiped from all faces ;" and where an eternity of glorious and celestial happiness shall infinitely outweigh the temporary and trivial sufferings of mortality.

During the fifty years which succeeded the reduction of Rochelle, the protestants suffered every indignity, injustice, and cruelty, which their barbarous persecutors could devise.   They were at the mercy of every petty despot, who, " dressed in a little brief authority," wished to gratify his malice, or signalize the season of his power, by punishing the *heretics*, and evincing his attachment to the *infallible church*.   The consequences of this may easily be imagined ; every petty vexation which can render private life miserable, every species of plunder and extortion, and every wanton exertion of arbitrary power, were employed to harass and molest the protestants of all ranks, sexes, and ages.

At length, in 1684, the impious and blasphemous tyrant Louis XIV., who, in imitation of the worst Roman emperors, wished to receive divine honours, and was flattered by his abject courtiers into the belief that he was more than human, determined to establish his claim to the title of *le grand*, which their fulsome adulation had bestowed on him by the extirpation of the *heretics* from his dominions. Pretending, however, to wish for their conversion to the *true faith*, he gave them the alternative of voluntarily becoming papists, or *being compelled to it.*

On their refusal to apostatize, they were *dragooned ;*

that is, the dragoons, the most ruffianly and barbarous of his *Christian* majesty's troops were quartered upon them, with orders to *live at discretion*. Their ideas of *discretion* may easily be conceived, and accordingly the unhappy protestants were exposed to every species of suffering which lust, avarice, cruelty, bigotry, and brutality can engender in the breasts of an ignorant, depraved, and infuriated soldiery, absolved from all restraint, and left to the diabolical promptings of their worst passions, whose flames were fanned by the assurances of the bishops, priests, and friars, that they were fulfilling a sacred duty, by punishing the enemies of God and religion!

An order was issued by the king, for the demolition of the protestant churches, and the banishment of the protestant ministers. Many other reformers were also ordered to leave the kingdom in a few days; and we are told by Monsieur Claude, the celebrated author of "*Les Plaintes des Protestans*," who was himself banished at this time, that the most frivolous pretexts were employed to detain those who were about to quit France, so that by remaining in that country beyond the time allowed by the edict, they might be sent to the galleys as a punishment for infringing an order which they were thus prevented from complying with.

On the whole, more than five hundred thousand persons escaped or were banished. And these industrious citizens, whom the blind bigotry of a besotted tyrant had driven from their native land, found shelter and protection in England, Germany, and other countries, which they amply repaid by the introduction of many useful arts and processes; in particular, it is to them that we are indebted for the commencement of the silk manufacture in Great Britain.

In the meanwhile those who were either purposely detained, or were unable to escape, were condemned to the galleys; and after being imprisoned in the most horrible dungeons, and fed only on bread and water, and that very scantily, were marched off in large bodies, handcuffed, and chained together, from one extremity of the kingdom to another. Their sufferings during this dreadful journey were indescribable. They were exposed to every vicissitude of weather, almost without covering; and frequently, in the midst of winter, were obliged to pass the nights on the bare earth, fainting from hunger and thirst, agonized by disease, and writhing from the lash of their merciless conductors. The consequence was, that scarcely half the original number reached their place of destination; those who did were immediately exposed to new sufferings and additional calamities.

They were put on board the galleys, where they were subjected to the absolute control of the most inhuman and barbarous wretches who ever disgraced the human form. The labour of rowing, as performed in the galleys, is described as being the most excessive that can be imagined; and the sufferings of the poor slaves were increased a hundred fold by the scourgings inflicted on them by their savage taskmasters. The recital of their miseries is too horrible to be dwelt upon: we shall therefore pass to that period when the Lord, of his infinite mercy, gave ear to the cries of his afflicted servants, and graciously raised them up a deliverer in Anne, queen of England, who, filled with compassion for the unhappy fate of so many of her fellow-protestants, ordered her ambassador at the court of France to make a spirited remonstrance in their favour, which Louis, whose affairs were then in a very critical situation, was under the necessity of complying with; and he accordingly despatched orders to all the seaports for the immediate release of every galley slave condemned for his religion.

When this order was received at Marseilles, where the majority of the protestants were detained, the priests, and most particularly the Jesuits, were much chagrined at the prospect of thus losing their victims, and determined to use all means in their power to prevent the order from being carried into effect. They prevailed on the intendant, a violent and cruel bigot, to delay its execution for eight days, till they could receive an answer to an address which they immediately despatched to the king, exhorting him to abandon his intention of releasing the *heretics*, and representing the dreadful judgments which, they asserted, might be expected to fall on himself and his kingdom, as the punishment of so great a dereliction from his duty as the *eldest son of the church.* At least, they desired, if his majesty were determined to release the protestants, that

he would not allow them to remain in or even pass through France; but would compel them to leave their ports by sea, and never again to enter his dominions, on pain of revisiting the galleys.

Although Louis could not comply with the first part of the petition of these truly Papistical bigots, the latter part was too congenial to his own inclinations to be rejected. The protestants were ordered to sail from the ports at which they had been confined; and the difficulty of obtaining vessels for their conveyance, which the malignant priests used all their arts to augment, occasioned a long delay, during which the poor prisoners were suffering all the agonies of uncertainty—that " hope deferred, which maketh the heart sick,"—and which led them to fear that something might still intervene to prevent their so much desired emancipation. But their heavenly Father, ever mindful of those who suffer for his sake, at length removed every obstacle which bigotry and malice could interpose, and delivered them from the hand of the oppressor. They went forth rejoicing, praising and blessing His holy name, who had wrought for them this great deliverance.

A deputation of those who had been released by the interposition of queen Anne, waited upon her majesty in London, to return their most grateful thanks, on behalf of themselves and their brethren, for her Christian interference in their favour. She received them very graciously, and assured them that she derived more pleasure from the consciousness of having lessened the miseries of her fellow-protestants, than from the most brilliant events of her reign.

These exiles also established themselves in England which by their industry and ingenuity acquired new riches every day, while France, by expelling them, received a blow from which her commercial and trading interests never recovered. Thus even on earth did the Almighty punish the bigoted and cruel, and reward the pious and beneficent. But how fearful shall be the judgment of the persecutors in that great day when every action shall be weighed in the balance of Eternal Justice! How awful the denunciation—" Depart from me, ye cursed! I know you not!" Will the plea of *religious zeal* be then allowed ?   Will not the true motives of their barbarity be exposed to Him " from whom no secret is hid ?"   Undoubtedly they will; and lamentably ignorant are they of the genuine spirit of Christianity, who imagine that cruelty and persecution form any part of it.   Let them look to the conduct of its Divine Founder; to his meekness, his charity, his universal benevolence; let them consider these, and blush to call themselves his followers, and tremble at the doom which his justice will award to those who have perverted his maxims of mercy and of peace into denunciations of hostility and extirpation.

Martyrdom of John Calas, of Toulouse.

By this interesting story, the truth of which is certified in historical records, we have ample proofs, if any were requisite, that the abominable spirit of persecution will always prevail wherever popery has an ascendency.   This shocking act took place in a polished age, and proves that neither experience nor improvement can root out the inveterate prejudices of the Roman catholics, or render them less cruel or inexorable to the protestants.

John Calas was a merchant, of the city of Toulouse, where he had settled and lived in good repute, and had married an Englishwoman of French extraction.

• Calas and his wife were both protestants, and had five sons, whom they educated in the same religion; but Lewis, one of the sons, became a Roman catholic, having been converted by a maid servant who had lived in the family above thirty years.   The father, however, did not express any resentment or ill-will upon the occasion, but kept the maid in the family, and settled an annuity upon the son.   In October 1761, the family consisted of John Calas and his wife, one woman servant, Mark Anthony Calas, the eldest son, and Peter Calas, the second son.   Mark Anthony was bred to the law, but could not be admitted to practice, on account of his being a protestant: hence he grew melancholy, read all the books which he could procure relative to suicide, and seemed determined to destroy himself.   To this may be added, that he led a very dissipated life, and was greatly addicted to gaming.   On this account his father frequently reprehended him, **and some-times** in terms of severity, which considerably **added to** the gloom that oppressed him.

M. Gober La Vaisse, a young gentleman about **nineteen** years of age, the son of a celebrated advocate of **Toulouse,** having been some time at Bourdeaux, came back **to Tou-louse** to see his father, on the 13th of October **1761; but** finding that he was gone to his country house, at **some dis-tance** from the city, he went to several places, **endeavour-ing** to hire a horse to carry him thither. No **horse, how-ever,** was to be obtained; and about five o'clock **in the** evening, he was met by John Calas the father, **and the** eldest son Mark Anthony, who was his friend. **Calas, the** father, invited him to supper, as he could not **set out for** his father's that night, and La Vaisse consented. **All** three, therefore, proceeded to Calas's house **together, and** when they came thither, finding that Mrs. Calas **was still** in her own room, which she had not quitted tha**t day, La** Vaisse went up to see her. After the first **compliments,** he told her he was to sup with her, by her husb**and's invi-tation,** at which she expressed her satisfaction, **and a few** minutes after left him, to give some orders to **her maid.** When that was done, she went to look for her son **Anthony,** whom she found sitting alone in the shop, very **pensive :** she gave him some money, and desired him to go **and buy** some Roquefort cheese, as he was a better judge of **the** quality of cheese than any other person in **the family.** She then returned to her guest La Vaisse, who **very soon** after went again to the livery stable, to see if **any horse** was come in, that he might secure it for the next **morning.**

In a short time Anthony returned, having **bought the** cheese, and La Vaisse also coming back about **the same** time, the family and their guest sat down to **supper, the** whole company consisting of Calas and his wife, **Anthony** and Peter Calas the sons, and La Vaisse, no **other person** being in the house, except the maid-servant, who **has been** mentioned already. This was about seven o'clock **: the** supper was not long ; but before it was over, Anthony **left** the table and went into the kitchen, (which **was on the** same floor) as he was accustomed to do. **The maid** asked him if he was cold ? He answered, " **Quite the** contrary, I burn :" and then left her. In the **meantime** his friend and family left the room they had supped in, and went into a bed-chamber; the father and La Vaisse sat down together on a sofa, the younger son Peter in an elbow chair, and the mother in another chair; and without making any inquiry after Anthony, continued in conversation together, till between nine and ten o'clock, when La Vaisse took his leave, and Peter, who had fallen asleep, was awakened to attend him with a light.

There was on the ground floor of Calas' house a shop and warehouse; the latter of which was divided from the shop by a pair of folding-doors. When Peter Calas and La Vaisse came down stairs into the shop, they were extremely shocked to see Anthony hanging in his shirt, from a bar which he had laid across the top of the two folding-doors, having half opened them for that purpose. On discovering this horrid spectacle, they shrieked out, which brought down Calas the father, the mother being seized with such a terror as kept her trembling in the passage above. The unhappy old man rushed forward, and taking the body in his arms, the bar to which the rope was fastened, slipped off from the folding-door of the warehouse, and fell down. Having placed the body on the ground, he loosed and took off the cord in an agony of grief and anguish not to be expressed, weeping, trembling, and deploring his loss. The two young men, who had not had presence of mind to attempt taking down the body, were standing by stupid with amazement and horror. In the meantime the mother, hearing the confused cries and complaints of her husband, and finding no one come to her, found means to get down stairs. At the bottom she saw La Vaisse, and hastily demanded what was the matter. This question roused Calas in a moment, and instead of answering her, he urged her to go again up stairs, to which, with much reluctance, she consented; but the conflict of her mind being such as could not be long borne, she sent down the maid to know what was the matter. When the maid discovered what had happened she continued below, either because she feared to carry an account of it to her mistress, or because she busied herself in doing some good office to her master, who was still embracing the body of his son, and bathing it in his tears. The mother, therefore, being thus left alone, went down and mixed in the scene that has been already described, with such emotions as it must naturally produce. In the meantime Peter had been sent for La Moire, a surgeon in the neighbourhood. La Moire was not at home, but his apprentice, named Grosse, came instantly. Upon examination he found the body quite dead ; and upon taking off the neckcloth, which was of black taffeta, he saw the mark of the cord, and immediately pronounced that the deceased had been strangled. This particular had not been told, for the poor old man, when Peter was going for La Moire, cried out, " Save at least the honour of my family ; do not go and spread a report that your brother has made away with himself."

A crowd of people by this time were gathered about the house, and one Casing, with another friend or two of the family, had come in. Some of those who were in the street had heard the cries and exclamations within, but knew not the occasion ; and having by some means heard that Anthony Calas was suddenly dead, and that the surgeon who had examined the body, declared he had been strangled, they took it into their heads he had been murdered ; and as the family were protestants, they presently supposed that the young man was about to change his religion, and had been put to death for that reason. The cries they had heard they fancied were those of the deceased, while he was resisting the violence done to him. The tumult in the street increased every moment : some said that Anthony Calas was to have abjured the next day ; others, that protestants are bound by their religion to strangle or cut the throats of their children when they are inclined to become catholics. Others who had found out that La Vaisse was in the house when the accident happened, very confidently affirmed, that the protestants at their last assembly, appointed a person to be their common executioner upon these occasions, and that La Vaisse was the man who, in consequence of the office to which he had been appointed, had come to Calas's house to hang his son.

Now the poor father, who was overwhelmed with grief for the loss of his child, was advised by his friends to send for the officers of justice to prevent his being torn to pieces by the ignorant and bigoted mob. A messenger was accordingly despatched to the capitoul, or first magistrate of the place; and another to an inferior officer, called an assessor. The capitoul had already set out, having been alarmed by the rumour of a murder. He entered Calas' house with forty soldiers, took the father, Peter the son, the mother, La Vaisse, and the maid, all into custody, and set a guard over them. He sent for M. de la Tour, a physician, and M. la Marque and Perronet, surgeons, who examined the body for marks of violence, but found none except the mark of the ligature on the neck; they found also the hair of the deceased done up in the usual manner, perfectly smooth, and without the least disorder; his clothes were also regularly folded up and laid upon the counter, nor was his shirt either unbuttoned or torn.

The capitoul, notwithstanding these appearances, thought proper to agree with the opinion of the mob, and took it into his head that old Calas had sent for La Vaisse, telling him he had a son to be hanged; that La Vaisse had come to perform the office of executioner; and that he had received assistance from the father and brother.

On account of these notions the capitoul ordered the body of the deceased to be carried to the town-house, with the clothes. The father and son were thrown into a dark dungeon; and the mother, La Vaisse, the maid, and Casing, were imprisoned in one that admitted the light. The next day, what is called the verbal process was taken at the town-house, instead of the spot where the body was found, as the law directs, and was dated at Calas' house to conceal the irregularity. This verbal process is somewhat like the coroner's inquest in England; witnesses are examined, and the magistrate makes his report similar to the verdict of a coroner's jury in England. The witnesses examined by the capitoul were the physician and surgeon, who proved Anthony Calas to have been strangled. The surgeon having been ordered to examine the stomach of the deceased, deposed also, that the food which was found there had been taken four hours before his death. Finding that no proof of the murder could be procured, the capitoul had recourse to a monitory or general information, in which the crime was taken for granted, and all persons were required to give such testimony against it as they were able, particularizing the points to which they were to speak. This recites, that La Vaisse was commissioned by the protestants to be their executioner in ordinary when any of their children were to be hanged for changing their religion; it recites also, that when the protestants thus hang their children, they compel them to kneel, and one of the interrogatories was, whether any person had seen Anthony Calas kneel before his father when he strangled him; it recites likewise, that Anthony died a Roman Catholic, and requires evidence of his catholicism.

These ridiculous opinions being adopted and published by the principal magistrate of a considerable city, the church of Geneva thought itself obliged to send an attestation of its abhorrence of opinions so abominable and absurd, and of its astonishment that they should be suspected of such opinions by persons whose rank and office required them to have more knowledge and better judgment.

However, before this monitory was published, the mob had got a notion that Anthony Calas was the next day to have entered into the fraternity of the White Penitents. The capitoul immediately adopted this opinion also, without the least examination, and ordered Anthony's body to be buried in the middle of St. Stephen's church, which was accordingly done; forty priests and all the White Penitents assisting in the funeral procession.

A short time after the interment of the deceased, the White Penitents performed a solemn service for him in their chapel; the church was hung with white, and a tomb was raised in the middle of it, on the top of which was placed a human skeleton, holding in one hand a paper, on which was written, " Abjuration of heresy," and in the other a palm, the emblem of martyrdom.

The Franciscans performed a service of the same kind for him the next day; and it is easy to imagine how much the minds of the people were inflamed by this strange folly of their magistrates and priests.

Still the capitoul continued the prosecution with unrelenting severity; and though the grief and distraction of the family, when he first came to the house, were alone sufficient to have convinced any reasonable being, that they were not the authors of the event which they deplored, yet having publicly attested that they were guilty, in his monitory, without proof, and no proof coming in, he thought fit to condemn the unhappy father, mother, brother, friend, and servant, to the torture, and put them all into irons, on the 18th of November. Casing was released, upon proof that he was not in Calas' house till after Anthony was dead.

From these dreadful proceedings the sufferers appealed to the parliament, which immediately took cognizance of the affair, and annulled the sentence of the capitoul as irregular ; but the prosecution still continued.

As soon as the trial came on, the hangman, who had been taken to Calas' house, and shown the folding doors and the bar, deposed, that it was impossible Anthony should hang himself as was pretended. Another witness swore, that he looked through the keyhole of Calas' door into a room, where he saw men running hastily to and fro. A third swore, that his wife had told him, a woman named Maundril had told her, that a certain woman unknown had declared she heard the cries of Anthony Calas at the further end of the city.

From this absurd evidence the majority of the parliament were of opinion, that the prisoners were guilty, and therefore ordered them to be tried by the criminal court of Toulouse.

There was among those who presided at the trial one La Borde, who had zealously espoused the popular prejudices ; and though it was manifest to demonstration that the prisoners were either all innocent or all guilty, he voted that the father should first suffer the torture, ordinary and extraordinary, to discover his accomplices, and be then broken alive upon the wheel ; to receive the last stroke when he had lain two hours, and then to be burnt to ashes. In this opinion he had the concurrence of six others ; three were for the torture alone ; two were of opinion that they should endeavour to ascertain on the spot whether Anthony could hang himself or not ; and one voted to acquit the prisoner. After long debates the majority was for the torture and wheel, and probably condemned the father by way of experiment, whether he was guilty or not, hoping he would, in the agony, confess the crime, and accuse the other prisoners, whose fate, therefore, they suspended. It is, however, certain, that if they had evidence against the father that would have justified the sentence they pronounced against him, that very evidence would have justified the same sentence against the rest; and that they could not justly condemn him alone, they being all in the house together when Anthony died.

However, poor Calas, who was 68 years of age, was condemned to this dreadful punishment. He suffered the torture with great constancy, and was led to execution in a frame of mind which excited respect and admiration.

Father Bourges and father Coldagues, the two Dominicans who attended him in his last moments, wished their latter end might be like his, and declared that they thought him not only wholly innocent of the crime laid to his charge, but an exemplary instance of true Christian patience, charity, and fortitude.

He gave but one shriek, when he received the first stroke; after which he uttered no complaint. Being at length placed on the wheel, to wait for the moment which was to end his life and his misery together, he declared himself full of an humble hope of a glorious immortality, and a compassionate regard for the judges who had condemned him. When he saw the executioner prepared to give him the last stroke, he made a fresh declaration of his innocence to father Bourges; but while the words were yet in his mouth, the capitoul, the author of this catastrophe, and who came upon the scaffold merely to gratify his desire of being a witness of his punishment and death, ran up to him, and bawled out, " Wretch, there are the fagots which are to reduce your body to ashes; speak the truth." M. Calas made no reply, but turned his head a little aside, and that moment the executioner did his office.

Donat Calas, a boy of fifteen years of age, the youngest son of the unfortunate victim, was apprentice to a merchant at Nismes, when he heard of the dreadful punishment by which seven prejudiced judges of Toulouse had put his worthy father to death.

So violent was the popular outcry against this family in Languedoc, that every body expected to see the children of Calas broke upon the wheel, and the mother burnt alive. So weak had been the defence made by this innocent family, oppressed by misfortunes, and terrified at the sight of lighted piles, racks, and wheels. Young Donat Calas dreading to share the fate of the rest of his family, was advised to fly into Switzerland. He did so, and there found a gentleman, who, at first, could only pity and relieve him, without daring to judge of the rigour exercised against his father, mother, and brothers. Shortly after, one of the brothers, who was only banished, likewise threw himself into the arms of the same person, who, for more than a month, took all possible means to be assured of the innocence of this family. But when he was once convinced, he thought himself obliged in conscience to employ his friends, his purse, his pen, and his credit, to repair the fatal mistake of the seven judges of Toulouse, and to have the proceedings revised by the king's counsel. This revision lasted three years, and at the end of that time, fifty masters of the Court of Requests unanimously declared the whole family of Calas innocent, and recommended them to the benevolent justice of his majesty. The duke de Choiseul, who never let slip an opportunity of signalizing the greatness of his character, not only assisted this unfortunate family with money from his own purse, but obtained for them a gratuity of 36,000 livres from the king.

The arrêt which justified the family of Calas, and changed their fate, was signed on the 9th of March, 1765. The 9th of March, 1762, was the very day on which the innocent and virtuous father of that family had been executed. All Paris ran in crowds to see them come out of prison, and clapped their hands for joy, while the tears streamed down their cheeks.

PART IV

CHAPTER I.

Origin, Progress, and Cruelties of the Inquisition.

History of the Inquisition.

WHEN the reformed religion began to diffuse the pure light of the gospel throughout Europe, the bigoted Roman

Catholics fearing the exposure of the frauds and abuses of their church, determined to leave nothing unattempted to crush the Reformation in its infancy; pope Innocent III. therefore instituted a number of *inquisitors*, or persons who were to make inquiry after, apprehend, and punish the professors of the reformed faith. At the head of these inquisitors was one Dominic, who was canonized by the pope, in order to render his authority the more respectable. He and the other inquisitors visited the various Roman Catholic countries, and treated the protestants with the utmost severity: but at length the pope not finding them so useful as he had expected, resolved upon the establishment of fixed and regular courts of inquisition; the first office of which was established in the city of Toulouse, and Dominic became the first inquisitor.

Cruelties of the Inquisition.

Courts of inquisition were also erected in several other countries; but the Spanish inquisition became the most powerful and the most dreadful of any. Even the kings of Spain themselves, though arbitrary in all other respects, were taught to dread its power; and the horrid cruelties exercised by the inquisition, compelled multitudes, who differed in opinion from the catholics, carefully to conceal their sentiments. The Dominicans and Franciscans were

the most zealous of all the monks: these, therefore, the
pope invested with an exclusive right of presiding over and
managing the different courts of inquisition. The friars
of those two orders were always selected from the very
dregs of the people, and therefore were not much troubled
with scruples of conscience; they were obliged by the
rules of their respective orders to lead very austere lives,
which rendered their manners unsocial, and better qualified
them for their barbarous employment.

The pope gave the inquisitors the most unlimited powers
as judges delegated by him, and immediately representing
his person: they were permitted to excommunicate, or
sentence to death whom they thought proper, upon the
slightest information of heresy; were allowed to publish
crusades against all whom they deemed heretics, and enter
into leagues with sovereign princes to join those crusades
with their forces. About the year 1244, their power was
further increased by the emperor Frederic II., who declared himself the protector and friend of all inquisitors,
and published two cruel edicts, viz.: that all heretics who
continued obstinate should be burnt; and that all who repented should be imprisoned for life. This zeal in the emperor for the inquisitors and the Roman Catholic persuasion, arose from a report which had been propagated
throughout Europe, that he intended to turn Mahometan;
the emperor therefore judiciously determined by the height
of bigotry and cruelty, to show his attachment to *popery.*

The officers of the inquisition are three inquisitors, or
judges, a proctor fiscal, two secretaries, a magistrate, a
messenger, a receiver, a gaoler, an agent of confiscated
possessions, and several assessors, counsellors, executioners, physicians, surgeons, door-keepers, familiars, and visiters, who are all sworn to profound secrecy. The chief
accusation against those who are subject to this tribunal is
heresy, which comprises all that is spoken or written
against any of the articles of the creed, or the traditions
of the Romish church. The other articles of accusation
are renouncing the Roman catholic persuasion, and believing that persons of any other religion may be saved, or
even admitting that the tenets of any but papists are in
the least reasonable. There are two other things which
incur the most severe punishments, viz.: to disapprove of

any action done by the inquisition, or disbelieve any thing said by an inquisitor.

Heresy comprises many subdivisions; and upon a suspicion of any of these the party is immediately apprehended. Advancing an offensive proposition; failing to impeach others who may advance such; contemning church ceremonies; defacing idols; reading books condemned by the inquisition: lending such books to others to read; deviating from the ordinary practices of the Romish church; letting a year pass without going to confession; eating meat on fast-days; neglecting mass; being present at a sermon preached by a heretic; not appearing when summoned by the inquisition; lodging in the house of, contracting a friendship with, or making a present to a heretic; assisting a heretic to escape from confinement, or visiting one in confinement, are all matters of suspicion, and prosecuted accordingly. All Roman catholics are commanded under pain of excommunication to give immediate information even of their nearest and dearest friends, if they judge them to be heretics, or inclining to heresy. All who give the least assistance to protestants are called fautors, or abettors of heresy, and the accusations against these are for comforting such as the inquisition have begun to prosecute; assisting, or not informing against such if they should happen to escape; concealing, abetting, advising, or furnishing heretics with money; visiting, or writing to, or sending them subsistence; secreting or burning books and papers which might serve to convict them. The inquisition also takes cognizance of such as are accused of being magicians, witches, blasphemers, soothsayers, wizards, common swearers; and of such who read or even possess the Bible in the vulgar tongues, the Talmud of the Jews, or the Alcoran of the Mahometans.

Upon all occasions the inquisitors carry on their processes with the utmost severity. They seldom show mercy to a protestant; and a Jew who turns Christian is far from being secure; for if he is known to keep company with another new converted Jew, a suspicion arises that they privately practice together some Jewish ceremonies; if he keep company with a person who was lately a protestant, but now professes popery, they are accused of plotting together; but if he associate with a Roman catholic, an ac

13

cusation is often laid against him for only pretending to be a papist, and the consequence is a confiscation of his effects, and the loss of his life if he complain.

A defence is of little use to the prisoner; for a suspicion only is deemed sufficient cause of condemnation, and the greater his wealth the greater his danger. Most of the inquisitors' cruelties are owing to their rapacity: they destroy life to possess the property; and under pretence of zeal, plunder individuals of their rights. A prisoner of the inquisitors is never allowed to see the face of his accuser, or any of the witnesses against him, but every method is taken by threats and tortures to oblige him to accuse himself. If the jurisdiction of the inquisition be not fully allowed, vengeance is denounced against such as call it in question; or if any of its officers are opposed, those who oppose them are almost certain to be sufferers for their temerity; the maxim of the inquisition being to strike terror, and awe those who are the objects of its power into obedience. High birth, distinguished rank, or eminent employments are no protection from its severeties; and its lowest officers can make the most exalted nobleman tremble at their authority.

Such are the circumstances which subject a person to the rage of the inquisition; and the modes of beginning the process are, 1. to proceed by imputation, or prosecute on common report; 2. by the information of any indifferent person who chooses to impeach another; 3. on the information of spies who are retained by the inquisition; and, 4. on the confession of the prisoner himself.

The inquisitors never forget or forgive; length of time cannot efface their resentments; nor can the humblest concessions or most liberal presents obtain a pardon: they carry the desire of revenge to the grave, and wish to have both the property and lives of those who have offended them. Hence, when a person once accused to the inquisition, after escaping, is retaken, pardon is next to an impossibility. If a positive accusation be given, the inquisitors direct an order to the executioner, who takes a certain number of familiars with him to assist in the execution. Father, son, brother, sister, husband or wife, must quietly submit; none dare resist or even speak: as either would subject them to the same punishment as the devoted victim. No respite is allowed, but the prisoner is instantaneously hurried away.

This dreadful engine of tyranny may at any time be introduced into a country where the catholics have the upper hand ; and hence, how careful ought we to be, who are not cursed with such an arbitrary court, to prevent its introduction. In treating of this subject, an elegant author pathetically says, " How horrid a scene of perfidy and inhumanity ? What kind of community must that be whence gratitude, love, and mutual forbearance with regard to human frailties are banished ! What must that tribunal be which obliges parents not only to erase from their minds the remembrance of their own children, to extinguish all those keen sensations of tenderness and affection wherewith nature inspires them, but even to extend their inhumanity so far as to force them to commence their accusers, and consequently to become the cause of the cruelties inflicted upon them ! What ideas ought we to form to ourselves of a tribunal which obliges children not only to stifle every soft impulse of gratitude, love, and respect, due to those who gave them birth, but even forces them, and that under the most rigorous penalties, to be spies over their parents, and to discover to a set of merciless inquisitors the crimes, the errors, and even the little lapses to which they are exposed by human frailty! In a word, a tribunal which will not permit relations, when imprisoned in its horrid dungeons, to give each other the succours, or perform the duties which religion enjoins, must be of an infernal nature. What disorder and confusion must such conduct give rise to in a tenderly affectionate family ! An expression innocent in itself, and, perhaps, but too true, shall, from an indiscreet zeal or a panic of fear, give infinite uneasiness to a family ; shall ruin its peace entirely, and perhaps cause one or more of its members to be the unhappy victims of the most barbarous of all tribunals. What distractions must necessarily break forth in a house where the husband and wife are at variance, or the children loose and wicked ! Will such children scruple to sacrifice a father who endeavours to restrain them by his exhortations, by reproofs, or paternal corrections? Will they not rather, after plundering his house to support their extravagance and riot, readily deliver up their unhappy parent to all the horrors of a tribunal founded on the blackest injustice? A riotous husband, or a loose wife, has an easy opportunity, assisted by means of the persecution in question, to rid themselves of one who is a check to their vices, by delivering him or her up to the rigours of the inquisition."

When the inquisitors have taken umbrage against an innocent person, all expedients are used to facilitate his condemnation; false oaths and testimonies are employed to prove the accused to be guilty; and all laws and institutions are sacrificed to the bigoted revenge of papacy.

When a person accused is taken, his treatment is deplorable. The gaolers first begin by searching him for books and papers which might tend to his conviction, or for instruments which might be employed in self-murder or escape, and on this pretext they even rob him of his wearing apparel. When he has been searched and robbed, he is committed to prison. Innocence on such an occasion is a weak reed; nothing being easier than to ruin an innocent person.

The mildest sentence is imprisonment for life; yet the inquisitors proceed by degrees at once subtle, slow, and cruel. The gaoler first of all insinuates himself into the prisoner's favour, by pretending to wish him well and advise him well; and among other pretended kind hints, tells him to petition for an audit. When he is brought before the consistory, the first demand is, "What is your request?" To this the prisoner very naturally answers, that he would have a hearing. Hereupon one of the inquisitors replies, "Your hearing is this; confess the truth, conceal nothing, and rely on our mercy." Now, if the prisoner make a confession of any trifling affair, they immediately found an indictment on it; if he is mute they shut him up without light, or any food but a scanty allowance of bread and water, till his obstinacy is overcome; and if he declare he is innocent, they torment him till he either die with the pain or confess himself guilty.

On the re-examination of such as confess, they continually say, "You have not been sincere, you tell not all; you keep many things concealed, and therefore must be remanded to your dungeon." When those who have stood mute are called for re-examination, if they continue silent such tortures are ordered as will either make them speak, or kill them; and when those who proclaim their innocence are re-examined, a crucifix is held before them, and they are solemnly exhorted to take an oath of their confession of faith. This brings them to the test; they must either swear they are Roman catholics, or acknowledge they are not. If they acknowledge they are not they are proceeded against as heretics. If they acknowledge they are Roman catholics, a string of accusations is brought against them, to which they are obliged to answer extempore: no time being given even to arrange their answers. On having verbally answered, pen, ink, and paper are given them, in order to produce a written answer, which must in every degree coincide with the verbal answer. If the verbal and written answers differ, the prisoners are charged with prevarication; if one contain more than the other, they are accused of wishing to conceal certain circumstances; if they both agree they are charged with premeditated artifice.

After a person impeached is condemned, he is either severely whipped, violently tortured, sent to the galleys, or sentenced to death; and in either case his effects are confiscated. After judgment a procession is performed to the place of execution, which ceremony is called an *Auto da Fé*, or Act of Faith.

Auto da Fé at Madrid.

The following is an account of an *Auto da Fé* at Madrid, in the year 1682.

The officers of the inquisition, preceded by trumpets, kettle-drums, and their banner, marched on the 30th of May, in cavalcade, to the palace of the great square, where they declared by proclamation, that on the 30th of June the sentence of the prisoners would be put in execution. There had not been a spectacle of this kind at Madrid for several years, for which reason it was expected by the inhabitants with as much impatience as a day of the greatest festivity and triumph.

When the day arrived, a prodigious number of people appeared, dressed as splendidly as their circumstances would allow. In the great square was raised a high scaf-

13*

fold; and thither, from seven in the morning till the evening, were brought criminals of both sexes, all the inquisitions in the kingdom sending their prisoners to Madrid. Twenty men and women of these prisoners, with one renegado Mahometan, were ordered to be burned; fifty Jews and Jewesses, having never before been imprisoned, and repenting of their crimes, were sentenced to a long confinement, and to wear a yellow cap; and ten others indicted for bigamy, witchcraft, and other crimes, were sentenced to be whipped, and then sent to the galleys; these last wore large pasteboard caps, with inscriptions on them, having a halter about their necks, and torches in their hands.

On this solemn occasion the whole court of Spain was present. The grand inquisitor's chair was placed in a sort of tribunal far above that of the king. The nobles here acted the part of the sheriff's officers in England, leading such criminals as were to be burned, and holding them when fast bound with thick cords; the rest of the criminals were conducted by the familiars of the inquisition.

Among those who were to suffer was a young Jewess of exquisite beauty, only seventeen years of age. Being on the same side of the scaffold where the queen was seated, she addressed her, in hopes of obtaining a pardon, in the following pathetic speech: "Great queen! will not your royal presence be of some service to me in my miserable condition? Have regard to my youth; and, oh! consider that I am about to die for professing a religion imbibed from my earliest infancy!" Her majesty seemed greatly to pity her distress, but turned away her eyes, as she did not dare to speak a word in behalf of a person who had been declared a heretic by the inquisition.

Mass now began, in the midst of which the priest came from the altar placed near the scaffold, and seated himself in a chair prepared for that purpose. Then the chief inquisitor descended from the amphitheatre, dressed in his cope, and having a mitre on his head. After bowing to the altar he advanced toward the king's balcony, and went up to it, attended by some of his officers, carrying a cross and the gospels, with a book containing the oath by which the kings of Spain oblige themselves to protect the cathohe faith, to extirpate heretics, and support with all their power the prosecutions and decrees of the inquisition. On the approach of the inquisitor, and on his presenting this book to the king, his majesty rose up, bareheaded, and swore to maintain the oath, which was read to him by one of his counsellors: after which the king continued standing till the inquisitor had returned to his place; when the secretary of the holy office mounted a sort of pulpit, and administered a like oath to the counsellors and the whole assembly. The mass was begun about twelve at noon, and did not end till nine in the evening, being protracted by a proclamation of the sentences of the several criminals, which were all separately rehearsed aloud one after another. Next followed the burning of the twenty-one men and women, whose intrepidity in suffering that horrid death was truly astonishing: some thrust their hands and feet into the flames with the most dauntless fortitude, and all of them yielded to their fate with such resolution that many of the amazed spectators lamented that such heroic souls *had not been more enlightened!* The situation of the king was so near to the criminals, that their dying groans were very audible to him: he could not, however, be absent from this dreadful scene, as it is esteemed a religious one; and his coronation oath obliges him to give a sanction by his presence to all the acts of the tribunal.

Inquisition of Portugal.

The inquisition of Portugal is exactly upon a similar plan to that of Spain, having been instituted about the same time, and put under the same regulations, and the proceedings nearly resemble each other. The house, or rather palace, of the inquisition is a noble edifice. It contains four courts, each about forty feet square, round which are about three hundred dungeons or cells. The dungeons on the ground floor are for the lowest class of prisoners, and those on the second floor are for persons of superior rank. The galleries are built of freestone, and hid from view both within and without by a double wall of about fifty feet high. So extensive is the whole prison, and it contains so many turnings and windings, that none but those well acquainted with it can find the way through its various avenues. The apartments of the chief inquisitor are spacious and elegant ; the entrance is through a large gate, which leads into a court-yard, round which are several chambers, and some large saloons for the king, royal family, and the rest of the court to stand and observe the executions during an Auto da Fé.

A testoon (sevenpence half-penny English money) is allowed every prisoner daily ; and the principal gaoler, accompanied by two other officers, monthly visits every prisoner to inquire how he would have his allowance laid out. This visit, however, is only a matter of form, for the gaoler usually lays out the money as he pleases, and commonly allows the prisoner daily a porringer of broth, half a pound of beef, a small piece of bread, and a trifling portion of cheese.

Sentinels walk about continually to listen ; if the least noise is heard, they call to and threaten the prisoner ; if the noise is repeated, a severe beating ensues. The following is a fact : a prisoner having a violent cough, one of the guards came and ordered him not to make a noise ; to which he replied that it was not in his power to forbear. The cough increasing, the guard went into the cell, stripped the poor creature naked, and beat him so unmercifully that he soon after died.

Sometimes a prisoner passes months without knowing of what he is accused, or having the least idea when he is to be tried. The gaoler at length informs him, that he must petition for a trial. This ceremony being gone through, he is taken for examination. When they come to the door of the tribunal, the gaoler knocks three times, to give the judges notice of their approach. A bell is rung by one of the judges, when an attendant opens the door, admits the prisoner, and seats him on a stool.

The prisoner is then ordered by the president to kneel down, and lay his right hand upon a book, which is presented to him close shut. This being complied with, the following question is put to him : " Will you promise to conceal the secrets of the holy office, and to speak the truth ?" Should he answer in the negative, he is remanded to his cell, and cruelly treated. If he answer in the affirmative, he is ordered to be again seated, and the examination proceeds ; when the president asks a variety of questions, and the clerk minutes both them and the answers.

When the examination is closed, the bell is again rung, the gaoler appears, and the prisoner is ordered to withdraw, with this exhortation: "Tax your memory, recollect all the sins you have ever committed, and when you are again brought here, communicate them to the holy office." The gaolers and attendants, when apprized that the prisoner has made an ingenuous confession, and readily answered every question, make him a low bow, and treat him with an affected kindness, as a reward for his candour.

He is brought in a few days to a second examination, with the same formalities as before. The inquisitors often deceive prisoners by promising the greatest lenity, and even to restore their liberty, if they will accuse themselves: the unhappy persons, who are in their power, frequently fall into this snare, and are sacrificed to their own simplicity. Instances have occurred of some, who, relying on the faith of the judges, have accused themselves of what they were totally innocent of, in expectation of obtaining their liberty, and thus became martyrs to their own folly.

There is another artifice made use of by the inquisitors: if a prisoner has too much resolution to accuse himself, and too much sense to be ensnared by their sophistry, they proceed thus: a copy of an indictment against the prisoner is given him, in which, among many trivial accusations, he is charged with the most enormous crimes of which human nature is capable. This rouses his temper, and he exclaims against such falsehoods. He is then asked which of the crimes he can deny. He naturally mentions the most atrocious, and begins to express his abhorrence of them, when the indictment being snatched out of his hand, the president says, "By your denying only those crimes which you mention, you implicitly confess the rest, and we shall therefore proceed accordingly." Sometimes they make a ridiculous affectation of equity, by pretending that the prisoner may be indulged with a counsellor if he chooses to demand one. Such a request is sometimes made and a counsellor appointed; but upon these occasions, as the trial itself is a mockery of justice, so the counsellor is a mere cypher; for he is not permitted to say any thing that might offend the inquisition, or to advance a syllable that might benefit the prisoner.

Though the inquisitors allow the torture to be used only three times, yet at those three it is so severely inflicted that the prisoner either dies under it, or continues always after a cripple. The following is a description of the severe torments occasioned by the torture, from the account of one who suffered it the three respective times, but happily survived its cruelties.

The prisoner, on refusing to comply with the iniquitous demands of the inquisitors, by confessing all the crimes they charged him with, was immediately conveyed to the torture-room, which, to prevent the cries of the sufferers from being heard by the other prisoners, is lined with a kind of quilting which covers all the crevices and deadens the sound. The prisoner's horror was extreme on entering this infernal place, when suddenly he was surrounded by six wretches, who after preparing the tortures, stripped him naked to his drawers. He was then laid upon his back on a kind of stand, elevated a few feet from the door. They began by putting an iron collar round his neck, and a ring to each foot, which fastened him to the stand. His limbs being thus stretched out, they wound two ropes round each arm, and two round each thigh, which ropes being passed under the scaffold, through holes made for that purpose, were all drawn tight at the same instant of time by four of the men, on a given signal. The pains which immediately succeeded were intolerable; the ropes, which were of the small size, cut through the prisoner's flesh to the bone, making the blood gush out at eight different places. As he persisted in not making any confession of what the inquisitors required, the ropes were drawn in this manner four times successively.

A physician and a surgeon attended, and often felt his temples, in order to judge of the danger he might be in; by which means his tortures were for a small time suspended, that he might have sufficient opportunity of recovering his spirits to sustain each ensuing torture. During this extremity of anguish, while the tender frame is being torn, as it were, in pieces, while at every pore it feels the sharpest pangs of death, and the agonized soul is just ready to burst forth and quit its wretched mansion, the ministers of the inquisition have the obduracy to look on without emotion, and calmly to advise the poor distracted creature to confess his imputed guilt, on doing which they tell him he may obtain a free pardon, and receive absolution. All this, however, was ineffectual with the prisoner, whose mind was strengthened by a sweet consciousness of innocence and the divine consolation of religion.

While he was thus suffering, the physician and surgeon were so barbarous as to declare that if he died under the torture he would be guilty by his obstinacy of self-murder. In short, at the last time of the ropes being drawn tight, he grew so exceedingly weak by the stoppage of the circulation of his blood, and the pains he endured, that he fainted away, upon which he was unloosed and carried back to his dungeon.

These inhuman wretches finding that the torture inflicted, as above described, instead of extorting a discovery from the prisoner, only served the more frequently to excite his supplication to Heaven for patience and power to persevere in truth and integrity, were so barbarous, in six weeks after, as to expose him to another kind of torture more severe if possible than the former; the manner of inflicting which was as follows : they forced his arms backwards, so that the palms of his hands were turned outward behind him ; when by means of a rope that fastened them together at the wrist, and which was turned by an engine, they drew them by degrees nearer each other, in such a manner that the back of each hand touched and stood exactly parallel to each other. In consequence of this violent contortion both his shoulders were dislocated, and a considerable quantity of blood issued from his mouth. This torture was repeated thrice ; after which he was again taken to the dungeon and delivered to the physician and surgeon, who, in setting the dislocated bones, put him to the most exquisite torment.

About two months after the second torture, the prisoner being a little recovered, was again ordered to the torture-room, and there made to undergo another kind of punishment. The executioners fastened a thick iron chain twice round his body, which crossing upon his stomach, terminated at the wrists. They then placed him with his back against a thick board, at each extremity whereof was a pulley, through which there ran a rope that caught the ends of the chain at his wrists. Then the executioner stretching the end of this rope, by means of a roller placed at a distance behind him, pressed or bruised his stomach in proportion as the ends of the chain were drawn tighter They tortured him in this manner to such a degree that his wrists as well as his shoulders were quite dislocated. They were however soon set by the surgeons ; but the barbarians not yet satisfied with this infernal cruelty, made him immediately undergo the like torture a second time, which he sustained, (though, if possible, attended with keener pains,) with equal constancy and resolution. He was then again remanded to his dungeon, attended by the surgeon to dress his bruises and adjust the parts dislocated ; and here he continued till their Auto da Fé, or gaol delivery, when he was happily discharged.

It may be judged, from the before mentioned relation, what dreadful agony the sufferer must have endured. Most of his limbs were disjointed ; so much was he bruised and exhausted as to be unable for some weeks to lift his hand to his mouth, and his body became greatly swelled from the inflammation caused by such frequent dislocations. After his discharge he felt the effects of this cruelty for the remainder of his life, being frequently seized with thrilling and excruciating pains to which he had never been subject till after he had the misfortune to fall into the power of the merciless and bloody inquisition.

The unhappy females who fall into their hands have not the least favour shown them on account of the softness of their sex, but are tortured with as much severity as the male prisoners, with the additional mortification of having the most shocking indecencies added to the most savage barbarities.

Should the above mentioned modes of torturing force a confession from the prisoner, he is remanded to his horrid dungeon, and left a prey to the melancholy of his situation, to the anguish arising from what he has suffered, and to the dreadful idea of future barbarities. Should he refuse to confess, he is in the same manner remanded to his dungeon, and stratagem is used to draw from him what the torture fails to do. A companion is allowed to attend him, under the pretence of waiting upon and comforting his mind till his wounds are healed; this person, who is always selected for his cunning, insinuates himself into the good graces of the prisoner, laments the anguish he feels, sympathizes with him, and taking an advantage of the hasty expressions forced from him by pain, does all he can to dive into his secrets. This companion sometimes pretends to be a prisoner like himself, and imprisoned on similar charges. This is to draw the unhappy person into a mutual confidence, and persuade him in unbosoming his grief to betray his private sentiments.

Frequently these snares succeed, as they are the more alluring by being glossed over with the appearance of friendship and sympathy. Finally, if the prisoner cannot be found guilty, he is either tortured or harassed to death, though a few have sometimes had the good fortune to be discharged, but not without having suffered the most dreadful cruelties.

The inquisition also takes cognizance of all new books; and tolerates or condemns with the same *justice* and *impartiality* by which all its proceedings are distinguished.

When a book is published it is carefully read by some of the familiars; who, too ignorant and bigoted to distinguish truth, and too malicious to relish beauties, search not for the merits but for the defects of an author, and pursue the slips of his pen with unremitting diligence. They read with prejudice, judge with partiality, pursue errors with avidity, and strain that which is innocent into an offensive meaning. They misapply, confound, and pervert the sense; and when they have gratified the malignity of their disposition, charge their blunders upon the author, that a prosecution may be founded upon their false conceptions and designed misinterpretations.

Any trivial charge causes the censure of a book; but it is to be observed that the censure is of a three-fold nature, viz.:

1. When the book is wholly condemned.

2. When it is partly condemned; that is, when certain passages are pointed out as exceptionable, and ordered to be expunged.

3. When it is deemed incorrect; the meaning of which is, that a few words or expressions displease the inquisitors.

14

These, therefore are ordered to be altered, and such alterations go under the name of corrections.

There is a catalogue of condemned books annually published, under the three different heads of censures already mentioned, which being printed on a large sheet of paper, is hung up in the most public and conspicuous places. After which people are obliged to destroy all such books as come under the first censure, and to keep none belonging to the other two censures, unless the exceptionable passages have been expunged, and the corrections made, as in either case disobedience would be of the most fatal consequence; for the possessing or reading the proscribed books are deemed very atrocious crimes.

The publisher of such books is usually ruined in his circumstances, and sometimes obliged to pass the remainder of his life in the inquisition.

Where such an absurd and detestable system exercises its deadening influence over the literature of a nation, can we be surprised that the grossest ignorance and the most bigoted superstition prevail? How can that people become enlightened among whom the finest productions of genius are prohibited, all discussion prevented, the most innocent inquiries liable to misconstruction and punishment, the materials for thinking proscribed, and even *thought* itself chained down and checked by the fear of its escaping into expression, and thus bringing certain and cruel punishment on him who has dared to exercise his reason, the noblest gift of his Almighty Creator? Surely every well wisher to the human race must rejoice in the downfall of this most barbarous and infernal of all tribunals; and must view with indignation and abhorrence the iniquitous attempts now making to re-establish it in those unhappy countries which so long groaned under its sway.

CHAPTER IV.

Barbarities exercised by the Inquisitions of Spain and Portugal.

FRANCIS ROMANES, a native of Spain, was employed by the merchants of Antwerp to transact some business for them at Bremen. He had been educated in the Romish persuasion, but going one day into a protestant church, he was struck with the truths which he heard, and beginning to perceive the errors of popery, he determined to search further into the matter. Perusing the sacred scriptures, and the writings of some protestant divines, he perceived how erroneous were the principles which he had formerly embraced; and renounced the impositions of popery for the doctrines of the reformed church, in which religion appeared in all its genuine purity. Resolving to think only of his eternal salvation, he studied religious truths more than trade, and purchased books rather than merchandise, convinced that the riches of the body are trifling to those of the soul. He therefore resigned his agency to the merchants of Antwerp, giving them an account at the same time of his conversion; and then resolving, if possible, to convert his parents, he went to Spain for that purpose; but the Antwerp merchants writing to the inquisitors, he was seized upon, imprisoned for some time, and then condemned to be burnt as a heretic. He was led to the place of execution in a garment painted over with devils, and had a paper mitre put upon his head by way of derision. As he passed by a wooden cross one of the priests bade him kneel to it, but he absolutely refused so to do, saying, " It is not for Christians to worship wood." Having been placed upon a pile of wood the fire quickly reached him, whereupon he lifted up his head suddenly; the priests thinking he meant to recant, ordered him to be taken down. Finding, however, that they were mistaken, and that he still retained his constancy, he was placed again upon the pile, where as long as he had life and voice remaining, he kept repeating the seventh psalm.

Horrid Treachery of an Inquisitor

A lady, with her two daughters and her niece, were apprehended at Seville for professing the protestant religion. They were all put to the torture; and when that was over one of the inquisitors sent for the youngest daughter, pretended to sympathise with her and pity her sufferings; then binding himself with a solemn oath not to betray her, he said, "If you will disclose all to me, I promise you I will procure the discharge of your mother, sister, cousin, and yourself." Made confident by his oath, and entrapped by promises, she revealed the whole of the tenets they professed; when the perjured wretch, instead of acting as he had sworn, immediately ordered her to be put to the rack, saying, "Now you have revealed so much I will make you reveal more." Refusing, however, to say any thing further, they were all ordered to be burnt: which sentence was executed at the next Auto da Fé.

The keeper of the castle of Triano, belonging to the inquisitors of Seville, happened to be of a disposition more mild and humane than is usual with persons in his situation. He gave all the indulgence he could to the prisoners, and showed them every favour in his power, with as much secrecy as possible. At length, however, the inquisitors became acquainted with his kindness, and determined to punish him severely for it, that other gaolers might be deterred from showing the least traces of that compassion which ought to glow in the breast of every human being. With this view they immediately threw him into a dismal dungeon, and used him with such dreadful barbarity that he lost his senses. His deplorable situation, however, procured him no favour; for, frantic as he was, they brought him from prison, at an Auto da Fé, to the usual place of punishment, with a sanbenito (or garment worn by criminals) on, and a rope about his neck. His sentence was then read, and ran thus: that he should be placed upon an ass, led through the city, receive two hundred stripes, and then be condemned for six years to the galleys. This unhappy, frantic wretch, just as they were about to begin his punishment, suddenly sprung from the back of the ass, broke the cords that bound him, snatched a sword from one of the guards, and dangerously wounded an officer of the inquisition. Being overpowered by multitudes, he was prevented from doing further mischief, seized, bound more securely to the ass, and punished according to his sentence. But so inexorable were the inquisitors, that for the rash effects of his madness four years were added to his slavery in the galleys.

Trial and Sufferings of Mr. Isaac Martin.

In the year 1714, about Lent, Mr. Martin arrived at Malaga, with his wife and four children. On the examination of his baggage his Bible and some other books were seized. He was accused in about three months time of being a Jew, for these curious reasons, that his own name was Isaac, and one of his sons was named Abraham. The accusation was laid in the bishop's court, and he informed the English consul of it, who said it was nothing but the malice of some of the Irish papists, whom he advised him always to shun. The clergy sent to Mr. Martin's neighbours to know their opinion concerning him: the result of which inquiry was this, " We believe him not to be a Jew, but a heretic." After this, being continually pestered by priests, particularly those of the Irish nation, to change his religion, he determined to dispose of what he had and retire from Malaga. But when his resolution became known, at about nine o'clock at night he heard a knocking at his door. He demanded who was there. The persons without said they wanted to enter. He desired they would come again the next morning; but they replied, if he would not open the door they would break it open; which they did. Then about fifteen persons entered, consisting of a commissioner, with several priests and familiars belonging to the inquisition. Mr. Martin would fain have gone to the English consul, but they told him the consul had nothing to do in the matter, and then said, " Where are your beads and firearms?" To which he answered, "I am an English protestant, and as such carry no private arms, nor make use of beads." They took away his watch, money, and other things, carried him to the bishop's prison, and put on him a pair of heavy fetters. His distressed family was at the same time turned out of doors till the

14*

house was stripped ; and when they had taken every thing away, they returned the key to his wife.

About four days after his commitment, Mr. Martin was told he must be sent to Granada to be tried ; he earnestly begged to see his wife and children before he went, but this was denied. Being doubly fettered, he was mounted on a mule, and set out toward Granada. By the way the mule threw him upon a rocky part of the road, and almost broke his back.

On his arrival at Granada, after a journey of three days, he was detained at an inn till it was dark, for they never put any one into the inquisition during daylight. At night he was taken to the prison, and led along a range of galleries till he arrived at a dungeon. The gaoler nailed up a box of books, belonging to him, which had been brought from Malaga, saying, they must remain in that state till the lords of the inquisition chose to inspect them, for prisoners were not allowed to read books. He also took an inventory of every thing which Mr. Martin had about him, even to his very buttons ; and having asked him a great number of frivolous questions, he at length gave him these orders : " You must observe as great silence here as if you were dead ; you must not speak, nor whistle, nor sing, nor make any noise that can be heard ; and if you hear any body cry or make a noise, you must be still and say nothing upon pain of two hundred lashes." Mr. Martin asked if he might have liberty to walk about the room ; the gaoler replied he might, but it must be very softly. After giving him some wine, bread, and a few walnuts, the gaoler left him till the morning. It was frosty weather, the walls of the dungeon were between two and three feet thick, the floor was bricked, and a great deal of wind came through a hole of about a foot in length, and five inches in breadth, which served as a window. The next morning the gaoler came to light his lamp, and bade him light a fire in order to dress his dinner. He then took him to a turn, or such a wheel as is found at the doors of convents, where a person on the other side turns the provisions round. He had then given him half a pound of mutton, two pounds of bread, some kidney beans, a bunch of raisins, and a pint of wine, which was the allowance for three days. He had likewise two pounds of charcoal, an earthen stove, and a few other articles.

In about a week he was ordered to an audience; he followed the gaoler, and coming to a large room saw a man sitting between two crucifixes; and another with a pen in his hand, who was, as he afterward learned, the secretary. The chief lord inquisitor was the person between the two crucifixes, and appeared to be about sixty years of age. He ordered Mr. M. to sit down upon a little stool that fronted him. A frivolous examination then took place; the questions related to his family, their religion, &c., and his own tenets of faith. The prisoner admitted that he was a protestant, told the inquisitor that the religion of Christ admitted of no persecution, and concluded with saying that he hoped to remain in that religion. He underwent five examinations without any thing serious being alleged against him.

In a few days after he was called to his sixth audience, when, after a few immaterial interrogatories, the inquisitor told him the charges against him should be read, and that he must give an immediate and prompt answer to each respective charge.

The accusations against him were then read; they amounted to twenty-six, but were principally of the most trivial nature, and the greater number wholly false, or, if founded on facts, so distorted and perverted by the malice of his accusers, as to bear little resemblance to the real occurrences to which they related. Mr. Martin answered the whole of them firmly and discreetly, exposing their weakness, and detecting their falsehood.

He was then remanded to his dungeon; was shaved on Whitsun-eve, (shaving being allowed only three times in the year,) and the next day one of the gaolers gave him some frankincense to be put into the fire, as he was to receive a visit from the lords of the inquisition. Two of them accordingly came, asked many trivial questions, concluding them as usual, with, " We will do you all the service we can." Mr. Martin complained greatly of their having promised him a lawyer to plead his cause; " When instead of a proper person," said he, " there was a man whom you called a lawyer, but he never spoke to me, nor I to him: If all your lawyers are so quiet in this country, they are the quietest in the world, for he hardly said any thing but yes and no to what your lordship said." To which one of the inquisitors gravely replied, "Lawyers are not allowed to speak here." At this the gaoler and secretary went out of the dungeon to laugh, and Mr. Martin could scarce refrain from smiling in their faces, to think that his cause was to be defended by a man who scarce dared to open his lips. Some time after he was ordered to dress himself very clean : as soon as he was ready one of the gaolers came and told him that he must go with him ; but that first he must have a handkerchief tied about his eyes. He now expected the torture ; but after another examination was remanded to his dungeon.

About a month afterward, he had a rope put round his neck, and was led by it to the altar of the great church. Here his sentence was pronounced, which was, that for the crimes of which he stood convicted, the lords of the holy office had ordered him to be banished out of the dominions of Spain, upon the penalty of two hundred lashes, and being sent five years to the galleys : and that he should at present receive two hundred lashes through the streets of the city of Grenada.

Mr. Martin was sent again to his dungeon that night, and the next morning the executioner came, stripped him, tied his hands together, put a rope about his neck, and led him out of the prison. He was then mounted on an ass, and received his two hundred lashes, amidst the shouts and peltings of the people. He remained a fortnight after this in gaol, and at length was sent to Malaga. Here he was put in gaol for some days, till he could be sent on board an English ship ; which had no sooner happened, than news was brought of a rupture between England and Spain, and that ship, with many others, was stopped. Mr. Martin, not being considered as a prisoner of war, was put on board of a Hamburgh trader, and his wife and children soon came to him, but he was obliged to put up with the loss of his effects, which had been embezzled by the inquisition.

His case was published by the desire of Secretary Craggs, the archbishops of Canterbury and York, the bishops of London, Winchester, Ely, Norwich, Sarem,

Chichester, St. Asaph, Lincoln, Bristol, Peterborough, Bangor, &c.

Discovery of some Enormities of the Inquisition.

In the beginning of the last century, when the crown of Spain was contested for by two princes, France espoused the cause of one competitor and England of the other. The duke of Berwick, (a natural son of James II., of England) commanded the Spanish and French forces, and defeated the English at the battle of Almanza. The army was then divided into two parts ; the one, consisting of Spaniards and French, headed by the duke of Berwick, advanced toward Catalonia ; the other body, consisting of French troops only, commanded by the duke of Orleans, proceeded to the conquest of Arragon. On the troops approaching the city of Arragon, the magistrates came to offer the keys to the duke of Orleans ; but he told them haughtily they were rebels, and that he would not accept the keys, for he had orders to enter the city through a breach. Accordingly, he made a breach in the walls with his cannon, and then entered the city through it, together with his whole army. When he had made regulations here, and ordered that heavy contributions should be levied, he departed to subdue other places, leaving a strong garrison, under the command of his lieutenant-general M. De Legal. This gentleman, though brought up a Roman Catholic, was totally free from superstition : he united great talents with great bravery, and was at once the accomplished gentleman and skilful officer.

The money levied upon the magistrates and principal inhabitants, and upon every house was paid as soon as demanded ; but when the persons applied to the heads of the convents and monasteries, they found the ecclesiastics very unwilling to part with their cash.

M. De Legal sent to the Jesuits a peremptory order to pay two thousand pistoles immediately. The superior of the Jesuits returned for answer, that for the clergy to pay money to the army was against all ecclesiastical immunities ; and that he knew of no argument that could authorize such a procedure. M. De Legal then sent four companies of dragoons to quarter themselves in the college, with this sarcastic message: " To convince you of the necessity of paying the money, I have sent four substantia arguments to your college, drawn from the system of military logic; and, therefore, hope you will not need any further admonition to direct your conduct."

The Jesuits, greatly perplexed at these proceedings despatched an express to court to the king's confessor, who was of their order; but the dragoons were much more expeditious in plundering and doing mischief than the courier in his journey: so that the Jesuits, seeing every thing going to ruin, thought proper to adjust the matter, and paid the money before the return of the messenger. The Augustines and Carmelites, taking warning by what had happened to the Jesuits, prudently went and paid the money, and by that means escaped the study of military arguments, and of being taught logic by the dragoons.

On the other hand, the Dominicans, who are all agents of the inquisition, imagined that that very circumstance would be their protection; but they were mistaken, for M. De Legal neither feared nor respected the inquisition.   The chief of the Dominicans sent word to the military commander, that his order was poor, and had not any money whatever to pay the donative; " For," said he, " the whole wealth of the Dominicans consists only in the silver images of the apostles and saints which are placed in our church, and to remove which would be accounted sacrilege."

This insinuation was meant to terrify the French commander; he however sent word that the silver images would make admirable substitutes for money, and would be more in character in his possession than in that of the Dominicans themselves; " For," said he, " while you possess them, they stand up in niches, useless and motionless, without being of the least benefit to mankind; but when they come into my possession, they shall be useful. I will put them in motion; for I intend to have them coined, when they may travel like the apostles."

The inquisitors were astonished at this treatment, which they never expected to receive, even from crowned heads; they therefore determined to deliver their precious images in a solemn procession, that they might excite the people to an insurrection.   The Dominican friars were accordingly ordered to march to De Legal's house, with the silver apostles and saints, in a mournful manner, having lighted tapers with them, and bitterly crying all the way, " Heresy ! heresy !"

When M. De Legal heard of these proceedings, he ordered four companies of grenadiers to line the street which led to his house; each grenadier was ordered to have his loaded fuzee in one hand, and a lighted taper in the other: so that the troops might either repel force with force, or do honour to the farcical ceremony. The friars did all they could to raise a tumult, but the people were too much afraid of the troops; the silver images were therefore delivered up to M. De Legal, who sent them to the mint to be coined.

The inquisitors however, determined to excommunicate M. De Legal, unless he would release their precious saints from imprisonment in the mint before they were melted down. The French commander absolutely refused to do this, upon which the inquisitors drew up the form of excommunication, and ordered their secretary to go and read it to him.

This commission the secretary punctually performed, and read the excommunication deliberately and distinctly. The French commander heard him with great patience, and politely told him he would answer it the next day. As soon as the secretary was gone, M. De Legal ordered his own secretary to prepare a form of excommunication exactly like that sent by the inquisition: but instead of his name, to put in those of the inquisitors.

The next morning he ordered four regiments under arms, and commanded them to accompany his secretary, and act according to his direction. The secretary went to the inquisition, and insisted upon admittance; which, after a great deal of altercation, was granted. As soon as he entered, he read, in an audible voice, the excommunication sent by M. De Legal against the inquisitors. They were all present, and heard it with astonishment. They cried out against De Legal, as a heretic; and said this was a most daring insult against the Catholic faith. But, to surprise them still more, the French secretary told them, they must remove from their present lodgings; for the French commander wanted to quarter his troops there, as it was the most commodious place in the whole city. On this the inquisitors exclaimed loudly, when the secretary put them under a strong guard, and sent them to a place appointed by M. De Legal to receive them. Here, finding their threats disregarded, they begged that they might be permitted to retire from the city, taking with them their private property, which was granted, and they immediately set out for Madrid, where they made the most bitter complaints to the king; but the monarch told them he could not grant them any redress, as the injuries they had received were from the troops of his grandfather, the king of France, by whose assistance alone he could be firmly established in his kingdom.

In the meantime, M. De Legal set open all the doors of the inquisition, and released the prisoners, who amounted in the whole to four hundred; and among these were *sixty beautiful young women*, who formed a *seraglio* for the three principal inquisitors.

This discovery, which laid open the enormity of the inquisitors, greatly alarmed the archbishop, who desired M. De Legal to send the women to his palace, and he would take proper care of them; and at the same time he published an ecclesiastical censure against all such as should ridicule or blame the holy inquisition. But the French commander sent word to the archbishop, that the prisoners had either ran away, or were securely concealed by their friends, or his own officers; that it was impossible for him to send them back again; and, therefore, the inquisition having committed such atrocious actions, must now put up with their exposure and shame.

One of the ladies thus delivered from captivity was afterward married to the French officer who opened the door of her dungeon and released her. She related many singular circumstances respecting the *holy fathers* to her husband and to M. Gavin, who afterward made them public in his work entitled "The Master Key to Popery."

From the foregoing narrative it will be perceived that the inquisitors, under the exterior garb of sanctity and self-denial, are guilty of the greatest enormities. Lust, pride, avarice, and cruelty, are their predominant passions; and such is the blindness and bigotry of the deluded people over whom they extend their despotic sway, that not a voice is raised, nor a murmur heard, against the most horrible barbarities, if they be sanctified by the specious pretext of zeal for the Catholic faith, and executed by the familiars of the *Holy Office*.

It might have been expected that their influence over the minds of the higher orders of society would have been less powerful; and that some one would have been found among the sovereigns of Spain or Portugal, sufficiently enlightened to see through the imposture, and courageous enough to assert his own rights and those of his subjects against the hypocritical tyrants who trampled on both. But such is the benumbing effect of this horrible tribunal, so powerful has it become by the weakness and folly of the people, that the only prince who dared to threaten its existence, was put to death by the machinations of the inquisitors, before his accession to the throne gave him an opportunity of executing his noble purpose. This unfortunate prince was Don Carlos, son of Philip the Second, and grandson of Charles the Fifth.

Don Carlos possessed all the good qualities of his grandfather, without any of the bad ones of his father. He had sense enough to see into the errors of popery, and abhorred the very name of the inquisition. He inveighed publicly against it, ridiculed the affected piety of the inquisitors, and declared, that if he ever came to the crown he would abolish the inquisition, and exterminate its agents. This irritated and alarmed the inquisitors; and they accordingly determined on his destruction. They therefore employed all their emissaries to spread the most artful insinuations against the prince; and at length raised such a spirit of discontent among the people, that the king was under the necessity of removing Don Carlos from court. They even pursued his friends, and obliged the king to banish Don John, duke of Austria, his brother, together with his own nephew, the prince of Parma, because both these illustrious persons had a most sincere attachment to their kinsman, Don Carlos.

Shortly after, the prince having shown great lenity and favour to the protestants in the Netherlands, the inquisitors gladly seized the opportunity of declaring, that as the persons in question were heretics, the prince himself must be one, since he gave them countenance. This they

15

gained so great an ascendency over the mind of the king, who was an absolute slave to superstition, that he sacrificed the feelings of nature to the force of bigotry, and from fear of incurring the anger of the inquisition, passed sentence of death on his only son.

The prince had what was termed an indulgence; that is, he was permitted to choose the manner of his death. He chose bleeding and the hot bath; when the veins of his arms and legs being opened, he expired gradually, falling a martyr to the malice of the inquisitors, and the besotted bigotry of his father.

CHAPTER III.

Persecutions in Bohemia and Germany.

THE severity exercised by the Roman catholics over the reformed Bohemians, induced the latter to send two ministers and four laymen to Rome, in the year 977, to seek redress from the pope. After some delay their request was granted, and their grievances redressed. Two things in particular were permitted to them, viz.; to have divine service in their own language, and to give the cup in the sacrament to the laity. The disputes, however, soon broke out again, the succeeding popes exerting all their power to resume their tyranny over the minds of the Bohemians; and the latter, with great spirit, aiming to preserve their religious liberties.

Some zealous friends of the gospel applied to Charles, king of Bohemia, A. D. 1375, to call a council for an inquiry into the abuses that had crept into the church, and to make a thorough reformation. Charles, at a loss how to proceed, sent to the pope for advice; the latter, incensed at the affair, only replied, "Punish severely those presumptuous and profane heretics." The king, accordingly, banished every one who had been concerned in the application; and to show his zeal for the pope, laid many additional restraints upon the reformed Christians of the country.

The martyrdom of John Huss and Jerome of Prague

greatly increased the indignation of the believers, and gave animation to their cause. These two great and pious men were condemned by order of the council of Constance, when fifty-eight of the principal Bohemian nobility interposed in their favour. Nevertheless they were burnt; and the pope, in conjunction with the council of Constance, ordered the Romish clergy everywhere to excommunicate all who adopted their opinions, or murmured at their fate. In consequence of these orders great contentions arose between the papists and reformed Bohemians, which produced a violent persecution against the latter. At Prague it was extremely severe, till at length the reformed, driven to desperation, armed themselves, attacked the senate-house, and cast twelve of its members, with the speaker, out of the windows. The pope hearing of this went to Florence and publicly excommunicated the reformed Bohemians, exciting the emperor of Germany, and all other kings, princes, dukes, &c., to take up arms in order to extirpate the whole race; promising, by way of encouragement, full remission of all sins to the most wicked person who should kill one Bohemian protestant. The result of this was a bloody war: for several popish princes undertook the extirpation, or at least expulsion, of the proscribed people; while the Bohemians, arming themselves, prepared to repel them in the most vigorous manner. The popish army prevailing against the protestant forces at the battle of Cuttenburgh, they conveyed their prisoners to three deep mines near that town, and threw several hundreds into each, where they perished in a miserable manner.

A bigoted popish magistrate, named Pichel, seized twenty-four protestants, among whom was his daughter's husband. On their all confessing themselves of the reformed religion, he sentenced them to be drowned in the river Abbis. On the day of the execution a great concourse of people attended; and Pichel's daughter threw herself at her father's feet, bedewed them with tears, and implored him to pardon her husband. The obdurate magistrate sternly replied, " Intercede not for him, child, he is a heretic, a vile heretic." To which she nobly answered, " Whatever his faults may be, or however his opinions may differ from yours, he is still my husband, a thought which at a time like this should alone employ my whole consideration." Pichel flew into a violent passion, and said. " You are mad! cannot you, after his death, have a much worthier husband?" " No, sir," replied she, " my affections are fixed upon him, and death itself shall not dissolve my marriage vow." Pichel, however, continued inflexible, and ordered the prisoners to be tied with their hands and feet behind them, and in that manner thrown into the river. This being put into execution, the young lady watched her opportunity, leaped into the waves, and embracing the body of her husband, both sunk together.

Persecution by the Emperor Ferdinand.

The emperor Ferdinand, whose hatred to the protestants was unlimited, not thinking he had sufficiently oppressed them, instituted a high court of reformers, upon the plan of the inquisition, with this difference, that the reformers were to remove from place to place. The greater part of this court consisted of Jesuits, and from its decisions there was no appeal. Attended by a body of troops they made the tour of Bohemia, and seldom examined or saw a prisoner; but suffered the soldiers to murder the protestants as they pleased, and then to make report of the matter afterward.

The first who fell a victim to their barbarity was an aged minister, whom they killed as he lay sick in bed, Next day they robbed and murdered another, and soon after shot a third while preaching in his pulpit.

They ravished the daughter of a protestant before his face, and then tortured her father to death. They tied a minister and his wife back to back and burnt them. Another minister they hung upon a cross-beam, and making a fire under him, broiled him to death. A gentleman they hacked into small pieces; and they filled a young man's mouth with gunpowder, and setting fire to it, blew his head to pieces.

But their principal rage being directed against the clergy, they seized a pious protestant minister, whom they tormented daily for a month, in the following manner: they placed him amidst them, and derided and mocked him: they spit in his face and pinched him in various parts of his body; they hunted him like a wild beast, till ready to expire with fatigue; they made him run the gauntlet, each striking him with a twig, their fists, or ropes; they scourged him with wires; they tied him up by the heels, with his head downward, till the blood started out of his nose, mouth, &c.; they hung him up by the arms till they were dislocated, and then had them set again; burning papers dipped in oil, were placed between his fingers and toes; his flesh was torn with red-hot pincers; he was put to the rack; they pulled off the nails of his fingers and toes; he was bastinadoed on his feet; a slit was made in his ears and nose; they set him upon an ass, and whipped him through the town; his teeth were pulled out; boiling lead was poured upon his fingers and toes; and, lastly, a knotted cord was twisted about his forehead in such a manner as to force out his eyes. In the midst of these enormities, particular care was taken lest his wounds should mortify, and his sufferings be thus shortened, till the last day, when the forcing out of his eyes caused his death.

The other acts of these monsters were various and diabolical. At length, the winter being far advanced, the high court of reformers, with their military ruffians, thought it proper to return to Prague; but on their way meeting with a protestant pastor, they could not resist the temptation of feasting their barbarous eyes with a new kind of cruelty. This was to strip him naked, and to cover him alternately with ice and burning coals. This novel mode of torture was immediately put in practice, and the unhappy victim expired beneath the torments which delighted his inhuman persecutors.

Some time after, a secret order was issued by the emperor for apprehending all noblemen and gentlemen who had been principally concerned in supporting the protestant cause, and in nominating Frederic, elector palatine of the Rhine, to be the king of Bohemia. Fifty of these were suddenly seized in one night and brought to the castle of Prague; while the estates of those who were absent were confiscated, themselves made outlaws, and their names fixed upon a gallows as a mark of public ignominy.

The high court of reformers afterward proceeded to try those who had been apprehended, and two apostate protestants were appointed to examine them. Their exami-

15*

ners asked many unnecessary and impertinent questions, which so exasperated one of the noblemen, that he exclaimed, opening his breast at the same time, " Cut here, search my heart, you shall find nothing but the love of religion and liberty : these were the motives for which I drew my sword, and for those I am willing to die."

As none of the prisoners would renounce their faith, or acknowledge themselves in error, they were all pronounced guilty ; the sentence was, however referred to the emperor. When that monarch had read their names, and the accusations against them, he passed judgment on all, but in a different manner ; his sentences being of four kinds, viz. : death, banishment, imprisonment for life, and imprisonment during pleasure. Twenty of them being ordered for execution, were informed they might send for Jesuits, monks, or friars, to prepare for their awful change, but that no communication with protestants would be permitted them. This proposal they rejected, and strove all they could to comfort and cheer each other upon the solemn occasion. The morning of the execution being arrived, a cannon was fired as a signal to bring the prisoners from the castle to the principal market-place, in which scaffolds were erected; and a body of troops drawn up to attend. The prisoners left the castle, and passed with dignity, composure, and cheerfulness, through soldiers, Jesuits, priests, executioners, attendants, and a prodigious concourse of people assembled to see the exit of these devoted martyrs. In pursuance of their sentence the whole twenty were beheaded, meeting death with a fortitude worthy of the cause in which they suffered.

Account of John Huss.

John Huss was born in the village of Hussenitz, in Bohemia, about the year 1380. His parents gave him the best education they could bestow, and having acquired a tolerable knowledge of the classics, at a private school, he was sent to the university of Prague, where the powers of his mind and his diligence in study soon rendered him conspicuous.

In 1408, he commenced bachelor of divinity, and was successively chosen pastor of the church of Bethlehem, in

Prague, and dean and rector of the university. The duties of these stations he discharged with great fidelity, and became at length so conspicuous for the boldness and truth of his preaching that he attracted the notice and raised the malignity of the pope and his creatures.

His influence in the university was very great, not only on account of his learning, eloquence, and exemplary life, but also on account of some valuable privileges he had obtained from the king in behalf of that seminary.

The English reformer, Wickliffe, had so kindled the light of reformation, that it began to illumine the darkest corners of popery and ignorance. His doctrines were received in Bohemia with avidity and zeal, by great numbers of people, but by none so particularly as John Huss, and his friend and fellow-martyr, Jerome of Prague.

The reformists daily increasing, the archbishop of Prague issued a decree to prevent the further spreading of Wickliffe's writings. This, however, had an effect quite the reverse to what he expected, for it stimulated the converts to greater zeal, and at length almost the whole university united in promoting them.

Strongly attached to the doctrines of Wickliffe, Huss strenuously opposed the decree of the archbishop, who, notwithstanding, obtained a bull from the pope authorizing him to prevent the publishing of Wickliffe's writings in his province. By virtue of this bull, he proceeded against four doctors, who had not delivered up some copies, and prohibited them from preaching. Against these proceedings, Huss, with some other members of the university, protested, and entered an appeal from the sentences of the archbishop. The pope no sooner heard of this, than he granted a commission to cardinal Colonna, to cite John Huss to appear at the court of Rome, to answer accusations laid against him, of preaching heresies. From this appearance, Huss desired to be excused, and so greatly was he favoured in Bohemia, that king Winceslaus, the queen, the nobility, and the university, desired the pope to dispense with such an appearance; as also that he would not suffer the kingdom of Bohemia to lie under the accusation of heresy, but permit them to preach the gospel with freedom in their places of worship.

Three proctors appeared for Huss before cardinal

Colonna.   They made an excuse for his absence, and said,
they were ready to answer in his behalf.   But the cardinal
declared him contumacious, and accordingly excommunicated him.   On this the proctors appealed to the pope,
who appointed four cardinals to examine the process:
these commissioners confirmed the sentence of the cardinal, and extended the excommunication, not only to Huss,
but to all his friends and followers.   Huss then appealed
from this unjust sentence to a future council, but without
success ; and, notwithstanding so severe a decree, and an
expulsion from his church in Prague, he retired to Hussenitz, his native place, where he continued to promulgate
the truth, both from the pulpit, and with the pen.

He here compiled a treatise, in which he maintained,
that reading the books of protestants could not be absolutely forbidden.   He wrote in defence of Wickliffe's book on
the Trinity ; and boldly declared against the vices of the
pope, the cardinals, and the clergy of those corrupt times.
Besides these, he wrote many other books all of which
were penned with such strength of argument, as greatly
facilitated the spreading of his doctrines.

In England the persecutions against the protestants had
been carried on for some time with relentless cruelty.
They now extended to Germany and Bohemia, where
Huss, and Jerome of Prague, were particularly singled
out to suffer in the cause of religion.

In the month of November, 1414, a general council
was assembled at Constance, in Germany, for the purpose
of determining a dispute then existing between three persons who contended for the papal throne.[*]

John Huss was summoned to appear at this council ;
and to dispel any apprehensions of danger, the emperor sent
him a safe-conduct, giving him permission freely to come
to, and return from the council.   On receiving this information, he told the persons who delivered it, "That he
desired nothing more than to purge himself publicly of

* These were, John, proposed and set up by the Italians; Gregory, by
the French ; and Benedict, by the Spaniards.   The council continued four
years, in which the severest laws were enacted to crush the protestants.
Pope John was deposed and obliged to fly, the most heinous crimes being
proved against him ; among which were, his attempt to poison his predecessor, his being a gamester, a liar, a murderer, an adulterer, and guilty of
unnatural offences.

the imputation of heresy; and that he esteemed himself happy in having so fair an opportunity of it, as at the council to which he was summoned to attend."

In the latter end of November, he set out to Constance, accompanied by two Bohemian noblemen, who were among the most eminent of his disciples, and who followed him merely through respect and affection. He caused some placards to be fixed upon the gates of the churches of Prague, in which he declared, that he went to the council to answer all allegations that might be made against him. He also declared, in all the cities through which he passed, that he was going to vindicate himself at Constance, and invited all his adversaries to be present.

On his way he met with every mark of affection and reverence from people of all descriptions. The streets and even the roads, were thronged with people, whom respect, rather than curiosity, had brought together. He was ushered into the towns with great acclamations; and he passed through Germany in a kind of triumph. "I thought," said he, "I had been an outcast. I now see my worst friends are in Bohemia."

On his arrival at Constance, he immediately took lodgings in a remote part of the city. Soon after, came one Stephen Paletz, who was engaged by the clergy at Prague to manage the intended prosecution against him. Paletz was afterwards joined by Michael de Cassis, on the part of the court of Rome. These two declared themselves his accusers, and drew up articles against him, which they presented to the pope, and the prelates of the council.

Notwithstanding the promise of the emperor, to give him a safe-conduct to and from Constance, he regarded not his word: but, according to the maxim of the council, that "Faith is not to be kept with heretics," when it was known he was in the city, he was immediately arrested, and committed prisoner to a chamber in the palace. This breach was particularly noticed by one of Huss's friends, who urged the imperial safe-conduct; but the pope replied, *he* never granted any such thing, nor was he bound by that of the *emperor.*

While Huss was under confinement, the council acted the part of inquisitors. They condemned the doctrines of Wickliffe, and, in their impotent malice, ordered his remains to be dug up and burnt to ashes; which orders were obeyed.

In the meantime the nobility of Bohemia and Poland used all their interest for Huss; and so far prevailed as to prevent his being condemned unheard, which had been resolved on by the commissioners appointed to try him.

Before his trial took place, his enemies employed a Franciscan friar, who might entangle him in his words, and then appear against him. This man, of great ingenuity and subtlety, came to him in the character of an idiot, and with seeming sincerity and zeal, requested to be taught his doctrines. But Huss soon discovered him, and told him that his manners wore a great semblance of simplicity; but that his questions discovered a depth and design beyond the reach of an idiot. He afterward found this pretended fool to be Didace, one of the deepest logicians in Lombardy.

At length he was brought before the council, when the articles exhibited against him were read: they were upwards of forty in number, and chiefly extracted from his writings.*

On his examination being finished he was taken from the court, and a resolution was formed by the council to burn him as a heretic, unless he retracted. He was then committed to a filthy prison, where, in the daytime, he was so laden with fetters on his legs that he could hardly move; and every night he was fastened by his hands to a ring against the walls of the prison.

He continued some days in this situation, in which time many noblemen of Bohemia interceded in his behalf. They drew up a petition for his release, which was presented to the council by several of the most illustrious nobles of Bohemia; notwithstanding which, so many enemies had Huss in that court, that no attention was paid to it, and the persecuted reformer was compelled to bear with the punishment inflicted on him by that merciless tribunal.

Shortly after the petition was presented, four bishops and two lords were sent by the emperor to the prison, in

---

* That the reader may form a judgment of his writings, we here give one of the articles for which he was condemned: "An evil and a wicked pope is not the successor of Peter, but of Judas."

order to prevail on Huss to make a recantation. But he called God to witness that he was not conscious of having preached or written any thing against his truth, or the faith of the orthodox church. The deputies then represented the great wisdom and authority of the council; to which Huss replied, " Let them send the meanest person of that council, who can convince me by argument from the word of God, and I will submit my judgment to him." This pious answer had no effect, because he would not take the authority of the council upon trust, without the least shadow of an argument offered. The deputies, therefore, finding they could make no impression on him, departed, greatly astonished at the strength of his resolution.

On the 4th of July he was, for the last time, brought before the council. After a long examination he was desired to abjure, which he refused without the least hesitation. The bishop of Lodi then preached a sermon, the text of which was, " Let the body of sin be destroyed," (concerning the destruction of heretics,) the prologue to his intended punishment. After the close of the sermon his fate was determined, his vindication rejected, and judgment pronounced. The council censured him for being obstinate and incorrigible, and ordained, " That he should be degraded from the priesthood, his books publicly burnt, and himself delivered to the secular power."

He received the sentence without the least emotion; and at the close of it he kneeled down with his eyes lifted toward heaven, and, with all the magnanimity of a primitive martyr, thus exclaimed : " May thy infinite mercy, O my God ! pardon this injustice of mine enemies. Thou knowest the injustice of my accusations : how deformed with crimes I have been represented ; how I have been oppressed with worthless witnesses, and a false condemnation ; yet, O my God ! let that mercy of thine, which no tongue can express, prevail with thee not to avenge my wrongs." These excellent sentences were received as so many expressions of heresy, and only tended to inflame his adversaries. Accordingly, the bishops appointed by the council, stripped him of his priestly garments degraded him, and put a paper mitre on his head, on which were painted devils, with this inscription : " A ringleader of heretics."

This mockery was received by the heroic martyr with an air of unconcern, which appeared to give him dignity rather than disgrace. A serenity appeared in his looks, which indicated that his soul had cut off many stages of a tedious journey in her way to the realms of everlasting happiness.

The ceremony of degradation being over, the bishops delivered him to the emperor, who committed him to the care of the duke of Bavaria. His books were burnt at the gates of the church ; and on the 6th of July he was led to the suburbs of Constance, to be burnt alive.

When he had reached the place of execution, he fell on his knees, sung several portions of the Psalms, looked steadfastly toward heaven, and repeated, " Into thy hands, O Lord ! do I commit my spirit : thou hast redeemed me, O most good and faithful God."

As soon as the chain was put about him at the stake, he said, with a smiling countenance, " My Lord Jesus Christ was bound with a harder chain than this for my sake, why then should I be ashamed of this old rusty one ?"

When the fagots were piled around him, the duke of Bavaria desired him to abjure. " No," said he, " I never preached any doctrine of an evil tendency ; and what I taught with my lips I now seal with my blood." He then said to the executioner, " You are now going to burn a *goose*, (*Huss* signifying *goose* in the Bohemian language,) but in a century you will have a *swan* whom you can neither roast nor boil." If this were spoken in prophecy, he must have meant Martin Luther, who flourished about a century after, and who had a *swan* for his arms.

As soon as the fagots were lighted, the heroic martyr sung a hymn, with so loud and cheerful a voice, that he was heard through all the cracklings of the combustibles, and the noise of the multitude. At length his voice was interrupted by the flames, which soon put a period to his life.

Account of Jerome of Prague.

This hero in the cause of truth, was born at Prague, and educated in its university, where he soon became distinguished for his learning and eloquence. Having completed his studies, he travelled over great part of Europe, and visited many of the seats of learning, particularly the universities of Paris, Heidelburg, Cologne, and Oxford. At the latter he became acquainted with the works of Wickliffe, and translated many of them into his own language.

On his return to Prague he openly professed the doctrines of Wickliffe, and finding that they had made a considerable progress in Bohemia, from the industry and zeal of Huss, he became an assistant to him in the great work of reformation.

On the 4th of April, 1415, Jerome went to Constance. This was about three months before the death of Huss. He entered the town privately, and consulting with some of the leaders of his party, was easily convinced that he could render his friend no service.

Finding that his arrival at Constance was publicly known, and that the council intended to seize him, he retired, and went to Iberling, an imperial town, a short distance from Constance. While here, he wrote to the emperor, and declared his readiness to appear before the council, if a safe-conduct were granted to him; this, however, was refused.

After this, he caused papers to be put up in all the public places in Constance, particularly on the doors of the cardinals' houses. In these he professed his willingness to appear at Constance in the defence of his character and doctrine, both which, he said, had been greatly falsified. He further declared, that if any error should be proved against him, he would retract it; desiring only that the faith of the council might be given for his security.

Receiving no answer to these papers, he set out on his return to Bohemia, taking the precaution to carry with him a certificate, signed by several of the Bohemian nobility, then at Constance, testifying that he had used every prudent means in his power, to procure an audience.

He was, however, notwithstanding this, seized on his way, without any authority, at Hirsaw, by an officer belonging to the duke of Sultzbach, who hoped thereby to receive commendations from the council for so acceptable a service.

The duke of Sultzbach immediately wrote to the council, informing them what he had done, and asking directions

16

how to proceed with Jerome.   The council, after expressing their obligations to the duke, desired him to send the
prisoner immediately to Constance.   He was, accordingly
conveyed thither in irons, and on his way, was met by the
elector palatine, who caused a long chain to be fastened
to him, by which he was dragged, like a wild beast, to the
cloister, whence, after an examination, he was conveyed
to a tower, and fastened to a block, with his legs in stocks.
In this manner he remained eleven days and nights, till
becoming dangerously ill in consequence, his persecutors,
in order to gratify their malice still farther, relieved him
from that painful state.

He remained confined till the martyrdom of his friend
Huss ; after which, he was brought forth and threatened
with immediate torments and death if he remained obstinate.   Terrified at the preparations which he beheld, he,
in a moment of weakness, forgot his resolution, abjured his
doctrines, and confessed that Huss merited his fate, and
that both he and Wickliffe were heretics.   In consequence
of this, his chains were taken off, and he was treated more
kindly ; he was, however still confined, but in hopes of
liberation.   But his enemies suspecting his sincerity, proposed another form of recantation to be drawn up and proposed to him.   To this, however, he refused to answer,
except in public, and was accordingly, brought before the
council, when, to the astonishment of his auditors, and to
the glory of truth, he renounced his recantation, and re
quested permission to plead his own cause, which was refused ; and the charges against him were read, in which
he was accused of being a derider of the papal dignity, an
opposer of the pope, an enemy to the cardinals, a persecutor of the prelates, and a hater of the Christian religion.

To these charges Jerome answered with an amazing
force of elocution and strength of argument.   After which
he was remanded to his prison.

The third day from this his trial was brought on, and
witnesses were examined.   He was prepared for his defence, although he had been nearly a year shut up in
loathsome prisons, deprived of the light of day, and almost starved for want of common necessaries.   But his
spirit soared above these disadvantages.

The most bigoted of the assembly were unwilling he

should be heard, dreading the effect of eloquence in the cause of truth on the minds of the most prejudiced. At length, however, it was carried by the majority, that he should have liberty to proceed in his defence; which he began in such an exalted strain, and continued in such a torrent of elocution, that the most obdurate heart was melted, and the mind of superstition seemed to admit a ray of conviction.

Bigotry, however, prevailed, and his trial being ended, he received the same sentence as had been passed upon his martyred countryman, and was, in the usual style of popish duplicity, delivered over to the civil power; but being a layman, he had not to undergo the ceremony of degradation.

Two days his execution was delayed in hopes that he would recant; in which time the cardinal of Florence used his utmost endeavours to bring him over. But they all proved ineffectual: Jerome was resolved to seal his doctrine with his blood.

On his way to the place of execution he sung several hymns; and on arriving there he knelt down and prayed fervently. He embraced the stake with great cheerfulness and resolution; and when the executioner went behind him to set fire to the fagots, he said, "Come here, and kindle it before my eyes; for had I been afraid of it, I had not come here, having had so many opportunities to escape."

When the flames enveloped him, he sung a hymn; and the last words he was heard to say, were, "This soul in flames I offer. Christ, to thee!"

CHAPTER IV.

General Persecutions in Germany.

MARTIN LUTHER, by unmasking popery, and by the vigour with which he prosecuted his doctrines, caused the papal throne to shake to its foundation. So terrified was the pope at his rapid success, that he determined, in order to stop his career, to engage the emperor, Charles V., in his scheme of utterly extirpating all who had embraced the reformation. To accomplish which, he gave the emperor 200,000 crowns; promised to maintain 12,000 foot, and 5000 horse, for six months, or during a campaign; allowed the emperor to receive one half of the revenues of the clergy in Germany during the war; and permitted him to pledge the abbey lands for 500,000 crowns, to assist in carrying on hostilities. Thus prompted and supported, the emperor, with a heart eager both from interest and prejudice for the cause, undertook the extirpation of the protestants; and for this purpose raised a formidable army in Germany, Spain, and Italy.

The protestant princes in the meantime were not idle; but formed a powerful confederacy, in order to repel the impending blow. A great army was raised, and the command given to the elector of Saxony and the landgrave of Hesse. The imperial forces were commanded by the emperor in person, and all Europe waited in anxious suspense the event of the war.

At length the armies met, and a desperate engagement ensued, in which the protestants were defeated, and the elector of Saxony and landgrave of Hesse, both taken prisoners. This calamitous stroke was succeeded by a persecution, in which the most horrible cruelties were inflicted on the protestants, and suffered by them with a fortitude which religion only can impart.

Among others, Henry Yoes and John Esch were apprehended and brought to examination; when, confessing and defending their adoption of the tenets of Luther, they were both condemned to the flames, and soon after suffered with the fortitude of real Christians.

An eloquent and pious preacher, named Henry Stutphen, was taken out of his bed at night, and compelled to walk barefoot a considerable way, so that his feet were terribly cut. On desiring a horse, his conductors said, in derision, "A horse for a heretic! no, no, heretics may go barefoot." On arriving at the place of destination, he was comdemned to be burnt; and while suffering in the flames he was cut and slashed in a terrible manner.

Many were murdered at Halle. Middleburgh being taken by assault, all the protestants were put to the sword. Great numbers were also burned at Vienna.

Peter Spengler, a divine of the town of Schalet, was thrown into the river and drowned.

Wolfgang Scuch, and John Huglin, two worthy ministers, were burned; likewise Leonard Keyser, a student of the university of Wirtemburg; and George Carpenter, a Bavarian, was hanged.

The persecutions in Germany having been suspended many years, again broke out in 1630, on account of a war between the emperor and the king of Sweden; the latter being a protestant prince, the protestants of Germany, in consequence, espoused his cause, which greatly exasperated the emperor against them.

The imperial army having laid siege to the town of Passewalk, (then defended by the Swedes,) took it by storm, and committed the most monstrous outrages on the occasion. They pulled down the churches, pillaged and burnt the houses, massacred the ministers, put the garrison to the sword, hanged the townsmen, ravished the women, smothered the children, &c., &c.

In 1631, a most bloody scene took place at the protestant city of Magdeburg. The generals Tilly and Pappenheim, having taken it by storm, upwards of 20,000 persons, without distinction of rank, sex, or age, were slain during the carnage, and 6,000 drowned in attempting to escape over the river Elbe. After which, the remaining inhabitants were stripped naked, severely scourged, had their ears cropped, and being yoked together like oxen were turned adrift.

On the popish army's taking the town of Hoxter, all the inhabitants, with the garrison, were put to the sword.

When the imperial forces prevailed at Griphenburgh, they shut up the senators in the senate chamber, and surrounding it by lighted straw, suffocated them.

Franhendal, notwithstanding it surrendered upon articles of capitulation suffered as cruelly as other places, and at Heidelburg many were shut up in prison and starved.

To enumerate the various species of cruelty practised by the imperial troops, under count Tilly, would excite disgust and horror. That sanguinary monster, in his progress through Saxony, not only permitted every excess in his soldiers, but actually commanded them to put all their

16*

enormities in practice.   Some of these are so unparalleled,
that we feel ourselves obliged to mention them.

In Hesse-Cassel, some of the troops entered a hospital,
in which were principally mad women, when stripping all
the poor wretches naked, they made them run about the
streets for their diversion, and then put them to death.

In Pomerania, some of the imperial troops entering a
small town, seized upon all the young women and girls of
upward of ten years, and then placing their parents in a
circle, they ordered them to sing psalms, while they
ravished their children, or else they swore they would
cut them to pieces afterward.   They then took all the
married women who had young children, and threatened,
if they did not consent to the gratification of their lusts, to
burn their children before their faces, in a large fire which
they had kindled for that purpose.

A band of Tilly's soldiers met with a company of merchants belonging to Basil, who were returning from the
great market of Strasbourg, and attempted to surround
them; all escaped, however, but ten, leaving their property
behind.   The ten who were taken begged hard for their
lives, but the soldiers murdered them, saying, " You must
die because you are heretics, and have got no money.

Wherever Tilly came, the most horrid barbarities and
cruel depredations ensued; famine and conflagration
marked his progress.   He destroyed all the provisions he
could not take with him, and burnt all the towns before he
left them; so that murder, poverty, and desolation followed
him.

Peace, at length, chiefly through the medium of England,
was restored to Germany, and the protestants for several
years enjoyed the free exercise of their religion.

Even as late as 1732, above 30,000 protestants were,
contrary to the treaty of Westphalia, driven from the archbishopric of Saltzburg, in the depth of winter, with scarce
clothes to cover them, and without provisions.   These
people emigrated to various protestant countries, and settled in places where they could enjoy the free exercise of
their religion, free from popish superstition and papal des-
potism.

Persecutions in the Netherlands.

The glorious light of the gospel spreading over every part of the continent, and chasing thence the dark night of ignorance, increased the alarm of the pope, who urged the emperor to commence a persecution against the protestants; when many thousands fell martyrs to superstitious malice and barbarous bigotry; among whom were the following:

A pious protestant widow, named Windelinuta, was apprehended on account of her religion, when several monks unsuccessfully endeavoured to persuade her to recant. Their attempts, however, proving ineffectual, a Roman catholic lady of her acquaintance desired to be admitted to the dungeon in which she was confined, promising to exert herself toward inducing the prisoner to abjure her religion. On being admitted to the dungeon, she did her utmost to perform the task she had undertaken; but finding her endeavours fruitless, she said, "Dear Windeluta, if you will not embrace our faith, at least keep the things which you profess secret within your own bosom, and strive to prolong your life." To which the widow replied, "Madam, you know not what you say; for with the heart we believe to righteousness, but with the tongue confession is made unto salvation." Still holding her faith against every effort of the powers of darkness, her goods were confiscated, and she was condemned to be burnt. At the place of execution a monk presented a cross to her, and bade her kiss and worship God. To which she answered, "I worship no wooden God, but the eternal God who is in heaven." She was then executed, but at the intercession of the beforementioned lady, it was granted that she should be strangled before the fagots were kindled.

At Colen, two protestant clergymen were burnt; a tradesman of Antwerp, named Nicholas, was tied up in a sack, thrown into the river and drowned; and Pistorius, an accomplished scholar and student, was carried to the market of a Dutch village and burnt.

A minister of the reformed church was ordered to attend the execution of sixteen protestants who were to be beheaded. This gentleman performed the melancholy office with great propriety, exhorted them to repentance, and gave them comfort in the mercies of their Redeemer.   As soon as they were beheaded, the magistrate cried out to the executioner, " There is another remaining ; you must behead the minister ; he can never die at a better time than with such excellent precepts in his mouth, and such laudable examples before him."   He was accordingly beheaded. though many of the Roman Catholics themselves reprobated this piece of treacherous and unnecessary barbarity.

George Scherter, a minister of Saltzburg, was committed to prison for instructing his flock in the truth of the gospel. While in confinement he wrote a confession of his faith ; soon after which he was condemned, first to be beheaded, and afterward to be burnt to ashes, which sentence was accordingly put in execution.

Percival, a learned man of Louviana, was murdered in prison ; and Justus Insparg was beheaded for having Luther's sermons in his possession.

Giles Tolleman, a cutler of Brussels, was a man of singular humanity and piety.   He was apprehended as a protestant, and many attempts were made by the monks to persuade him to recant.   Once, by accident, a fair opportunity of escaping from prison offered itself to him, but of which he did not avail himself.   Being asked the reason, he replied, " I would not do the keepers so much injury ; as they must have answered for my absence had I got away."   When he was sentenced to be burnt, he fervently thanked God for allowing him, by martyrdom, to glorify his name.   Observing at the place of execution a great quantity of fagots, he desired the principal part of them might be given to the poor, saying, " A small quantity will suffice to consume me."   The executioner offered to strangle him before the fire was lighted, but he would not consent, telling him that he did not fear the flames ; and, indeed, he gave up the ghost with such composure amidst them, that he hardly seemed sensible of pain.

In Flanders, about 1543 and 1544, the persecution raged with great violence.   Many were doomed to perpetual imprisonment, others to perpetual banishment ; but the greater number were put to death either by hanging drowning, burning, the rack, or burying alive.

John de Boscane, a zealous protestant, was apprehended in the city of Antwerp. On his trial he undauntedly professed himself to be of the reformed religion, on which he was immediately condemned. The magistrate, however, was afraid to execute the sentence publicly, as he was popular through his great generosity, and almost universally revered for his inoffensive life and exemplary piety. A private execution was, therefore, determined on, for which an order was given to drown him in prison. The executioner, accordingly, forced him into a large tub; but Boscane struggling, and getting his head above the water, the executioner stabbed him in several places with a dagger till he expired.

John de Buisons, on account of his religion, was, about the same time, secretly apprehended. In this city the number of protestants being great, and the prisoner much respected, the magistrates, fearful of an insurrection, ordered him to be beheaded in prison.

In 1568 were apprehended at Antwerp, Scoblant, Hues, and Coomans. The first who was brought to trial was Scoblant, who, persisting in his faith, received sentence of death. On his return to prison, he requested the jailor not to permit any friar to come near him, saying, " They can do me no good, but may greatly disturb me. I hope my salvation is already sealed in Heaven, and that the blood of Christ, in which I firmly put my trust, hath washed me from my iniquities, I am now going to tear off this mantle of clay, to be clad in robes of eternal glory. I hope I may be the last martyr of papal tyranny, and that the blood already spilt will be sufficient to quench its thirst of cruelty; that the church of Christ may have rest here, as his servants will hereafter." On the day of execution he took a pathetic leave of his fellow prisoners. At the stake he uttered with great fervency the Lord's prayer, and sung the fortieth psalm; then commending his soul to God, the flames soon terminated his mortal existence.

A short time after Hues died in prison, upon which occasion Coomans thus vents his mind to his friends; " I am now deprived of my friends and companion; Scoblant is martyred, and Hues dead by the visitation of the Lord; yet I am not alone: I have with me the God of Abraham, of Isaac, and of Jacob: he is my comfort, and shall be my reward." When brought to trial, Hues freely confessed himself of the reformed religion, and answered with a manly firmness to every charge brought against him, proving his doctrine from the gospel. "But," said the judge, "will you die for the faith you profess?" "I am not only willing to die," replied Coomans, "but also to suffer the utmost stretch of inventive cruelty for it : after which my soul shall receive its confirmation from God himself, in the midst of eternal glory." Being condemned, he went cheerfully to the place of execution, and died with Christian fortitude and resignation.

Assassination of the Prince of Orange.

Baltazar Gerard, a native of Franche Comte, a bigoted and furious Roman Catholic, thinking to advance his own fortune and the popish cause by one desperate act, resolved upon the assassination of the prince of Orange. Having provided himself with firearms, he watched the prince as he passed through the great hall of his palace to dinner, and demanded a passport. The princess of Orange, observing in his tone of voice and manner something confused and singular, asked who he was, saying, she did not like his countenance. The prince answered, it was one that demanded a passport, which he should have presently. Nothing further transpired until after dinner, when on the return of the prince and princess through the same hall he assassin, from behind one of the pillars, fired at the prince; the balls entering at the left side, and passing through the right, wounded in their passage the stomach and vital parts. The prince had only power to say, " Lord have mercy upon my soul, and upon this poor people," and immediately expired.

The death of this virtuous prince, who was considered as the father of his people, spread universal sorrow throughout the United Provinces. The assassin was immediately taken, and received sentence to be put to death in the most exemplary manner; yet such was his enthusiasm and blindness for his crime, that while suffering for it, he coolly said, " Were I at liberty I would repeat the same."

In different parts of Flanders numbers fell victims to popish jealousy and cruelty. In the city of Valence in particular, fifty-seven of the principal inhabitants were butchered in one day for refusing to embrace the Romish superstition ; beside whom, great numbers remained in confinement till they perished.

CHAPTER V.

Persecutions in Italy in the sixteenth and seventeenth centuries.

In the year 1560, pope Pius the Fourth commenced a general persecution of the protestants throughout the Italian states, when great numbers of every age, sex, and condition, suffered martyrdom. Concerning the cruelties practised upon this occasion, a learned and humane Roman catholic thus speaks in a letter to a nobleman :

" I cannot, my lord, forbear disclosing my sentiments with respect to the persecution now carrying on. I think it cruel and unnecessary ; I tremble at the manner of putting to death, as it resembles more the slaughter of calves and sheep, than the execution of human beings. I will relate to your lordship a dreadful scene, of which I was myself an eye-witness : seventy protestants were cooped up in one filthy dungeon together ; the executioner went

in among them, picked out one from among the rest,
blindfolded him, led him out to an open place before the
prison, and cut his throat with the greatest composure.

Butchery of seventy Protestants.

He then calmy walked into the prison again, bloody as he
was, and with the knife in his hand selected another, and
despatched him in the same manner; and this, my lord,
he repeated till the whole number were put to death.   I
leave it to your lordship's feelings to judge of my sensations upon the occasion; my tears now wash the paper
upon which I give you the recital.   Another thing I must
mention, the patience with which they met death : they
seemed all resignation and piety, fervently praying to God
and cheerfully encountering their fate.   I cannot reflect
without shuddering, how the executioner held the bloody
knife between his teeth ; what a dreadful figure he appeared, all covered with blood, and with what unconcern he
executed his barbarous office !"

Persecutions in Piedmont.

Early in the seventeenth century, Pope Clement the
Eighth sent missionaries in the valleys of Piedmont, with
a view to induce the protestants to renounce their religion

These missionaries erected monasteries in several parts of the valleys, and soon became very troublesome to the reformed, to whom the monasteries appeared not only as fortresses to curb, but as sanctuaries for all such to fly to as had injured them in any degree.

The insolence and tyranny of these missionaries increasing, the protestants petitioned the duke of Savoy for protection. But instead of granting any redress, the duke published a decree, in which he declared that one witness should be sufficient in a court of law against a protestant ; and that any witness who convicted a protestant of any crime whatever, should be entitled to a hundred crowns as a reward.

In consequence of this, as may be imagined, many protestants fell martyrs to the perjury and avarice of the papists, who would swear any thing against them for the sake of the reward, and then fly to their own priests for absolution from their false oaths.

These missionaries endeavoured to get the books of the protestants into their power, in order to burn them ; and on the owners concealing them, wrote to the duke of Savoy, who, for the heinous crime of not surrendering their bibles, prayer-books, and religious treatises, sent a number of troops to be quartered on them, which occasioned the ruin of many families.

To encourage as much as possible the apostacy of the protestants, the duke published a proclamation, granting an exemption for five years from all taxes to every protestant who should become a catholic. He likewise established a court called the council for extirpating the heretics ; the object and nature of which are sufficiently evident from its name.

After this the duke published several edicts, prohibiting the protestants from acting as schoolmasters or tutors ; from teaching any art, science, or language ; from holding any places of profit, trust, or honour ; and, finally, commanding them to attend mass. This last was the signal for a persecution, which, of course, soon followed.

Before the persecution commenced, the missionaries employed kidnappers to steal away the children of the protestants, that they might privately be brought up Roman catholics ; but now they took away the children by open

17

force, and if the wretched parents resisted they were immediately murdered.

The duke of Savoy, in order to give force to the persecution, called a general assembly of the Roman catholic nobility and gentry, whence issued a solemn edict against the reformed, containing many heads, and including several reasons for extirpating them, among which the following were the principal : The preservation of the papal authority ; that the church livings might be all under one mode of government ; to make a union among all parties ; in honour of all the saints, and of the ceremonies of the church of Rome.

This was followed by a most cruel order, published on January 25, 1655, which decreed that every family of the reformed religion, of whatever rank, residing in Lucerne, St. Giovanni, Bibiana, Campiglione, St. Secondo, Lucernetta, La Torre, Fenile, or Bricherassio, should, within three days after the publication thereof, depart from their habitations to such places as were appointed by the duke, on pain of death and confiscation.

This order produced the greatest distress among the unhappy objects of it, as it was enforced with the greatest severity in the depth of a very severe winter, and the people were driven from their habitations at the time appointed, without even sufficient clothes to cover them ; by which many perished in the mountains through the severity of the weather or for want of food. Those who remained behind after the publication of the decree, were murdered by the popish inhabitants, or shot by the troops, and the most horrible barbarities were perpetrated by these ruffians, encouraged by the Roman catholic priests and monks, of which the following may serve as a specimen.

Martha Constantine, a beautiful young woman, was first ravished, and then killed by cutting off her breasts. These some of the soldiers fried, and set before their comrades, who eat them without knowing what they were. When they had done eating, the others told them what they had made a meal of, in consequence of which a quarrel ensued, and a battle took place. Several were killed in the fray, the greater part of whom were those concerned in the horrid massacre of the woman, and the inhuman deception on their comrades.

Peter Simonds, a protestant of about eighty years of age, was tied neck and heels, and then thrown down a precipice. In his fall the branch of a tree caught hold of the ropes and suspended him in the midway, so that he languished for several days, till he perished of hunger.

Esay Garcino, refusing to renounce his religion, the soldiers cut him into small pieces, saying in ridicule, they had minced him. A woman, named Armand, was torn limb from limb, and then the respective parts were hung upon a hedge.

Several men, women, and children were flung from the rocks and dashed to pieces. Among others, Magdalen Bertino, a protestant woman of La Torre, was stripped naked, her head tied between her legs, and she was then thrown down a precipice. Mary Raymondet, of the same town, had her flesh sliced from her bones till she expired; Magdalen Pilot, of Villaro, was cut to pieces in the cave of Castolus; Ann Charboniere had one end of a stake thrust up her body, and the other end being fixed in the ground, she was left in that manner to perish; and Jacob Perrin, the elder of the church of Villaro, with David, his brother, was flayed alive.

Giovanni Andrea Michialin, an inhabitant of La Torre with four of his children, was apprehended; three of them were hacked to pieces before him, the soldiers asking him, at the death of every child, if he would recant, which he constantly refused. One of the soldiers then took up the last and the youngest by the legs, and putting the same question to the father, he replied as before, when the inhuman brute dashed out the child's brains. The father, however, at the same moment started from them, and fled; the soldiers fired after him, but missed him; and he escaped to the Alps, and there remained concealed.

Giovanni Pelanchion, on refusing to abjure his faith, was tied by one leg to the tail of a mule, and dragged through the streets of Lucerne, amid the acclamations of an inhuman mob, who kept stoning him, and crying out, "He is possessed of the devil." They then took him to the river side, chopped off his head, and left that and his body unburied, upon the bank of the river.

A beautiful child, ten years of age, Magdalen Fontaine, was ravished and murdered by the soldiers. Another girl, of about the same age, they roasted alive at Villa Nova, and a poor woman hearing the soldiers were coming toward her house, snatched up the cradle in which her infant son was asleep, and fled toward the woods. The soldiers, however, saw and pursued her, when she lightened herself by putting down the cradle and child, which the soldiers no sooner came to, than they murdered the infant, and continuing the pursuit, found, the mother in a cave, where they first ravished, and then cut her to atoms.

Jacobo Michelino, chief elder of the church of Bobbio, and several other protestants, were hung up by hooks fixed in their flesh, and left so to expire. Giovanni Rostagnal, a venerable protestant, upward of fourscore years of age, had his nose and ears cut off, and the flesh cut from his body, till he bled to death.

Daniel Saleago and his wife, Giovanni Durant, Lodwich Durant, Bartholomew Durant, Daniel Revel, and Paul Reynard, had their mouths stuffed with gunpowder which being set fire to, their heads were blown to pieces.

Jacob Birone, a schoolmaster of Rorato, was stripped naked; and after having been so exposed, had the nails of his toes and fingers torn off with red-hot pincers, and holes bored through his hands with the point of a dagger. He next had a cord tied round his middle, and was led through the streets with a soldier on each side of him. At every turning the soldier on his ride-hand side cut a gash in his flesh, and the soldier on his left-hand side struck him with a bludgeon, both saying, at the same instant, "Will you go to mass? Will you go to mass?" He still replied in the negative, and being at length taken to the bridge, they cut off his head on the ballustrades, and threw both that and his body into the river.

Paul Garnier, a protestant beloved for his piety, had his eyes put out, was then flayed alive, and being divided into four parts, his quarters were placed on four of the principal houses of Lucerne. He bore all his sufferings with the most exemplary patience, praised God as long as he could speak, and plainly evinced the courage arising from a confidence in God.

Daniel Cardon, of Rocappiata, being apprehended by some soldiers, they cut off his head. Two poor old blind women, of St. Giovanni, were burnt alive; and a widow of La Toïre, with her daughter, was driven into the river, and stoned to death there.

A man named Paul Giles attempting to run away from some soldiers, was shot in the neck : they then slit his nose, sliced his chin, stabbed him, and gave his carcass to the dogs.

Some of the Irish troops having taken eleven men of Garcigliana prisoners, they heated a furnace red hot, and forced them to push each other in till they came to the last man, whom they themselves pushed in.

Michael Gonet, a man about ninety years old, was burnt to death ; Baptista Oudri, another old man, was stabbed ; and Bartholemew Frasche had his heels pierced through which ropes being put, he was dragged by them to the goal, where in consequence of his wounds mortifying, he soon died.

Magdalena de la Peire being pursued by some of the soldiers, and taken, was cast down a precipice, and dashed to pieces. Margaret Revella and Mary Pravillerin, two very old women, were burnt alive ; Michael Bellino, with Ann Bochardno, were beheaded ; Joseph Chairet, and Paul Carniero, were flayed alive.

Daniel Maria, and all his family, being ill of a fever, several papist ruffians broke into his house, telling him they were practical physicians, and would give them all present ease ; which they did, by murdering the whole family.

Lucy the wife of Peter Besson, being in an advanced state of pregnancy, determined, if possible, to escape from such dreadful scenes as everywhere surrounded her ; she accordingly took two young children, one in each hand, and set off toward the Alps. But on the third day of the journey she was taken in labour among the mountains, and delivered of an infant, who perished through the inclemency of the weather, as did the other two children ; for all three were found dead by her side, and herself just expiring, by the person to whom she related the above circumstances.

Cipriana Bustia being asked if he would renounce his religion, and turn Roman catholic, replied, " I would rather renounce life, or turn dog ;" to which a priest answered, " For that expression you shall both renounce life, and be given to the dogs." They accordingly drag-

17*

ged him to prison, where they confined him till he perished of hunger, after which they threw his corpse into the street before the prison, and it was devoured by dogs.

Joseph Pont was severed in two; Margaret Soretta was stoned to death; and Antonio Bertiua had his head cleft asunder.

Martyrdom of Francis Gross.

Francis Gross had his flesh slowly cut from his body into small pieces, and put into a dish before him; two of his children were minced before his sight, while his wife was fastened to a post, to behold these cruelties practised on her husband and offspring. The tormenters, at length, tired of exercising their cruelties, decapitated both husband and wife.

The Sieur Thomas Margher fled to a cave, where being discovered, the soldiers shut up the mouth, and he perished with famine. Judith Revelin, with seven children, were barbarously murdered in their beds.

Jacob Roseno was commanded to pray to the saints, which he refusing the soldiers beat him violently with bludgeons to make him comply, but he continuing steady to his faith, they fired at him. While in the agonies of death they cried to him, "Will you pray to the saints?" to which he answered "No!" when one of the soldiers, with a broad sword, clove his head asunder, and put an end to his sufferings.

A young woman named Susanna Ciacquin, being attempted to be ravished by a soldier, made a stout resistance, and in the struggle pushed him over a precipice, when he was dashed to pieces by the fall. His comrades immediately fell upon her with their swords and cut her to atoms.

Giovanni Pullius being apprehended as a protestant by the soldiers, was ordered by the marquis of Pianessa to be executed in a place near the convent. When brought to the gallows several monks attended to persuade him to renounce his religion. But finding him inflexible, they commanded the executioner to perform his office, which he did, and so launched the martyr into the world of glory.

Paul Clement, an elder of the church of Rossana, being apprehended by the monks of a neighbouring monastery, was carried to the market-place of that town, where some protestants had just been executed. On beholding the dead bodies, he said calmly, "You may kill the body, but you cannot prejudice the soul of a true believer : with respect to the dreadful spectacles which you have here shown me, you may rest assured, that God's vengeance will overtake the murderers of those poor people, and punish them for the innocent blood they have spilt." The monks were so exasperated at this reply, that they ordered him to be hung directly : and while he was hanging the soldiers amused themselves by shooting at the body.

Daniel Rambaut, of Villaro, the father of a numerous family, was seized, and with several others, committed to the goal of Paysana. Here he was visited by several priests, who, with continual importunities, strove to persuade him to turn papist, but this he peremptorily refused, and the priests finding his resolution, and enraged at his answers, determined to put him to the most horrible tortures, in the hope of overcoming his faith ; they therefore ordered one joint of his fingers to be cut off every day, till all the fingers were gone; they then proceeded in the same manner with his toes ; afterward they alternately cut off, daily, a hand and a foot ; but finding that he bore his sufferings with the most unconquerable fortitude, and maintained his faith with steadfast resolution, they stabbed him to the heart, and then gave his body to be devoured by dogs.

Peter Gabriolo, a protestant gentleman of considerable eminence, being seized by a troop of soldiers, and refusing to renounce his religion, they hung several bags of gunpowder about his body, and then setting fire to them, blew him up.

Anthony, the son of Samuel Catieris, a poor dumb lad and extremely inoffensive, was cut to pieces by a party of the troops; and soon after the same ruffians entered the house of Peter Moniriat, and cut off the legs of the whole family, leaving them to bleed to death, they being unable to assist each other in that melancholy plight.

Daniel Benech being apprehended, had his nose slit, and his ears cut off; after which he was divided into quarters, and each quarter hung upon a tree. Mary Monino had her jaw-bones broken, and was then left to languish till she was starved to death.

Mary Pelanchion, a widow, of the town of Villaro, was seized by a party of the Irish brigades, who having beat her cruelly, and ravished her, dragged her to a high bridge which crossed the river, and stripping her naked, hung her by the legs to the bridge, with her head downward toward the water, and then going into boats, they shot her.

Mary Nigrino, and her daughter, a poor idiot, were cut to pieces in the woods, and their bodies left to be devoured by wild beasts: Susanna Bales, a widow of Villaro, was immured and starved to death; and Susanna Calvio, running away from some soldiers, and hiding herself in a barn, they set fire to the straw, by which she was burnt to death.

Daniel Bertino, a child, was burnt; Paul Armand was hacked to pieces; Daniel Michialino having his tongue plucked out, was left to perish in that condition; and Andreo Bertino, a lame and very old man, was mangled in a most shocking manner, and at length had his belly ripped open, and his bowels carried about on the point of a halberd.

A protestant lady named Constantia Bellone was apprehended on account of her faith, and asked by a priest if she would renounce the devil and go to mass? to which she replied, "I was brought up in a religion by which I was always taught to renounce the devil; but should I comply with your desire, and go to mass, I should be sure to meet him there in a variety of shapes." The priest was highly incensed at this, and told her to recant or she should suffer cruelly. She, however, boldly answered, ' That she valued not any sufferings he could inflict, and in spite of all the torments he could invent, she would keep her faith inviolate." The priest then ordered slices of her flesh to be cut off from various parts of her body. This she bore with the most singular patience, only saying to the priest, " What horrid and lasting torments will you suffer in hell, for the trifling and temporary pains which I now endure !" Exasperated at this expression, the priest ordered a file of musketeers to draw up and fire upon her, by which she was soon despatched.

Judith Mandon was fastened to a stake, and sticks thrown at her from a distance. By this inhuman treatment her limbs were beat and mangled in a most terrible manner. At last one of the bludgeons striking her head, she was at once freed from her pains and her life.

Paul Genre and David Paglia, each with his son, attempting to escape to the Alps, were pursued and overtaken by the soldiers in a large plain. Here they hunted them for their diversion, goading them with their swords, and making them run about till they dropped down with fatigue. When they found that their spirits were quite exhausted, the soldiers hacked them to pieces, and left their mangled bodies on the spot.

Michael Greve, a young man of Bobbio, was apprehended in the town of La Torre, and being led to the bridge, was thrown over into the river. Being an expert swimmer, he swam down the stream, thinking to escape, but the soldiers and mob followed on both sides, and kept stoning him, till receiving a blow on one of his temples, he sunk and was drowned.

David Armand was forced to lay his head down on a block, when a soldier with a large hammer beat out his brains. David Baridona was apprehended at Villaro, and carried to La Torre, where, refusing to renounce his religion, he was tormented by brimstone matches being tied between his fingers and toes, and set fire to, and afterward, by having his flesh plucked off with red hot pincers, till he expired. Giovanni Barolina, with his wife, were thrown into a pool of stagnant water, and compelled, by means of pitch-forks and stones, to duck down their heads till they were suffocated with the stench.

A number of soldiers assaulted the house of Joseph Garniero, and before they entered, fired in at the window, and shot Mrs. Garniero, who was at that instant suckling her child. She begged them to spare the life of the infant, which they promised to do, and send it immediately to a Roman catholic nurse. They then seized the husband and hanged him at his own door, and having shot the wife through the head, left her body weltering in its blood.

Isaiah Mondon, an aged and pious protestant, fled from the merciless persecutors to a cleft in a rock, where he suffered the most dreadful hardships; for, in the midst of the winter he was forced to lie on the bare stone, without any covering; his food was the roots he could scratch up near his miserable habitation, and the only way by which he could procure drink, was to put snow in his mouth till it melted. Here, however, some of the soldiers found him, and after beating him unmercifully, they drove him toward Lucerne, goading him all the way with the points of their swords. Being exceedingly weakened by his manner of living, and exhausted by the blows he had received, he fell down in the road. They again beat him to make him proceed, till on his knees he implored them to put him out of his misery. This they at last agreed to do; and one of them shot him through the head, saying, "There, heretic, take thy request."

To screen themselves from danger, a number of men, women, and children fled to a large cave, where they continued for some weeks in safety, two of the men going by stealth to procure provisions. These were, however, one day watched, by which the cave was discovered, and soon after a troop of Roman catholics appeared before it. Many of these were neighbours and intimate acquaintance, and some even relations to those in the cave. The protestants, therefore, came out and implored them by the ties of hospitality and of blood, not to murder them. But the bigoted wretches told them they could not show any mercy to heretics, and, therefore, bade them all prepare to die. Hearing this, and knowing the obduracy of their enemies, the protestants fell on their knees, lifted their hearts to heaven, and patiently awaited their fate; which the papists soon decided by cutting them to pieces.

Heroic Defence of the Protestants of Roras.

The blood of the faithful being almost exhausted in all the towns and villages of Piedmont, there remained but one place that had been exempted from the general slaughter. This was the little commonalty of Roras, which stood upon an eminence. Of this one of the duke of Savoy's officers determined, if possible, to make himself master; with that view he detached three hundred men to surprise it.

The inhabitants, however, had intelligence of the approach of these troops, and captain Joshua Gianavel, a brave protestant officer, put himself at the head of a small body of the citizens, and waited in ambuscade to attack the enemy in a narrow passage, the only place by which the town could be approached.

As soon as the troops appeared, and had entered the passage, the protestants commenced a well-directed fire against them, and kept themselves concealed behind bushes. A great number of the soldiers were killed, and the rest receiving a continual fire, and not seeing any to whom they might return it, made a precipitate retreat.

The members of this little community immediately sent a memorial to the marquis of Piannessa, a general officer of the duke, stating, "That they were sorry to be under the necessity of taking up arms; but that the secret approach of a body of troops, without any previous notice sent of the purpose of their coming, had greatly alarmed them; that as it was their custom never to suffer any of the military to enter their little community, they had repelled force by force, and should do so again; but in all other respects they professed themselves dutiful, obedient, and loyal subjects to their sovereign the duke of Savoy."

The marquis, in order to delude and surprise them, answered, "That he was perfectly satisfied with their behaviour, for they had done right, and even rendered a service to their country, as the men who had attempted to pass the defile were not his troops, but a band of desperate robbers, who had for some time infested those parts, and been a terror to the neighbouring country." To give a greater colour to his treachery, he published a proclamation to the same purpose, expressive of thanks to the citizens of Roras.

The very day after, however, he sent five hundred men to take possession of the town, while the people, as he thought, were lulled into security by his artifice.

Captain Gianavel, however, was not thus to be deceived; he, therefore, laid a second ambuscade for these troops, and compelled them to retire with great loss.

Foiled in these two attempts, the sanguinary marquis determined on a third, still more formidable; but, with his usual duplicity, he published another proclamation, disowning any knowledge of the second attempt.

He soon after sent seven hundred chosen men upon the expedition, who, in spite of the fire from the protestants, forced the defile, entered Roras, and began to murder every person they met with, without distinction of sex or age. Captain Gianaval, at the head of his friends, though he had lost the defile, determined to dispute the passage through a fortified pass that led to the richest and best part of the town. Here he succeeded, by keeping up a continual fire, which did great execution, his men being all good marksmen. The Roman catholic commander was astonished and dismayed at this opposition, as he imagined that he had surmounted all difficulties. He, however, strove to force the pass, but being able to bring up only twelve men in front at a time, and the protestants being secured by a breastwork, he saw all his hopes frustrated.

Enraged at the loss of so many of his troops, and fearful of disgrace if he persisted in attempting what appeared so impracticable, he thought it wiser to retreat. Unwilling, however, to withdraw his men by the defile at which he had entered, on account of the danger, he designed to retreat toward Villaro, by another pass called Piampra, which, though hard of access, was easy of descent. Here, however, he again felt the determined bravery of captain Gianavel, who having posted his little band here greatly annoyed the troops as they passed, and even pursued their rear till they entered the open country.

The marquis of Pianessa, finding all his attempts baffled, and all his artifices discovered, resolved to throw off the mask; and therefore proclaimed that ample rewards should be given to any who would bear arms against the obdurate heretics of Roras, and that any officer who would exterminate them, should be honoured accordingly.

Captain Mario, a bigoted Roman catholic and a desperate ruffian, stimulated by this, resolved to undertake the enterprise. He, therefore, levied a regiment of one thousand men, and with these he resolved to attempt gaining the summit of a rock which commanded the town. But the protestants, aware of his design, suffered his troops to proceed without molestation till they had nearly reached the summit of the rock, when they made a furious attack upon them; one party keeping up a well-directed and constant fire, and others rolling down large stones. Thus were they suddenly stopped in their career. Many were killed by the musketry, and more by the stones, which beat them down the precipices. Several fell sacrifices to their own fears, for by attempting a precipitate retreat, they fell down and were dashed to pieces; and captain Mario himself, having fallen from a craggy place into a river at the foot of the rock, was taken up senseless, and after lingering some time expired.

After this, another body of troops from the camp at Villaro made an attempt upon Roras, but were likewise defeated and compelled to retreat to their camp.

Captain Gianavel, for each of these signal victories, made a suitable discourse to his men, kneeling down with them to return thanks to the Almighty for his providential protection; and concluding with the 11th psalm.

The marquis of Pianessa, now enraged to the highest degree at being thus foiled by a handful of peasants, determined on their expulsion or destruction.

To this end he ordered all the Roman catholic militia of Piedmont to be called out and disciplined. To these he joined eight thousand regular troops, and dividing the whole into three distinct bodies, he planned three formidable attacks to be made at once, unless the people of Roras, to whom he sent an account of his great preparations, would comply with the following conditions:

To ask pardon for taking up arms. To pay the expenses of all the expeditions sent against them. To acknowledge the infallibility of the pope. To go to mass. To pray to

18

the saints. To deliver up their ministers and schoolmasters. To go to confession. To pay loans for the delivery of souls from purgatory; and to give up Captain Gianavel and the elders of the church at discretion.

The brave inhabitants, indignant at these proposals, answered, " That sooner than comply with them they would suffer their estates to be seized, their houses to be burnt ; and themselves to be murdered."

Enraged at this, the marquis sent them the following laconic letter :

" *To the obstinate Heretics of Roras.*

" You shall have your request, for the troops sent against you have strict injunctions to plunder, burn and kill. " PIANESSA."

The three armies were accordingly put in motion, and the first attack ordered to be made by the rocks of Villaro ; the second by the pass of Bagnol ; and the third by the defile of Lucerne.

As might be expected, from the superiority of numbers, the troops gained the rocks, pass, and defile, entered the town, and commenced the most horrid depredations. Men they hanged, burnt, racked to death, or cut to pieces ; women they ripped open, crucified, drowned, or threw from the precipices; and children they tossed upon spears, minced, cut their throats, or dashed out their brains. On the first day of their gaining the town, one hundred and twenty-six suffered in this manner.

Agreeably to the orders of the marquis, they likewise plundered the estates, and burnt the houses of the people. Several protestants, however, made their escape, under the conduct of the brave Gianavel, whose wife and children were unfortunately made prisoners, and sent to Turin under a strong guard.

The marquis, thinking to conquer at least the mind of Gianavel, wrote him a letter, and released a protestant prisoner that he might carry it to him. The contents were, that if the captain would embrace the Roman catholic religion, he should be indemnified for all his losses since the commencement of the war, his wife and children should be immediately released, and himself honourably promoted in the duke of Savoy's army; but if he refused to accede to the proposals made to him, his wife and children should be put to death; and so large a reward should be given to take him, dead or alive, that even some of his own confidential friends should, from the greatness of the sum, be tempted to betray him.

To this Gianavel returned the following answer:

" MY LORD MARQUIS.

" There is no torment so great, or death so cruel, that I would not prefer to the abjuration of my religion; so that promises lose their effects, and menaces do but strengthen me in my faith.

" With respect to my wife and children, my lord, nothing can be more afflicting to me than the thoughts of their confinement, or more dreadful to my imagination, than their sufferings and violent death. I keenly feel all the tender sensations of a husband and a parent; I would suffer any torment to rescue them; I would die to preserve them.

" But having said thus much, my lord, I assure you that the purchase of their lives must not be the price of my salvation. You have them in your power it is true; but my consolation is, that your power is only a temporary authority over their bodies: you may destroy the mortal part, but their immortal souls are out of your reach and will live hereafter to bear testimony against you for your cruelties. I therefore recommend them and myself to God, and pray for a reformation in your heart.

" JOSHUA GIANAVEL."

He then with his followers retired to the Alps, where, being afterward joined by several protestant officers, with a considerable number of fugitive protestants, they conjointly defended themselves, and made several successful attacks upon the Roman Catholic towns and forces; carrying terror by the valour of their exploits and the boldness of their enterprises.

Nevertheless, the disproportion between their forces and those of their enemies was so great, that no reasonable expectations could be entertained of their ultimate success;

which induced many protestant princes and states, in various parts of Europe, to interest themselves in favour of these courageous sufferers for religious and civil liberty.

Among these intercessors, the protestant cantons of Switzerland early distinguished themselves; and as their mediation was rejected by the duke of Savoy, they raised considerable sums of money, by private subscriptions, for the relief of the fugitives and the assistance of the brave defenders of their native valleys. Nor did they limit their kindness to pecuniary relief; they despatched a messenger to the United Provinces, for the purpose of procuring subscriptions, and the interference of the Dutch government in favour of the Piedmontese, both of which they at length obtained. They then made another attempt to prevail on the duke of Savoy to grant his protestant subjects liberty of conscience, and to restore them to their ancient privileges; but this, after much evasion on the part of the duke, also failed.

But that God whom they worshipped in purity of spirit, now raised them up a more powerful champion in the person of Oliver Cromwell, Lord Protector of England. This extraordinary man, however criminal in the means by which he obtained power, certainly deserves the praise of having exercised it with dignity and firmness; and if his usurpation be censured, it must be acknowledged that he raised England to a station among the neighbouring powers to which it had never before attained. From the throne which he had just seized, he dictated to the most potent monarchs of Europe; and never was his influence more justly exercised than in behalf of the persecuted protestants of Piedmont. He caused subscriptions to be set on foot throughout England in their favour; he sent an envoy to the court of France, and wrote to all the protestant powers of Europe, to interest them in the same good cause. He despatched an ambassador to the court of Turin, who was received with great respect by the duke, who pretended to justify his treatment of the Piedmontese, under the pretence of their being rebellious.

But Cromwell would not suffer himself to be trifled with: his ambassador gave the duke to understand that if negociation failed, arms would be had recourse to: and as the kings of Denmark and Sweden, the Dutch government and many of the German states, encouraged by the example of the Protector, now came forward in the same cause, the duke found himself under the necessity of dismissing the English ambassador, with a very respectful message to his master, assuring him that "the persecutions had been much misrepresented and exaggerated: and that they had been occasioned by his rebellious subjects themselves: nevertheless, to show his great respect for his highness he would pardon them, and restore them to their former privileges."

This was accordingly done; and the protestants returned to their homes, grateful for the kindness that had been shown to them, and praising the name of the Lord who is as a tower of strength to those who put their trust in him.

During the lifetime of Cromwell, they lived in peace and security; but no sooner had his death relieved the papists from the terror of his vengeance, than they began anew to exercise that cruel and bigoted spirit which is inherent in popery: and although the persecutions were not avowedly countenanced by the court, they were connived at and unpunished: insomuch that whatever injury had been inflicted on a protestant, he could obtain no redress from the corrupted judges to whom he applied for that protection which the laws nominally granted to him.

At length in the year 1686, all the treaties in favour of the protestants were openly violated, by the publication of an edict prohibiting the exercise of any religion but the Roman catholic, on pain of death.

The protestants petitioned for a repeal of this cruel edict; and their petitions were backed by their ancient friends the protestant cantons of Switzerland. But the cries of his subjects, and the intercession of their allies, were equally unavailing; the duke replied that "his engagements with France obliged him to extirpate the *heretics* from Piedmont."

Finding supplications useless, the protestants flew to arms; and being attacked by the duke's army and some French troops, on the 22d of April, 1686, they, after an obstinate engagement of several hours, obtained a complete victory, killing great numbers of the French and Savoyards.

Exasperated by this defeat, the duke immediately col-

18*

lected a large army, which he augmented with a reinforce
ment of French and Swiss troops; and was so successfu
in several engagements against the protestants, that the
latter, despairing of success, consented to lay down their
arms and quit the country, on his solemn promise of safety
themselves, their families, and property.

No sooner were they disarmed, than the treacherous
papists, acting upon their maxim that no faith is to be kept
with heretics, massacred a large body of them, in cold
blood, without distinction of age or sex: and burnt and
ravaged the country in every direction.

The horrors perpetrated by these faithless and bigoted
monsters almost exceed belief. We will not weary and
disgust our readers with the recital: suffice it to say, that
every variety of rapine, lust, and cruelty, was exhausted
by these demons in human shape. Those protestants who
were fortunate enough to escape, found an asylum in the
Swiss cantons and in Germany, where they were treated
kindly and lands granted to them for their residence.

The natural consequence of these horrible proceedings
was, that the fruitful valleys of Piedmont were depopulated
and desolate, and the barbarous monster who had caused
this devastation, now feeling its ill effects, tried, by all
means in his power, to draw Roman Catholic families from
all parts of Europe, to repeople the valleys, and to culti-
vate the fields which had been blasted by the malignant
breath of bigotry.

Some of the exiles, in the meanwhile, animated by that
love of country which glows with peculiar warmth in their
breasts, determined to make an attempt to regain a part
of their native valleys, or to perish in the attempt. Accordingly, nine hundred of them, who had resided during
their exile near the lake of Geneva, crossing it in the
night, entered Savoy without resistance, and seizing two
villages obtained provisions, for which they paid, and immediately passed the river Arve, before the duke had notice
of their arrival in the country.

When he became acquainted with this, he was astonished at the boldness of the enterprise, and despatched
troops to guard the defiles and passes; which, however,
were all forced by the protestants, and great numbers of
the Savoyard troops defeated.

Alarmed by this intelligence and still more by a report that a great body of the exiles was advancing from Branden- burg to support those already in Savoy, and that many protestant states meant to assist them in their attempts to regain a footing in their native country, the duke published an edict by which he restored them to all their former privileges.

This just and humane conduct was, however, so displeasing to that bigoted and ferocious tyrant, Louis XIV. of France, that he sent an order to the duke of Savoy to extirpate every protestant in his dominions; and to assist him in the execution of this horrible project, or to punish him if he were unwilling to engage in it, M. Catinet was despatched at the head of an army of 16,000 men. This insolent dictation irritated the duke; he determined no longer to be the slave of the French king, and solicited the aid of the emperor of Germany and the king of Spain, who sent large bodies of troops to his assistance. Being also joined, at his own request, by the protestant army, he hesitated no longer to declare war against France; and in the campaign which followed, his protestant subjects were of infinite service by their valour and resolution. The French troops were at length driven from Piedmont, and the heroic protestants were reinstated in their former possessions, their ancient privileges confirmed, and many new ones granted to them. The exiles now returned from Germany and Switzerland; and were accompanied by many French refugees, whom the cruel persecutions of Louis had driven from their native land in search of the toleration denied to them at home. But this infuriated bigot, not yet glutted with revenge, insisted on their being expelled from Piedmont; and the duke of Savoy, anxious for peace, was compelled to comply with this merciless demand, before the French king would sign the treaty. The wanderers, thus driven from the south of Europe, sought and found an asylum from the hospitality of the elector of Brandenburg, and consoled themselves for the loss of a genial climate and a delightful country, in the enjoyment of the more substantial blessings of liberty of conscience and security of property.

PART V.

Causes which led to the Reformation.

CHAPTER I.

Usurpation of the Popes during the Middle Ages.

IN the preceding pages we have had occasion to treat of
the rise and progress of popery, from the commencement
of its usurpations to the tenth century.   From this period,
till the reformation was attempted by Wickliffe, the abominations of these arch and unchristian heretics increased
with rapid strides, till at length all the sovereigns of Europe were compelled to do them the most servile homage.
It was in the reign of Edgar, king of England, that monks
were first made spiritual ministers, though contrary to the
decrees and custom of the church ; and in the time of this
sovereign they were allowed to marry, there being no law
forbidding it, before the papacy of Gregory VII.
  To relate the tyrannical innovations upon the religion
of Christ during the space of more than three hundred
years, would be the province of a writer on church history,
and is quite incompatible with our limits. Suffice it to say,
that scarcely a foreign war or civil broil convulsed Europe
during that period, which did not originate in the infernal
artifices of popes, monks, and friars. They frequently fell
victims to their own machinations ; for, from the year 1004,
many popes died violent deaths : several were poisoned :
Sylvester was cut to pieces by his own people ; and the
reigns of his successors were but short.   Benedict, who
succeeded John XXI., thought proper to resist the emperor Henry III., and place in his room Peter, king of Hungary ; but afterward being alarmed by the success of
Henry, he *sold* his seat to Gratianus, called Gregory VI.
At this time there were three popes in Rome, all striving
against each other for the supreme power, viz. : Benedict
IX., Sylvester III., and Gregory VI.   But the emperor
Henry, coming to Rome, displaced these three monsters at

once, and appointed Clement the Second: enacting that henceforth no bishop of Rome should be chosen but by the consent of the emperor. Though this law was necessary for public tranquillity, yet it interfered too much with the ambitious views of the cardinals, who accordingly exerted themselves to get it repealed; and failing in this, on the departure of the emperor for Germany, they poisoned Clement, and at once violated the law by choosing another pope, without the imperial sanction.

This was Damascus II., who being also poisoned, within a few days from his appointment, much contention took place. Whereupon the Romans sent to the emperor, desiring him to give them a bishop; upon which he selected Bruno, a German, called Leo IX. This pope was also poisoned in the first year of his popedom.

After his death Theophylactus made an effort to be pope, but Hildebrand, to defeat him, went to the emperor, and persuaded him to assign another bishop, a German, who ascended the papal chair under the title of Victor II.

The second year of his papacy, this pope also followed his predecessors, like them being poisoned.

On the death of Victor, the cardinals elected Stephen IX. for pope, contrary to their oath, and the emperor's assignment. From this period, indeed, their ascendency was so great that the most powerful sovereigns of Europe were obliged to do them homage; and Nicholas, who succeeded Stephen, established the council of the Lateran.

In this council first was promulgated the terrible sentence of excommunication against all such as " do creep into the seat of Peter by money or favour, without the full consent of the cardinals;" cursing them and their children with the anger of Almighty God; and giving authority and power to cardinals, with the clergy and laity, to depose all such persons, and call a council general, wheresoever they will against them.

Pope Nicholas only reigned three years and a half, and then, like his predecessors, was poisoned.

Submission of the Emperor Henry IV. to the Pope

To such a height had papal insolence now attained, that, on the emperor Henry IV. refusing to submit to some decrees of pope Gregory VII., the latter excommunicated him, and absolved all his subjects from their oath of allegiance to him; on this he was deserted by the nobility, and dreading the consequences, though a brave man, he found it necessary to make his submission. He accordingly repaired to the city of Canusium, where the pope then was, and went barefooted with his wife and child to the gate; where he remained from morning to night fasting, humbly desiring absolution, and craving to be let in. But no ingress being given him, he continued thus three days together; at length answer came, that his holiness had yet no leisure to talk with him. The emperor patiently waited without the walls, though in the depth of winter. At length his request was granted, through the entreaties of Matilda, the pope's paramour. On the fourth day, being let in, for a token of his true repentance, he yielded to the pope's hands his crown, and confessed himself unworthy of the empire, if he ever again offended against the pope, desiring for that time to be absolved and forgiven. **The pope answered, he would neither forgive him, nor release the bond of his excommunication, but upon condition that he would**

abide by his arbitrement in the council, and undergo such penance as he should enjoin him; that he should answer to all objections and accusations laid against him, and that he should never seek revenge; that it should be at the pope's pleasure whether his kingdom should be restored or not. Finally, that before the trial of his cause, he should neither use his kingly ornaments, nor usurp the authority to govern, nor to exact any oath of allegiance from his subjects, &c. These things being promised to the pope by an oath, the emperor was released upon from excommunication.

King John surrenders his Crown to the Pope.

The ascendency of the popes was never more fully evinced than by a remarkable fact in the history of England. King John having incurred the hatred of his barons and people by his cruel and tyrannical measures, they took arms against him, and offered the crown to Louis, son of the French king. By seizing the possessions of the clergy, John had also fallen under the displeasure of the pope, who accordingly laid the kingdom under an interdict, and absolved his subjects from their allegiance. Alarmed at this the tyrant earnestly sued for peace with his holiness, hoping by his mediation to obtain favourable terms from the barons, or by his thunders to terrify them into submission. He made the most abject supplications, and the pope, ever willing to increase the power of the church, sent cardinal Pandulf as legate to the king at Canterbury, to whom John resigned his crown and dominions; and the cardinal, after retaining the crown five days in token of possession, returned it to the king on condition of his making a yearly payment of one thousand marks to the court of Rome, and holding the dominions of England and Ireland *in farm* from the pope.

But if John expected any benefit from this most disgraceful transaction, he was disappointed; and instead of enjoying the crown which he had so basely surrendered and received again, the short remainder of his life was disturbed **by continual insurrections, and he at last either died of grief, or by poison administered to him by a monk of the convent of Swinezhead in Lincolnshire. The latter cause** assigned by many historians, and we are told that the king, suspecting some fruit, which was presented to him at the above convent to be poisoned, ordered the monk who brought it to eat of it, which he did, and died in a few hours after.

An Emperor trodden under foot by the Pope.

The papal usurpations were extended to every part of Europe. In Germany, the emperor Frederic was compelled to submit to be trodden under the feet of Pope Alexander, and dared not make any resistance. In England, however, a spirit of resentment broke out in various reigns, in consequence of the oppressions and horrible conduct of those anti-christian blasphemers, which continued with more or less violence till the time of the great Wickliffe, of whom we shall speak more fully in the following pages.

Account of Wickliffe, and of the Martyrs who suffered in defence of his Doctrines.

The first attempts made in England toward the reformation of the church, took place in the reign of Edward III., about A. D. 1350, when John Wickliffe appeared. This early star of the English church was public reader of divinity in the university of Oxford, and by the learned of his day, was accounted deeply versed in theology, and all kinds of philosophy. This even his adversaries allowed, as Walden, his bitterest enemy, writing to pope Martin, says, that he was wonderfully astonished at his strong arguments, with the places of authority which he had gathered, with the vehemence and force of his reasons, &c. At the time of his appearance the greatest darkness pervaded the church. Scarcely any thing but the name of Christ remained; his true doctrine being as far unknown to the most part, as his name was common to all. As to faith, consolation, the end and use of the law, the office of Christ, our impotency and weakness, the greatness and strength of sin, of true works, grace, and free justification by faith, wherein Christianity consists, they were either unknown or disregarded. Scripture learning and divinity were known but to a few, and that in the schools only where they were turned and converted into sophistry. Instead of Peter and Paul, men occupied their time in studying Aquinas and Scotus; and, forsaking the lively power of God's spiritual word and doctrine, were altogether led and blinded with outward ceremonies and human traditions, insomuch that scarcely any other thing was seen in the churches, taught or spoken of in sermons, or intended or sought after in their whole lives, but the heaping up of ceremonies upon ceremonies; and the people were taught to worship no other thing but that which they saw, and almost all they saw they worshipped. But Wickliffe was inspired with a purer sense of religion; and knowing it to be his duty to impart the gracious blessing to others, he published his belief with regard to the several articles of religion in which he differed from the common doctrine. Pope Gregory XI., hearing this, condemned some of his tenets, and commanded the archbishop of Canterbury and the bishop of London to oblige him to subscribe the condemnation of them; and in case of refusal, to summon him to Rome. This commission could not easily be executed, Wickliffe having powerful friends, the chief of whom was John of Gaunt, duke of Lancaster, son of Edward III. The archbishop holding a synod at St. Paul's, Wickliffe appeared, accompanied by the duke of Lancaster and lord Percy, marshal of England, when a dispute arising whether Wickliffe should answer sitting or standing, the duke of Lancaster proceeded to threats, and treated the bishop with very little ceremony. The people present thinking the bishop in danger, sided with him, so that the duke and the earl marshal thought it prudent to retire, and to take Wickliffe with them. After this an insurrection ensued, the clergy and their emissaries spreading a report that the duke of Lancaster had persuaded the king to take away the privileges of the city of London, &c., which fired the people to such a degree that they broke open the Marshalsea, and freed all the prisoners; and not contented with this, a vast number of them went to the duke's palace in the Savoy, when missing his person, they plundered his house. For this outrage the duke of Lancaster caused the lord mayor and aldermen to be removed from their offices, imagining that they had not used their authority to quell the mutineers. After this the bishops met-

19

ing a second time, Wickliffe explained to them his sentiments with regard to the sacrament of the eucharist, in opposition to the belief of the papists; for which the bishops only enjoined him silence, not daring at that time to proceed to greater extremities against him.

Wickliffe Translates the Bible.

Wickliffe paying less regard to the injunctions of the bishops than to his duty to God, continued to promulgate his doctrines, and gradually to unveil the truth to the eyes of men.   He wrote several books, which, as may be supposed, gave great alarm and offence to the clergy.   But God raising him up a protector in the duke of Lancaster, he was secure from their malice.   He translated the Bible into English, which amid the ignorance of the times, may be compared to the sun breaking forth in a dark night. To this Bible he prefixed a bold preface, wherein he reflected on the immoralities of the clergy, and condemned the worship of saints, images, and the corporal presence of Christ in the sacrament: but what gave the greatest offence to the priests, was, his exhorting all people to read the scriptures, in which the testimonies against all those corruptions appeared so strongly.

About the same time the common people, goaded to desperation by the oppressions of the nobility and clergy, rose in arms and committed great devastation; and, among other persons of distinction, they put to death Simon of Sudbury, archbishop of Canterbury.   He was succeeded by William Courtney, who was no less diligent than his predecessor had been in attempting to root out *heretics.* Notwithstanding all opposition, however, Wickliffe's sect increased, and daily grew to greater force, until the time that William Barton, vice-chancellor of Oxford, who had the whole rule of that university, assisted by some monastic doctors, issued an edict, prohibiting all persons under a heavy penalty, from associating themselves with any of Wickliffe's favourers; and threatening Wickliffe himself with excommunication and imprisonment, unless he, after three days canonical admonition or warning, did repent and amend.   Upon this Wickliffe wished to appeal to the king, but the duke of Lancaster forbade him; whereupon he was forced again to make confession of his doctrine; in which confession, by explaining his assertions, he mitigated the rigour of his enemies.

Still his followers greatly multiplied. Many of them, indeed, were not men of learning; but being wrought upon by the conviction of plain reason, they were the more steadfast in their persuasion. In a short time his doctrine made a great progress, being not only espoused by vast numbers of the students of Oxford, but also by many of the nobility, particularly by the duke of Lancaster and lord Percy, earl marshal, as before mentioned.

Wickliffe may thus be considered as the great founder of the reformation in England. He was of Merton college in Oxford, where he took his doctor's degree, and became so eminent for his fine genius and great learning, that Simon Islip, archbishop of Canterbury, having founded Canterbury college, now Christ church, in Oxford, appointed him rector; which employment he filled with universal approbation, till the death of the archbishop. Langholm, successor to Islip, being desirous of favouring the monks, and introducing them into the college, attempted to remove Wickliffe, and put Woodhall, a monk, in his place. But the fellows of the college being attached to Wickliffe, would not consent to this. Nevertheless, the affair being carried to Rome Wickliffe was deprived in favour of Woodhall. This did not at all lessen the reputation of the former, every one perceiving it was a general affair, and that the monks did not so much strike at Wickliffe's person, as at all the secular priests who were members of the college. And, indeed, they were all turned out to make room for the monks. Shortly after Wickliffe was presented to the living of Lutterworth, in the county of Leicester, where he remained unmolested till his death, which happened December 31, 1385. But after the body of this good man had lain in the grave forty-one years, his bones were taken up by the decree of the synod of Constance, publicly burnt, and his ashes thrown into a river. The condemnation of his doctrine did not prevent its spreading all over the kingdom, and with such success, that according to Spelman, "two men could not be found together, and one not a Lollard or Wickliffite."

Tenets of Wickliffe.

The following are among the articles of Wickliffe which were condemned as heretical:

The substance of material bread and wine doth remain in the sacrament of the altar after the consecration.

The accidents do not remain without the subject in the same sacrament, after the consecration.

That Christ is not in the sacrament of the altar truly and really, in his proper and corporal person.

That if a bishop or a priest be in deadly sin, he doth not order, consecrate, nor baptize.

That if a man be duly and truly contrite and penitent, all exterior and outer confession is but superfluous and unprofitable unto him.

That it is not found or established by the gospel, that Christ did make or ordain mass.

If the pope be a reprobate and evil man, and consequently a member of the devil, he hath no power by any manner of means given unto him over faithful Christians.

That since the time of Urban the Sixth, there is none to be received for pope, but every man is to live after the manner of the Greeks, under his own law.

That it is against the scriptures, that ecclesiastical ministers should have any temporal possessions.

That no prelate ought to excommunicate any man except he knew him first to be excommunicate of God.

That he who doth so excommunicate any man, is thereby himself either a heretic or excommunicated.

That all such which do leave off preaching or hearing the word of God, or preaching of the gospel for fear of excommunication, they are already excommunicated, and in the day of judgment shall be counted as traitors unto God.

That it is lawful for any man either deacon or priest, to preach the word of God, without authority or license of the apostolic see or any other of his catholics.

That so long as a man is in deadly sin, he is neither bishop nor prelate in the church of God.

Wickliffe wrote several works, which in the year 1410 were burnt at Oxford, the abbot of Shrewsbury being then commissary. And in Bohemia, likewise, his books were burnt by the archbishop of Prague.

Burning of the Wickliffites.

In the council of the Lateran, a decree was made with regard to heretics, which required all magistrates to extirpate them upon pain of forfeiture and deposition. The canons of this council being received in England, the prosecution of heretics became a part of the common law; and a writ (styled *de heretico comburendo*) was issued under king Henry IV. for burning them upon their conviction; and it was enacted, that all who presumed to preach without the license of the bishops should be imprisoned, and be brought to trial within three months. If, upon conviction, they offered to abjure, and were not relapses, they were to be imprisoned and fined at pleasure; but if they refused to abjure, or were relapses, they were to be delivered over to the secular arm: and the magistrates were to burn them in some public place. About this time William Sautre, parish priest of St. Osith in London, being condemned as a relapse, and degraded by Arundel, archbishop of Canterbury, a writ was issued, wherein burning is called the common punishment, and referring to the customs of other nations. This was the first example of that sort in England.

The clergy alarmed lest the doctrines of Wickliffe should ultimately become established, used every exertion in their power to check them. In the reign of Richard II. the bishops had obtained a general license to imprison heretics, without being obliged to procure a special order from court, which however the house of commons caused to be revoked. But as the fear of imprisonment could not check the pretended evil dreaded by the Bishops, Henry IV., whose particular object was to secure the affection of the clergy, earnestly recommended to the parliament the concerns of the church. How reluctant soever the house of commons might be to prosecute the Lollards, the credit of the court, and the cabals of the clergy, at last obtained a most detestable act, for the burning of obstinate heretics; which bloody statute was not repealed till the year 1677. It was immediately after the passing

19*

of this statute that the ecclesiastical court condemned
William Sautre above mentioned.

Increase of Wickliffe's Doctrine.

Notwithstanding the opposition of the popish clergy,
Wickliffe's doctrine continued to spread greatly in Henry
IV.'s reign, even to such a degree, that the majority
of the house of commons were inclined to it; whence they
presented two petitions to the king, one against the clergy
and the other in favour of the Lollards. The first set
forth, that the clergy made ill use of their wealth, and
consumed their income in a manner quite different from
the intent of the donors; that their revenues were excessive, and consequently that it would be necessary to lessen
them; that so many estates might easily be seized as
would provide for 150 earls at the rate of 3000 marks a
year each, 1500 barons at 100 marks each, 6200 knights
at 40 marks, and 100 hospitals; that by this means the
safety of the kingdom might be better provided for, the
poor better maintained, and the clergy more devoted to
their duty. In the second petition the commons prayed,
that the statute passed against the Lollards, in the second
year of this reign, might be repealed, or qualified with
some restrictions. As it was the king's interest to please
the clergy, he answered the commons very sharply, that
he neither could nor would consent to their petitions. And
with regard to the Lollards, he declared he wished the
heretics were extirpated out of the land. To prove the
truth of this, he signed a warrant for burning Thomas
Badby.

Martyrdom of Thomas Badby in the year 1409.

Thomas Badby was a layman, and by trade a tailor. He
was arraigned in the year 1409, on the charge of heresy,
for having embraced the sentiments of Wickliffe. Though
standing as it were alone, he made a bold declaration of his
faith, and exclaimed against the idolatry and impious practices of the Roman church; though his life was promised
him, together with an annual pension out of the king's
treasury, on condition of recanting, he nobly rejected the

offre, and died like a faithful soldier of Christ, commending his soul to his care. He was burned in a tub at Smithfield.

Martyrdom of John Badby.

Martyrdom of Sir John Oldcastle.

The persecutions of the Lollards in the reign of Hen y V., were owing to the cruel instigations of the clergy, w o thought that the most effectual way to check the progress of Wickliffe's doctrine, would be to attack the then chi f protector of it, viz.: Sir John Oldcastle, baron of Cobham; and to persuade the king that the Lollards were engaged in conspiracies to overturn the state. It was even reported that they intended to murder the king, together with the princes, his brothers, and most of the lords spiritual and temporal, in hopes that the confusion which must necessarily arise in the kingdom, after such a massacre, would prove favourable to their religion. Upon this a false rumour was spread, that Sir John Oldcastle had got together 20,000 men in St. Giles' in the Fields, a place then overgrown with bushes. The king himself went thither at midnight, and finding no more than fourscore or a hundred persons, who were privately met upon a religious account, he fell upon them and killed many. Some of them being afterward examined, were prevailed upon, by promises or threats, to confess whatever their enemies desired ; and these accused Sir John Oldcastle.

The king hereupon thought him guilty ; and in that belief set a thousand marks upon his head, with a promise of perpetual exemption from taxes to any town which should secure him. Sir John was apprehended and imprisoned in the Tower ; but escaping from thence he fled into Wales, where he long concealed himself. But being afterward seized in Powisland, in North Wales, by lord Powis, he was brought to London, to the great joy of the clergy, who were highly incensed against him, and resolved to sacrifice him, to strike a terror into the rest of the Lollards. Sir John was of a very good family, had been sheriff of Hertfordshire under Henry IV., and summoned to parliament among the barons of the realm in that reign. He had been sent beyond the sea, with the earl of Arundel, to assist the duke of Burgundy against the French. In a word, he was a man of extraordinary merit, notwithstanding which he was condemned to be hanged up by the waist with a chain, and burnt alive. This most barbarous sentence was executed amid the curses and imprecations of the priests and monks, who used their utmost endeavours to prevent the people from praying for him. Such was the tragical end of Sir John Oldcastle, who left the world with a resolution and constancy that answered perfectly to the brave spirit with which he had ever maintained the cause of truth and of his God.

Not satisfied with his single death, the clergy induced the parliament to make fresh statutes against the Lollards. It was enacted among other things that whosoever read the scriptures in English should forfeit land, chattels, goods, and life, and be condemned as heretics to God, enemies to the crown, and traitors to the kingdom ; that they should not have the benefit of any sanctuary ; and that, if they continued obstinate, or relapsed after being pardoned, they should first be hanged for treason against the king, and then burned for heresy against God. This act was no sooner passed, but a violent persecution was raised against the Lollards ; several of them were burnt alive, some fled the kingdom, and others were weak enough to abjure their religion, to escape the torments prepared for them.

CHAPTER II.

Great Schism in the Church of Rome.

A circumstance occured at this period, by the providence of God, which greatly tended to facilitate the progress of truth. This was a great schism in the church o. Rome, which originated as follows : After the death of Gregory XI., who expired in the midst of his anxiety to crush Wickliffe and his doctrines, Urban the Sixth succeeded to the papal chair. This pope was so proud and insolent, and so intent on the advancement of his nephews and kindred, which he frequently accomplished by injuring other princes, that the greatest number of his cardinals and courtiers deserted him, and set up another pope against him, named Clement, who reigned eleven years. After him Benedict the Thirteenth, who reigned twenty-six years. Again, on the contrary side, after Urban the Sixth, succeeded Boniface the Ninth, Innocent the Eighth, Gregory the Twelfth, Alexander the Fifth, and John the Thirteenth. To relate all the particulars of this miserable schism, would reqare volumes ; we shall merely take notice of a few of the principal occurrences from which the reader may form an idea of the bloodshed and misery brought on the Christian world by the ambition and wickedness of these pretended representatives of our blessed Saviour ; and may judge how widely they departed from his blessed maxims of peace and good will to all men. Otho, duke of Brunswick and prince of Tarentum, was taken and murdered. Joan, his wife, queen of Jerusalem and Sicily, who had sent to pope Urban, beside other gifts, 40,000 ducats in gold, was afterward, by his order, committed to prison, and there strangled. Many cardinals were racked and tortured to death ; battles were fought between the rival popes, in which great multitudes were slain. Five cardinals were beheaded together, after long torments. The bishop o Aquilonensis being suspected by pope Urban, for not riding faster when in his company, was slain on the spot by the pope's order.   Thus did these demons in human form torment each other for the space of thirty-nine years, until the council of Constance.

Progress of the Reformation in the Reign of Henry VIII.

The reader will doubtless attend to the transactions recorded in this reign, with peculiar interest.   It was in this period that God, through the instrumentality of the king, liberated England from the papal yoke, and it became as it were a religious world dependant on itself.

The wars between the two houses of York and Lancaster had produced such fatal revolutions, and thrown England into such frequent convulsions, that the nation, with great joy, hailed the accession of Henry VII., to the throne, who being himself descended from the house of Lancaster, by his marriage with the heiress of the house of York, freed them from the fear of any further civil wars.   But the covetousness of his temper, the severity of his ministers, and his jealousy of the house of York, made him so generally odious to his people, that his death was little lamented.

Henry VIII. succeeded, with all the advantages he could have desired ; and his disgracing Empson and Dudley, the cruel ministers of his father's avaricious designs, his appointing restitution to be made of the sums that had been unjustly exacted of the people, and his ordering justice to be done on those rapacious ministers, gave all people hopes of happy times ; and when ministers by the king's orders were condemned and executed for invading the liberties of the people, under the covert of the king's prerogative, it made the nation conclude that they should hereafter live secure under the protection of such a prince, and that the violent remedies of parliamentary judgments should be no more necessary, except as in this case, to confirm what had been done before in the ordinary courts of justice.

The king also, either from the magnificence of his own temper, or the observation he had made of the ill effects of his father's parsimony, distributed his rewards and largesses with an unmeasured bounty ; so that he quickly expended those treasures, which his father had left; but till the ill effects of this appeared, it raised in his court and subjects the greatest hopes possible of a prince whose first actions showed an equal mixture of justice and generosity.

The king had been educated with more than ordinary care: learning being then in its dawning, after a night of long and gross ignorance, his father having given orders that both his elder brother and he should be well instructed in matters of knowledge. The learning then most in credit among the clergy was the scholastical divinity, which, by a show of subtlety, recommended itself to curious persons; and being very suitable to a vain and contentious temper, agreed best with his disposition; and further, it being likely to draw the most flattery, became the chief subject of his studies, in which he grew not only to be eminent for a prince, but he might really have passed for a learned man had his quality been never so mean. He delighted in the purity of the Latin tongue, and understood philosophy, and was so great a master in music, that he composed well. He was a bountiful patron to all learned men, more particularly to Erasmus and Polydore Virgil, and delighted much in those returns which hungry scholars make to liberal princes; for he loved flattery out of measure, and he had enough of it to have surfeited a man of any modesty; for all the world, both at home and abroad, contended who should exceed most indecently in setting out his praises. The clergy carried it; for as he had merited most at their hands, both by espousing the interests of the papacy, and by his entering the lists with Luther, so those that hoped to be advanced by those arts, were as little ashamed in magnifying him out of measure, as he was in receiving their gross commendations.

Character of Cardinal Wolsey.

One of the most remarkable men of this, or perhaps of any other age, was Cardinal Wolsey. He was of mean extraction, but possessed great abilities, and had a wonderful dexterity in insinuating himself into men's favour. He had but a little time been introduced to the king before he obtained an entire ascendency over him, and the direc-

tion of all his affairs, and for fifteen years continued to be the most absolute favourite ever known in England. He saw the king was much set on his pleasures and had a great aversion to business, and the other counsellors being unwilling to bear the load of affairs, were troublesome to him, by pressing him to govern by his own counsels; but Wolsey knew the methods of favourites better, and so was not only easy, but assistant to the king in his pleasures, and undertook to free him from the trouble of government, and to give him leisure to follow his appetites.

He was master of all the offices at home, and treaties abroad, so that all affairs went as he directed them. He soon became obnoxious to parliaments, and therefore tried but one during his ministry, where the supply was granted so scantily, that afterward he chose rather to raise money by loans and benevolences, than by the free gift of the people in Parliament. He in time became so scandalous for his ill life, that he grew to be a disgrace to his profession; for he not only served the king, but also shared with him in his pleasures. He was first made bishop of Tournay in Flanders, then of Lincoln, after that he was promoted to the see of York, and had both the abbey of St. Albans, and the bishopric of Bath and Wells in commendam; the last he afterward exchanged for Durham, and upon Fox's death he quitted Durham, that he might take Winchester; and besides all this, the king by a special grant gave him power to dispose of all the ecclesiastical preferments in England; so that in effect he was the pope of the British world, and no doubt but he copied skilfully enough after those patterns that were set him at Rome. Being made a cardinal, and setting up a legatine court, he found it fit for his ambition to have the great seal likewise, that there might be no clashing between those two jurisdictions. He had in one word, all the qualities necessary for a great minister, and all the vices usual in a great favourite.

The manner of promotion to bishoprics and abbeys was then the same that it had been almost ever since the investitures by the ring and staff were taken out of the hands of princes. Upon a vacancy the king seized on all the temporalities, and granted a license for an election, with a special recommendation of the person; who being returned, the royal assent was given, and it was sent to Rome, that bulls might be procured, and then the bishop elect was consecrated : after that he came to the king, and renounced every clause in his bulls that was contrary to the king's prerogative or to the law, and swore fealty ; and then were the temporalities restored. Nor could bulls be sued out at Rome without a license under the great seal ; so that the kings of England had reserved the power to themselves of promoting to ecclesiastical benefices, notwithstanding all the invasions the popes had made on the temporal power of princes.

Contest concerning Ecclesiastical Immunity.

The immunity of churchmen for crimes committed by them till they were first degraded by the spiritual court, occasioned a contest in the beginning of this reign between the secular and ecclesiastical courts. A law was passed under Henry VII., that clerks convict should be burnt in the hand. A temporary law was also made in the beginning of Henry VIII.'s reign, that murderers and robbers, not being bishops, priests, nor deacons, should be denied the benefit of clergy : but this was to last only till the next parliament, and so being not continued by it, the act determined. The abbot of Winchelcomb preached severely against it, as being contrary to the laws of God, and the liberties of the holy church, and said, that all who assented to it, had fallen under the censures of the church. And afterward he published a book to prove that all clerks even of the lower orders were sacred, and could not be judged by the temporal courts. This being done during the sitting of parliament, the temporal lords and the commons addressed the king, desiring him to repress the insolence of the clergy. Accordingly a public hearing was appointed before the king and all the judges : Dr. Standish a Franciscan, argued against the immunity, and proved that clerks, equally with laymen, had been in all times brought to trial in England ; and that it was necessary for the peace and safety of mankind that all criminals should be punished. The abbot argued on the other side, and said it was contrary to a decree of the church, and was a sin of itself. Standish answered that all decrees were not observed; for, notwithstanding the decrees for residence bishops did not reside at their cathedrals; and since no decree did bind till it was received, this concerning immunity, which was never received in England did not bind. After they had fully argued the matter, the laity were of opinion that Standish had the best of the argument: and therefore moved the king that the bishops might be ordered to make the abbot preach a recantation sermon. But they refused to do it, and said they were bound by their oaths to maintain his opinion. Standish was upon this much hated by the clergy, but the matter was dropped; yet the clergy carried the point, for the law was not continued.

Hun Imprisoned for Heresy, and Murdered.

Not long after this, an event occurred that was productive of great consequences. Richard Hun, a merchant in London, was sued by his parish priest for a mortuary in the legate's court; on this, his friends advised him to sue the priest in the temporal court for a præmunire for bringing the king's subjects before a foreign and illegal court. This incensed the clergy so much that they contrived his destruction. Accordingly, hearing that he had Wickliffe's Bible in his house, he was upon that put in the bishop's prison for heresy; but being examined upon sundry articles, he confessed some things, and submitted himself to mercy; upon which they ought, according to the law, to have enjoined him penance, and discharged him, this being his first crime; but he could not be prevailed on by the terror of this to let his suit fall in the temporal court; so one night his neck was broken with an iron chain, and he was wounded in other parts of his body, and then knit up in his own girdle, and it was given out that he had hanged himself; but the coroner's inquest, by examining the body, and by several other evidences, particularly by the confession of the sumner, gave their verdict that he was murdered by the bishop's chancellor, Dr. Horsey, and the sumner, and the bell-ringer. The spiritual court proceeded against the dead body, and charged Hun with all the heresy in Wickliffe's preface to the Bible, because that was found in his possession; so he was condemned as a heretic, and his body was burnt. The indignation of the people was raised to the highest pitch against this action, in which they implicated the whole body of the clergy, whom they esteemed no more their pastors, but barbarous murderers. The rage went so high that the bishop of London complained that he was not safe in his own house. The bishops, chancellor, and sumner were indicted as principals in the murder. In parliament an act passed, restoring Hun's children; but the commons sent up a bill concerning his murder, which was laid aside by the peers, where the spiritual lords had the majority.

The clergy looked on the opposition that Standish had made to their immunities as that which gave rise to Hun's first suit; and the convocation cited him to answer for his conduct; but he claimed the king's protection, since he had done nothing, but only pleaded in the king's name. The clergy pretended they did not prosecute him for his pleading, but for some of his divinity lectures, contrary to the liberty of the church, which the king was bound to maintain by his coronation oath: but the temporal lords, the judges, and the commons prayed the king also to maintain the laws according to his coronation oath, and to give Standish his protection. The king upon this being in great perplexity, required Veysy, afterward bishop of Exeter, to declare upon his conscience and allegiance the truth in that matter. His opinion was against the immunity; so another public hearing being appointed, Standish was accused for teaching, " That the inferior orders of the clergy were not sacred; that their exemption was not founded on a divine right, but that the laity might punish them; that the canons of the church did not bind till they were received; and that the study of the canon law was useless." Of these he denied some, and justified other particulars. Veysy being required to give his opinion, alleged, " That the laws of the church did only oblige where they were received: as the law of the celibacy of the clergy, received in the West, did not bind the Greek churches that never received it: so the exemption of the clerks not being received, did not bind in England." The judges gave their opinion next, which was, " That those who prosecuted Standish were all in a præmunire." So the court broke up. But in another hearing, in the presence of the greatest part of both nouses of parliament, the cardinal said in the name of the clergy, " That though they intended to do nothing against the king's prerogative, yet the trying of clerks seemed to be contrary to the liberty of the church, which they were bound by their oaths to maintain." So they prayed that the matter might be referred to the pope.

The king answered that he thought Standish had answered them fully: the bishop of Winchester said he would not stand to his opinion at his peril. Standish upon that said, " What can one poor friar do against all the clergy of England?" The archbishop of Canterbury said, " Some of the fathers of the church had suffered martyrdom upon that account;" but the chief justice replied, " That many holy kings had maintained that law, and many holy bishops had obeyed it." In conclusion the king declared that he would maintain his rights, and would not submit them to the decrees of the church otherwise than as his ancestors had done. Horsey was appointed to be brought to his trial for Hun's murder, and upon his pleading not guilty, no evidence was to be brought, and so he was to be discharged. The discontents of the people greatly increased at this, and very much disposed them to all that was done afterward, for overthrowing the ecclesiastical tyranny.

This was the first disagreement between the clergy and laity in this king's reign. In all other points he was at this time attached to the pope's interests, who sent him the common compliments of roses, and such other trifles by which that see had treated princes so long as children. But no compliment wrought so much on the king's vanity as the title of " Defender of the Faith," sent him by pope Leo upon the book which he wrote against Luther concerning the sacraments.

Progress of Luther's Doctrine.

The rise and progress of the doctrines of Luther are well known; the scandalous sale of indulgences gave the first occasion to all that followed between him and the church of Rome; in which, had not the corruptions and cruelties of the clergy been so visible and scandalous, so small a cause could never have produced so great a revolution.

The bishops were grossly ignorant; they seldom resided in their dioceses, except on great festivals; and all the effect their residence at such times could have was to corrupt others by their ill example. They attached themselves to princes and aspired to the greatest offices. The abbots and monks were wholly given up to luxury and idleness, and their unmarried state gave infinite scandal to the world; for it appeared that the restraining them from having wives of their own made them conclude that they had a right to all other men's. The inferior clergy were no better: and not having places of retreat to conceal their vices in, as the monks had, they became more public. In short, all ranks of churchmen were so universally despised and hated, that the world was very easily possessed with prejudice against the doctrines of men whom they knew to be capable of every vice; and the worship of God was so defiled with gross superstition that all men were easily convinced that the church stood in great need of a reformation. This was much increased when the books of the fathers began to be read, in which the difference between the former and latter ages of the church did very evidently appear. It was found that a blind superstition came first in the room of true piety; and when by its means the wealth and interest of the clergy were highly advanced, the popes had upon that established their tyranny; under which all classes of people had long groaned. All these things concurred to make way for the advancement of the reformation; and the books of the German reformers being brought into England and translated, many were prevailed on by them. Upon this a furious persecution was set on foot, to such a degree that six men and women were burnt in Coventry in passion week, only for teaching their children the creed, the Lord's prayer, and the ten commandments in English. Great numbers were every where brought into the bishops' courts; of whom some were burnt, but the greater part abjured.

The king laid hold on this occasion to become the champion of the church, and wrote against Luther, as mentioned above. His book, beside the title of "De-

20*

fender of the Faith," drew upon him all that flattery could
invent to extol it; yet Luther, not daunted by such an antagonist, answered it, and treated him as much below the
respect that was due to a king, as his flatterers had raised
him above it.   Tindal's translation of the New Testament,
with notes, drew a severe condemnation from the clergy,
there being nothing in which they were more concerned,
than to keep the people unacquainted with that book.
Thus much may serve to show the condition of affairs in
England both in church and state, when the process of the
king's divorce was first set on foot.

History of Henry's Marriage with Catharine.

As this incident is so replete with consequences, a particular relation of its cause will not, it is presumed, be unacceptable to the reader.

Henry VII. had entered into a firm alliance with Ferdinand of Spain, and agreed on a match between his son,
prince Arthur, and Catharine, the Infanta of Spain.   She
came into England, and was married in November; but
on the second of April after, the prince died.   They were
not only bedded in ceremony the night of the marriage,
but continued still to lodge together; and the prince gave
occasion to believe that the marriage was consummated.

The king being unwilling to restore so great a portion
as 200,000 ducats, which the princess brought as her
dowry, proposed a second match for her with his
younger son Henry.   Warham objected against the lawfulness of it; but Fox, bishop of Winchester, was for it, and
the opinion of the pope's authority was then so well established, that it was thought a dispensation from Rome was
sufficient to remove all objections.   Accordingly, one was
obtained, grounded upon the desire of the two young persons to marry together, and for the preservation of peace
between the crowns of England and Spain.

The pope was then at war with Louis the Twelfth of
France, and so would refuse nothing to the king of England, being, perhaps, not unwilling that princes should contract such marriages, by which the legitimation of their
issue depending on the pope's dispensation, they would be
thereby obliged in interest to support that authority.   Upon

this a marriage followed, the prince being yet under age; but the same day in which he became of age, he did, by his father's orders, make a protestation that he retracted and annulled his marriage.

Henry the Seventh, on his death bed, charged his son to break it off entirely, being perhaps apprehensive of such a return of confusion upon a controverted succession to the crown, as had been during the wars of the houses of York and Lancaster; but after his father's death, Henry the Eighth being then eighteen years of age, married her: she bore him two sons, who died soon after they were born; and a daughter, Mary, afterward queen of England. After this the queen contracted some diseases that made her unacceptable to the king; who, at the same time beginning to have some scruples of conscience with regard to the lawfulness of his marriage, determined to have the affair investigated.

The King's scruples concerning his Marriage.

He seemed to lay the greatest weight on the prohibition in the levitical law, of marrying the brother's wife, and being conversant in Thomas Aquinas's writings, he found that he and the other schoolmen looked on those laws as moral, and forever binding; and consequently the pope's dispensation was of no force, since his authority went not so far as to dispense with the laws of God. All the bishops of England, Fisher of Rochester only excepted, declared under their hands and seals, that they judged the marriage unlawful. The ill consequences of wars that might follow upon a doubtful title to the crown, were also much considered. It is not probable that Henry's affection for any other lady was the origin of these proceedings; but rather that, conceiving himself upon the point of being freed of his former marriage, he gave free scope to his affections, which settled on Anne Boleyn.

This lady was born in the year 1507, and at seven years of age was sent to France, where she remained twelve years, and then returned to England. She was much admired in both courts, was more beautiful than graceful, and more cheerful than discreet. She wanted none of the charms of wit or person, and must have had extraordinary attractions, since she could so long retain her place in such a king's affection.

Knight, then secretary of state, was sent to Rome to prepare the pope to grant a dispensation from the former marriage. Knight made application to the pope in the most secret manner he could, and had a most favourable answer, for the pope promised frankly to dissolve the marriage; but another promise being exacted of him by the emperor Charles V., nephew of Catharine, not to proceed in that affair, he was reduced to great straits, being then at his mercy, and yet unwilling to offend the king of England: he therefore studied to gain time, and promised that if the king would have a little patience, he should not only have that which he asked, but every thing that was in his power to grant.

Some scruples were made concerning the bull that was demanded, till, by great presents, it was at length obtained; and then the pope signed a commission for Wolsey to try the cause and judge in it, and also a dispensation, and put them in Knight's hands, but with tears prayed him that there might be no proceedings upon them, till the emperor were put out of a capacity of executing his revenge upon him, and whenever that were done he would own this act of justice which he did in the king's favour.

The pope was at this time offended with Cardinal Wolsey; for he understood that during his captivity Wolsey had been in an intrigue to get himself chosen vicar of the papacy, and was to have sat at Avignon, which might have produced a new schism. Staphileus, dean of the Rota, being then in England, was prevailed on by the promise of a bishopric, and a recommendation to a cardinal's hat, to promote the king's affair; and by him the cardinal wrote to the pope, in a most earnest strain, for a despatch of this business; and he desired that an indifferent and tractable cardinal might be sent over, with a full commission to join with him and to judge the matter; proposing Campegio to the king's ambassadors as the fittest man.

The cardinal in his letters to Cassali, who was in great favour with the pontiff, offered to take the blame on his own soul, if the pope would grant this bull; and with an earnestness, as hearty and warm as can be expressed in words, he pressed the thing, and added, that if the pope continued inexorable, he perceived the king would proceed another way.

These entreaties had such an effect, that Campegio was declared legate, and ordered to go to England, and join in commission with Wolsey for judging this matter. He accordingly set out from Rome, and carried with him a decretal bull for annulling the marriage, which he was authorized to show to the king and Wolsey; but was required not to give it out of his hands to either of them.

Campegio comes to England.

In October he arrived in England, and advised the king to relinquish the prosecution of his suit; and then counselled the queen, in the pope's name, to enter into a religious community; but both were in vain; and he by affecting an impartiality, almost lost both sides. But he in great measure pacified the king, when he showed him the bull he had brought over for annulling the marriage; yet he would not part with it out of his hands, neither to the king nor the cardinal; upon which great solicitation was employed at Rome, that Campegio might be ordered to show it to some of the king's counsellors, and to go on and end the business, otherwise Wolsey would be ruined and England lost: yet all this did not prevail on the pope, who knew that the king intended to get the bull out of Campegio's hands, and then to leave the pontiff to the emperor's indignation: but though he positively refused to grant that, yet, he said, he left the legates in England free to judge as they saw cause, and promised that he would confirm their sentence.

The affair proceeding very slowly, ambassadors were despatched to Rome with new propositions for a speedy termination. On this, the pope gave new assurances that though he would not grant a bull by which the divorce should be immediately his own act, yet he would confirm the legate's sentence.

About this time, the pope was taken suddenly ill, upon which the Imperialists began to prepare for a conclave: but Farnese, and the cardinal of Mantua, opposed them, and seemed to favour Wolsey; whom, as his correspondents wrote to him, "they reverenced as a Deity." Upon

this he despatched a courier to Gardiner, then on his way
to Rome, with large directions how to manage the election;
it was reckoned, that on the king of France joining heartily
with Henry, of which he seemed confident, there were
only six cardinals wanting to make the election sure, and
besides sums of money, and other rewards, that were to
be distributed among them, he was to give them assurance
that the cardinal's preferments should be divided among
them. These were the secret methods of attaining that
chair: and indeed it would puzzle a man of an ordinary
degree of credulity, to think that one chosen by such
means could presume to be Christ's vicar, and the infallible
judge of controversies. The recovery, however, of the
pope, put an end to those intrigues.

The Queen appeals to the Pope.

At length the legates began the process, when the queen
protested against them as incompetent judges. They, however, proceeded according to the forms of law, although
the queen had appealed from them to the pope, and objected alike to the place, to the judges, and her lawyers: yet
they pronounced her contumacious, and went on to examine witnesses, chiefly as to the consummation of her marriage with prince Arthur. But now, since the process was
thus going on, the emperor's agents pressed the pope vehemently for an avocation, and all possible endeavours were
used by the king's agents to hinder it; it was told him, that
there was a treaty on foot between the king and the Lutheran princes of Germany; and that upon declaring himself so partial as to grant the avocation, this would certainly
be concluded. But the pope thought the king so far engaged
in honour in the points of religion, that he would not be
prevailed upon to unite with Luther's followers; he did not,
therefore, imagine that the effects of his granting the avocation would be so fatal as was represented. In conclusion,
therefore, after the emperor had engaged to him to restore
his family to the government of Florence, the pope resolved
to publish his treaty with him: he told the English ambassadors that he was forced to it; both because all the lawyers told him it could not be denied, and that he could
not resist the emperor's forces, which surrounded him or.

all hands. Their endeavours to gain a little time by delays were as fruitless as their other arts had been, for on the 15th of July the pope signed it, and on the 19th sent it by an express messenger to England.

The legates, Campegio in particular, drew out the matter by all the delays they could contrive, and gained much time. At last, sentence being to be pronounced, Campegio, instead of pronouncing it, adjourned the court till October, and said that they being a part of the consistory, must observe their times of vacation. This gave the king and his court great offence when they saw what was like to be the issue of a process on which his majesty was so much bent, and in which he was so far engaged, both in honour and interest. The king governed himself upon this occasion with more temper than was expected: he dismissed Campegio civilly, only his officers searched his coffers when he went beyond sea, with design, as was thought, to see if the decretal bull could be found. Wolsey was now upon the point of being disgraced, though the king seemed to treat him with all his former confidence.

CHAPTER III.

Account of Cranmer.

AT this period Dr. Cranmer, a fellow of Jesus College in Cambridge, meeting accidentally with Gardiner and Fox at Waltham, and entering into discourse upon the royal marriage, suggested that the king should engage the chief universities and divines of Europe to examine the lawfulness of his marriage; and if they gave their resolutions against it, then it being certain that the pope's dispensation could not derogate from the law of God, the marriage must be declared null. This novel and reasonable scheme they proposed to the king, who was much pleased with it, as he saw this way was better in itself, and would mortify the pope. Cranmer was accordingly sent for, and on conversing with him, the king conceived a high opinion both of his learning and prudence, as well as of his probity and sincerity, which took such root in his mind, that no artifices nor calumnies were ever able to remove it.

Wolsey is disgraced.

From this moment began the decline of Wolsey. The great seal was taken from him and given to Sir Thomas More : and he was sued in a præmunire for having held the legatine courts by a foreign authority, contrary to the laws of England : he confessed the indictment, pleaded ignorance, and submitted himself to the king's mercy ; so judgment passed on him : then was his rich palace and royal furniture seized on for the royal use ; yet the king received him again into his protection, and restored to him the temporalities of the sees of York and Winchester and above 6000l. in plate and other goods. Articles were, however, preferred against him in the house of lords, where he had but few friends ; but Cromwell, who had been his secretary did so manage the matter in the house of commons that it came to nothing. This failing, his enemies procured an order to be sent to him to go into Yorkshire : thither he went in great state, with one hundred and sixty horses in his train, and seventy-two carts following him. There he lived some time ; but the king being informed that he was practising with the pope and the emperor, sent the earl of Northumberland to arrest him for high treason and bring him up to London. On the way he sickened, and died at Leicester, making great protestations of his constant fidelity to the king, particularly in the matter of his divorce : and " wishing he had served God as faithfully as he had done the king ; for then he would not have cast him off in his gray hairs as the king had done :" words that declining favourites are apt to reflect on, but seldom remember in the height of their fortune.

The Universities declare against the King's Marriage.

The king now intending to proceed in the method proposed by Cranmer, sent to Oxford and Cambridge to procure their conclusions. At Oxford it was referred by the major part of the convocation to thirty-three doctors and bachelors of divinity, whom that faculty was to name: they were empowered to determine the question, and put the seal of the university to their conclusion. And they gave their opinions that the marriage of the brother's wife was contrary both to the laws of God and nature. At Cambridge the convocation referred the question to twenty-nine; of which number, two-thirds agreeing, they were empowered to put the seal of the university to their determination. These agreed in opinion with those of Oxford. The jealousy of Dr. Cranmer's favouring Lutheranism caused the fierce popish party to oppose every thing in which he was engaged. They were also afraid of Anne Boleyn's advancement, who was believed to be tinctured with these opinions. Crook, a learned man, was employed in Italy to procure the resolution of divines there; in which he was so successful that besides the great discoveries he made in searching the manuscripts of the Greek fathers concerning their opinions in this point, he engaged several persons to write for the king's cause: and also got the Jews to give their opinions of the laws in Leviticus that they were moral and obligatory; yet, when a brother died without issue, his brother might marry his widow within Judea, for preserving their families and succession; but they thought that might not be done out of Judea. The state of Venice would not declare themselves, but said they would be neutral, and it was not easy to persuade the divines of the republic to give their opinions till a brief was obtained of the pope permitting all divines and canonists to deliver their opinions according to their consciences. The pope abhorred this way of proceeding, though he could not decently oppose it: but he said, in great scorn, that no friar should set limits to his power. Crook was ordered to give no money, nor make promises to any till they had freely delivered their opinion; which he is said to have faithfully observed.

He sent over to England a hundred several books and papers, with many subscriptions; all condemning the king's marriage as unlawful in itself. At Paris the Sorbonne made their determination with great solemnity; after mass all the doctors took an oath to study the ques-

tion and to give their judgment according to their consciences; and after three weeks study, the greater part
agreed on this: "that the king's marriage was unlawful
and that the pope could not dispense with it." At Orleans.
Angiers, and Toulouse, they determined to the same
purpose.

Calvin thought the marriage null, and all agreed that the
pope's dispensation was of no force. Osiander was employed to engage the Lutheran divines, but they were
afraid of giving the emperor new grounds of displeasure.

Melancthon thought the law in Leviticus was dispensable,
and that the marriage might be lawful; and that in those
matters states and princes might make what laws they
pleased; and though the divines of Leipsic after much
disputing about it, did agree that those laws were. moral,
yet they could never be brought to justify the divorce with
the subsequent marriage; but the pope was more com-
pliant, for he offered to Cassali to grant the king dispensation for having another wife, with which the Imperialists
seemed not dissatisfied.

The king's cause being thus fortified by so many resolutions in his favour, he made many members of parliament
in a prorogation time sign a letter to the pope, complaining that notwithstanding the great merits of the king, the
justice of his cause, and the importance of it to the safety
of the kingdom, yet the pope made still new delays; they
therefore pressed him to despatch it speedily, otherwise
they would be forced to seek other remedies, though they
were not willing to drive things to extremities till it was
unavoidable. The letter was signed by the cardinal, the
archbishop of Canterbury, four bishops, twenty-two abbots, forty-two peers, and eleven commoners.

To this the pope wrote an answer: he took notice of
the vehemence of their style: he freed himself from the
imputations of ingratitude and injustice: he acknowledged
the king's great merits; and said he had done all he could
in his favour: he had granted a commission, but could not
refuse to receive the queen's appeal; all the cardinals
with one consent judged that an avocation was necessary.
Since that time the delays lay not with him, but with the
king; that he was ready to proceed, and would bring it

to as speedy an issue as the importance of it would admit of; and for their threatenings they were neither agreeable to their wisdom, nor their religion.

The king, now disgusted at his dependence on the pope, issued a proclamation against any that should purchase, bring over, or publish any bull from Rome contrary to his authority: and after that he made an abstract of all the reasons and authorities of the fathers or modern writers against his marriage, to be published both in Latin and English.

Both sides having produced the strength of their cause, it evidently appeared that, according to the authority given to the tradition in the church of Rome, the king had clearly the right on his side.

Amidst these disputes the queen continued firm to her resolution of leaving the matter in the pope's hands, and would not listen to any propositions for referring the matter to the arbitration of a number chosen on both sides.

The kings of England claimed the same latitude of power in ecclesiastical matters, as the Roman emperors had exercised before the fall of that empire: anciently they had by their authority divided bishoprics, granted the investitures, and made laws relating both to ecclesiastical causes and persons. When the popes began to extend their power beyond the limits assigned them by the canons, great opposition arose to them in England; but they managed the advantages they found, either from the weakness or ill circumstances of princes so steadily, that at length they subdued the world: and if they had not by their cruel exactions so oppressed the clergy, that they were driven to seek shelter under the covert of the temporal authority, the world was so overwhelmed by superstition and credulity, that not only the whole spiritual power, but even the temporal authority of the princes was likely to have fallen under popish tyranny. But the discontented clergy supported the secular power as much as they had before advanced that of the papal. Boniface VIII. had raised his pretentions to that impudent pitch that he declared all power both ecclesiastical and civil was derived from him; and this he established as an article of faith necessary to salvation; on which he and his successors took upon them to dispose of all ecclesiastical benefices by their bulls and provisions. To restrain these invasions of the rights of princes, laws were made in England, which condemned them for the future : but no punishment being declared for the transgressors, the courtiers at Rome were not frighted at so general a law: so that these abuses still continued: but in the reign of Edward III., a more severe act was made, by which all that transgressed were to be imprisoned, to be fined at pleasure, and to forfeit all their benefices.

The Clergy sued in a Præmunire.

These long forgotten statutes were now revived, to bring the clergy into a snare: it was designed, by the terror of this, to force them into an entire submission, and to oblige them to redeem themselves by the grant of a considerable subsidy. They pleaded ignorance ; it was a public error, and they ought not therefore to be punished for it. To this it was answered, that the laws which they had transgressed were still in force, and so no ignorance could excuse the violation of them. The convocation of Canterbury made their submission, and in their address to the king, he was called the protector and supreme head of the church of England ; and but some objecting to that, it was added, " in so far as it is agreeable to the law of Christ." This was signed by nine bishops, fifty abbots and priors, and the greater part of the lower house : and with it they offered the king a subsidy of £100,000, to procure his favour, and promised for the future not to make nor execute any constitutions without his licence.

The convocation of York did not pass this so easily ; they objected to the word *head*, as agreeing to none but Christ ; whereupon the king wrote them a long expostulatory letter, and told them with what limitations those of Canterbury had passed that title ; upon which they all submitted, and offered £18,840, which was accepted ; and thus the clergy were again received into the king s protection, and pardoned.

The King leaves the Queen.

After the prorogation of this session of parliament, new applications were made to the queen to persuade her to depart from her appeal; but she remained fixed in her resolution, and said she was the king's lawful wife, and would abide by it till the court of Rome should declare the contrary. Upon that, the king desired her to choose any of his houses in the country to live in, and resolved never to see her more.

The Pope writes to the King, and is answered.

In January, 1532, the pope, upon the motion of the Imperialists, wrote to the king, complaining that notwithstanding a suit was depending concerning his marriage, yet he had put away his queen, and kept one Anne as his wife, contrary to a prohibition served on him; he therefore exhorted him to live with his queen again, and to put away Anne. Upon this the king sent Dr. Bennet to Rome with a large despatch, in which he complained that the pope proceeded in that matter upon the suggestion of others, who were ignorant and rash men, and had carried himself inconstantly and deceitfully in it, and not as became Christ's vicar: he had granted a commission, had promised never to recall it, and had sent over a decretal bull defining the cause. Either these were unjustly granted, or unjustly recalled. It was plain that he acted more with regard to his interests, than according to conscience; and that, as the pope had often confessed his own ignorance in these matters, so he was not furnished with learned men to advise him, otherwise he would not defend a marriage which almost all the learned men and universities in England, France and Italy, had condemned as unlawful. He would not question his authority, unless he were compelled to it, and would do nothing but reduce it to its first and ancient limits.

This haughty letter made the pope resolve to proceed and end this matter, either by a sentence or a treaty. The king was cited to answer to the queen's appeal at Rome in person, or by proxy: accordingly, Sir Edward Karne was sent thither in the new character of the king's excu

21*

sator, to excuse the king s appearance, upon such grounds as could be founded on the canon law, and upon the privi leges of the crown of England. The Imperialists pressed the pope to give sentence, but the wiser cardinals, who observed that the nation would adhere to the king, if he should be provoked to shake off the pope's yoke, suggested milder counsels.

In conclusion, the pope seemed to favour the king's ex-cusatory plea, upon which the Imperialists made great complaints. But this amounted to no more, than that the king was not bound to appear in person : therefore the cardinals, who were in his interest, advised the king to send over a proxy for answering to the merits of the cause. Bonner was also sent to England to assure the king, that the pope was now so much in the French interest, that he might confidently refer his matter to him.

At that time the king sent for the speaker of the house of commons, and told him he found the prelates were but half subjects ; for they swore at their consecration an oath to the pope, inconsistent with their allegiance and oath to him. By their oath to the pope, they swore to be in no council against him, nor to disclose his secrets ; but to maintain the papacy, and the rights and authorities of the church of Rome, against all men. In their oath to the king, they renounced all clauses in their bulls contrary to the king's royal dignity, and swore to be faithful to him, and to live and die with him against all others, and to keep his counsel ; acknowledging that they held their bishoprics only of him. It was evident they could not keep both those oaths, in case of a breach between the king and the pope. But the plague broke off the consultations of par liament at this time. Soon after, Sir Thomas More, see-ing a rupture with Rome coming on so fast, desired leave to lay down his office, which was upon that conferred on Sir Thomas Audley. More was satisfied with the king's keeping up the laws formerly made in opposition to the papal encroachments, and so had concurred in the suit of the præmunire ; but now the matter went further, and not being able to keep pace with the king's measures, he re turned to a private life

Interview of the Kings of England and France.

An interview soon followed between the kings of France and England; in which, Francis promised Henry to second him in his suit; encouraged him to proceed to a second marriage without delay; and assured him of his assistance and support: meantime, the pope offered to the king, to send a legate to any indifferent place out of England, to form the process, reserving only the giving sentence to himself; and proposed to him, and all princes, a general truce, to be followed by a general council.

The king answered, that such was the present state of the affairs of Europe, that it was not seasonable to call a general council; and that it was contrary to his prerogative to send a proxy to appear at Rome; that by the decrees of general councils, all causes ought to be judged on the place and by a provincial council; and that it was fitter to judge it in England, than any where else: and that by his coronation oath he was bound to maintain the dignities of his crown, and the rights of his subjects; and not to appear before any foreign court. Sir Thomas Elliot was, therefore, sent over with instructions, to move that the cause might be judged in England.

The King marries Anne Boleyn.

Soon after this, the king married Anne Boleyn; Rowland Lee (afterward bishop of Coventry and Lichfield) officiated, none being present but the duke of Norfolk; and her father, mother, brother, and Cranmer. It was thought that the former marriage being null, the king might proceed to another: and perhaps they hoped, that as the pope had formerly proposed this method, so he would now approve of it. But though the pope had joined himself to France, yet he was still so much in fear of the emperor, that he dared not provoke him. A new citation was therefore issued out, for the king to answer to the queen's complaints; but Henry's agents protested, that their master was a sovereign prince, and England a free church, over which the pope had no just authority; and that the king could expect no justice at Rome, where the emperor's power was so great.

The Parliament condemns Appeals to Rome.

At this time, the parliament met again, and passed an act, condemning all appeals to Rome ; and enacting, that thenceforth all causes should be judged within the kingdom, and that sentences given in England were to have full effect : and all that executed any censures from Rome were to incur the pain of præmunire.

Cranmer made Archbishop of Canterbury.

Warham, archbishop of Canterbury, having died the preceding year, was succeeded by Cranmer who was then in Germany, disputing in the king's cause with some of the emperor's divines.   The king resolved to advance him to that dignity, and sent him word of it, that so he might make haste over : but a promotion so far above his thoughts, had not its common effect on him : he had a true and primitive sense of so great a charge ; and instead of aspiring to it feared it ; and returning very slowly to England, used all his endeavours to be excused from that advancement. Bulls were sent for to Rome, in order to his consecration which the pope granted, and on the 30th of March, Cranmer was consecrated by the bishops of Lincoln, Exeter and St. Asaph.   The oath to the pope was of hard digestion to him.   He therefore made a protestation, before he took it, that he conceived himself not bound up by it in any thing that was contrary to his duty to God, to his king, or to his country ; and this he repeated when he took it.

The King's Marriage condemned by the Convocation.

The convocation had then two questions before them ; the first was, concerning the lawfulness of the king's marriage, and the validity of the pope's dispensation ; the other was, of matter of fact, whether Prince Arthur had consummated the marriage.   For the first, the judgments of nineteen universities were read ; and after a long debate, there being twenty-three only in the lower house, fourteen were against the marriage, seven for it, and two voted dubiously.   In the upper house Stokesly, bishop of

London, and Fisher, maintained the debate long: the one for the affirmative, and the other the negative: at last it was carried *nemine contradicente*, (the few that were of the other side it seems withdrawing) against the marriage, 216 being present. The other question was referred to the canonists; and they all, except five or six, reported, that the presumptions were violent; and these, in a matter not capable of plain proof, were always received in law.

The convocation having thus judged in the matter, the ceremony of pronouncing the divorce judicially was now only wanting. The new queen being pregnant, was a great evidence of her having preserved her chastity previously to her marriage. On Easter eve she was declared queen of England: and soon after, Cranmer, with Gardiner, who had been made upon Wolsey's death bishop of Winchester, and the bishops of London, Lincoln, Bath and Wells, with many divines and canonists, went to Dunstable; Queen Catherine living then near it, at Ampthill. The king and queen were cited; he appeared by proxy but the queen refused to take any notice of the court: so after three citations she was declared contumacious, and the merits of the cause were examined. At last, on the 23d of May, sentence was given, declaring the marriage to have been null from the beginning.

Coronation of Anne Boleyn.

Some days after this, another judgment was given, confirming the king's marriage with queen Anne, and on the first of June she was crowned. All people admired her conduct, who, during so many years, managed the spirit of so violent a king in such a manner, as neither to surfeit him with too many favours, nor to provoke him with too much rigour. They that loved the reformation, looked for better days under her protection; but many priests and friars, both in sermons and discourses, condemned the king's proceedings. Henry sent ambassadors to the various courts of Europe, to justify what he had done: he sent also to queen Catharine, charging her to assume no other title but that of princess dowager; but to this she refused obedience, saying, she would not take that infamy

on herself; and so resolved, that none should serve about
her who did not treat her as queen.

At Rome the cardinals of the Imperial faction complained much of the attempt made on the pope's power, and
urged him to proceed to censures. But there was only
sentence given, annulling all that the archbishop of Canterbury had done; and the king was required under pain of
excommunication, to place things again in the state in
which they formerly were; and this notification was affixed
at Dunkirk. The king sent an embassy to the French
monarch, who was then setting out to Marseilles, to meet
the pope; their errand was to dissuade him from the journey, unless the pope promised Henry satisfaction: Francis
said he was engaged in honour to go on; but assured them
he would mind the king's concerns with as much zeal as if
they were his own.

Birth of the Princess Elizabeth.

In September the queen brought forth a daughter, afterward the renowned queen Elizabeth; and the king having
before declared lady Mary princess of Wales, did now the
same for her: though, since a son might exclude her from
it, she could not be heir apparent, but only heir presump-
tive to the crown.

The eventful moment was now at hand, when the incident should take place that would cause the separation of
England from the Church of Rome. There was a secret
agreement between the pope and Francis, that if king
Henry would refer his cause to the consistory, excepting
only the cardinals of the Imperial faction, as partial, and
would in all other things return to his obedience to the see
of Rome, the sentence should be given in his favour.
When Francis returned to Paris, he sent over the bishop
of that city to the king, to tell what he had obtained of
the pope in his favour, and the terms on which it was promised; this wrought so much on the king, that he presently consented to them: upon which the bishop of Paris,
though it was now in the middle of winter, went to Rome
'n consequence. Upon his arrival there, the matter seemed
agreed; for it was promised, that upon the king's sending

a promise under his hand, to place things in their former
state, and his ordering a proxy to appear for him, judges
should be sent to Cambray for making the process, and
then sentence should be given.   Upon the notice given of
this and of a day fixed for the return of the courier, the
king despatched him with all possible haste ; and now the
business seemed at an end.   But the courier had the sea
and Alps to pass, and in winter it was not easy to observe
a limited day so exactly.   The appointed day came, and
no courier arrived ; upon which the imperialists gave out
that the king was abusing the pope's easiness ; and pressed
him vehemently to proceed to a sentence : the bishop of
Paris requested only a delay of six days.   But the design
of the imperialists was to hinder a reconciliation ; for if
the king had been set right with the pope, there would
have been so powerful a league formed against the emperor, as would have frustrated all his measures : and therefore it was necessary for his politics to embroil them.   Seduced by the artifice of this intriguing prince, the pope,
contrary to his ordinary prudence, brought the matter before the consistory ; and there the imperialists having the
majority, it was driven on with so much precipitation,
that they did in one day that which, according to form,
should have occupied three.

They gave the final sentence, declared the king's marriage with queen Catharine good, and required him to live
with her as his wife, otherwise they would proceed to censures.   Two days after this, the courier came with the
king's submission in due form ; he also brought earnest
letters from Francis in the king's favour.   This wrought
on all the indifferent cardinals, as well as those of the
French faction, so much that they prayed the pope to recall what was done.   A new consistory was called ; but
the imperialists urged, with greater vehemence than ever,
that they would not give such scandal to the world as to
recall a definitive sentence past of the validity of a marriage, and give the heretics such advantages by their un-
steadiness in matters of that nature : it was therefore carried, that the former sentence should take place, and the
execution of it be committed to the emperor.   When this
was known in England, it determined the king in his resolution of shaking off the papal yoke; in which he had

made so great a progress, that the parliament had passed all the acts concerning it, before he received the news from Rome ; for he judged that the best way to secure his cause was to let Rome see his power, and with what vigour he could make war.

CHAPTER IV.

Arguments for rejecting the Pope's power.

IN England the foundations on which the papal authority was built, had been examined with extraordinary care of late years ; and several books were written on that subject. It was demonstrated that all the apostles were made equal in the powers that Christ gave them, and he often condemned their contests about superiority, but never declared in St. Peter's favour. St. Paul withstood him to his face, and reckoned himself not inferior to him. If the dignity of a person left any authority with the city in which he sat, then Antioch must carry it as well as Rome ; and Jerusalem, where Christ suffered, was to be preferred to all the world, for it was truly the mother-church. The other privileges ascribed to St. Peter, were either only a precedence of order, or were occasioned by his fall, as that injunction, "Feed my sheep," it being a restoring him to the apostolical function. St. Peter had also a limited province, the circumcision, as St. Paul had the uncircumcision, of far greater extent ; which showed that Peter was not considered as the universal pastor.

Several sees, as Ravenna, Milan, and Aquileia, pretended exemption from the papal authority. Many English bishops had asserted that the popes had no authority against the canons, and to that day no canon the pope made was binding till it was received ; which showed the pope's authority was not believed to be founded on a divine authority : and the contests which the kings of England had had with the popes concerning investitures, bishops doing homage, appeals to Rome, and the authority of papal bulls and provisions, showed that the pope's power was believed to be subject to laws and custom, and so not derived from Christ and St. Peter; and as laws had given them some power, and princes had been forced in ignorant ages to submit to their usurpations, so they might, as they saw cause, change those laws, and resume their rights.

The next point inquired into was the authority that kings had in matters of religion and the church. In the New Testament, Christ was himself subject to the civil powers, and charged his disciples not to affect temporal dominion. They also wrote to the churches to be subject to the higher powers, and call them supreme, and charge every soul to be subject to them: so in scripture the king is called head and supreme, and every soul is said to be under him, which joined together makes up his conclusion that he is the supreme head over all persons. In the primitive church the bishops only made rules or canons, but pretended to no compulsive authority, but what came from the civil magistrate. Upon the whole matter, they concluded that the pope had no power in England, and that the king had an entire dominion over all his subjects, which extended even to the regulation of ecclesiastical matters.

These questions being fully discussed in many disputes and published in several books, all the bishops, abbots, and friars of England, Fisher only excepted, were so far satisfied with them, that they resolved to comply with the changes the king was resolved to make.

The Pope's power rejected by Parliament.

At the next meeting of parliament there were but seven bishops and twelve abbots present, the rest being unwilling to concur in making this change, though they complied with it when it was made. Every Sunday during the session a bishop preached at St. Paul's, and declared that the pope had no authority in England: before this they had only said that a general council was above him, and that the exactions of his court, and appeals to it, were unlawful; but now they went a strain higher, to prepare the people for receiving the acts then in agitation. On the 9th of March the commons began the bill for taking away the pope's power, and sent it to the lords on the 14th, who passed it on the 20th without any dissent. In it they set forth the exactions of the court of Rome, grounded on the

22

pope's power of dispensing; and that as none could dispense with the laws of God, so the king and parliament only had the authority of dispensing with the laws of the land; and that therefore such licenses or dispensations as were formerly in use, should be for the future granted by the two archbishops; some of these were to be confirmed under the great seal; and they appointed that thereafter all intercourse with Rome, on those subjects should cease. They also declared that they did not intend to alter any article of the catholic faith of Christendom, or of that which was declared in the scripture necessary to salvation. They confirmed all the exemptions granted to monasteries _the popes, but subjected them to the king's visitation, and gave the king and his council power to examine and reform all indulgences and privileges granted by the pope. This act subjected the monasteries entirely to the king's authority, and put them in no small confusion. Those who loved the reformation rejoiced both to see the pope's power rooted out, and to find the scripture made the standard of religion.

After this act, another passed in both houses, in six days time, without any opposition, settling the succession of the crown, confirming the sentence of divorce, and the king's marriage with queen Anne, and declaring all marriages within the degrees prohibited by Moses to be unlawful: all that had married within them were appointed to be divorced, and their issue illegitimated; and the succession to the crown was settled upon the king's issue by the present queen, or, in default of that, to the king's right heirs for ever. All were required to swear to maintain the contents of this act; and if any refused to swear to it, or should say any thing to the slander of the king's marriage, he was to be judged guilty of misprision of treason, and to be punished accordingly.

About this time one Phillips complained to the house of commons of the bishop of London, for using him cruelly in prison upon suspicion of heresy; the commons sent up his petition to the lords, but received no answer; they therefore sent some of their members to the bishop, desiring him to answer the complaints put in against him: but he acquainted the house of lords with it; and they with one consent voted that none of their house ought to ap-

pear or answer to any complaint at the bar of the house
of commons. On which the commons let this particular
case fall, and sent up a bill, to which the lords agreed,
regulating the proceedings against heretics; repealing the
statute of Henry IV.; and declaring that none were to be
committed for heresy but upon a presentment made by
two witnesses; none were to be accused for speaking
against things that were grounded only upon the pope's
canons; bail was to be taken for heretics, and they were
to be brought to trial in open court; and if upon conviction they did not abjure, or were relapses, they were to
be burnt; the king's writ being first obtained. This was
a great check to the bishops' tyranny, and gave great satisfaction to the friends of the reformation.

The convocation sent in a submission at the same time,
by which they acknowledged, that all the convocations
ought to be assembled by the king's writ; and promised
never to make nor execute any canons without the king's
assent. They also desired, that since many of the received
canons were found to be contrary to the king's prerogative
and the laws of the land, there might be a committee, named
by the king, of thirty-two, the one half out of both houses
of parliament, and the other of the clergy, empowered to
abrogate or regulate them, as they should see cause. This
was confirmed in parliament; the act against appeals was
renewed; and an appeal was allowed from the archbishop
to the king, upon which the lord chancellor was to grant
a commission for a court of delegates.

Another act passed for regulating the elections and consecrations of bishops, condemning all bulls from Rome,
and appointing that upon a vacancy the king should
grant a license for an election, and should by a missive
letter signify the person's name whom he would have
chosen; and within twelve days after these were delivered,
the dean and chapter, or prior and convent, were required
to return an election of the person named by the king
under their seals. The bishop elect was upon that to
swear fealty, and a writ was to be issued out for his consecration in the usual manner; after that he was to do
homage to the king, upon which both the temporalities and
spiritualities were to be restored, and bishops were to exercise their jurisdictions as they had done before. All

who transgressed this act were made guilty of a præ munire.

A private act passed, depriving cardinal Campegio and Jerome de Gianuccii of the bishoprics of Salisbury and Worcester : the reasons given for it were, because they did not reside in their dioceses, for preaching the laws of God, and keeping hospitality, but lived at the court of Rome, and drew £3000 a year out of the kingdom.

While these measures were pursuing by the government, Tindal of Antwerp, who had been compelled to flee from England, by the assistance of several others translated the New Testament into English, and improved every opportunity of sending them from thence to England, by means of which the minds of the people were preparing for the change that was soon to follow.

Story and Martyrdom of Thomas Bilney.

Thomas Bilney was brought up at Cambridge from a child. On leaving the university he preached in several places; and in his sermons spoke with great boldness against the pride and insolence of the clergy. This was during the ministry of cardinal Wolsey, who, hearing of his attacks, caused him to be seized and imprisoned. Overcome with fear, Bilney abjured, was pardoned, and returned to Cambridge in the year 1530. Here he fell into great horror of mind, in consequence of his instability and denial of the truth. He became ashamed of himself, bitterly repented of his sin, and growing strong in faith, resolved to make some atonement by a public avowal of his apostacy, and confession of his sentiments. To prepare himself for his task, he studied the scriptures with deep attention for two years ; at the expiration of which he again quitted the university, went into Norfolk, where he was born, and preached up and down that county against idolatry and superstition ; exhorting the people to a good life, to give alms, to believe in Christ, and to offer up their souls to him in the sacrament. He openly confessed nis own sin of denying the faith ; and using no precaution as he went about, was soon taken by the bishop's officers, condemned as a relapse, and degraded. Sir Thomas More sent down the writ to burn him. Parker, afterward archbishop, was an eye-witness of his sufferings; and affirms that he bore all his hardships with great fortitude and resignation, and continued very cheerful after his sentence. He eat up the poor provision that was brought him heartily, saying, he must keep up a ruinous cottage till it fell. He had these words of Isaiah often in his mouth, "When thou walkest through the fire thou shalt not be burnt;" and by burning his finger in the candle he prepared himself for the stake; saying, the fire would only consume the stubble of his body, and would purify his soul.

On the 10th of November he was brought to the stake, where he repeated the creed, prayed earnestly, and with the deepest sense repeated these words, "Enter not into judgment with thy servant, oh, Lord!" Dr. Warner, who attended, embraced him, shedding many tears, and wishing he might die in as good a frame of mind as Bilney then was. The friars requested him to inform the people that they were not instrumental to his death, which he did; so that the last act of his life was one of charity and forgiveness.

The officers then put the reeds and fagots about his body, and set fire to the first, which made a great flame, and disfigured his face: he held up his hands, and struck his breast, crying sometimes " Jesus;" sometimes " Credo!" but the flame was blown away from him several times, the wind being very high, till at length the wood taking fire, the flame was stronger, and so he yielded up the ghost.

His body being shrunk up, leaned down on the chain, till one of the officers with his halberd struck out the staple of the chain behind him, on which it fell down into the bottom of the fire, where it was covered with wood, and consumed.

The sufferings, the confession, and the heroic death of this martyr, inspirited and animated others to imitate his conduct.

Byfield and others Burnt.

Byfield, who had formerly abjured, was taken dispersing Tindal's books; and he, with one Tewkesbury were condemned by Stokesly, and burnt. Two men and a woman

suffered also the same fate at York.   Upon these proceed
ings, the parliament complained to the king ; but this did
not check the sanguinary proceedings of the clergy.   One
Bainham, a counsellor of the Temple, was taken on suspicion of heresy, whipped in the presence of sir Thomas
More, and afterward racked in the Tower, yet he could
not be wrought on to accuse any, but through fear he abjured.   After this, however, being discharged, he was in
great trouble of mind, and could find no quiet till he went
publicly to church, where he openly confessed his sins,
and declared the torments he felt in his conscience for
what he had done.   Upon this he was again seized on, and
condemned for having said that Thomas Becket was a
murderer, and was damned if he did not repent ; and that
in the sacrament, Christ's body was received by faith, and
not chewed with the teeth.   Sentence was passed upon
him, and he was burnt.   Soon after this More delivered up
the great seal, in consequence of which the reformed
preachers had a short respite.

But the persecution was soon revived, and its rage
stopped not at the living, but ventured itself even on the
dead.   Lord Tracy made a will, by which he left his soul
to God, in hopes of mercy through Christ, without the
help of any saint ; and therefore he declared that he would
leave nothing for soul-masses.   This will, being brought to
the bishop of London's court to be proved after his death,
provoked the clergy so much that he was condemned as a
heretic, and an order was sent to the chancellor of Worcester to raise his body : but he went beyond his instructions, and burnt it, which could not be justified, since the
deceased was not a relapse.   Tracy's heir sued him for it
and he was turned out of his place, and fined £400.

The clergy proclaimed an indulgence of forty days pardon to any that carried a fagot to the burning of a heretic,
that so cruelty might seem the more meritorious.

The reformed now enjoyed a respite of two years, when
the crafty Gardiner represented to the king that it would
tend much to his advantage if he would take some occasion to show his hatred of heresy.   Accordingly a young
man named Frith was chosen for a sacrifice to this affected
zeal for religion.

The Reformers favoured by the Court.

The nobility and gentry were generally well satisfied
with the change in ecclesiastical affairs; but the body of
the people, being more under the power of the priests
were filled with great fears on the subject. It was said
among them that the king now joined himself to heretics;
that the queen, Cranmer, and Cromwell, favoured them.
It was left free to dispute what were articles of faith, and
what were only the decrees of popes; and the most important changes might be made, under the pretence that
they only rejected those opinions which were supported by
the papal authority.

The monks and friars saw themselves left at the king's
mercy. Their bulls could be no longer useful to them
The trade of new saints, or indulgences was now at an
end; they had also some intimations that Cromwell was
forming a project for suppresssing them; so they thought
it necessary for their own preservation to embroil the
king's affairs as much as was possible: therefore, both in
confessions and discourses, they laboured to infuse into
the people a dislike of his proceedings: but these prac
tices at home, and the intrigues of cardinal Pole abroad,
the libels that were published, and the rebellions that were
raised in England, wrought so much on the king's temper,
naturally imperious and boisterous, that he became too
prone to acts of severity, and his new title of *head of the
church* seemed to have increased his former vanity, and
made him fancy that all his subjects were bound to regulate their belief by the measures he set them. The bishops
and abbots did what they could to free the king of any
jealousies he might have of them; and of their own accord
before any law was made about it, swore to maintain his
supremacy.

Cromwell made Vicar-General.

The first act of his new power was the making Cromwell vicar-general, and visiter of all the monasteries and
churches of England, with a delegation of the king's supremacy to him; he was also empowered to give commissions subaltern to himself; and all wills, where the estate

was in value above £200, were to be proved in his court This was afterward enlarged: he was made the king's vicegerent in ecclesiastical matters, had the precedence of all persons except the royal family; and his authority was in all points the same as had been formerly exercised by the pope's legates.

Pains were taken to engage all the clergy to declare for the supremacy. At Oxford a public determination was made, to which every member assented, that the pope had no more authority in England than any other foreign bishop. The Franciscans at Richmond made some opposition; they said, by the rule of St. Francis, they were bound to obey the holy see. The bishop of Lichfield told them that all the bishops in England, all the heads of houses, and the most learned divines had signed that proposition. St. Francis made his rule in Italy, where the bishop of Rome was metropolitan, but that ought not to extend to England: and it was shown that the chapte cited by them was not written by him, but added since yet they continued positive in their refusal to sign it.

General visitation of the Monasteries.

It was well known that the monks and friars, though they complied with the time, yet hated this new power of the king's; the people were also startled at it: so one Dr. Leighton, who had been in Wolsey's service with Cromwell, proposed a general visitation of all the religious houses in England; and thought that nothing would reconcile the nation so much to the king's supremacy, as to see some good effect flow from it. Others deemed this was too bold a step, and feared it would provoke the religious orders too much. Yet it was known that they were guilty of such disorders, as nothing could so effectually check as inquiry. Cranmer led the way to this by a metropolitical visitation, for which he obtained the king's license; he took care to see that the pope's name was struck out of all the offices of the church, and that the king's supremacy was generally acknowledged.

In October the general visitation of the monasteries was begun; and the visiters were instructed to inquire whether the houses had their full number according to their foundation? If they performed divine worship at the appointed hours? what exemptions they had? what were their statutes? how their superiors were chosen? whether they lived according to the severities of their orders? how their lands and revenues were managed? what hospitality was kept? what care was taken of the novices? what benefices were in their gift, and how they disposed of them? how the enclosures of the nunneries were kept? whether the nuns went abroad, or if men were admitted to come to them? how they employed their time, and what priests they had as their confessors?

The visiters were also ordered to deliver some injunctions in the king's name, as to his supremacy, and the act of succession; and were authorized to absolve every one from any rules or oaths of obedience to the pope.

They were also ordered to take care that the abbots should not have choice dishes, but plain tables for hospitality; and that the scriptures should be read at meals; that they should have daily lectures of divinity; and maintain some of every house at the university, and to require that the abbot of each monastery should instruct the monks in true religion, and show them that it did not consist in outward ceremonies, but in clearness of heart, purity of life, and the worshipping of God in spirit and truth. Rules were given about their revenues, and against admitting any under twenty years of age; and the visiters were empowered to punish offenders, or to bring them to answer before the visiter-general.

The visiters went over England, and found in many places monstrous disorders. The most horrible and disgusting crimes were found to be practiced in many of the houses; and vice and cruelty were more frequently the inmates of these pretended *sanctuaries* than religion and piety. The report contained many abominable things, not fit to be mentioned: some of these were printed, but the greater part was lost.

The first house that was surrendered to the king was Langden, in Kent; the abbot of which was found in bed with a woman, who went in the habit of a lay brother. To prevent greater evil to himself, he and ten of his monks signed a resignation of their house to the king. Two other monasteries in the same county, Folkstone and

Dover, followed their example.   And in the following year four others made the like surrenders.

Death of Queen Catharine.

On January 8, 1536, queen Catharine died.   She had been resolute in maintaining her title and state, saying, that since the pope had judged her marriage was good, she would die rather than do any thing to prejudice it.   She desired to be buried among the Observant friars, who had most strongly supported her, and suffered for her cause. She ordered 500 masses to be said for her soul; and that one of her women should go a pilgrimage to our lady of Walsingham, and give two hundred nobles on her way to the poor.   When she found death approaching, she wrote to the emperor, recommended her daughter to his care. also to the king, with this inscription, " My dear lord, king, and husband."   She forgave him all the injuries he had done her; and wished him to have regard to his soul. She recommended her daughter to his protection, and desired him to be kind to her three maids, and to pay her servants a year's wages; and concluded with, " Mine eyes desire you above all things."   She expired at Kimbolton, in the fiftieth year of her age, having been thirty-three years in England.   She was devout and exemplary; patient and charitable.   Her virtues and her sufferings created an esteem for her in all ranks of people.   The king ordered her to be buried in the abbey of Peterborough, and was somewhat affected at her death; but the natural barbarity of his temper prevented him from feeling much remorse on the reflection that he had embittered the existence of a woman who loved and reverenced him.

The same year the parliament confirmed the act empowering thirty-two persons to revise the ecclesiastical laws; but no time being limited for finishing it, it had no effect.   The chief business of this session, was the suppressing of all monasteries whose revenues did not exceed £200 a year   The act sets forth the great disorders of those houses, and the many unsuccessful attempts made to reform them.   The religious that were in them were ordered to be placed in the greater houses, and the revenues given to the king.   The king was also empowered to make new foundations of such of the suppressed houses as he pleased, which were in all three hundred and seventy This parliament, after six years continuance, was now dis solved.

A Translation of the Bible proposed.

In a convocation which sat at this time, a motion was made for translating the Bible into English, which had been promised when Tindal's translation was condemned, but was afterward laid aside by the clergy as neither necessary nor expedient. It was said, that those whose office it was to teach the people the word of God, did all they could to suppress it. Moses, the prophets, and the apostles wrote in the vulgar tongue : Christ directed the peo ple to search the scriptures ; and as soon as any nation was converted to the Christian religion, the Bible was translated into their language ; nor was it ever taken out of the hands of the people, till the Christian religion was so corrupted, that it was deemed impolitic to trust them with a book, which would so manifestly discover those errors ; and the legends, as agreeing better with those abuses, were read instead of the word of God.

Cranmer thought that putting the Bible in the people's hands would be the most effectual means for promoting the reformation ; and therefore moved that the king might be prayed to order it. But Gardiner, and all the other party opposed this vehemently. They said all the extravagant opinions lately broached in Germany arose from the indiscreet use of the scriptures. Some of those opinions were at this time disseminated in England, both against the divinity and incarnation of Christ, and the usefulness of the sacraments. They therefore argued, that during these distractions the use of the scriptures would prove a great snare, and proposed that instead of them, that there might be some short exposition of the Christian religion put into the people's hands, which might keep them in a certain subjection to the king and the church. But in spite of their arguments, the question of the translation was carried in the convocation in the affirmative.

The courtiers were much divided on this point ; some said, if the king gave way to it, he would never be able

after that to govern his people, and that they would break
into many divisions.   But on the other hand, it was maintained, that nothing would make the difference between
the pope's power and the king's supremacy appear more
eminently, than for the one to give the people the free use
of the word of God; while the other kept them in darkness, and ruled them by a blind obedience.   It would do
much also in extinguishing the interests that either the
pope or the monks had among the people.   The Bible
would teach them, that they had been long deceived by impostures, which had no foundation in the scriptures.   These
reasons, strengthened by the queen's representations to the
king, prevailed so far with him, that he gave order for setting about this important affair with all possible haste;
and within three years the impression of it was finished.

The popish party saw, with disappointment and concern, that the queen was the great obstacle to their designs.
She grew not only in the king's esteem, but in the love of
the nation.   During the last nine months of her life she
bestowed above £14,000 in alms to the poor, and seemed
to delight in doing good.   Soon after Catharine's death,
Anne bore a dead son, which was believed to have made
an unfavourable impression on the king's mind.   It was also
considered, that now queen Catharine was dead, the king
might marry another, and regain the friendship of the pope
and the emperor, and that the issue by any other marriage
would never be questioned.   With these reasons of state
the king's affections joined: for he was now in love (if so
heartless a monster was capable of feeling love) with Jane
Seymour, whose disposition was tempered between the
gravity of Catharine and the gayety of Anne.   The latter
used all possible arts to reinflame his dying affection; but
he was weary of her, and therefore determined on her destruction; to effect which he soon found a pretence.   Lady
Rochford, wife to the brother of Anne, basely accused her
husband of a criminal intercourse with his sister; and
Norris, Weston and Brereton, the king's servants, with
Smeton, a musician, were accused of the same crime.

She was confined to her Chamber, and the five persons
before mentioned were sent to the Tower, whither the
next day, she was also carried.   On the river some privy
counsellors came to examine her, but she made deep pro

testations of her innocence; and on landing at the Tower she fell on her knees, and prayed God to assist her; protesting her innocence of the crimes laid to her charge. Those who were imprisoned on her account denied every thing, except Smeton, who, from hopes of favour and acquittal, confessed that he had been criminally connected with her; but denied it when he was afterward brought to execution.

The queen was of a lively temper, and having resided long in the French court, had imbibed somewhat of the levities of that people. She was also free from pride, and hence, in her exterior, she might have condescended too much to her familiar servants.

Every court-sycophant was now her enemy; and Cranmer formed the only honourable exception. An order was therefore procured, forbidding him to come to court; yet he wrote the king a long letter upon this critical juncture, wherein he acknowledged, that " if the things reported of the queen were true, it was the greatest affliction that ever befel the king, and therefore exhorted him to bear it with patience and submission to the will of God; he confessed he never had a better opinion of any woman than of her; and that, next the king, he was more bound to her than all persons living, and therefore he begged the king's leave to pray that she might be found innocent; he loved her not a little, because of the love which she seemed to bear to God and his gospel; but if she was guilty, all that loved the gospel must hate her, as having been the greatest slander possible to the gospel; but he prayed the king not to entertain any prejudice to the gospel on her account. nor give the world to say, that his love to that was founded on the influence she had with him." But the king was inexorable. The prisoners were put on their trial; when Smeton pleaded guilty, as before; the rest pleaded not guilty; but all were condemned.

Trial and Execution of the Queen.

On the 15th of May the queen and her brother, lord Rochford, were tried before the duke of Norfolk, as high steward, and a court of twenty-seven peers. The crime charged on her was, that she had procured her brother and

four others to lie with her; and had often said to them,
that the king never had her heart; and this was to the
slander of the issue begotten between the king and her,
which was treasonable to slander the issue of the king,
so that the act made in the 25th of the marriage was now turned to
her ruin. They would not now acknowledge her the
king's lawful wife, and they charged her not heard the treason
committed in the 25th of Edward III. It does not appear what
her answer was to this, and I suppose her conviction being secretly foregone... Norris being ac-
cused... and for her...
it... was condemned... and to
be... as to... Lady Wingfield, who... to have
been... the only... of all these... has... now
been... very... doubtful.

The court of Norreys, her husband was one of the judges. He
had formerly been in love with the queen, and either from
jealousy... his jealousy, or from some other cause, he became so... so sick that he could not stay out the trial.
It was... said that this earl had said to the earl of
Wiltshire, that he had engaged himself so far with her, that

... of the... which was perhaps done by some
judges... the words of the future tense; but no
judge said that... the words of the present tense, could

annu the subsequent marriage. Perhaps the queen did not understand that difference, or probably the fear of a terrible death wrought so much on her, that she confessed the contract; but the earl denied it positively, and took the sacrament upon it, wishing that it might turn to his damnation if there were ever either contract or promise of marriage between them. Upon her own confession, however, her marriage with the king was judged null from the beginning, and she was condemned, although nothing could be more contradictory; for if she was never the king's wife, she could not be guilty of adultery, there being no breach of the rites of wedlock, if they were never truly married. But the king was resolved both to be rid of her, and to illegitimatise his daughter by her.

The day before her death, she sent her last message to the king, asserting her innocence, recommending her daughter to his care, and thanking him for his advancing her first to be a marchioness, then a queen, and now, when he could raise her no higher on earth, for sending her to be a saint in Heaven. The lieutenant of the Tower wrote to Cromwell, that it was not fit to publish the time of her execution, for the fewer that were present, the better it would be, since he believed she would declare her innocence at the hour of her death; for that morning she had made great protestations of it when she received the sacrament, and seemed to long for death with great joy and pleasure. On being told that the executioner, who had been sent for expressly from France, was very skilful, she expressed great happiness; for she said she had a very short neck, at which she laughed.

A little before noon, she was brought to the place of execution; there were present some of the chief officers and great men of the court. She was, it seems, prevailed on, out of regard to her daughter, to make no reflections on the cruel treatment she met with, nor to say any thing touching the grounds on which sentence passed against her. She only desired that all would judge the best; she highly commended the king, and then took her leave of the world. She remained for some time in her private devotions, and concluded, "To Christ I commend my soul!" upon which the executioner struck off her head; and so little respect was paid to her body, that it was with brutal insolence put

in a chest of elm tree, made to send arrows into Ireland,
and then buried in the chapel of the Tower.   Norris then
had his life promised him if he would accuse her.   But
this faithful and virtuous servant said he knew she was
innocent, and would die a thousand deaths rather than de-
fame her; so he and the three others were beheaded, and
all of them continued to the last to vindicate her.   The
day after queen Anne's death the king married Jane Seymour, who gained more upon him than all his wives ever
did; but she was fortunate that she did not outlive his love
to her.

The Pope proposes a reconciliation with the King.

Pope Clement the Seventh was now dead, and cardinal
Farnese succeeded him by the name of Paul the Third,
who made an attempt to reconcile himself with the king;
but, when that was rejected, thundered out a most terrible
sentence of deposition against him.   Yet now, since the
two queens upon whose account the breach was made were
out of the way, he thought it a fit time to attempt the recovery of the papal interest, and ordered Cassali to let the
king know that he had been driven, very much against his
mind, to pass sentence against him, and that now it would
be easy for him to recover the favour of the apostolic see.
But the king, instead of hearkening to the proposition,
caused two acts to be passed, by one of which it was
made a præmunire for any one to acknowledge the authority of the pope, or to persuade others to it; and, by the
other, all bulls, and all privileges flowing from them, were
declared null and void; only marriages or consecrations
made by virtue of them were excepted.   All who enjoyed
privileges by these bulls were required to bring them into
the chancery, upon which the archbishop was to make a
new grant of them, which, being confirmed under the great
seal, was to be of full force in law.

Debates of the Convocation.

The convocation sat at the same time, and was much
employed.   Latimer preached a Latin sermon before
them; he was the most celebrated preacher of that time;

the simplicity of his matter, and his zeal in expressing it, being preferred to more elaborate compositions. The convocation first confirmed the sentence of divorce between the king and queen Anne. Then the lower house made an address to the upper house, complaining of sixty-seven opinions, which they found were very much spread in the kingdom. These were either the tenets of the old Lollards, or of the new Reformers, or of the Anabaptists; and many of them were only indiscreet expressions, which might have flowed from the heat and folly of some rash zealots, who had endeavonred to disgrace both the received doctrines and rites. They also complained of some bishops who were wanting in their duty to suppress such abuses. This was understood as a reflection on Cranmer, Shaxton, and Latimer, the first of whom it was thought was now declining, in consequence of the fall of queen Anne.

But all these projects failed, for Cranmer was now fully established in the king's favour; and Cromwell was sent to the convocation, with a message from his majesty, that they should reform the rites and ceremonies of the church according to the rules set down in scripture, which ought to be preferred to all glosses or decrees of popes.

There was one Alesse, a Scotchman, whom Cromwell entertained in his house, who being appointed to deliver his opinion, showed that there were no sacraments instituted by Christ but baptism and the Lord's supper. Stokesly answered him in a long discourse upon the principles of the school divinity; upon which Cranmer took occasion to show the vanity of that sort of learning, and the uncertainty of tradition: and that religion had been so corrupted in the latter ages, that there was no finding out the truth but by resting on the authority of the scriptures. Fox, bishop of Hereford, seconded them, and told him that the world was now awake, and would be no longer imposed on by the niceties and dark terms of the schools; for the laity now did not only read the scriptures in the vulgar tongues, but searched the originals themselves; therefore they must not think to govern them as they had been governed in the times of ignorance. Among the bishops, Cranmer, Goodrick, Shaxton, Latimer, Fox, Hilsey, and Barlow, pressed the reformation; but Lee, archbishop of York, Stokesley, Tunstall, Gardiner. Longland, and several others opposed

23*

it as much. The contest would have been much sharper, had not the king sent some articles to be considered of by them, when the following mixture of truth and error was agreed upon.

1. That the bishops and preachers ought to instruct the people according to the scriptures, the three creeds, and the four first general councils.

2. That baptism was necessary to salvation, and that children ought to be baptized for the pardon of original sin, and obtaining the Holy Ghost.

3. That penance was necessary to salvation, and that it consisted in confession, contrition, and amendment of life with the external works of charity, to which a lively faith ought to be joined ; and that confession to a priest was necessary where it might be had.

4. That in the eucharist under the forms of bread and wine, the very flesh and blood of Christ was received.

5. That justification was the remission of sins, and a perfect renovation in Christ ; and that not only outward good works, but inward holiness, was absolutely necessary. As for the outward ceremonies, the people were to be taught, 1. That it was meet to have images in churches, but they ought to avoid all such superstition as had been usual in times past, and not to worship the image, but only God. 2. That they were to honour the saints, but not to expect those things from them which God only gives. 3. That they might pray to them for their intercession, but all superstitious abuses were to cease ; and if the king should lessen the number of saint's days, they ought to obey him. 4. That the use of the ceremonies was good, and that they contained many mystical significations that tended to raise the mind toward God ; such were vestments in divine worship, holy water, holy bread, the carrying of candles and palms and ashes, and creeping to the cross, and hallowing the font, with other exorcisms. 5. That it was good to pray for departed souls, and to have masses and obsequies said for them ; but the scriptures having neither declared in what place they were, nor what torments they suffered, that was uncertain, and to be left to God ; therefore all the abuses of the pope's pardons, or saying masses in such and such places, or before such images, were to be put away.

These articles were signed by Cromwell, the two archbishops, sixteen bishops, forty abbots and priors, and fifty of the lower house. The king afterward added a preface, declaring the pains that he and the clergy had been at for the removing the differences in religion which existed in the nation, and that he approved of these articles, and required all his subjects to accept them, and he would be thereby encouraged to take further pains in the like matters for the future.

On the publication of these things, the favourers of the reformation, though they did not approve of every particular, yet were well pleased to see things brought under examination; and since some things were at this time changed, they did not doubt but more changes would follow; they were glad that the scriptures and the ancient creeds were made the standards of the faith, without adding tradition, and that the nature of justification and the gospel-covenant was rightly stated; that the immediate worship of images and saints was condemned, and that purgatory was left uncertain: but the necessity of auricular confession and the corporeal presence, the doing reverence to images and praying to saints, were of hard digestion to them; yet they rejoiced to see some grosser abuses removed, and a reformation once set on foot. The popish party, on the other hand, were sorry to see four sacraments passed over in silence, and the trade in masses for the dead put down.

At the same time other things were in consultation, though not finished. Cranmer offered a paper to the king, exhorting him to proceed to further reformation, and that nothing should be determined without clear proofs from scripture, the departing from which had been the occasion of all the errors that had been in the church. Many things were now acknowledged to be erroneous, for which some not long before had suffered death. He therefore proposed several points to be discussed, as, Whether there were a purgatory? Whether departed saints ought to be invocated, or tradition to be believed? Whether images ought to be considered only as representations of history? and Whether it were lawful for the clergy to marry? He prayed the king not to give judgment in these points till

he heard them well examined : but all this was carried no
further at that period.

At this time visiters were appointed to survey all the
lesser monasteries : they were to examine the state of
their revenues and goods and take inventories of them,
and to take their seals into their keeping ; they were to
try how many of the religious would return to a secular
course of life ; and these were to be sent to the archbishop
of Canterbury, or the lord chancellor, and an allowance
was to be given them for their journey ; but those who intended to continue in that state were to be removed to
some of the great monasteries.   A pension was also to be
assigned to the abbot or prior during life ; and the visiters
were particularly to examine what leases had been made
during the last year.   Ten thousand of the religious were
by this means driven to seek for their livings with forty
shillings, and a gown a man.   Their goods and plate were
estimated at £100,000, and the valued rents of their
houses were £32,000 ; but they were above ten times as
much.   The churches and cloisters were in most places
pulled down, and the materials sold.

This procedure gave great discontent ; and the monks
were now as much pitied, as they were formerly hated.
The nobility and gentry, who provided for their younger
children or friends by putting them in those sanctuaries,
were sensible of their loss.   The people, who as they travelled over the country found abbeys to be places of reception to strangers, saw what they were to lose.   But the
superstitious, who thought their friends must now lie still
in purgatory, without relief from the masses, were out of
measure offended.   But to remove this discontent, Cromwell advised the king to sell these lands at very easy rates
to the nobility and gentry, and to oblige them to keep up
the wonted hospitality.   This would both be grateful to
them, and would engage them to assist the crown in the
maintenance of the changes that had been made ; since
their own interests would be interwoven with those of their
sovereign.   And, a clause in the act empowering the king
to found anew such houses as he should think fit, there
were fifteen monasteries and sixteen nunneries newly
founded.   These were bound to obey such rules as the

king should send them, and to pay him tenths and first fruits. But all this did not pacify the people, for there was still a great outcry. The clergy studied much to inflame the nation, and urged that a heretical prince deposed by the pope was no more to be acknowledged, and that it was a part of the papal power to depose kings, and give away their dominions.

There were some injunctions given out by Cromwell, which increased this discontent. All churchmen were required every Sunday for a quarter of a year, and twice every quarter after that, to preach against the pope's power, and to explain the six articles of the convocation. They were forbidden to extol images, relics, or pilgrimages; but to exhort to works of charity. They were also required to teach the Lord's prayer, the creed, and the ten commandments in English, and to explain these carefully, and instruct the children well in them. They were to perform the divine offices reverently, to study the scriptures much, and be exemplary in their lives. Those who did not reside were to give the fortieth part of their income to the poor, and for every hundred pounds a year they were to maintain a scholar at some grammar-school, or the university; and if the parsorage-house was in decay they were ordered to apply a fifth part of their benefice for repairing it.

Rebellions in Lincolnshire and in Yorkshire.

While these things were passing in the convocation, the common people, instigated by the priests, raised a rebellion in Lincolnshire and Yorkshire, which at first appeared formidable, but by the prudent measures of the king and ministry was soon suppressed, almost without the loss of blood.

Impostures of images and relics discovered.

They disclosed to the world many impostures about pretended relics, and wonderful images, to which pilgrimages had been made. At Reading was preserved the wing of an angel, who, according to the monks, brought over the point of the spear that pierced our Saviour's side;

and as many pieces of the *real* cross were found, as when joined together would have made half a dozen.

The "Rood of Grace," at Boxley, in Kent, had been much esteemed, and drawn many pilgrims to it, on account of its possessing the wonderful powers of bowing its head, rolling its eyes, smiling, and frowning, to the great astonishment and terror of the credulous multitude, who imputed it to a divine power : but all this was now discovered to be a cheat, and it was brought up to St. Paul's cross; where all the springs were shown by which its motions were governed.

At Hales, in Gloucestershire, some of the blood of Christ was shown in a vial ; and it was believed that none could see it who were in mortal sin. Those who could bestow liberal presents were, of course, gratified, by being led to believe that they were in a state of grace. This miracle consisted in the blood of a duck renewed every week, put in a vial, very thick on one side and thin on the other, and either side turned toward the pilgrim, as the priests were satisfied or not with his oblations. Several other similar impostures were discovered, which contributed much to the undeceiving of the people.

The rich shrine of Thomas a Becket at Canterbury was destroyed, and an immense quantity of gold and precious stones, offered by the deluded victims of superstition in honour of that factious priest and " saint after the pope's own heart," were confiscated and carried away.

When these proceedings were known at Rome, the pope immediately fulminated against the king all the thunders of his spiritual store-house ; absolved his subjects from their allegiance, and his allies from their treaties with him; and exhorted all Christians to make war against and extirpate him from the face of the earth. But the age of crusades was past, and this display of impotent malice produced only contempt in the minds of the king and his advisers, who steadily proceeded in the great work of reformation ; and the translation of the Bible into English being now completed, it was printed and ordered to be read in all churches, with permission for every person to read it who might be so disposed.

But, notwithstanding the king's disagreement with the pope on many subjects, there was one point on which they were alike—they were both intolerant, furious bigots; and while the former was excommunicated as a *heretic* he was himself equally zealous in rooting out *heresy*, and burning all who presumed to depart from the standard of faith which he had established

Gardiner, bishop of Winchester, strengthened this disposition of the king, and persuaded him, under the pretext of a zeal for religion, to persecute the Sacramentarists, or those who denied the corporeal presence in the sacrament.

Martyrdom of John Lambert.

In consequence of this determination, John Lambert, a teacher of languages in London, who had drawn up ten arguments against the tenets of Dr. Taylor, on the above subject, as delivered in a sermon at St. Peter's church, and presented them to the Doctor, was brought before the archbishop's court to defend his writings; and, having appealed to the king, the royal theologian, who was proud of every occasion of displaying his talents and learning resolved to hear him in person. He therefore issued a commission, ordering all his nobility and bishops to repair to London, to assist him against heretics.

A day was appointed for the disputation, when a great number of persons of all ranks assembled to witness the proceedings, and Lambert was brought from his prison by a guard, and placed directly opposite to the king.

Henry being seated on his throne, and surrounded by the peers, bishops, and judges, regarded the prisoner with a stern countenance, and then commanded Day, bishop of Chichester, to state the occasion of the present assembly.

The bishop made a long oration, stating that, although the king had abolished the papal authority in England, it was not to be supposed that he would allow heretics with impunity to disturb and trouble the church of which he was the head. He had therefore determined to punish all schismatics; and being willing to have the advice of his bishops and counsellors on so great an occasion, had assembled them to hear the arguments in the present case.

The oration being concluded, the king ordered Lambert to declare his opinion as to the sacrament of the Lord's

Supper, which he did, by denying it to be the body of Christ.

The king then commanded Cranmer to refute his assertion, which the latter attempted: but was interrupted by Gardiner, who vehemently interposed, and, being unable to bring argument to his aid, sought by abuse and virulence to overpower his antagonist, who was not allowed to answer the taunts and insults of the bishop.

Tonstal and Stokesly followed in the same course, and Lambert, beginning to answer them, was silenced by the king. The other bishops then each made a speech in confutation of one of Lambert's arguments, till the whole ten were answered, or rather, railed against; for he was not permitted to defend them, however misrepresented.

At last, when the day was passed, and torches began to be lighted, the king desiring to break up this pretended disputation, said to Lambert, " What sayest thou now, after all these great labours which thou hast taken upon thee, and all the reasons and instructions of these learned men? Art thou not yet satisfied? Wilt thou live or die? What sayest thou? Thou hast yet free choice."

Lambert answered, " I yield and submit myself wholly unto the will of your majesty." " Then," said the king, " commit thyself unto the hands of God, and not into mine."

Lambert replied, " I commend my soul into the hands of God, but my body I wholly yield and submit unto your clemency." To which the king answered, " If you do commit yourself unto my judgment, you must die, for I will not be a patron unto heretics;" and, turning to Cromwell, he said, " Read the sentence of condemnation against him," which he accordingly did.

Upon the day appointed for this holy martyr to suffer, he was brought out of the prison at eight o'clock in the morning to the house of Cromwell, and carried into his inner chamber, where, it is said, Cromwell desired his forgiveness for what he had done. Lambert being at last admonished that the hour of his death was at hand, and being brought out of the chamber into the hall, saluted the gentlemen present, and sat down to breakfast with them, snowing neither sadness nor fear. When breakfast was

ended, he was carried straight to the place of execution at Smithfield.

The manner of his death was dreadful: for after his legs were consumed and burned up to the stumps, and but a small fire was left under him, two of the inhuman monsters who stood on each side of him, pierced him with their halberds, and lifted him up as far as the chain would reach; while he, raising his half consumed hands cried unto the people in these words: "None but Christ, none but Christ;" and so being let down again from their halberds, fell into the fire and there ended his life.

The popish party greatly triumphed at this event, and endeavoured to improve it. They persuaded the king of the good effects it would have on his people, who would in this see his zeal for the faith; and they forgot not to magnify all that he had said, as if it had been uttered by an oracle, which proved him to be both "Defender of the Faith and Supreme Head of the Church." All this wrought so much on the king, that he resolved to call a parliament for the contradictory purposes of suppressing the still remaining monasteries, and extirpating the "new opinions."

The Act of the Six Articles.

The parliament accordingly met on the 28th of April, 1538; and after long debates, passed what was called " a bill of religion," containing six articles, by which it was declared, that the elements in the sacrament were the real body and blood of Christ; that communion was necessary only in one kind; that priests ought not to marry; that vows of chastity ought to be observed; that private masses were lawful and useful; and that auricular confession was necessary.

This act gave great satisfaction to the popish party, and induced them to consent more readily to the act for suppressing the monasteries, which immediately followed; by virtue of which, their total dissolution soon after took place. The king founded six new bishoprics from a small portion of their immense revenues, and lavished the remainder on his profligate courtiers and favourites.

In 1540 a bill was passed for the suppression of the

24

knights of St. John of Jerusalem, both in England and
Ireland.

Fall of Cromwell.

In this year, also, Cromwell, who had so long been a
favourite of the king, and had held the highest offices, was
suddenly disgraced, and committed to the Tower. He had
many enemies; the nobility, from jealousy at beholding a
man of obscure birth promoted to the peerage, and enjoying great power and influence; and the popish clergy
from the belief that the suppression of the monasteries and
the innovations on their religion were principally produced
by his counsels. The fickle tyrant whom he had so long
and faithfully served, was also displeased with him as the
adviser of his marriage with Anne of Cleves, whom he
was now anxious to get rid of, in order to obtain the hand
of Catharine Howard, niece of the duke of Norfolk. He
suspected him likewise of secretly encouraging an opposition to the six articles, and hoped, by sacrificing a man
who was obnoxious to the catholics, to regain their affections, forfeited by his sanguinary and rapacious proceedings.

Cromwell experienced the common fate of fallen ministers; his pretended friends forsook him, and his enemies pursued their revenge against him without opposition,
except from Cranmer, who, with a rare fidelity, dared
to avow an attachment to him, even at this time, and
wrote a very earnest letter to the king in his favour. But
Henry was not easily turned from his purpose, and being
resolved on the ruin of Cromwell, was not to be dissuaded
from his design.

In the house of lords a bill of attainder was passed with
the most indecent haste; but in the commons it met with
opposition, and, after a delay of ten days, a new bill was
framed, and sent up to the lords, in which Cromwell was
designated as " the most corrupt traitor ever known;" his
treasons, as afterward specified, consisting in the countenance and favour he had shown to the reformers. On
these grounds he was attainted both for treason and heresy.

The king now proceeded with his divorce; and, although
there was no reason to dispute the legality of his marriage

with Anne of Cleves, still, as she was disagreeable to his royal taste, his sycophants were too well taught to offer the least opposition to his wishes. The convocation unanimously dissolved the marriage, and gave him liberty to marry again; indeed it is probable, that if he had desired to have two or more wives at once, the measure would have been sanctioned, so base and servile were the courtiers and priests by whom this monstrous tyrant was surrounded. The queen continued to reside in England, being declared "The adopted sister" of the king, and having a pension of £4000 per annum.

Cromwell was executed on the 28th of July, and his fall gave a great check to the reformation in England; Cranmer being left almost alone to struggle against a host of enemies.

Notwithstanding the power of the pope was at an end in the kingdom, and a great progress was already made toward a reformation, still a spirit of persecution was cherished by the reformers themselves, against all such as dared to think more liberally than themselves, and in this were they encouraged by the artful insinuations of the papists, who represented to the king the good effects that would result from such measures in effecting the suppression of heresy, and bringing about a reconciliation with the pope. The martyrdom of Lambert was therefore soon followed by that of Dr. Barnes, Thomas Garret, William Jerome, Bernard and Merton, Robert Testwood, Anthony Pearsons, Adam Damlip, Anne Askew, Thomas Benet, with a great number of others, for presuming to differ from the king on the subject of the real body and blood of Christ in the sacrament of the Lord's Supper, and some other points. These all suffered martyrdom by burning; the particulars of the first three we have only room to mention.

Martyrdom of Dr. Robert Barnes.

Dr. Barnes was educated in the university of Louvain, in Brabant. On his return to England he went to Cambridge, where he was made prior and master of the house of the Augustines. The darkest ignorance pervaded the university at the time of his arrival there: but he, zealous to

promote knowledge and truth, began to instruct the stu
dents in the classical languages, and, with the assistance
of Parnel, his scholar, whom he had brought from Louvain,
soon caused learning to flourish, and the university to bear
a very different aspect.

These foundations being laid, he began to read openly
the epistles of St. Paul, and to teach in greater purity the
doctrine of Christ. He preached and disputed with great
warmth against the luxuries of the higher clergy, particularly against cardinal Wolsey, and the lamentable hypocrisy of the times. But still he remained ignorant of the
great cause of these evils, namely, the idolatry and superstition of the church; and while he declaimed against the
stream, he himself drank at the spring, and bowed down
to idols. At length, happily becoming acquainted with
Bilney, he was by that martyr wholly converted unto
Christ.

The first sermon he preached of this truth was on the
Sunday before Christmas-day, at St. Edward's church, in
Cambridge. His theme was the epistle of the same Sun-
day, " *Gaudete in Domino.*" &c. For this sermon he
was immediately accused of heresy by two fellows of
King's Hall, before the vice-chancellor. Then Dr. Notto-
ris, a bitter enemy to Christ, moved Barnes to recant; but
he refused, as appears in his book which he wrote to king
Henry in English, confuting the judgment of cardinal
Wolsey, and the residue of the papistical bishops.

After preaching some time, Barnes was arrested openly
in the convocation-house: brought to London, and the
next morning carried to the palace of cardinal Wolsey,
at Westminster, where after waiting the whole day, he
was at night brought before the cardinal in his chamber
of state. " Is this," said Wolsey, " Dr Barnes, who is
accused of heresy?"—" Yes, and please your grace," replied the cardinal's secretary, " and I trust you will find
him reformable, for he is learned and wise.'

" What, Mr. Doctor," said Wolsey, " had you not a
sufficient scope in the scriptures to teach the people, but
that my golden shoes, my poll-axes, my pillars, my golden
cushions, my crosses, did so sore offend you, that you must
make us *ridiculum caput* amongst the people, who that
day laughed us to scorn? Verily it was a sermon fitter to

be preached on a stage than in a pulpit; for at last you said, 'I wear a pair of red gloves, I should say bloody gloves,' quoth you, 'that I should not be cold in the midst of my ceremonies.'"

Dr. Barnes answered, "I spake nothing but the truth, out of the scriptures, according to my conscience, and according to the old doctors." And then he delivered him six sheets of paper written to confirm and corroborate his sentiments.

The cardinal received them smiling, saying, "We perceive then that you intend to stand to your articles, and to show your learning."

"Yea," said Barnes, "that I do by God's grace, with your lordship's favour."

He answered, "Such as you bear us little favour and the catholic church. I will ask you a question; whether do you think it more necessary that I should have all this royalty, because I represent the king's majesty in all the high courts of this realm, to the terror and keeping down of all rebellious treasons, traitors, all the wicked and corrupt members of this commonwealth, or to be as simple as you would have us, to sell all these things, and to give them to the poor, who shortly will cast them into the dirt; and to pull away this princely dignity, which is a terror to the wicked, and to follow your council?"

"I think it necessary," said Barnes, "to be sold and given to the poor. For this is not becoming your calling; nor is the king's majesty maintained by your pomp and poll-axes, but by God, who saith, kings and their majesty reign and stand by me."

Then answered the cardinal, "Lo, master doctors, here is the learned wise man that you told me of." Then they kneeled down and said, "We desire your grace to be good unto him, for he will be reformable."

"Then," said he, "stand you up; for your sakes and the university we will be good unto him.—How say you, master doctor, do you not know that I am able to dispense in all matters concerning religion within this realm, as much as the pope may?" He said, "I know it to be so."

"Will you then be ruled by us? and we will do all things for your honesty, and for the honesty of the university."   24*

He answered, "I thank your grace for your good wil', I will stick to the holy scripture, and to God's book, according to the simple talent that God hath lent me."

"Well," said he, "thou shalt have thy learning tried at the uttermost, and thou shalt have the law."

He was then committed to the custody of the sergeant at arms, who had brought him to London and by whom he was the next morning brought before the bishops; who, on examining the articles of his faith, which he had delivered to the cardinal, asked him if he would sign them, which he did, and was thereupon committed to the Fleet.

On the Saturday following he was again brought before the bishops, who called upon him to know whether he would abjure or burn. He was then greatly agitated, and felt inclined rather to burn than abjure; but was persuaded by some persons to abjure, which he at length consented to do, and the abjuration being put into his hand, he abjured as it was there written, and then he subscribed it with his own hand; yet his judges would scarcely receive him into the bosom of the church as they termed it. Then they put him to an oath, and charged him to do all that they commanded him, which he accordingly promised.

He was then again committed to the Fleet; and the next morning was brought to St. Paul's church, with five others who had abjured. Here the cardinal, bishops, and clergy being assembled in great pomp, the bishop of Rochester preached a sermon against the doctrines of Luther and Barnes, during which the latter was commanded to kneel down and ask forgiveness of God, and the catholic church, and the cardinal's grace; after which he was ordered, at the end of the sermon, to declare that he was used more charitably than he deserved, his heresies being so horrible and so detestable: once more he kneeled, desiring of the people forgiveness and to pray for him. This farce being ended, the cardinal departed under a canopy, with the bishops and mitred abbots, who accompanied him to the outer gate of the church, when they returned. Then Barnes, and the others who had abjured, were carried thrice about the fire, after which they were brought to the bishops, and kneeled down for absolution. The bishop of Rochester standing up, declared that Dr. Barnes with the others were received into the church again. After which they were recommitted to the Fleet during the cardinal's pleasure.

Dr. Barnes having remained in the Fleet half a year, was placed in the custody of the Austin Friars in London; from whence he was removed to the Austin Friars of Northampton, there to be burned; of which intention, however, he was perfectly ignorant. Being informed of the base designs of his enemies, however, he, by a stratagem, escaped, and reached Antwerp, where he dwelt in safety, and was honoured with the friendship of the best and most eminent reformers of the time, as Luther, Melancthon, the duke of Saxony, and others. Indeed, so great was his reputation, that the king of Denmark sent him as one of his ambassadors to England; when sir Thomas More, at that time lord chancellor, wished to have him apprehended on the former charge. Henry, however, would not allow of this, considering it as a breach of the most sacred laws, to offer violence to the person of an ambassador, under any pretence. Barnes therefore remained in England unmolested; and departed again without restraint. He returned to Wittemberg, where he remained to forward his works in print which he had begun, after which he returned again to England, and continued a faithful preacher in London, being well entertained and promoted during the ascendency of Anne Boleyn. He was afterward sent ambassador by Henry to the duke of Cleves, upon the business of the marriage between Anne of Cleves and the king; and gave great satisfaction in every duty which was entrusted to him.

Not long after the arrival of Gardiner from France, Dr. Barnes and other reformed preachers, were apprehended and carried before the king at Hampton Court, where Barnes was examined. The king being desirous to bring about an agreement between him and Gardiner, granted him leave to go home with the bishop to confer with him. But they not agreeing, Gardiner and his party sought to entangle and entrap Barnes and his friends in further danger, which not long after was brought to pass. For, by certain complaints made to the king of them, they were enjoined to preach three sermons the following Easter at the Spittle; at which sermons, besides other reporters which were sent thither, Stephen Gardiner also was there present, sitting with the mayor, either to bear record of their recantation, or else, as the Pharisees came to Christ, to ensnare them in their talk, if they should speak any thing amiss. Barnes preached first; and at the conclusion of his sermon, requested Gardiner, if he thought he had said nothing contradictory to truth, to hold up his hand in the face of all present; upon which Gardiner immediately held up his finger. Notwithstanding this, they were all three sent for to Hampton Court, whence they were conducted to the Tower, where they remained till they were brought out to death.

Story of Thomas Garret.

Thomas Garret was a curate of London. About the year 1526, he came to Oxford, and brought with him sundry books in Latin, treating of the Scriptures, with the first part of *Unio dissidentium*, and Tindal's first translation of the New Testament in English, which books he sold to several scholars in Oxford.

After he had been there awhile, and had disposed of those books, news came from London that he was sought for in that city, to be apprehended as a heretic, and to be imprisoned for selling those heretical publications, as they were termed. For it was not unknown to cardinal Wolsey, the bishop of London, and others, that Mr. Garret had a great number of those books, and that he was gone to Oxford to sell them, to such as he knew to be lovers of the gospel. Wherefore they determined to make a privy search through all Oxford, to apprehend and imprison him, and to burn all his books, and him too if they could. But, happily, one of the proctors gave Mr. Garret secret warning of this privy search, and advised that he should immediately and privately depart from Oxford.

By means of another friend, a curacy was procured for him in Dorsetshire, and he set out for that country, but being waylaid by his enemies, was unable to proceed, and therefore returned to Oxford, where he was, on the same night, apprehended in his bed, and was ordered, by the commissary of the University, to be confined in his own chamber, till further directions were received respecting him. He escaped in disguise, but was retaken, and being convicted as a heretic, carried a fagot in token of his abjuration, at St. Mary's church, in Oxford; after which we meet with nothing further respecting him till his apprehension with Dr. Barnes.

Story of William Jerome.

William Jerome was vicar of Stepney, and being convinced of, and disgusted at, the errors of the church of Rome, he preached with great zeal, and set up the pure and simple doctrines of the gospel against the perversions and traditions of man. Thus proceeding, he soon became known to the enemies of truth, who watched him with malignant jealousy.

At length, in a sermon at St. Paul's, on the fourth Sunday in Lent, wherein he dwelt upon the justification by faith, he so offended the legal preachers of the day, that he was summoned before the king at Westminster, and there accused of heresy.

It was urged against him, that he had insisted, according to St. Paul, in Galatians iv. "That the children of Sarah (allegorically used for the children of the promise) were all born free, and, independent of baptism, or of penance, were, through faith, made heirs of God." A Dr. Wilson argued against him, and strongly opposed this doctrine. But Jerome defended it with all the force of truth, and said, "that although good works were the means of salvation, yet that they followed as a consequence of faith, whose fruits they were, and which discovered their root, even as good fruit proves a good tree."

Notwithstanding his arguments, so inveterate were his enemies, and so deluded was the king, that he was committed to the Tower, in company with the other two soldiers of Christ, Barnes and Garret.

Burning of Barnes Garret and Jerome

Here they remained, while a process ensued against them by the king's council in parliament, by whom, without any hearing, or knowledge of their fate, they were attainted of heresy, and sentenced to be burned. On the 30th of the following June, therefore, they were brought from the Tower to Smithfield, where, before they were committed to the fire, they addressed the people.

"I am come hither," said Dr. Barnes, "to be burned as a heretic, and you shall hear my belief, whereby you may perceive what erroneous opinions I hold. God I take to record, I never (to my knowledge) taught any erroneous doctrine, but only those things which scripture led me unto; neither in my sermons have I ever maintained or given occasion for any insurrection; but with all diligence evermore did I study to set forth the glory of God, the obedience to our sovereign lord the king, and the true and sincere religion of Christ; and now hearken to my faith.

"I believe in the holy and blessed Trinity, three persons, and one God, that created and made all the world; and that this blessed Trinity sent down the second person, Jesus Christ, into the womb of the most blessed and purest virgin Mary. I believe that he was conceived of the Holy Ghost, and took flesh of her, and that he suffered hunger, thirst, cold, and other passions of our body, sin excepted, according to the saying of St. Peter, ' He was made in all things like to his brethren, except sin.' And I believe that this his death and passion was the sufficient ransom for sin. And I believe, that through his death he overcame sin, death, and hell; and that there is none other satisfaction unto the Father, but this his death and passion only; and that no work of man did deserve anything of God, but his passion only, as touching our justification; for I know the best work that ever I performed is impure and imperfect.

He then, lifting up his hands, prayed God to forgive him his trespasses, saying, "I confess, that my evil thoughts and cogitations are innumerable; wherefore I beseech thee, O Lord, not to enter into judgment with me, for, if thou straitly mark our iniquities, who is able to abide thy judgment? Wherefore I trust in no good work that ever I did, but only in the death of Christ. I do not doubt but through him to inherit the kingdom of heaven. But imagine not, that I speak against good works, for they are to be done, and verily they that do them not, shall never come into the kingdom of God. We must do them, because they are commanded us of God, to show and se forth our profession, not to deserve or merit; for that is only by the death of Christ.

"I believe that there is a holy church, and a company of all them that do profess Christ; and that all who have suffered and confessed his name, are saints, and that they praise and laud God in heaven, more than I or any man's tongue can express."

A person present asked him his opinion upon praying to saints. "I believe," said he, "they are in heaven with God, and that they are worthy of all the honour that scripture willeth them to have. But I say, throughout scripture we are not commanded to pray to any saints. Therefore I neither can nor will preach to you that saints ought to be prayed unto; for then should I preach unto you a doctrine of mine own head. Notwithstanding, whether they pray for us or no, that I refer to God. And if saints do pray for us, then I trust to pray for you within this half hour, Mr. Sheriff, and for every Christian living in the faith of Christ, and dying in the same as a saint. Wherefore, if the dead may for the quick, I will surely pray for you."

Then said he to the sheriff, "Have ye any articles against me for which I am condemned?" The sheriff answered, "No." Then said he, "Is there here any man else that knoweth wherefore I die, or that by my preaching hath taken any error? Let them now speak, and I will make them answer." But no man answered. Then said he, "Well, I am condemned by the law to die, and as I understand by an act of parliament, but wherefore I cannot tell; perhaps it is for heresy; for we are like to burn. But they that have been the occasion of it, I pray God forgive them, as I would be forgiven myself. And Dr. Stephen, bishop of Winchester, if he have sought or wrought this my death, either by word or deed, I pray God to forgive him as heartily, as freely, as charitably, and as sincerely, as Christ forgave them that put him to death. And if any of the council, or any other, have sought or wrought it through malice or ignorance, I pray God forgive their ignorance, and illuminate their eyes, that they may see and ask mercy for it. I beseech you all to pray for the king's grace, as I have done ever since I was in prison, and do now, that God may give him prosperity,

and that he may long reign among you; and after him
that godly prince Edward, that he may finish those things
which his father hath begun.   I have been reported to be
a preacher of sedition, and disobedience unto the king;
but here I say to you, that you are all bound by the commandment of God to obey your prince with all humility,
and with all your heart, and that not only for fear of the
sword, but also for conscience sake before God."

He then begged all men to forgive him; to bear witness
that he detested and abhorred all evil opinions and doctrines against the word of God, and that he died in the
faith of Jesus Christ, by whom he doubted not but to be
saved.   With these words, he desired all the spectators to
pray for him, and then he prepared himself to suffer.

Jerome and Garret professed in like manner their be-
'ief, reciting all the articles of the Christian faith, briefly
declaring their minds upon every article, as the time would
suffer, whereby the people might understand that there
was no cause nor error in their faith for which they could
justly be condemned; protesting, moreover, that they denied nothing that was either in the Old or New Testament,
set forth by the king, whom they prayed the Lord long to
continue among them, with his son prince Edward.

Jerome then addressed the people as follows: I say unto
you, good brethren, that God hath bought us all with no
small price, neither with gold nor silver, or other such
things of small value, but with his most precious blood.
Be not unthankful therefore to him again, but do as much
as to Christian men belongeth to fulfil his commandments;
that is, love your brethren.   Love hurteth no man, love
fulfilleth all things.   If God hath sent thee plenty, help thy
neighbour that hath need.   Give him good counsel.   If he
lack, consider if thou wert in necessity, thou wouldst gladly
be refreshed.   And again, bear your cross with Christ.
Consider what reproof, slander, and reproach, he suffered of
his enemies, and how patiently he suffered all things. Con
sider, that all that Christ did was of his mere goodness, and
not of our deserving.   For if we could merit our own salvation, Christ would not have died for us.   But for Adam's
breaking of God's precepts, we had been all lost, if Christ
had not redeemed us again.   And like as Adam broke the
precepts, and was driven out of Paradise, so we, if we

break God's commandments, shall have damnation, if we do not repent and ask mercy. Now, therefore, let all Christians put no trust nor confidence in their own works, but in the blood of Christ, to whom I commit my soul to guide, beseeching you all to pray to God for me, and for my brethren here present with me, that our souls, leaving these wretched bodies, may constantly depart in the true faith of Christ."

After he had concluded, Garret thus spoke : " I also detest and refuse all heresies and errors, and if either by negligence or ignorance, I have taught or maintained any, I am sorry for it, and ask God mercy. Or if I have been vehement or rash in preaching, whereby any person hath taken offence, error or evil opinion, I desire of him, and all other persons whom I have any way offended, forgiveness. Notwithstanding, to my remembrance, I have never preached wittingly or willingly, anything against God's holy word, or contrary to the true faith ; but have ever endeavoured, with my little learning and wit, to set forth the honour of God and the right obedience to his laws, and also the king's : if I could have done better I would. Wherefore, Lord, if I have taken in hand to do that thing which I could not perfectly perform, I desire thy pardon for my bold presumption. And I pray God send the king's grace good and godly counsel, to his glory, to the king's honour, and the increase of virtue in this realm. And thus do I now yield my soul up unto Almighty God, trusting and believing, that he of his infinite mercy, according to his promise made in the blood of his Son, Jesus Christ, will take it and pardon all my sins, of which I ask him mercy, and desire you all to pray with and for me, that I may patiently suffer this pain, and die in true faith, hope and charity."

The three martyrs then took each other by the hand, and after embracing, submitted themselves to the tormentors, who, fastening them to the stake, soon lighted the fagots, and terminated their mortal life and care.

25

CHAPTER VI.

Attempt against Cranmer.

The cruelty of the measures of the king against the dissenters hinted at in the preceding chapter, gave the popish party great hopes of succeeding, and to complete their victory, they attempted the destruction of Cranmer, and the queen, whom they considered the greatest obstacles to their success. They persuaded the king that Cranmer was the source of all the heresies in England; but Henry's esteem for him was such, that no one would appear to give evidence against him; they therefore desired that he might be committed to the Tower, and then it would appear how many would inform against him

The king seemed to approve this plan, and they resolved to execute it the next day: but in the night Henry sent for Cranmer, and told him what was resolved concerning him. Cranmer thanked the king for giving him notice of it and submitted to it, only desiring that he might be heard in answer for himself; and that he might have impartial judges, competent to decide. Henry was surprised to see him so little concerned in his own preservation: but told him, since he took so little care of himself, that he must take care of him. He therefore gave him instructions to appear before the council, and to desire to see his accusers before he should be sent to the Tower; and that he might be used by them, as they would desire to be used in a similar case; and if he could not prevail by the force of reason, then he was to appeal to the king in person, and was to show the royal seal ring, which he took from his finger, and gave him, which they would know so well that they would do nothing after they once saw it.

Accordingly on being summoned next morning, he came over to Whitehall; there he was detained, with great insolence, in the lobby of the council chamber before he was called in; but when that was done, and he had acted as the king had ordered him, and at last showed the ring, his enemies rose in great confusion, and went to the king. He upbraided them severely for what they had done, and expressed his esteem and kindness for Cranmer in such terms, that they were glad to get off, by pretending that they had no other design but that of having his innocence declared by a public trial. From this vain attempt they were so convinced of the king's unalterable favour to him, that they told no try of their designs against him.

But what they could not effect against Cranmer, they thought might be more safely tried against the queen, who was known to love the "new learning," as the reformation was then called. She used to have sermons in her privy chamber, which could not be so secretly carried, but that it came to the knowledge of her royal spouse; yet her conduct in all other things was so exact, and she expressed such a tender care of the king's person, that it was observed she had gained much upon him; but his peevishness growing with his distempers, made him sometimes impatient even to her.

He used often to talk with her of matters of religion, and sometimes she sustained the argument for the reformers so strenuously, that he was offended at it; yet as soon as that appeared she let it fall. But once the debate continued long, the king expressed his displeasure at it to Gardiner, with whom she went away. The crafty bishop took hold of this opportunity to persuade the king that she was a great cherisher of heretics. Wriothesly joined with him in the same artifice; and filled the angry king's head with suspicions, insomuch that he signed the articles upon which she was to be impeached. But the chancellor carelessly dropping the paper, it happened to be taken up by one of the queen's friends, who carried it to her.

The next night after supper, she went into the king's bedchamber, where she found him sitting and talking with certain gentlemen. He very courteously welcomed her, and breaking off his talk with the gentlemen, began of himself, contrary to his usual manner, to enter into talk of religion, seeming as it were desirous to hear the queen's opinion on certain matters which he mentioned.

The queen, perceiving to what this tended, mildly and with much apparent deference, answered him as follows:

"Your Majesty," says she, "doth right well know, neither am I myself ignorant, what great imperfection and weakness by our first creation is allotted unto us women, to be ordained and appointed as inferior, and subject unto man as our head, from which head all our direction ought to proceed ; and that as God made man to his own shape and likeness, whereby he, being endued with more special gifts of perfection, might rather be stirred to the contemplation of heavenly things, and to the earnest endeavour to obey his commandments ; even so also made he woman of man, of whom, and by whom, she is to be governed, commanded, and directed ; whose womanly weaknesses and natural imperfection ought to be tolerated, aided, and borne withal, so that by his wisdom such things as be lacking in her ought to be supplied.

"Since thence, therefore, that God hath appointed such a natural difference between man and woman, and your majesty being so excellent in gifts and ornaments of wisdom, and I a silly poor woman, so much inferior in all respects of nature unto you, how then cometh it now to pass that your majesty, in such diffuse causes of religion, will seem to require my judgment ? which, when I have uttered and said what I can, yet must I, and will I, refer my judgment in this and in all other cases, to your majesty's wisdom, as my only anchor, supreme head and governor here on earth, next under God to lean unto.'

"Not so, by Saint Mary," replied the king ; " you are become a doctor, Kate, to instruct us, as we take it, and not to be instructed or directed by us."

"If your majesty take it so," said the queen, " then hath your majesty very much mistaken, who have ever been of the opinion, to think it very unseemly and preposterous for a woman to take upon her the office of an instructer, or teacher to her lord and husband, but rather to learn of her husband, and to be taught by him ; and where I have, with your majesty's leave, heretofore been bold to hold talk with your majesty, wherein sometimes in opinions there hath seemed some difference, I have not done it so much to maintain opinion, as I did it rather to minister talk, not only to the end your majesty might with less grief pass over this painful time of your infirmity, being intentive to our talk, and hoping that your majesty should reap some ease thereby ; but also that I, hearing your majesty's learned discourse, might receive to myself some profit thereby ; wherein, I assure your majesty, I have not missed any part of my desire in that behalf always referring myself in all such matters unto your majesty as by ordinance of nature it is convenient for me to do."

"And is it even so, sweetheart?" cried the king; "and tended your arguments to no worse end? Then perfect friends we are now again, as ever at any time heretofore." And as he sat in his chair, embracing her in his arms, and kissing her, he added, that "it did him more good at that time to hear those words of her own mouth, than if he had heard present news of a hundred thousand pounds of money fallen unto him;" and with tokens of great joy, and promises and assurances never again to mistake her, he entered into a very pleasant discourse with the queen, and the lords and gentlemen standing by; and at last, the night being far advanced, he gave her leave to depart. And after she was gone, he greatly commended and praised her.

The time formerly appointed for her being taken into custody, being come, the king, waited upon by two gentlemen only of his bedchamber, went into the garden, whither the queen also came, being sent for by the king himself, with three ladies attending her. Henry immediately entered into pleasant conversation with the queen and attendants; when suddenly, in the midst of their mirth, the lord chancellor came into the garden with forty of the king's guard, intending to have taken the queen together with the three ladies to the Tower. The king, sternly beholding them, broke off his mirth with the queen, and stepping a little aside, called the chancellor to him, who upon his knees spake to the king, but what he said is not well known: it is, however, certain that the king's reply to him was, "Knave! yea, arrant knave, beast, and fool!" and then he commanded him presently to begone out of his presence; which words, being vehemently spoken by the king, the queen and her ladies overheard them.

The king, after the departure of the chancellor and his guards, immediately returned to the queen; when she perceiving him to be very much irritated, endeavoured to pacify him with kind words, in behalf of the lord chancellor, with whom he seemed to be offended, saying, "That albeit she knew not what just cause his majesty had at

25*

that time to be offended with him; yet she thought that ignorance, not wilfulness was the cause of his error."

"Ah, poor soul," replied the king, "thou little knowest how ill he deserveth this grace at thy hands. On my word sweetheart, he hath been toward thee an arrant knave, and so let him go." Thus the design against her was frustrated, and Gardiner, who had promoted it lost the king's favour entirely.

The King's Sickness and Death.

The king's distemper had been long growing upon him. He was become so corpulent that he could not go up and down stairs, but was let down and drawn up by an engine, when he intended to walk in his garden. He had an ulceration in his leg, which gave him much pain, the humours of his body discharging themselves that way, till at last a dropsy came on. He had grown so fierce and cruel, that those about him were afraid to let him know that his death seemed near, lest they might have been adjudged guilty of treason, in foretelling his death!

His will was made ready, and signed by him on the 30th of December. He ordered Gardiner's name to be struck out from the list of his executors. When sir Anthony Brown endeavoured to persuade him not to put that disgrace on an old servant, he continued positive in it: for he said *"he* knew his temper and could govern him; but it would not be in the power of others to do it, if he were put in so high a trust." The most material thing in the will, was, the preferring the children of his second sister, by Charles Brandon, duke of Suffolk, to the children of his eldest sister the queen of Scotland, in the succession to the crown. On his deathbed he finished the foundation of Trinity College, in Cambridge, and of Christ's Hospital, near Newgate: yet this last was not fully settled, till his son completed what he had begun.

On the 27th of January, 1547, his spirits sunk, and it was evident that he had not long to live. Sir Anthony Denny took courage to tell him that death was approaching and desired him to call on God for his mercy. He expressed in general his sorrow for his past sins, and his trust in the mercies of God in Christ Jesus. He ordered Cranmer to be sent for, but was speechless before he arrived; yet he gave a sign that he understood what he said to him, and soon after died, in the 56th year of his age, after he had reigned thirty-seven years and nine months. His death was concealed three days; and the parliament continued to sit till the 31st of January, when his decease was made public. It is probable the Seymours, uncles to the young king, concealed it so long, till they made a party for securing the government in their own hands.

The severities Henry used against many of his subjects, in matters of religion, made both sides write with great sharpness against him; his temper was imperious and cruel, he was sudden and violent in his passions, and hesitated at nothing by which he could gratify either his lust or his revenge. This was much provoked by the sentence of the pope against him, by the virulent books Cardinal Pole and others published, by the rebellions that were raised in England by the popish clergy, and the apprehensions he was in of the emperor's greatness, together with his knowledge of the fate of those princes, against whom the popes had thundered in former times; all which made him think it necessary to keep his people under the terror of a severe government; and by some public examples to secure the peace of the nation, and thereby to prevent a more profuse effusion of blood, which might have otherwise followed if he had been more gentle; and it was no wonder if, after the pope deposed him, he proceeded to great severities against all who supported the papal authority.

Almost the last act of his life was one of barbarous ingratitude and monstrous tyranny. This was the execution of the earl of Surrey, a brave and accomplished nobleman, who had served him with zeal and fidelity, but was now sacrificed to the groundless suspicions of this gloomy tyrant, on the pretence of his having assumed the arms of Edward the Confessor, which, from his being related to the royal family, he had a right to do, and which he had done during many years, without offence. Not satisfied with the death of this nobleman, the blood-thirsty despot, now tottering on the brink of the grave, determined to complete his worse than savage barbarity, by bringing to the block

the aged duke of Norfolk, father of his former victim, who
had spent a long life, and expended a princely fortune, in
his service.   There being no charge on which to found an
impeachment against him, a parliament was summoned to
attaint him; and so well did these servile wretches fulfil
their inhuman master's expectations, that the bill of attainder was passed in both houses in the short space of seven
days; and the royal assent being given by commission,
January 27, the duke was ordered for execution on the
next morning; but in the course of the night, the king
was himself summoned before the tribunal of the eternal
Judge.

PART VI.

Persecutions in Scotland, and Progress of the Reforma-
tion during the reign of King Edward.

CHAPTER I

Persecutions in Scotland during the 15th and part of
the 16th centuries.

HAVING brought our account of the sufferings and mar
tyrdoms of the English reformers down to the death of
Henry the Eighth, we shall now proceed to relate the cruel
persecutions of God's faithful servants in Scotland to the
same period; but it will previously be necessary to give a
short sketch of the progress of the reformation in that
country.

The long alliance between Scotland and France, had
rendered the two nations extremely attached to each other;
and Paris was the place where the learned of Scotland
had their education.   Yet early in the fifteenth century,
learning was more encouraged in Scotland, and universities were founded in several episcopal sees.   About the

same time some of Wickliffe's followers began to show themselves in Scotland; and an Englishman, named Resby, was burnt in 1407 for teaching some opinions contrary to the pope's authority.

Some years after that, Paul Craw, a Bohemian, who had been converted by Huss, was burnt for infusing the opinions of that martyr into some persons at St. Andrews.

About the end of the fifteenth century, Lollardy, as it was then called, spread itself into many parts of the diocese of Glasgow, for which several persons of quality were accused; but they answered the archbishop of that see with so much boldness and truth, that he dismissed them, having admonished them to content themselves with the faith of the church, and to beware of new doctrines.

The same spirit of ignorance, immorality, and superstition, had overrun the church of Scotland that was so much complained of in other parts of Europe. The total neglect of the pastoral care, and the scandalous lives of the clergy, filled the people with such prejudices against them, that they were easily disposed to hearken to new preachers, among the most conspicuous of whom was Patrick Hamilton.

Story and Martyrdom of Patrick Hamilton.

This noble martyr was nephew, by his father, to the earl of Arran, and by his mother, to the duke of Albany. He was educated for the church, and would have been highly preferred, having an abbey given him for prosecuting his studies. But, going over to Germany, and studying at the university of Marpurg, he soon distinguished himself by his zeal, assiduity, and great progress, particularly in the scriptures, which were his grand object, and to which he made everything else subservient. He also became acquainted with Luther and Melancthon; and being convinced, from his own researches, of the truth of their doctrines, he burned to impart the light of the gospel to his own countrymen, and to show them the errors and corruptions of their church. For this great purpose he returned to Scotland.

After preaching some time, and holding up the truth to his deluded countrymen, he was at length invited to St.

Andrews, to confer upon the points in question. But his
enemies could not stand the light, and finding they could
not defend themselves by argument, resolved upon revenge.
Hamilton was accordingly imprisoned. Articles were exhibited against him, in which he was charged with having
denied free-will; advocated justification by faith alone;
and declared that faith, hope, and charity, are so linked
together, that one cannot exist in the breast without the
other.

Upon his refusing to abjure these doctrines, Beaton,
archbishop of St. Andrews, with the archbishop of Glasgow, three bishops, and five abbots, condemned him as an
obstinate heretic, delivered him to the secular power, and
ordered his execution to take place that very afternoon;
for the king had gone in pilgrimage to Ross, and they
were afraid, lest, upon his return, Hamilton's friends might
have interceded effectually for him. When he was tied to
the stake, he expressed great joy in his sufferings, since
by these he was to enter into everlasting life.

A train of powder being fired, it did not kindle the fuel,
but only burnt his face, which occasioned a delay till more
powder was brought; and in that time the friars continually
urged him to recant, and pray to the Virgin, saying the
Salve regina. Among the rest, a friar named Campbel,
who had been often with him in prison, was very officious.
Hamilton answered him, that he knew he was not a heretic, and had confessed to him in private, and charged him
to answer for that at the throne of Almighty God. By
this time the gunpowder was brought, and the fire being
kindled, he died, repeating these words, "Lord Jesus, receive my spirit! How long, oh! Lord! how long shall
darkness overwhelm this kingdom? and how long wilt
thou suffer the tyranny of these men?" He suffered death
in the year 1527.

The views and doctrines of this glorious martyr were
such as could not fail to excite the highest admiration of
every real believer; and they were expressed with such
brevity, such clearness, and such peculiar vigour and
beauty, forming in themselves a complete summary of the
gospel, that they afforded instruction to all who sought to
know more of God.

The force of the truths preached by Hamilton, the firm

ness of his death, and the singular catastrophe of friar Campbel, made strong impressions on the people; and many received the new opinions. Seaton, a Dominican, the king's confessor, preaching in Lent, set out the nature and method of true repentance, without mixing the directions which the friars commonly gave on that subject; and when another friar attempted to show the defectiveness of what he had taught, Seaton defended himself in another sermon, and reflected on those bishops who did not preach, calling them dumb dogs. But the clergy dared not meddle with him, till they had by secret insinuations ruined his credit with the king; and the freedom he used in reproving him for his vices, quickly alienated James from him; upon which he withdrew into England, and wrote to the king, taxing the clergy for their cruelty, and praying him to restrain it.

Martyrdom of Henry Forest.

A few years after this event, Henry Forest, a young friar of Lithgow, was burnt for saying that Hamilton was a martyr, and that the doctrines he preached were true.

Norman Gurley and David Stratton were also put to death about the same time, for saying there was no such place as purgatory, and that the pope was Antichrist.

The year following, viz. 1539, two others were apprehended on suspicion of heresy, namely: Jerome Russel and Alexander Campbell, a youth of about eighteen years of age. Being tried before the archbishop, they were sentenced to be burnt on the following day, which was executed accordingly.

Martyrdom of six Persons.

In 1543, the archbishop of St. Andrews making a visitation into various parts of his diocese, several persons were accused at Perth of heresy. Among these the six following were condemned to die: William Anderson, Robert Lamb, James Finlayson, James Hunter, James Raveleson, and Helen Stark.

The accusations laid against them were to the following effect :

The four first were accused of having hung up the image of St. Francis, nailing ram's horns on his head, and fastening a cow's tail to his rump ; but the principal matter on which they were condemned was having regaled themselves with a goose on Allhallows-eve, a fast day, according to the Romish superstition.

James Raveleson was accused of having ornamented his house with the three-crowned diadem of Peter, carved in wood, which the archbishop conceived to be done in mockery to his cardinal's hat.

Helen Stark was accused of not having accustomed herself to pray to the Virgin Mary, more especially during the time she was in childbed.

On these accusations they were all found guilty, and immediately received sentence of death ; the four men for eating the goose to be hanged ; James Raveleson to be burnt ; and the woman, with her sucking infant, to be put into a sack, and drowned.

The four men, with the woman and child, suffered at the same time ; but James Raveleson was not executed till some days after.

On the day appointed for the execution of the former, they were all conducted, under a proper guard, to the place where they were to suffer, and were attended by a prodigious number of spectators.

As soon as they arrived at the place of execution, they all fervently prayed for some time; after which Robert Lamb addressed himself to the spectators, exhorting them to fear God, and to quit the practice of papistical abominations.

The four men were all hanged on the same gibbet; and the woman, with her sucking child, was conducted to a river adjoining, when, being fastened in a large sack, they were thrown into it and drowned.

They all suffered their fate with becoming fortitude and resignation, committing their departing spirits to that Redeemer who was to be their final judge, and who, they had reason to hope, would usher them into the realms of everlasting bliss.

When we reflect on the sufferings of these unhappy persons, we are naturally induced, both as men and Christians, to lament their fate, and to express our feelings by dropping the tear of commiseration. The putting to death four men, for little other reason than that of satisfying nature with an article sent by Providence for that very purpose, merely because it was on a day prohibited by ridiculous bigotry and superstition, is shocking indeed; but the fate of the innocent woman, and her still more harmless infant, makes human nature tremble at the contemplation of what mankind may become, when incited by bigotry to the gratification of the most diabolical cruelty.

Beside the abovementioned persons, many others were cruelly persecuted during the archbishop's stay at Perth, some being banished, and others confined in loathsome dungeons. In particular, John Rogers, a pious and learned man, was, by the archbishop's orders, murdered in prison, and his body thrown over the walls into the street; after which the archbishop caused a report to be spread, that he had met with his death in an attempt to make his

Life, Sufferings, and Martyrdom of George Wishart.

Mr. George Wishart was born in Scotland, and after receiving a grammatical education at a private school, he left that place, and finished his studies at the university of Cambridge.

The following character of him, during his residence in that university, was written by one of his scholars, and contains so just a picture of this excellent man, that we give it at length.

"About the year of our Lord 1543, there was in the university of Cambridge one Mr. George Wishart, commonly called Mr. George, of Bennet's college, who was a man of tall stature, bald-headed, and on the same wore a round French cap; judged to be of melancholy complexion by his physiognomy, black-haired, long-bearded, comely of personage, well spoken after his country of Scotland, courteous, lowly, lovely, glad to teach, desirous to learn, and was well travelled; having on him for his habit or clothing, never but a mantle or frieze gown to the shoes, a black millian fustian doublet, and plain black hose, coarse new canvass for his shirts, and white falling bands and cuffs at his hands. All the which apparel he gave to the poor, some weekly, some monthly, some quarterly, as he liked, saving his French cap, which he kept the whole year of my being with him.

"He was a man modest, temperate, fearing God, hating covetousness; for his charity had never end, night, noon, nor day; he forbare one meal in three, one day in four, for the most part, except something to comfort nature. He lay hard upon a puff of straw, and coarse new canvass sheets, which when he changed he gave away. He had commonly by his bed-side a tub of water, in the which (his people being in bed, the candle put out and all quiet) he used to bathe himself, as I being very young, being assured, often heard him, and in one light night discerned him. He loved me tenderly, and I him, for my age, as effectually. He taught with great modesty and gravity, so that some of his people thought him severe, and would have slain him, but the Lord was his defence. And he, after due correction for their malice, by good exhortation amended them and went his way. O that the Lord had eft him to me his poor boy, that he might have finished that he had begun! for in his religion he was as you see here in the rest of his life, when he went into Scotland with divers of the nobility, that came for a treaty to king Henry VIII. His learning was no less sufficient than his desire; always pressed and ready to do good in that he was able, both in the house privately, and in the school publicly, professing and reading divers authors.

"If I should declare his love to me, and all men, his charity to the poor, in giving, relieving, caring, helping, providing, yea, infinitely studying how to do good unto all, and hurt to none, I should sooner want words than just cause to commend him.

" All this I testify with my whole heart, and truth, of this godly man. He that made all, governeth all, and shall judge all, knoweth that I speak the truth, that the simple may be satisfied, the arrogant confounded, the hypocrite unclosed.—EMERY TYLNEY."

In order to improve himself as much as possible in the knowledge of literature, he travelled into various foreign countries, where he distinguished himself for his great learning and abilities, both in philosophy and divinity. His desire to promote true knowledge and science among men, accompanied the profession of it himself. He was very ready to communicate what he knew to others, and frequently read various authors, both in his own chamber, and in the public schools.

After being some time abroad, he returned to England, and took up his residence at Cambridge, where he was admitted a member of Bennet college. Having taken his degrees, he entered into holy orders, and expounded the gospel in so clear and intelligible a manner, as highly to delight his numerous auditors.

Being desirous of propagating the true gospel in his own country, he left Cambridge in 1544, and in his way to Scotland preached in most of the principal towns, to the great satisfaction of his hearers.

On his arrival in his native land, he first preached at Montrose, and afterward at Dundee. In this last place he made a public exposition of the epistle to the Romans, which he went through with so much grace, eloquence, and freedom, as delighted the reformers, and alarmed the papists.

In consequence of this exposition, one Robert Miln, a principal man of Dundee, went, by command of cardinal Beaton, to the church where Wishart preached, and in the midst of his discourse publicly told him "not to trouble the town any more, for he was determined not to suffer it."

This treatment greatly surprised Wishart, who, after a short pause, looking sorrowfully on the speaker and the audience, said, " God is my witness, that I never intended your trouble, but your comfort ; yea, your trouble is more grievous to me than it is to yourselves ; but I am assured, to refuse God's word, and to chase from you his messenger, shall not preserve you from trouble, but shall bring you into it ; for God shall send you ministers that shall neither fear burning nor banishment. I have offered you the word of salvation. With the hazard of my life I have remained among you : now ye yourselves refuse me ; and I must leave my innocence to be declared by my God. If it be long prosperous with you, I am not led by the spirit of truth ; but if unlooked-for trouble come upon you, acknowledge the cause, and turn to God, who is gracious and merciful. But if you turn not at the first warning, he will visit you with fire and sword." At the close of this speech he left the pulpit, and retired.

After this he went into the west of Scotland, where he preached God's word, which was gladly received by many ; till the archbishop of Glasgow, at the instigation of cardinal Beaton, came, with his train, to the town of Ayr, to suppress Wishart, and insisted on having the church to preach in himself. Some opposed this ; but Wishart said, " Let him alone, his sermon will not do much hurt ; let us go to the market-cross." This was agreed to, and Wishart preached a sermon that gave universal satisfaction to his hearers, and at the same time confounded his enemies.

He continued to propagate the gospel with the greatest alacrity, preaching sometimes in one place, and sometimes in another ; but coming to Macklene, he was, by force, kept out of the church. Some of his followers would have broken in ; upon which he said to one of them, " Brother,

Jesus Christ is as mighty in the fields as in the church; and himself often preached in the desert, at the sea-side, and other places. The like word of peace God sends by me: the blood of none shall be shed this day for preaching it."

He then went into the fields, where he preached to the people for above three hours; and such an impression did his sermon make on the minds of his hearers, that many of the most wicked men in the country became converts to the truth of the gospel.

A short time after this, Mr. Wishart received intelligence that the plague was broke out in Dundee. It began four days after he was prohibited from preaching there, and raged so extremely that incredible numbers died in the space of twenty-four hours. This being related to him, he, notwithstanding the persuasions of his friends, determined to go thither, saying, " They are now in troubles, and need comfort. Perhaps this hand of God, will make them now to magnify and reverence the word of God which before they lightly esteemed."

Here he was with joy received by the godly. He chose the East-gate for the place of his preaching; so that the healthy were within, and the sick without the gate. He took his text from these words, " He sent his word and healed them," &c. In this sermon he chiefly dwelt upon the advantage and comfort of God's word, the judgments that ensue upon the contempt or rejection of it, the freedom of God's grace to all his people, and the happiness of those of his elect, whom he takes to himself out of this miserable world. The hearts of his hearers were so raised by the divine force of this discourse, as not to regard death but to judge them the more happy who should then be called, not knowing whether they might have such a comforter again among them.

After this the plague abated: though in the midst of it, Wishart constantly visited those that lay in the greatest extremity, and comforted them by his exhortations.

When he took his leave of the people of Dundee, he said, " That God had almost put an end to that plague, and that he was now called to another place."

He went from thence to Montrose, where he sometimes
26*

preached, but spent most of his time in private meditation and prayer.

It is said, that before he left Dundee, and while he was engaged in the labours of love to the bodies, as well as to the souls, of those poor afflicted people, cardinal Beaton engaged a desperate popish priest, called John Weighton, to kill him; the attempt to execute which was as follows: one day, after Wishart had finished his sermon, and the people departed, the priest stood waiting at the bottom of the stairs, with a naked dagger in his hand under his gown. But Mr. Wishart having a sharp, piercing eye, and seeing the priest as he came from the pulpit, said to him, "My friend what would you have?" And immediately clapping his hand upon the dagger, took it from him. The priest being terrified, fell on his knees, confessed his intention, and craved pardon. A noise being hereupon raised, and it coming to the ears of those who were sick, they cried, "Deliver the traitor to us, we will take him by force;" and they burst in at the gate. But Wishart, taking the priest in his arms, said, "Whatsoever hurts him, shall hurt me; for he hath done me no mischief, but much good by teaching me more heedfulness for the time to come." By this conduct he appeased the people, and saved the life of the wicked priest.

Soon after his return to Montrose, the cardinal again conspired his death, causing a letter to be sent to him as if it had been from his familiar friend the laird of Kinnier, in which he was desired with all possible speed, to come to him, because he was taken with a sudden sickness. In the mean time the cardinal had provided sixty armed men, to lie in wait within a mile and a half of Montrose, in order to murder him as he passed that way.

The letter coming to Wishart's hand by a boy, who also brought him a horse for the journey, Wishart, accompanied by some of his friends set forward; but something particular striking his mind by the way, he returned back, which they wondering at, asked him the cause; to whom he said, "I will not go; I am forbidden of God; I am assured there is treason. Let some of you go to yonder place, and tell me what you find." They accordingly went, discovered the assassins, and hastily returning, they told Mr

Wishart: whereupon he said, "I know I shall end my life by that bloodthirsty man's hands, but it will not be in this manner."

A short time after this he left Montrose, and proceeded to Edinburgh, in order to propagate the gospel in that city. By the way he lodged with a faithful brother, called James Watson, of Inner-Goury. In the middle of the night he got up, and went into the yard, which two men hearing they privately followed him.

While in the yard he fell on his knees, and prayed for sometime with the greatest fervency; after which he arose and returned to his bed. Those who attended him, appearing as though they were ignorant of all, came and asked him where he had been? But he would not answer them. The next day they importuned him to tell them saying, "Be plain with us, for we heard your mourning, and saw your gestures."

On this he, with a dejected countenance, said, "I had rather you had been in your beds." But they still pressing upon him to know something, he said, "I will tell you; I am assured that my warfare is near at an end, and therefore pray to God with me, that I shrink not when the battle waxeth most hot.'

When they heard this they wept, saying, "This is small comfort to us."—"Then," said he, "God shall send you comfort after me. This realm shall be illuminated with the light of Christ's gospel, as clearly as any realm since the days of the apostles. The house of God shall be built in it; yea, it shall not lack, in despite of all enemies, the topstone; neither will it be long before this be accomplished. Many shall not suffer after me, before the glory of God shall appear, and triumph in despite of Satan. But, alas, if the people afterward shall prove unthankful, then fearful and terrible will be the plagues that shall follow."

The next day he proceeded on his journey, and when he arrived at Leith, not meeting with those he expected, he kept himself retired for a day or two. He then grew pensive, and being asked the reason he answered, "What do I differ from a dead man? Hitherto God hath used my labours for the instruction of others, and to the disclosing of darkness; and now I lurk as a man ashamed to show his face." His friends perceived that his desire was to preach, whereupon they said to him, "It is most comfort able for us to hear you, but because we know the danger wherein you stand, we dare not desire it." He replied. "If you dare hear, let God provide for me as best pleaseth him;" after which it was concluded, that the next day he should preach in Leith. His text was from the parable of the sower, Matt. xiii. The sermon ended, the gentlemen of Lothian, who were earnest professors of Jesus Christ, would not suffer him to stay at Leith, because the governor and cardinal were shortly to come to Edinburgh; but took him along with them; and he preached at Branston, Longniddry, and Ormistone. He also preached at Iveresk, near Muselburg: he had a great concourse of people, and among them Sir George Douglas, who after sermon said publicly, "I know that the governor and cardinal will hear that I have been at this sermon; but let them know that I will avow it, and will maintain both the doctrine and the preacher to the uttermost of my power."

Among others that came to hear him preach, there were two gray friars, who, standing at the church door, whispered to such as came in; which Wishart observing, said to the people, "I pray you make room for these two men, it may be they come to learn; and turning to them, he said, "Come near, for I assure you you shall hear the word of truth, which this day shall seal up to you either your salvation or damnation:" after which he proceeded in his sermon, supposing that they would be quiet; but when he perceived that they still continued to disturb the people that stood near them, he said to them the second time, with an angry countenance, "O ministers of Satan, and deceivers of the souls of men, will ye neither hear God's truth yourselves, nor suffer others to hear it? Depart, and take this for your portion; God shall shortly confound and disclose your hypocrisy within this kingdom; ye shall be abominable to men, and your places and habitations shall be desolate." He spoke this with much vehemency; then turning to the people, said, "These men have provoked the Spirit of God to anger;" after which he proceeded in his sermon, highly to the satisfaction of his hearers.

From hence he went and preached at Branstone, Languedine, Ormistone, and Inveresk, where he was followed by a great concourse of people. He preached also in many other places, the people flocking after him; and in all his sermons he foretold the shortness of the time he had to travel, and the near approach of his death. When he came to Haddington, his auditory began much to decrease, which was thought to happen through the influence of the earl of Bothwell, who was moved to oppose him at the instigation of the cardinal. Soon after this, as he was going to church, he received a letter from the west country gentlemen, which having read, he called John Knox, who had diligently waited upon him since his arrival at Lothian; to whom he said, " He was weary of the world, because he saw that men began to be weary of God: for," said he, " the gentlemen of the west have sent me word, that they cannot keep their meeting at Edinburgh."

Knox, wondering he should enter into conference about these things, immediately before his sermon, contrary to his usual custom, said to him, " Sir, sermon time approaches; I will leave you for the present to your meditations."

Wishart's sad countenance declared the grief of his mind. At length he went into the pulpit, and his auditory being very small, he introduced his sermon with the following exclamation: " O Lord! how long shall it be that thy holy word shall be despised, and men shall not regard their own salvation? I have heard of thee, O Haddington, that in thee there used to be two or three thousand persons at a vain and wicked play; and now, to hear the messenger of the eternal God, of all the parish can scarce be numbered one hundred present. Sore and fearful shall be the plagues that shall ensue upon this thy contempt. With fire and sword shalt thou be plagued; yea, thou Haddington in special, strangers shall possess thee: and ye, the present inhabitants, shall either in bondage serve your enemies, or else ye shall be chased from your own habitations; and that because ye have not known, nor will know, the time of your visitation."

This prediction was, in a great measure accomplished not long after, when the English took Haddington, made it a garrison, and forced many of the inhabitants to flee. Soon after this, a dreadful plague broke out in the town, of which such numbers died, that the place became almost depopulated.

Cardinal Beaton, being informed that Wishart was at the house of Mr. Cockburn, of Ormiston, in East Lothian, applied to the regent to cause him to be apprehended; with which, after great persuasion, and much against his will, he complied.

The earl accordingly went, with proper attendants, to the house of Mr. Cockburn, which he beset about midnight. The master of the house being greatly alarmed, put himself in a posture of defence, when the earl told him that it was in vain to resist, for the governor and cardinal were within a mile, with a power; but if he would deliver Wishart to him, he would promise upon his honour that he should be safe, and that the cardinal should not hurt him. Wishart said, "Open the gates, the will of God be done;" and Bothwell coming in, Wishart said to him, "I praise my God, that so honourable a man as you, my lord, receive me this night; for I am persuaded that for your honour's sake you will suffer nothing to be done to me but by order of law: I less fear to die openly, than secretly to be murdered." Bothwell replied, "I will not only preserve your body from all violence that shall be intended against you without order of law; but I also promise in the presence of these gentlemen, that neither the governor nor cardinal shall have their will of you; but I will keep you in my own house, till I either set you free, or restore you to the same place where I receive you." Then said Mr. Cockburn, "My lord, if you make good your promise, which we presume you will, we ourselves will not only serve you, but we will procure all the professors in Lothian to do the same."

This agreement being made, Mr. Wishart was delivered into the hands of the earl, who immediately conducted him to Edinburgh.

As soon as the earl arrived at that place, he was sent for by the queen, who being an inveterate enemy to Wishart, prevailed on the earl, notwithstanding the promises he had made, to commit him a prisoner to the castle.

The cardinal being informed of Wishart's situation, went to Edinburgh, and immediately caused him to be removed from thence to the castle of St. Andrews.

The inveterate and persecuting prelate, having now got our martyr fully at his own disposal, resolved to proceed immediately to try him as a heretic: for which purpose he assembled the prelates at St. Andrews' church on the 27th of February, 1546.

At this meeting the archbishop of Glasgow gave it as his opinion, that application should be made to the regent, to grant a commission to some nobleman to try the prisoner, that all the odium of putting so popular a man to death might not lie on the clergy.

To this the cardinal readily agreed: but upon sending to the regent, he received the following answer: "That he would do well not to precipitate this man's trial, but delay it until his coming; for as to himself, he would not consent to his death before the cause was very well examined; and if the cardinal should do otherwise, he would make protestation, that the blood of this man should be required at his hands."

The cardinal was extremely chagrined at this message from the regent; however he determined to proceed in the bloody business he had undertaken: and therefore sent the regent word, " That he had not written to him about this matter, as supposing himself to be in any way dependant upon his authority, but from the desire that the prosecution and conviction of heretics might have a show of public consent; which, since he could not this way obtain, he would proceed in that way which to him appeared the most proper."

In consequence of this, the cardinal immediately proceeded to the trial of Wishart, against whom no less than eighteen articles were exhibited, which were in substance as follows:

That he had despised the "holy mother-church;" had deceived the people; had ridiculed the mass; had preached against the sacraments, saying that there were not seven, but two only, viz.: baptism and the supper of the Lord; had preached against confession to a priest; had denied transubstantiation and the necessity of extreme unction; would not admit the authority of the pope or the councils; allowed the eating of flesh on Friday; condemned prayers to saints; spoke against the vows of monks, &c. saying that " whoever was bound to such vows, had vowed themselves to the state of damnation, and that it was lawful for priests to marry:" that he had said, " it was in vain to build costly churches to the honour of God, seeing that he remained not in churches made with men's hands; nor yet could God be in so small a space as between the priest's hands;"—and, finally, that he had avowed his disbelief of purgatory, and had said, " the soul of man should sleep till the last day, and should not obtain immortal life till that time."

Mr. Wishart answered these respective articles with great composure of mind, and in so learned and clear a manner, as greatly surprised most of those who were present.

A bigotted priest named Lauder, at the instigation of the archbishop, not only heaped a load of curses on him, but treated him with the most barbarous contempt, calling him " runagate, false heretic, traitor, and thief;" and, not satisfied with that, spit in his face, and otherwise maltreated him.

On this Mr. Wishart fell on his knees, and after making a prayer to God, thus addressed his judges :

" Many and horrible sayings unto me a Christian man, many words abominable to hear, have ye spoken here this day; which not only to teach, but even to think, I ever thought a great abomination."

After the examination was finished, the archbishop endeavoured to prevail on Mr. Wishart to recant; but he was too firmly fixed in his religious principles, and too much enlightened with the truth of the gospel, to be in the least moved.

In consequence of this the archbishop pronounced on him the dreadful sentence of death, which he ordered should be put into execution on the following day.

As soon as this cruel and melancholy ceremony was finished, our martyr fell on his knees and thus exclaimed :

" O immortal God, how long wilt thou suffer the rage and great cruelty of the ungodly to exercise their fury upon thy servants, which do further thy word in this world? Whereas they, on the contrary, seek to destroy the truth, whereby thou hast revealed thyself to the world. O Lord, we know certainly that thy true servants must needs suffer, for thy name's sake, persecutions, afflictions, and troubles in this present world; yet we desire that thou wouldst preserve and defend thy church, which thou hast chosen before the foundation of the world, and give thy people grace to hear thy word, and to be thy true servants in this present life."

Having said this, he arose, and was immediately conducted by the officers to the prison from whence he had been brought in the castle.

In the evening he was visited by two friars, who told him he must make his confession to them; to whom he replied, "I will not make any confession to you;" on which they immediately departed.

Soon after this came the sub-prior, with whom Wishart conversed in so feeling a manner on religious matters, as to make him weep. When this man left Wishart, he went to the cardinal, and told him he came not to intercede for the prisoner's life, but to make known his innocence to all men. At these words, the cardinal expressed great dissatisfaction, and forbid the sub-prior from again visiting Wishart.

Towards the close of the evening, our martyr was visited by the captain of the castle, with several of his friends; who bringing with them some bread and wine, asked him if he would eat and drink with them. "Yes," said Wishart, "very willingly, for I know you are honest men." In the mean time he desired them to hear him a little when he discoursed with them on the Lord's Supper, his sufferings and death for us, exhorting them to love one another, and to lay aside all rancour and malice, as became the members of Jesus Christ, who continually interceded for them with his father. After this he gave thanks to God, and blessing the bread and wine, he took the bread and brake it, giving some to each, saying, at the same time, "Eat this, remember that Christ died for us, and feed on it spiritually. Then taking the cup he drank, and bade them remember that Christ's blood was shed for them." After this he gave thanks, prayed for some time, took leave of his visiters, and retired to his chamber

On the morning of his execution there came to him two friars from the cardinal; one of whom put on him a black linen coat, and the other brought several bags of gunpowder, which they tied about different parts of his body.

In this dress he was conducted from the room in which he had been confined, to the outer chamber of the governor's apartments, there to stay till the necessary preparations were made for his execution.

The windows and balconies of the castle, opposite the place where he was to suffer, were all hung with tapestry and silk hangings, with cushions for the cardinal and his train, who were from thence to feast their eyes with the torments of this innocent man. There was also a large guard of soldiers, not so much to secure the execution, as to show a vain ostentation of power; besides which, cannon were placed on different parts of the castle.

All the preparations being completed, Wishart, after having his hands tied behind him, was conducted to the fatal spot. In his way thither he was accosted by two friars, who desired him to pray to the Virgin Mary to intercede for him. To whom he meekly said, "Cease; tempt me not, I entreat you."

As soon as he arrived at the stake, the executioner put a rope round his neck, and a chain about his middle; upon which he fell on his knees, and thus exclaimed:

"O thou Saviour of the world, have mercy upon me! Father of heaven, I commend my spirit into thy holy hands."

After repeating these words three times he arose, and turning himself to the spectators, addressed them as follows:

"Christian brethren and sisters, I beseech you be not offended at the word of God for the torments which you see prepared for me; but I exhort you, that ye love the word of God for your salvation, and suffer patiently, and with a comfortable heart, for the word's sake which is your undoubted salvation, and everlasting comfort. I pray you also, show my brethren and sisters, who have often heard me, that they cease not to learn the word of God, which I taught them according to the measure of grace given me, but to hold fast to it with the strictest attention; and show them that the doctrine was no old wives' fables, but the truth of God; for if I had taught men's doctrine, I should have had greater thanks from men: but for the word of God's sake I now suffer, not sorrowfully, but with a glad heart and mind. For this cause I was sent, that I should suffer this fire for Christ's sake; behold my face, you shall not see me change my countenance; I fear not the fire; and if persecution come to you for the word's sake, I pray you fear not them that can kill the body, and have no power to hurt the soul."

After this he prayed for his accusers, saying, "I beseech thee, Father of heaven, forgive them that have, from ignorance or an evil mind, forged lies of me: I forgive them with all my heart. I beseech Christ to forgive them, that have ignorantly condemned me."

Then, again turning himself to the spectators, he said, "I beseech you, brethren, exhort your prelates to learn the word of God, that they may be ashamed to do evil, and learn to do good; or there will come upon them the wrath of God, which they shall not eschew."

As soon as he had finished this speech, the executioner fell on his knees before him, and said, "Sir, I pray you forgive me, for I am not the cause of your death."

In return to this Wishart cordially took the man by the hand, and kissed him, saying, "Lo, here is a token that I forgive thee; my heart, do thine office."

He was then fastened to the stake, and the fagots being lighted, immediately set fire to the powder that was tied about him, and which blew into a flame and smoke.

The governor of the castle, who stood so near that he was singed with the flame, exhorted our martyr in a few words, to be of good cheer, and to ask pardon of God for his offences. To which he replied, "This flame occasions trouble to my body, indeed, but it hath in no wise broken my spirit. But he who so proudly looks down from yonder lofty place," pointing to the cardinal, "shall, ere long, be as ignominiously thrown down, as now he proudly lolls at his ease."

When he had said this, the executioner pulled the rope which was tied about his neck with great violence, so that he was soon strangled; and the fire getting strength, burnt with such rapidity that in less than an hour his body was totally consumed.

Thus died, in confirmation of the gospel of Christ, a sincere believer, whose fortitude and constancy, during his sufferings, can only be imputed to the support of divine aid, in order to fulfil that memorable promise, "As is thy day, so shall thy strength be also."

Cardinal Beaton put to death.

The prediction of Mr. Wishart concerning cardinal Beaton is related by Buchanan and others, but it has been doubted, by some later writers, whether he really made such prediction or not. Be that as it may, however, it is certain that the death of Wishart did, in a short time after, prove fatal to the cardinal himself; the particulars of which we subjoin.

Soon after the death of Mr. Wishart, the cardinal went to Finhaven, the seat of the earl of Crawford, to solemnize a marriage between the eldest son of that nobleman, and his own natural daughter, Margaret. While he was thus employed, he received intelligence that an English squadron was upon the coast, and that consequently an invasion was to be feared. Upon this he immediately returned to St. Andrews, and appointed a day for the nobility and gentry to meet, and consult what was proper to be done on this occasion. But as no further news was heard of the English fleet, their apprehensions of an invasion soon subsided.

In the mean time Norman Lesley, eldest son of the earl of Rothes, who had been treated by the cardinal with injustice and contempt, formed a design, in conjunction with his uncle John Lesley, who hated Beaton, and others who were inflamed against him on account of his persecution of the protestants, the death of Wishart, and other causes, to assassinate the prelate, though he now resided in the castle of St. Andrews, which he was fortifying at great expense, and had, in the opinion of that age, already rendered it almost impregnable.

The cardinal's retinue was numerous, the town was at his devotion, and the neighbouring country full of his dependants. However, the conspirators, who were only sixteen, having concerted their plan, met together early in the morning, on Saturday the 29th of May. The first thing they did, was to seize the porter of the castle, from whom they took the keys, and secured the gate. They then sent four of their party to watch the cardinal's chamber, that he might have no notice given him of what was doing; after which they went and called up the servants and attendants, to whom they were well known, and turned them out the gate to the number of fifty, as they did also upwards of a hundred workmen, who were employed in the fortifications and buildings of the castle; but the eldest son of the regent, whom the cardinal kept with him, under pretence of superintending his education, but in reality as a hostage, they kept for their own security.

All this was done with so little noise, that the cardinal was not waked till they knocked at his chamber door; upon which he cried out, "Who is there?" John Lesley answered, "My name is Lesley." "Which Lesley?" inquired the cardinal; "is it Norman?" It was answered that he must open the door to those who were there; but instead of this, he barricaded it in the best manner he could. However, finding that they had brought fire in order to force their way, and they having, as it is said by some, made him a promise of his life, he opened the door They immediately entered with their swords drawn, and John Lesley smote him twice or thrice, as did also Peter Carmichael; but James Melvil, as Mr. Knox relates the affair, perceiving them to be in choler, said, "This work, and judgment of God, although it be secret, ought to be done with greater gravity;" and presenting the point of the sword to the cardinal, said to him, "Repent thee of thy wicked life, but especially of the shedding the blood of that notable instrument of God, Mr. George Wishart, which albeit the flame of fire consumed before men, yet cries it for vengeance upon thee; and we from God are sent to revenge it. For here before my God, I protest, that neither the hatred of thy person, the love of thy riches nor the fear of any trouble thou couldst have done to me in particular, moved or moveth me to strike thee; but only because thou hast been and remainest an obstinate enemy of Christ Jesus and his holy gospel." Having said this, he with his sword run him twice or thrice through the body; who only said, "I am a priest! Fie! fie! all is gone!" and then expired, being about fifty-two years of age.

Thus fell cardinal Beaton, who had been as great a persecutor against the protestants in Scotland, as Bonner was in England; and whose death was as little regretted by all true professors of Christ's gospel.

The next and last person put to death in Scotland for the sake of Christ, was Walter Mille who was burnt in 1558.

27*

CHAPTER II.

Progress of the Reformation in the Reign of Edward VI.

EDWARD was the only son of king Henry, by his beloved wife Jane Seymour, who died the day after his birth, which took place on the twelfth of October, 1537, so that, when he came to the throne, in 1547, he was but ten years old.

At six years of age he was put into the hands of Dr. Cox and Mr. Cheke; the one was to form his mind, and teach him philosophy and divinity, the other, to teach him languages and mathematics: other masters were also appointed for the various parts of his education. He discovered very early a good disposition to religion and virtue, and a particular reverence for the scriptures; and was once greatly offended with a person, who, in order to reach something hastily, laid a great Bible on the floor, and stood upon it. He made great progress in learning, and at the age of eight years, wrote Latin letters frequently to the king, to queen Catharine Parre, to the archbishop of Canterbury, and his uncle, the earl of Hertford.

Upon his father's decease, the earl of Hertford and sir Anthony Brown were sent to bring him to the Tower of London: and when Henry's death was published, he was proclaimed king.

At his coming to the Tower, his father's will was opened, by which it was found that he had named sixteen noblemen and gentlemen to be the governors of the kingdom, and of his son's person till he should be eighteen years of age. These were the archbishop of Canterbury; lords Wriothesly, St. John, Russel, Hertford, and Lisle; Tonstall, bishop of Durham; sir Anthony Brown, sir William Paget, sir Edward North, sir Edward Montague, lord chief justice of the common pleas; judge Bromley, sir Anthony Denny, sir William Herbert, sir Edward Wotton, and Dr. Wotton, dean of Canterbury and York. They were also to give the king's sisters in marriage; who, if they married without their consent, were to forfeit their right of succession. A privy council was also named to be their assistant in the government.

As might have been expected, dissensions soon arose among so numerous a party; and, on its being proposed that one should be chosen out of the sixteen to whom ambassadors should address themselves, and who should have the chief direction of affairs; lord Wriothesly, the chancellor, was thought the precedence fell to him by his office, since the archbishop did not meddle much in secular affairs opposed this much, and said, "It was a chance of the king's will, who had made them all equal in power and dignity; and it any were raised above the rest in title, it would not be possible to keep him within due bounds, since great titles make way for high powers." Notwithstanding this, the earl of Hertford was declared governor of the king's person, and protector of the kingdoms; with this restriction, that he should do nothing but by the advice and consent of the rest. Upon this advancement, and the opposition made to it by several, parties were formed, the one headed by the protector, and the other by the chancellor; the favourers of the reformation were of the former, and those that opposed it of the latter.

The chancellor was ordered to renew the commissions of the judges and justices of peace, and king Henry's great seal was to be made use of, till a new one should be made. The day after this, all the executors took oaths to execute their trust faithfully, the privy counsellors were also brought into the king's presence, who all expressed their satisfaction in the choice of the protector; and it was ordered that all despatches to foreign princes should be signed only by him. All that held offices were required to come and renew their commissions, and to swear allegiance to the king; among the rest, came the bishops, and took out such commissions as were granted in the former reign, by which they were to hold their bishoprics only during the king's pleasure. Cranmer set an example to the rest in taking out one of these. This check upon the bishops was judged expedient in case they should oppose the reformation; but the ill consequences of such an unlimited power being foreseen, the bishops, who were afterward promoted, were not so fettered, but were to hold their bishoprics during life.

An accident soon occurred, which made way for great

changes in the church.   The curate and church-wardens
of St. Martin's in London, were brought before the council
for removing the crucifix, and other images, and putting
some texts of scripture on the walls of their church, in the
places where they stood ; they answered, that in repairing
their church, they had removed the images, which being
rotten they did not renew them, but put the words of scripture in their room : they had also removed others, which
they found had been abused to idolatry.   Great pains were
taken by the popish party to punish them severely, in
order to strike a terror into others ; but Cranmer was for
the removing of all images set up in churches, as being
expressly contrary both to the second commandment, and
the practice of the purest Christians for many ages : and
though, in compliance with the gross abuses of paganism,
much of the pomp of their worship was very early brought
into the Christian church, yet it was long before images
were introduced.   At first all images were condemned by
the fathers ; then they allowed the use, but condemned
the worshipping of them ; and afterward, in the eighth and
ninth centuries, the worshipping of them was, after a long
contest, both in the east and west, at last generally received.   Some, in particular, were believed to be more
wonderfully endowed, and this was much improved by the
cheats of the monks, who had enriched themselves by such
means.   And this abuse had now grown to such a height,
that heathenism itself had not been guilty of greater absurdities toward its idols.   Since all these abuses had risen
out of the use of them, and the setting them up being contrary to the command of God, and the nature of the Christian religion, which is simple and spiritual ; it seemed
most reasonable to cure the disease in its root, and to clear
the churches of images, that the people might be preserved
from idolatry.

These reasons prevailed so far, that the curate and
church-wardens were dismissed with a reprimand ; they
were ordered to beware of such rashness for the future,
and to provide a crucifix, and, till that could be had, were
ordered to cause one to be painted on the wall.   Upon
this, Dr. Ridley, in a sermon preached before the king,
inveighed against the superstition toward images and holy

water, and spread over the whole nation a general disposition to pull them down; which soon after commenced in Portsmouth.

Upon this Gardiner made great complaints; he said the Lutherans themselves went not so far, for he had seen images in their churches. He distinguished between image and idol as if the one, which he said only was condemned, were the representation of a false God, and the other of the true; and he thought, that as words conveyed by the ear begat devotion, so images, by the conveyance of the eye, might have the same effect on the mind. He also thought a virtue might be both in them and in holy water, as well as there was in Christ's garments, Peter's shadow, or Elisha's staff: and there might be a virtue in holy water, as well as in water of baptism.

To these arguments, which Gardiner wrote in several letters, the protector answered, that the bishops had formerly argued much in another strain, namely, that because the scriptures were abused by the vulgar readers, therefore they were not to be trusted to them; and so made a pretended abuse the ground of taking away that which, by God's special appointment, was to be delivered to all Christians. This held much stronger against images, forbidden by God. The brazen serpent set up by Moses, by God's own direction, was broken when abused to idolatry; for that was the greatest corruption of religion possible: but yet the protector acknowledged there was reason to complain of the forwardness of the people, who broke down images without authority: to prevent which, in future, orders were sent to the justices of peace to look well to the peace and government of the nation.

The funeral of the deceased king was performed, with the usual ceremonies, at Windsor. He had left six hundred pounds a year to the church of Windsor, for priests to say mass for his soul every day, and for four obits* a year, and sermons, and distribution of alms at every one of them, and for a sermon every Sunday, and a maintenance for thirteen poor knights, which was settled upon that church by his executors in due form of law.

The pomp of this endowment led people to examine

* *Obit* was the anniversary of a person's death.

into the *usefulness* of *soul-masses* and *obits.* Christ appointed the sacrament for a commemoration of his death among the living, but it was not easy to conceive how that was to be applied to departed souls; and it was evidently a project for drawing the wealth of the world into their hands. In the primitive church there was a commemoration of the dead, or an honourable remembrance of them made in the daily offices. But even this custom grew into abuse, and some inferred from it, that departed souls, unless they were signally pure, passed through a purgation in the next life, before they were admitted to heaven; of which St. Austin, in whose time the opinion began to be received, says, that it was taken up without any sure ground in scripture. But what was wanting in scripture-proof was supplied by visions, dreams, and tales, till it was generally received. King Henry had acted like one who did not much believe it, for he had deprived innumerable souls of the masses that were said for them in monasteries, by destroying those foundations. Yet he seems to have intended that if masses could avail the departed souls, he would himself be secure; and as he gratified the priests by this part of his endowment, so he pleased the people by appointing sermons and alms to be given on such days. Thus he died as he had lived, wavering between both persuasions.

But now the ceremony of the coronation took off the attention of the multitude from more serious thoughts. The protector was made duke of Somerset; the earl of Essex, marquis of Northampton; the lords Leslie and Wriothesly, earls of Warwick and Southampton; Seymour, Rich, Willoughby, and Sheffield, were made barons. In order to the king's coronation, the office for that ceremony was reviewed, and much shortened; one remarkable alteration was, that formerly the king used to be presented to the people at the corners of the scaffold, and they were asked if they would have him to be their king? Which looked like an election, rather than a ceremony of investing one that was already king. This was now changed, and the people were desired only to give their assent and good will to his coronation, as by the duty of allegiance they were bound to do. On the twentieth of February, 1517, he was crowned, and a general pardon was proclaimed, out of which the duke of Norfolk, cardinal Pole, and some others, were excepted.

The chancellor, who was looked on as the head of the popish party, now lost his place, by granting a commission to the master of the rolls and three masters of chancery, of whom two were civilians, to execute his office in the court of chancery as if he were present, only their decrees were to be brought to him to be signed before they should be enrolled.

The first business of consequence that required great consideration was the Smalcaldic war, then begun between the emperor and the princes of the protestant league : the effects of which, if the emperor prevailed, were like to be. not only the extirpating of Lutheranism, but his becoming the absolute master of Germany : which he chiefly wished as the first step to a universal monarchy, but disguised it to other princes : to the pope he pretended that his design was only to extirpate heresy ; to other sovereigns he pretended it was to repress a rebellion, and denied all designs of suppressing the new doctrines ; which he managed so artfully, that he divided Germany against itself, and got some Lutheran princes to declare for him, and others to be neutral : and having obtained a very liberal supply for his wars with France and the Turks, for which he granted an edict for liberty of conscience, he made peace with both these princes, and resolved to employ that treasure which the Germans had given him, against themselves. That he might deprive them of their allies, he used means to engage king Henry and Francis the First in a war ; but that was, chiefly by their interposition, composed. And now, when the war was likely to be carried on with great vigour, both those princes died ; Henry in January, and Francis in March following. Many of their confederates began to capitulate and forsake them ; and the divisions among their own commanders very much hindered their success.

The pope wished to engage the emperor in a war in Germany, that so Italy might be at peace : and in order to accomplish this object, he published the treaty which had been made between them, that so it might appear that the design of the war was to extirpate heresy, though the emperor was making great protestations to the contrar, in

Germany. He also opened the council of Trent, which Charles had long desired in vain; but it was now brought upon him when he least wished for it; for the protestants all declared, that they could not look upon it as a free general council, since it was so entirely at the pope's devotion, that not so much as a reformation of the grossest abuses was likely to be obtained. Nor could the emperor prevail with the council not to condemn the "new doctrines" as heresy; but the more he attempted to obstruct its proceedings, the more did the pope urge it on, to open the eyes of the Germans, and engage them all vigorously against the emperor; who, on his part, gave them such secret assurances of tolerating the Augsburgh confession, that the marquis of Brandenburgh declared for him, and his example was followed by several other princes. This was the state of affairs in Germany; which rendered it very difficult to determine what answer the protector should give the duke of Saxony's chancellor, whom he had sent over to obtain money for carrying on the war. It was, on the one hand, of great importance to the safety of England to preserve the German princes, and yet it was very dangerous to begin a war of such consequence under an infant king. At present the government only promised, within three months, to send 50,000 crowns to Hamburgh, and would do no more till new emergencies should lead them to new counsels.

The nation was in an ill condition for a war with such a mighty prince;—labouring under great distractions at home; the people generally crying out for a reformation, despising the clergy, and loving the new preachers. The priests were for the most part very ignorant, and scandalous in their lives: many of them had been monks, and those who were to pay them the pensions which were reserved to them at the destruction of the monasteries, till they should be provided, took care to get them in some small benefice. The greatest part of the parsonages were impropriated, for they belonged to the monasteries, and the abbots had only granted the incumbents, either the vicarage, or some small donative, and left them the perquisites raised by masses and other offices. At the suppression of those houses there was no care taken to make provision for the incumbents; so that they were in some measure compelled to continue in their idolatrous practices for subsistence.

Now these persons saw that a reformation of those abuses would deprive them of their means of existence; and, therefore, they were at first zealous against all changes; but the same principle made them comply with every change which was made rather than lose their benefices. The clergy were encouraged in their opposition to the reformation by the protection they expected from Gardiner, Bonner, and Tonstall, men of great reputation and in power; and, above all, the lady Mary, the next heir to the crown, openly declared against all changes till the king should be of age.

On the other hand, Cranmer resolved to proceed more vigorously: the protector was firmly united to him, as were the young king's tutors, and Edward himself was as much engaged as could be expected from so young a person; for both his knowledge and zeal for true religion were above his age. Several of the bishops also declared for a reformation, but Ridley, bishop of Rochester, was the person on whom Cranmer most depended. Latimer remained with him at Lambeth, and did great service by his sermons, which were very popular; but he would not return to his bishopric, choosing rather to serve the church in a more disengaged manner. Assisted by these persons, Cranmer resolved to proceed by degrees, and to give the reasons of every advance so fully, that he hoped by the blessing of God, to convince the nation of the fitness of whatsoever should be done, and thereby prevent the dangerous opposition that might otherwise be apprehended.

Visitation of all the Churches.

The power of the privy council had been much exalted in the last reign, by act of parliament; and one proviso made was, that the king's council should have the same authority when he was under age that he himself had at full age. It was, therefore, resolved to begin with a general visitation of all England, which was divided into six precincts: and two gentlemen, a civilian, a divine, and a register, were appointed for each of these. But before they

28

were sent out, a letter was written to all the bishops, giving them notice of it, suspending their jurisdiction while it lasted, and requiring them to preach no where but in their cathedrals, and that the other clergy should not preach but in their own churches, without license; by which it was intended to restrain such as were not acceptable to their own parishes, and to grant the others licenses to preach in any church of England. The greatest difficulty the reformers found was in the want of able and prudent men; most of the reformed preachers being too hot and indiscreet, and the few who were otherwise were required in London and the universities.

The only thing by which the people could be universally instructed was a book of homilies: therefore the twelve first homilies, in the book still known by that name, were compiled; in framing which the chief design was to acquaint the people rightly with the nature of the gospel covenant. Orders were also given, that a Bible should be in every church, which, though it had been commanded by Henry, yet had not been generally obeyed; and for understanding the New Testament, Erasmus's paraphrase was translated into English, and appointed to be placed with it. His great reputation and learning, and his dying in the communion of the Roman church, made this book preferable to any other of the kind.

The injunctions made by Cromwell in the former reign for instructing the people, for removing images, and putting down all other customs abused to superstition; for reading the Scriptures, saying the litany in English, for frequent sermons and catechising, for the exemplary lives of the clergy, their labours in visiting the sick, reconciling differences, and exhorting the people to charity, &c., were now renewed; and all who gave livings by simoniacal bargains, were declared to have forfeited their right of patronage to the king. A great charge was also given for the strict observation of the Lord's day, which was appointed to be spent wholly in the service of God, it not being enough to hear mass or matins in the morning, and spend the rest of the day in drunkenness and quarrelling, as was commonly practised: but it ought to be all employed, either in the duties of religion, or in acts of charity. Direction was also given for the saying of prayers, in which the king, as supreme head, and the queen, and the king's sisters, the protector and council, and all orders of persons in the kingdom, were to be mentioned. Injunctions were also given for the bishops to preach four times a year in all their dioceses, once in their cathedral, and thrice in any other church, unless they had a good excuse to the contrary: that their chaplains should preach often: and that they should give orders to none but such as were duly qualified.

The visiters at length ended the visitation, and in London and every part of England, the images, for refusing to bow down to which many a saint had been burnt, were now committed to the flames. Bonner at first protested that he would obey the injunctions, if they were not contrary to the laws of God and the ordinances of the church; but being called before the council, he retracted, and asked pardon; yet, for an example to others, he was some time confined. Gardiner wrote to one of the visiters, before they came to Winchester, that he could not receive the homilies; and if he must either quit his bishopric, or sin against his conscience, he resolved to choose the former. Upon this he was called before the council, and required to receive the book of homilies: but he objected to one of them, which taught that charity did not justify, contrary to the book published by the late king, and confirmed in parliament. He also complained of many things in Erasmus's paraphrase; and being pressed to declare whether he would obey the injunctions or not, he refused to promise it, and was in consequence sent to the Fleet. Cranmer treated in private with him, and they argued much about justification. Gardiner thought the sacraments justified, and that charity justified as well as faith. Cranmer urged that nothing but the merits of Christ justified, as they were applied by faith, which could not exist without charity.

Gardiner lay in prison till the act of general pardon set him at liberty. Many blamed the severity of these proceedings, as contrary both to law and equity, and said, that all people, even those who complained most of arbitrary power, were apt to usurp it when in authority. Lady Mary was so much alarmed that she wrote to the protector that such changes were contrary to the honour due to her father's memory, and that it was against their duty to the king to enter upon such points, and endanger the public peace before he was of age. To which he answered, " That her father had died before he could finish the good things he had intended concerning religion ; and had expressed his regret, both before himself and many others, that he left things in so unsettled a state ; and assured her, that nothing should be done but what would turn to the glory of God, and the king's honour."

New Acts of Parliament.

The parliament was opened the fourth of November, and the protector was by patent authorized to sit under the cloth of state, on the right hand of the throne ; and to have all the honours and privileges that so near a relative of the sovereign had ever had. Rich was lord chancellor. The first act that passed, five bishops only dissenting, was a repeal of all the statutes in the late reign, that had made any thing treason or felony which was not so before, and of the six articles, and the authority given to the king's proclamations, as also of the acts against Lollards. By this act, all who denied the king's supremacy, or asserted the pope's, for the first offence were to forfeit their goods ; for the second, were to be in a præmunire ; and were to be attainted of treason for the third. If any one attempted to deprive the king of his estate or title, he was was adjudged guilty of treason ; but none were to be accused of words, but within a month after they were spoken. The king's power of annulling all laws made, before he was twenty-four years of age, was also repealed, and restricted to the annulling them for the time to come.

Another act passed, with the same dissent, for the laity receiving the sacrament in both kinds, and that the people should always communicate with the priest ; and by it irreverence to the sacrament was condemned under severe penalties.

Another act was passed without any dissent, ordaining that the *congé d'élire*, and the election pursuant to it, should cease for the future, and that bishops should be named by the king's letters patent and thereupon be consecrated ;

and should hold their courts in the king's name, and not in their own, excepting only the archbishop of Canterbury's court : and they were to use the king's seal in all their writings, except in presentations, collations, and letters of orders, in which they might use their own seals.

Another act was made against rogues and vagabonds, decreeing that they should be *made slaves for two years,* by any who should seize on them : this was chiefly intended to operate against some vagrant monks, who went about the country infusing into the people a dislike of the government. But a state of slavery is so contrary to the feelings of every English heart, that no person could be found to act upon it ; and the odious statute was virtually repealed. An act was next proposed for giving the king all those chantries which his father had not seized on. Cranmer much opposed this ; " For," he said, " the poverty of the clergy was such that the state of learning and religion was like to suffer greatly if it should not be relieved ; and yet he saw no probable fund for that, but the preserving these till the king should come to age, and allow the selling them, for buying in of at least such a share of the impropriations as might afford them some more comfortable subsistence ;" yet, notwithstanding the dissent of himself, and seven other bishops, it was passed. The last act was for granting a general pardon, but clogged with some exceptions.

The convocation sat at the same time ; and moved that the commission begun in the late reign for reforming the ecclesiastical laws, might be revived, and that the inferior clergy might be admitted to sit in the house of commons, for which they alleged a clause in the bishop's writ, and ancient custom ; and since some prelates had, under the former reign, begun to alter the service of the church, they desired it might be brought to perfection ; and that some care might be taken for supplying the poor clergy, and relieving them from the taxes that lay so heavily on them. The claim of the inferior clergy to sit in the house of commons occasioned some debate, but to no effect.

It was resolved that some bishops and divines should be sent to Windsor, to finish some reformations in the public offices ; for the whole lower house of convocation, without a contradictory vote, agreed to the bill about the sacrament. A proposition being also set on foot concerning the lawfulness of the marriage of the clergy, thirty-five subscribed to the affirmative, and only fourteen dissented.

Gardner, being included in the act of pardon, was set at liberty; he promised to receive and obey the injunctions, objecting only to the homily of justification; yet he complied in that likewise; but it was visible that in his heart he abhorred all these proceedings, though he outwardly conformed.

Ceremonies Abolished.

Candlemas and Lent were now approaching, and the clergy and people were much divided with respect to the ceremonies usual at those times. By some injunctions in Henry's reign it had been declared that fasting in Lent was only binding by a positive law. Wakes and Plough-Mondays were also suppressed, and hints were given that other customs, which were much abused, should be shortly done away. The rabble loved these things, as matters of diversion, and thought divine worship without them would be but a dull business. But others looked on them as relics of heathenism, and thought they did not become the gravity and simplicity of the Christian religion.

Cranmer procured an order of council against the carrying of candles on Candlemas-day, of ashes on Ash-Wednesday, and palms on Palm-Sunday; which was directed to Bonner to be intimated to the bishops of the province of Canterbury, and was executed by him. But a proclamation followed against all who should make changes without authority. The creeping to the cross, and taking holy bread and water, were put down, and power was given to the archbishop of Canterbury to certify, in the king's name, what ceremonies should be afterward laid aside; and none were to preach out of their own parishes without license from the king or the visiters, the archbishop, or the bishop of the diocese. Soon after this, a general order followed for a removal of all images out of the churches, which occasioned great contests whether the images had been abused to superstition or not. Some thought the consecration of them was an abuse. Those also which represented the Trinity as a man with three faces in one head; or as an old man with a young man before him, and a dove over his head; and some, where the blessed Virgin was represented as admitted into it, gave so great scandal, that it was no wonder if men, as they grew more enlightened, could no longer endure them. The only occasion given to censure in this order, was, that all shrines, and the plate belonging to them, were appointed to be brought in for the king's use.

CHAPTER III.

A New Office for the Communion.

EIGHTEEN bishops and some other divines were now employed to examine and amend the offices of the church. They began with the Eucharist, and proceeded in the same manner as in the former reign. It was clearly found that the plain institution of the sacrament was much vitiated with a mixture of many heathenish rites and pomps, to raise the credit of the priests, in whose hands that great performance was lodged. This was at first done to draw over the heathen by those splendid rites to Christianity; but superstition, once begun, has no bounds; and ignorance and barbarity increasing in the middle ages, there was no regard had to any thing in religion, but as it was set off with pageantry; and the belief of the corporeal presence raised this to a still greater height. The office was in an unknown tongue; all the vessels and garments belonging to it were consecrated with much devotion; a great part of the service was secret, to make it look like a wonderful charm; the consecration itself was to be said very softly, for words that were not to be heard agreed best with a change that was not to be seen: the many gesticulations and the magnificent processions all tended to raise this pageantry higher. Masses were also said for all the affairs of human life. Trentals, a custom of having thirty masses a year on the chief festivals for redeeming souls out of purgatory, was that which brought the priests most money, for these were thought to be God's *best days*, in which access was easier to him! On saint's days, in the mass it was prayed, that by the saints' intercession the sacrifice might become the more acceptable, and procure a more ample indulgence; which could not be easily explained, if the sacrifice were the death of Christ. Beside the before-mentioned, a numberless variety of other rites and ceremonies, borrowed from the heathens, were made use of for corrupting the holiest institutions of the Christian religion.

The first step that was now taken was to make a new office for the communion, that is, the distribution of the sacrament, for the office of consecration was not at this time touched. In the exhortation, auricular confession to a priest is left free to be done or omitted, and all were required not to judge one another in that matter. There was also a denunciation made, requiring impenitent sinners to withdraw. The bread was to be still of the same form as that formerly used. In the distribution it was said, " The body of our Lord, &c., preserve thy body ; and the blood of our Lord, &c., preserve thy soul." This was printed, with a proclamation, requiring all to receive it with such reverence and uniformity as might encourage the king to proceed further, and not to run to other things before the king gave direction, assuring the people of his earnest zeal to set forth godly orders ; and therefore it was hoped they would wait for it : the books were sent all over England, and the clergy were appointed to administer the communion at the following Easter according to them.

Auricular Confession Examined.

Confession was next examined ; and it was found that the practice had commenced in the early ages of the church ; and penances had been imposed by the priests. Afterward, pilgrimages, and crusades against heretics, or princes deposed by the pope, were commanded instead of all other penances : the priests also managed confession and absolution so as to enter into all men's secrets, and to govern their consciences by them ; many reserved cases were made, in which the pope only gave absolution ; this occasioned the trade of *indulgences* to be put in their hands which they managed with as much confidence as mountebanks use in selling their medicines, with this superior advantage over other quacks, that the inefficacy of their devices was not so easily discovered.

Gardiner was now again brought into trouble; many complaints were made of him, that he disparaged the preachers sent with the king's license into his diocese, and that he secretly opposed all reformation. On being brought before the council, he denied most of the things objected to him, and offered to explain himself openly in a sermon before the king. This being granted, he justified many of the changes that had been made; but when he came to the sacrament, he contended so strongly for the corporeal presence, that a great disturbance took place in the church. This conduct being deemed seditious, he was sent to the Tower.

A New Liturgy Composed.

But now a more general reformation of the whole liturgy was under consideration, that all the nation might have a uniformity in the worship of God. Anciently the liturgies were short, and had few ceremonies in them: every bishop had one for his diocese; but in the African churches they began first to put them into a more regular form. Gregory the Great laboured much in this; yet he left Augustine, when he sent him into Britain, to his choice, either to use the Roman or French forms in England, as he found they were like to tend most to edification. Great additions had been made to the liturgy in every age; for the private devotions of some who were reputed saints, were added to the public offices: and mysterious significations were invented for every new rite, which swelled them to a vast bulk. It was now resolved to have a liturgy, which should bring the worship to a proper mean between the pomp of superstition, and naked simplicity. It was resolved to change nothing, merely in opposition to received practices, but rather (in imitation of what Christ did in the institution of the two sacraments of the gospel, that consisted of rites used among the Jews, but sanctified by him to higher purposes) to comply with what had been formerly in use, as much as was possible, thereby to gain the people.

All the consecrations of water, salt, &c., in the church

of Rome, being relics of heathenism, were laid aside.
The absolutions on account of the merits of the blessed
virgin and the saints, the sprinklings of water, fastings,
and pilgrimages, with many other things; and the absolution given to dead bodies, were looked upon as gross impostures, tending to make the world think that the priests
had the keys of heaven in their hands, and could carry
people thither on easier terms than the gospel prescribes.
This induced the people to purchase their favour, especially when they were dying; so that, as their fears were
then heightened, there was no other way left them, in the
conclusion of an ill life, to die with any hopes of eternal
happiness, but as they bargained with their priests; all
this was now rejected.

It was resolved to have the whole worship in the vulgar
tongue; as enabling all persons to join in " praising God
with understanding." As white had been the colour of
the priest's vestments, under the mosaical law, had early
been brought into the Christian churches, and was a proper expression of innocence, and it being fit that the worship of God should be performed in a decent habit, it was
continued.

The morning and evening prayers were but almost in
the same form as that in which they now stand, only there
was neither confession nor absolution. In the office for
the communion, there was a commemoration of thanksgiving for the blessed virgin and all departed saints, and
they were commended to God's mercy and peace. In the
consecration, the use of crossing the elements was retained; but there was no elevation, which was at first
used as a historical rite, to show Christ's being lifted up
on the cross; but it was afterward done, to excite the people to adore it. No stamp was to be on the bread, and it
was to be thicker than ordinary. It was to be put in the
people's mouths by the priests, though it had been anciently put in their hands; but after the corporeal presence was acknowledged, the people were not suffered to
touch it, and the priest's thumbs and fingers were pe-
culiarly anointed, to qualify them for that contact. In
baptism the child's head and breast were to be crossed,
and adjuration was to be made of the devil to depart from
him: children were to be thrice dipped, or, in case of

weakness, water was to be sprinkled on their faces, and then they were to be anointed. The sick might also be anointed if they desired it. At funerals, the departed soul was recommended to God's mercy.

The sacraments were formerly believed of such virtue, that they conferred grace by the very receiving them. Acting on this belief, the early Christians used to send portions of the eucharist to the sick, but without any pomp: which was a corruption of later times. But instead of the procession with the host, it was now appointed that the sacraments should be ministered to the sick, being consecrated by their bedsides; and, in case of weakness, children were allowed to be baptized in houses; though it was more suitable to the design of baptism which was the admission of a new member to the church to do it before the whole congregation.

The liturgy thus compiled, was published, with a preface concerning ceremonies.

When the book came before the public, several things were censured; as particularly the frequent use of the cross, and anointing. The former was at first used as a badge of a crucified Saviour, but was much corrupted by the priests in after ages, so that it was at length believed to have a virtue for driving away evil spirits, and preserving one from dangers; and acquired a kind of sacramental character, entirely unfounded in Scripture or reason; but the using it as a ceremony, expressing the believing in a crucified Saviour, could imply no superstition.

The protestant religion now appeared almost ruined in Germany, and this made the reformers turn their eyes to England. Calvin wrote to the protector, and pressed him to go on to a more complete reformation, and that prayers for the dead, the chrism, and extreme unction, might be laid aside. He desired him to trust in God, and go on, and wished there were more preaching, and in a more lively way than he heard was then in England: but prayed him to suppress that impiety and profanity that, as he was told, abounded in the nation.

In February 1549, an act passed, allowing the clergy to marry. It was declared, "That it were better for priests to live unmarried, free of all worldly cares; yet since the laws compelling it had occasioned great debauchery, they were all repealed." The pretence of chastity in the Romish priests had possessed the world with a high opinion of them, and had been a great reflection on the reformers, if the world had not clearly seen through it and been made very sensible of the ill effects of it, by the defilement it brought into their own families. Nor was there any point in which the reformers had searched the Scriptures more, to remove the prejudice that lay against them. In the Old Testament all the priests were not only married, but the office descended by inheritance. In the New Testament marriage was declared honourable in all: among the qualifications of bishops and deacons, their being the husbands of one wife, are reckoned up. Many of the apostles were married, and carried their wives about with them as also Aquila did Priscilla.

Another act was passed, confirming the liturgy, which was now finished; eight bishops and three temporal lords only protesting against it. There was a long preamble, setting forth the inconveniencies of the former offices, and the pains that had been taken to reform them; and that divers bishops and divines had, by the aid of the Holy Ghost, with a uniform agreement concluded on the new book: therefore they enacted that by Whitsunday next all divine offices should be performed according to it; and if any persons used other offices, for the first offence, they should be imprisoned six months, lose their benifices for the second, and be imprisoned during life for the third

Another act was also passed respecting fasting, declaring. " That though all days and meats were in themselves alike, yet fasting being a great help to virtue, and to the subduing the body to the mind, it was enacted, that Lent, and all Fridays and Saturdays, and ember-days, should be fish-days, under several penalties, excepting the weak, or those that had the king's license." Christ had told his disciples, that when he was taken from them, they should fast: so in the primitive church they fasted before Easter; but the same number of days was not observed in all places; afterward, other rules and days were established: but St. Austin complained, that many in his time placed all their religion in observing them. Fast days are turned to a mockery in the church of Rome, in which they dine on fish exquisitely drest and drink wine.

A new Visitation.

Both the laity and clergy gave the king subsidies, upon which the parliament was prorogued. The first thing attended to was the enforcing the act of uniformity. Some complaints were made of the priests' manner of officiating, who did it with such a tone of voice that the people could not understand what was said, any more than when the prayers were said in Latin. Prayers were, therefore, ordered to be said in parish churches in a plain voice, but in cathedrals the old way was still kept up, as agreeing better with the music used in them ; though this seemed not very decent in the confession of sins, nor in the litany, where a simple voice, gravely uttered, agreed better with those devotions than cadences and musical notes. Others continued to use all the gesticulations, crossings, and kneelings, to which they had formerly been accustomed. The people also continued the use of their beads, which had been brought in by Peter the Hermit, in the eleventh century, by which the repeating the angel's salutation to the Virgin was made a great part of their devotion, and was ten times said for one *Paternoster.* Instructions were given to the visiters to put all these down, and to inquire if any priests continued their trentals or masses for departed souls. Orders were also given, that there should be no private masses at altars in the corners of churches ; also that there should be but one communion in a day, unless in great churches, and at high festivals, in which they were allowed to have two, one in the morning, and another at noon.

The visiters made their report, that they found the book of common prayer received universally over the kingdom, except that the lady Mary continued to have mass said according to the abrogated forms. Upon this the council wrote to her to conform to the laws ; " for the nearer she was to the king in blood, she was so much the more obliged to give example to the rest of the subjects." She refused to comply with their desires, and sent to the emperor for his protection ; upon which he pressed the English ambassadors, who promised that she should be dispensed with, at least for the present. The emperor pretended afterwards that they had made him an absolute promise that he should never more be troubled about it, but they said it

29

was only a temporary one. She refused to acknowledge the laws made when the king was under age, and carried herself very haughtily ; for she well knew that the protector was then fearful of a war with France, which made the emperor's alliance more necessary to England : yet the council sent for the officers of her household, and required them to let her know, that the king's authority was the same while he was a child, as if he were at full age ; and that it was now lodged in them, and though, as single persons, they were all inferior to her, yet as they were the king's council, she was bound to obey them, especially when they executed the law ; which all subjects, of what rank soever, were bound to obey. At present, however, they durst go no further for fear of the emperor's displeasure.

Anabaptists in England.

There were some anabaptists at this time in England, who came from Germany. Of these there were two sorts ; the first only objected to the baptizing of children, and to the manner of it, by sprinkling instead of dipping. The other held many opinions, anciently condemned as heresies : they had raised a war in Germany, and had set up a new king at Munster ; but all these were called Anabaptists, from their opposition to infant baptism, though it was one of the mildest opinions they held. When they came to England, a commission was granted to some bishops, and others to search them out, and to proceed against them. Several of these persons, on being taken up and brought before them, abjured their errors, some of which were, " That there was not a trinity of persons ; that Christ was not God, and took not flesh of the Virgin ; and that a regenerate man could not sin."

Joan Boacher, called Joan of Kent, one of their proselytes, persisted in her error, and denied that Christ took flesh of the substance of his mother ; she was intolerably vain of her notions, and rejected with scorn all the instructions offered her ; she was therefore condemned as an obstinate heretic, and delivered to the secular power. But it was with the most extreme reluctance that the king signed the warrant for her execution ; he thought it was an instance of the same spirit of cruelty for which the reformers condemned the papists and notwithstanding all the arguments that were used with him, he was rather silenced than satisfied, and signed the warrant with tears in his eyes, saying to Cranmer, that since he resigned up himself to his judgment, if he sinned in it, it should lie at his door. This struck the archbishop; and both he and Ridley took great pains with her, and tried what reason, joined with gentleness, could do. But she growing still more and more insolent, at last was burnt, and ended her life very indecently breaking out often in jeers and reproaches.

Some time after this, George Van Parre, a Dutchman, was also condemned and burnt for denying the divinity of Christ, and saying that the Father only was God. He had led a very exemplary life, both for fasting, devotion, and a good conversation, and suffered with extraordinary composure of mind. Against the other sort of anabaptists no severities were used: but several books were written to justify infant baptism; and the practice of the church, so clearly begun, and so universally spread, was thought a good plea, especially as it was grounded on such arguments in Scripture, as demonstrated at least its lawfulness.

CHAPTER IV.

Rebellion in Devonshire and other Parts.

ABOUT this time a rebellion broke out in many parts of England, partly arising from a jealousy in the commons against the nobility and gentry, who finding more advantage by the trade of wool than by that of corn, generally enclosed their grounds, and turned them to pasture, by which a great number of persons were thrown out of employment, and a general consternation was spread throughout the country. The other cause was the unquenched enmity of the popish priests to the reformation, and their endeavours to revive in the minds of the blind multitude their former errors.

In Devonshire, the insurrection was very formidable, and the rebels became quickly ten thousand strong. Lord Russel was sent against them with a small force, and order ed to endeavour to prevail on them to disperse without shedding blood : but Arundel, a man of quality, being at their head, they were not a mere rabble, easily scattered, but had more of the discipline and consequent strength of a regular army. They, however, consented to treat with Lord Russel, and by him forwarded the following demands to the court : "That the old service and ceremonies might be set up again ; that the act of the six articles, and the decrees of general councils, might be again in force ; that the Bible in English should be called in ; that preachers should pray for the souls in purgatory ; that cardinal Pole should be recalled ; that the half of the abbey lands should be restored, to found two abbeys in every county ; and that gentlemen of 100 marks a year might have one servant ;" and they desired a safe-conduct for their chief leaders, in order to the redress of their particular grievances : they afterward reduced their demands to those only which related to religion.

Cranmer wrote an answer to these, showing "The novelty and superstition of those rites and ceremonies, and of all that method of worship of which they were so fond ; and that the amendments and changes had been made according to the Scriptures, and the customs of the primitive church : that their being partial to a worship which they understood not, and being desirous to be kept still in ignorance, without the Scriptures, proved that their priests had greater power over them than the common reason of all mankind had : as for the six articles, that act had never passed if the late king had not gone in person to the parliament, and argued for it : yet he soon saw his error, and was slack in executing it."

After this, a threatening letter was sent to them, in the king's name, upbraiding them for their rebellion and blind obedience to their priests. In it the authority of the king, although under age, was shown at large ; for by the pretence of the king's minority, the people generally were taught to believe that their rising in arms was not rebellion. In conclusion, they were earnestly invited to submit to the royal mercy, as others had done, whom the king had not only pardoned, but had redressed their just grievances.

A fast was proclaimed at court, where Cranmer preached with great freedom and vehemence : he reproved the assembly for their vicious lives, particularly those who pretended a love to the gospel; and set before them the judgments of God, which they might expect would overtake their misdeeds, if they did not repent and amend their lives.

The rebels still continuing in arms, troops were sent against them, and after some resistance in Oxfordshire, Devonshire, and Norfolk, they were at length every where routed, their leaders punished, and tranquillity restored.

Visitation of Cambridge.

A visitation of Cambridge followed soon after this. Ridley was the chief of the visiters; but when he found that a design was laid to suppress some colleges, under pretence of uniting them to others, and to convert some fellowships that were provided for divines, to the study of the civil law, he refused his assent. He said, "The church was already too much robbed, and yet some men's ravenousness was not yet satisfied. It seemed a design was laid to drive both religion and learning out of the land; therefore he desired leave to be gone." The other visiters complained of him to the protector, who wrote him a reproving letter: but he answered it with the freedom that became a bishop, who was resolved to suffer all things rather than sin against his conscience; and the protector was so well satisfied with him, that, for his sake, the college of Clare-hall, the suppression of which he had strongly objected to, was preserved.

Bonner Prosecuted.

Bonner was now brought into trouble. It was not easy to know how to deal with him, for he obeyed every order that was sent him, and yet it was known that he secretly hated and condemned all that was done; and as often as he could declare that safely, he did so, and by such means preserved his interest with the papists: and though he obeyed the orders of the council, yet he did it in so remiss a manner, that it was visibly against his inclination. He was, therefore called before the council, and charged with several particulars, that " Whereas he used to officiate himself on the great festivals, he had not done it since the new service was set out ; that he took no care to repress adultery, and that he never preached." On examination, proving very refractory and violent, he was deprived of his bishopric, and committed to prison during the king's pleasure.

Fall of the Protector.

The English affairs upon the continent this year were extremely unsuccessful, and the fault being laid on the protector, heavy complaints were made against him ; and his enemies, who were very numerous and powerful, openly declared their hostility. The earls of Southampton and of Warwick were the chief; the one hated him for dismissing him from the chancellorship, and the other because he was his rival in power and dignity.

The privy counsellors complained that he was become so arbitrary in his proceedings, that he little regarded the opposition that was made by the majority of the council, to any of his designs. All those things concurred to create him many enemies ; and, except Cranmer, Paget, and Smith, all turned against him.

The protector conducted the king to Hampton court, and put many of his own people about him, which increased the jealousies of the opposite party ; upon which nine of the privy council met at Ely-house, and assumed to themselves the authority of the council ; and secretary Petre being sent by the king, to ask an account of their meeting, instead of returning, joined himself to them. They made a full declaration of the protector's ill government ; and stated that " Therefore they resolved, themselves, to see the safety of the king and kingdom." Both the city of London, and the lieutenant of the Tower declared for them : they also sent letters all over England, desiring the assistance of the nobility and gentry, and seven more of the privy council joined them.

The protector had removed the king from Hampton-court to Windsor-castle, which was capable of some defence ; and had armed some of his own servants ; yet seeing himself abandoned by nearly all his friends, and finding the party against him growing to such a strength, that it would be in vain to struggle any longer, he offered to submit himself to the council. A proposition for a treaty was accordingly set on foot; and the lords of London were desired to send two of their number with their proposals. Cranmer, and the other two, wrote to the council, to persuade them to an agreement, and not to follow cruel suggestions.

Many false reports of the protector were spread abroad, as, that he had threatened, if they intended to put him to death, the king should die first; which served to increase the prejudices against him. The council wrote to Cranmer and Paget, charging them "To look well to the king's person, that he should not be removed from Windsor; and that the duke of Somerset's dependants might be put from him, and his own sworn servants admitted to wait:" they also protested that they would proceed with all the moderation and favour that was possible toward the duke. The council, understanding that all things were prepared as they had desired, sent three of their number, to see that the duke and five of his followers should be confined to their apartments; and on the 12th of October, the whole council went to Windsor and made great protestations of their duty to the king, which he received favourably, and assured them he took all that they had done in good part.

Accordingly, the duke of Somerset, with four of those who had been confined, were sent to the Tower, and many articles were objected to the duke, "That he being made protector, with this condition, that he should do nothing but by the consent of the other executors, had treated with ambassadors apart; had made bishops and lord-lieutenants without their knowledge; had held a court of requests in his house; embased the coin; neglected the places the king had in France; encouraged the commons in their late insurrections; and had given out commissions and proclaimed a pardon without their consent: that he had animated the king against the rest of the council, and had proclaimed them traitors, and had put his own servants armed about the king's person."

By these charges, it appears, that the crimes alleged against him were the effects of his sudden exaltation, which had made him forget that he was a subject. He, however, had carried his greatness with much innocence, since, in all the studied charges brought against him by his numerous enemies, no acts of cruelty, rapine, or bribery, were objected to him. His faults were rather errors and weaknesses, than crimes. His " embasing the coin" was done upon a common mistake of weak governments, who fly to that as their last refuge in the necessity of their affairs. In his imprisonment, he set himself to the study of moral philosophy and divinity, and wrote a preface to a book on patience, which had made a great impression on his mind. His fall was a great affliction to all who loved the reformation, and this was much increased, by their fears of two of his greatest enemies ; of whom Southampton was a known papist, and Warwick was looked on as a man of no religion.

But this event, while it depressed the reformers, raised the spirits of the papists : the duke of Norfolk and Gardiner hoped to be discharged. Bonner expected to be reestablished in his bishopric ; and the new service was neglected in many places : but the earl of Warwick, finding the king zealously attached to the reformation, affected to be a great promoter of that cause. A court of civilians was appointed to examine Bonner's appeal, and upon their report the council rejected it, and confirmed his sentence.

In November, the parliament met : in which a kind of riot act was passed, declaring it treason in any persons to assemble to the number of twelve, if, on being requested they did not disperse. The bishops made a heavy complaint of the growth of vice and impiety, and that their power was so much abridged that they could not repress it. Accordingly, a bill was read, enlarging their authority, which was passed by the lords ; but the commons rejected it, and instead of it, sent up a bill that empowered thirty-two persons who were to be named by the king, " the one half of the temporalty, and the other of the spirtualty, to compile a body of ecclesiastical laws within three years ; and that these, not being contrary to the common or statute law, and approved of by the king, should have the force of ecclesiastical laws."

Six bishops and six other clergymen were empowered to prepare a new form of ordination ; which being confirmed under the great seal, should take place after April next. Articles were also presented against the duke of Somerset, with a confession signed by him, in which he protested that his errors had flowed rather from indiscretion than malice, and denied all treasonable designs against the king, or the realm. He was fined in £2000 a year in land, and was deprived of all his goods and offices. He complained of the heaviness of this sentence, and " desired earnestly to be restored to the king's favour, trusting that he should make amends for his past follies." He was discharged in the beginning of February, soon after which he was pardoned, and was again brought both to the court and council in April.

The reformation now, after this confusion, recommenced with fresh vigour. The council sent orders throughout England, to require all to conform themselves to the new service, and to call in all the books of the old offices. An act was passed in parliament to the same effect. All the old books and images were appointed to be defaced, and all prayers to saints were to be struck out of the books of devotion published by the late king.

The committee appointed to prepare the book of ordinations, finished their work with unanimity. They found that, in the ancient church, there was nothing used in ordinations, but prayer and imposition of hands; the anointing and giving consecrated vestments being additions of later ages. In the council of Florence it was declared, that the rite of ordaining a priest, was the delivering the vessels for the eucharist, with a power to offer sacrifices to God for the dead and living, which was a novelty invented to support the belief of transubstantiation. All these additions were now cut off, ordination was restored to a greater simplicity; and the form was almost the same as that still in use in the church of England; only then, in ordaining a priest, the bishop was to lay one hand on his head, and with the other to give him a Bible, and a chalice, and bread in it. In the consecration of a bishop, the form was the same that we still employ, only then they retained the custom of giving the bishop a staff, saying these words, " Be to the flock of Christ a shepherd."

At this time pope Paul the Third died. In the conclave that followed, cardinal Farnese promoted the interest of cardinal Pole, whose wise behaviour at Trent had greatly raised him in the opinion of his contemporaries. It also appeared, that though he was of the emperor's faction, yet he did not serve him blindly. Some loaded him with the imputations of Lutheranism, and of incontinence; the last would not have hindered his advancement much, though true, yet he fully cleared himself from it: but the former lay heavier; for in his retirement at Viterbo, where he was legate, he had given himself much to the study of controversies; and Tranellius, Flaminio, and others suspected of Lutheranism, had lived in his house; and in the discussions at the council of Trent he seemed favourable to some of their opinions. But the great sufferings both of himself and family in England, seemed to set him above all suspicions.

When his friends had almost gained a sufficient number of suffrages, he seemed little concerned at it, and rather declined than aspired to the dignity. When a full number of the cardinals had agreed, and came to adore him, according to the ordinary ceremony, he received it with his usual coldness; and as they came in the night, he said, " God loved light," and therefore advised them to delay the adoration till day. The Italians, among whom ambition is thought to be the characteristic of a great mind, looked on this as an insufferable piece of dulness; so that the cardinals deserted him before day, and chose De Monte pope, who assumed the papal crown by the name of Julius the Third. His first promotion was very extraordinary, for he gave his own cardinal's hat to a servant who kept his monkey; and being asked the reason of it, he said " He saw as much in his servant to recommend him to be a cardinal, as the conclave saw in him to induce them to choose him pope." ·

In February, Ridley was made bishop of London and Westminster, with license to hold two prebends; and his patent was not during pleasure, but during life.

About this time there was a rumour of a marriage between the king, and a French princess, which grieved the reformers, who rather wished him to marry the daughter of the emperor Maximilian, who was believed to favour the reformation, and was esteemed one of the best men of the age. Dr. Latimer preached at court, and warned the king of the ill effects of bad marriages, which were made up only as bargains, without affection between the parties; and that they occasioned so much iniquity and so many divorces: he also complained of the luxury and vanity of the age, and pressed the setting up a primitive discipline in the church. He preached this as his last sermon, and therefore used great freedom.

The see of Gloucester now became vacant, and Hooper was named to it. He had some scruples about the episcopal vestments, and thought all those garments, having been consecrated with much superstition, were to be reckoned among the elements condemned by St. Paul, but Ridley justified the use of them, and said, "The elements condemned by St. Paul, were only the Jewish ceremonies; which he condemned, when they were imposed as essential; as that imported that the Mosaical law was not abrogated, and that the Messiah was not come."

Cranmer desired Bucer's opinion concerning the lawfulness of those habits, and the obligation lying on the subjects to obey the laws about them. His opinion was, that "Every creature of God was good, and that no former abuse could make a thing, indifferent in itself, become unlawful. Yet, since these garments had been abused to superstition, and were like to become a subject of contention, he wished they might be taken away by law; and that ecclesiastical discipline, and a more complete reformation, might be pursued, and a stop put to the robbing of churches; otherwise they might see in the present state of Germany, a dreadful prospect of that which England ought to look for. He wished that all good men would unite against the greater corruptions, and then lesser abuses would easily be redressed." Peter Martyr also delivered his opinion to the same purpose.

Hooper was suspended from preaching; but the Earl of Warwick wrote to Cranmer to dispense with him in that matter; who answered, that while the law continued in force, he could not do it without incurring a *præmunire.* Upon which the king wrote to the archbishop, allowing him to do it, and dispensing with the law.

The Common Prayer Book revised.

A design was now set on foot for a revision of the common prayer book : in order to which the opinion of that eminent reformer Bucer was asked.   He replied that " He approved the main parts of the former book, and wished there might be not only a denunciation against scandalous persons who came to the sacrament, but a discipline to exclude them ; that the habits might be laid aside ;   that no part of the communion office might be used, except when there was a sacrament ; that communions might be more frequent ; that the prayers might be said in a plain voice ; the sacrament put in the people's hands ; and that there might be no prayers for the dead." He also advised " a change of several phrases in the office of the communion that favoured transubstantiation too much ; and that baptism might be performed only in churches"; he thought " the hallowing the water, the chrism, and the white garment, were too scenical ; nor did he approve of abjuring the devil, nor of the godfather's answering in the child's name : he thought confirmation should be delayed till the person was of age, and came sincerely to renew the baptismal covenant ; and catechising should take place every holyday, both of children and adults.   He disliked private marriages, extreme unction, and making offerings at the churching of women : and thought there ought to be greater strictness used in the examination of those persons who came to receive orders."
At the same time he understood that the king expected a newyear's gift from him, of a book written particularly for his own use : he therefore, prepared a book concerning the kingdom of Christ ; in which he pressed much the setting up a strict discipline, the sanctification of the Lord's day, the appointing days of fasting, and that pluralities and non-residence of the clergy might be condemned ; that children might be catechised ; that the reverence due to churches might be preserved ; that the pastoral function might be restored to what it ought to be ; that bishops might throw off secular affairs, take care of their diocesses, and govern them by the advice of their presbyters ; that there might be rural bishops over twenty or thirty parishes

and that provincial councils might meet twice a year; that church lands should be restored, and that a fourth part should be assigned to the poor; that marriage without consent of parents, should be annulled; that a second marriage might be declared lawful, after a divorce for adultery, and for some other reasons; that care should be taken of the education of youth and for repressing luxury; that the law might be reformed; that no office might be sold, but given to the most deserving; that none should be put in prison for slight offences; and that the severity of some laws, as that which made theft capital, might be mitigated.

Edward was much pleased with these counsels; and upon them began to form a scheme for amending many things that were amiss in the government. This he wrote out with his own hand, and in a style and manner which were rather childish, though the thoughts were manly. He also wrote a journal of every thing that passed at home, and of the news from beyond sea. It has clear marks of being his own composition. He also wrote another book in French, being a collection of all the places of scripture against idolatry, with a preface, and a dedication to the protector.

At this time, Ridley made his first visitation of his diocess; the articles upon which he proceeded were chiefly relating to the service and ceremonies that were abolished. He also carried with him injunctions against some remainders of the former superstition, and exhortations to the people to be charitable, and to come frequently to the sacrament; and he expressed a wish that altars in the churches should be removed, and tables put in their room, in the most convenient place of the chancel. In the ancient church their tables were of wood; but the sacrament being afterward called a sacrifice, they came to be called altars. This gave rise to the opinion of an expiatory sacrifice in the mass, and therefore it was now thought fit to take away both the name and form of altars. Ridley only advised the curates to do this; but upon some contests arising concerning it, the council interposed, and ordered it to be done; sending with their order six reasons in justification of it, in which they showed that a table was more proper than an altar; especially since the opinion of an expiatory sacrifice was supported by the latter.

30

The government was now free of all disturbance : the coinage was reformed, and trade was encouraged. The factions in the court seemed also to be extinguished by a marriage between the earl of Warwick's son and the duke of Somerset's daughter

The popish clergy now complied with every change that was made. Oglethorpe, afterward bishop of Carlisle, being informed against as a favourer of the old superstition, made a declaration, that " he thought the order of religion then settled, was nearer the use of the primitive church than that which was formerly received ; and that he condemned transubstantiation as a late invention, and approved the communion in both kinds ; also the people's receiving it always with the priest."

Smith, who had written against the marriage of the clergy, and had been imprisoned, but was discharged by Cranmer's intercession, wrote a submission to him, acknowledging the mistake he had committed in his book, and the archbishop's kindness toward him : concluding with a wish that " he might perish, if he were not sincere," and calling on " God, as a witness against his soul, if he lied."

Day, the bishop of Chichester, preached at court against transubstantiation, and all opposition to the reformation seemed to have melted away ; but the calm was deceitful ; the papists still abhorred the changes which had been made, and although they thought it prudent at present to comply with them, they resolved to seize the earliest opportunity of throwing off the mask.

Martin Bucer died in the beginning of this year. He had entertained great apprehensions of a fatal revolution in England, on account of the bad lives of the people, the want of ecclesiastical discipline, and the neglect of the pastoral charge. Orders were sent from the court to Cambridge, to bury him with all the public honour to his memory that could be devised. Speeches and sermons were made by Haddon, the university orator, and by Parker and Redmayn. The last of these was one of the most extraordinary men both for learning and judgment in his time : he had differed in some points from Bucer, and yet he acknowledged, that there were none alive of whom he hoped to learn so much as he had done by his conversation with him.   Bucer was inferior to none of all the reformers in learning, and had a great zeal for the interests of the church; but he had not that fluency in disputing for which Peter Martyr was admired, and the popish doctors took advantage from that to treat him with more insolence.

Soon after this the process against Gardiner was brought to a conclusion: a commission was issued out to Cranmer, three bishops, and some civilians, to proceed against him, on the following charges: That he had refused to set out in his sermon the king's power, when he was under age, and had affronted the preachers, whom the king had sent to his diocess; that he had been negligent in executing the king's injunctions, and refused to confess his fault, or ask the king's pardon; and that the rebellions raised in England might have been prevented, if he had in time set forth the king's authority."

To this he answered, that " He was not required to do it by any order of council, but only in a private discourse:" but witnesses being examined upon these particulars, the delegates proceeded to sentence a deprivation against him, notwithstanding his appeal to the king in person; and he was remanded to the tower, where he continued till queen Mary discharged him.

CHAPTER V.

The thirty-nine Articles Published.

By this time the greater number of the bishops were sincere friends to the reformation: it was, therefore, resolved to proceed to a settlement of the doctrine of the church.   Many persons thought that should have been done in the first place; but Cranmer judged it better to proceed slowly in that matter: he thought the corruptions in the worship were to be first abolished; " since, while they remained, the addresses to God were so defiled that all people were involved in unlawful compliances."   He thought speculative opinions might be reformed last, since errors in them were not of such ill consequence: and he judged it necessary to explain these in many treatises and disputes, before alterations were made, in order that every one might be acquainted with what was intended to be done. Accordingly the bishops and clergy framed a body of articles, which contained the doctrine of the church of England: they divided them into forty-two, and afterward, some few alterations being made in the beginning of queen Elizabeth's reign, they were reduced to their present number, thirty-nine.

The Common Prayer Book Revised.

When this was settled, they commenced the review of the common prayer book. In the daily service they added the confession and absolution, "That so the worship of God might begin with a grave and humble confession; after which a solemn declaration of the mercy of God, according to the terms of the gospel," was to be pronounced by the priest. This was thought much better than the giving absolution in such formal words as, "I absolve thee;" which raised, in superficial worshippers, an opinion that the priest had authority to pardon sin, and made them think of nothing so much as how to purchase it at his hands. In the communion service they ordered a recital of the commandments, with a short devotion between every one of them. The chrism, the use of the cross in consecrating the eucharist, prayers for the dead, and some expressions that favoured transubstantiation, were rejected, and the book was put in the same order and method as that it which it continues to this day, with the exception of some inconsiderable variations. A rubric was added to the office of the communion, explaining the reason of kneeling in it, that it was only as an expression of reverence and gratitude, upon the receiving so particular a mark of the favour of God: but that no adoration was intended by it, and that they did not think Christ was corporeally present in it. In queen Elizabeth's time this was omitted, that such as conformed in other things, but still retained the belief of the corporeal presence, might not be offended at such a declaration: it was again inserted on the restoration of Charles II., for removing the scruples of those who excepted to that posture.

At this time six of the most eminent preachers were

appointed to reside at court by turns, two at a time, and the other four were sent, as intinerant preachers, into all the counties of England, for supplying the defects of the clergy, who were generally very weak and faulty.

Fall and death of the Duke of Somerset.

About this time the earl of Warwick, to strengthen his party against Somerset, prevailed on the king to confer new titles on several noblemen, and to raise some commoners to the peerage. He was himself created duke of Northumberland ; the marquis of Dorset was made duke of Suffolk ; Paulet, marquis of Winchester ; Herbert, earl of Pembroke ; Russel, earl of Bedford ; and Darcy, lord Darcy. An apparent reconciliation had taken place between Somerset and Northumberland ; but each distrusted the other, and was prepared to seize the first opportunity of crushing his rival. Northumberland's superior skill gave him the advantage ; and upon information of a pretended plot to assassinate him and some of his friends, the duke and dutchess of Somerset, with several other persons, were committed to the Tower. On the first of December, 1551, the duke was brought to his trial : the marquis of Winchester presided, and twenty-seven peers sat as judges, among whom were the dukes of Suffolk and Northumberland, and the earl of Pembroke. He was charged with a design to seize on the king's person, to assassinate Northumberland, to take possession of the tower and city of London, and to destroy the king's guards. It seemed a gross dereliction of justice for Northumberland to sit as a judge, when the crime objected was a design against his life ; but hatred of his rival carried him beyond the bounds of decency. Somerset, in his defence, denied all designs to raise the people, or to kill Northumberland ; "or if he had talked of it, it was in a passion, without any intention of doing so : and it was ridiculous to think, that he with a small troop could destroy the guards, who were 900 strong. The few armed men he had about him, were only for his own defence ; he had done no mischief to his enemies, though it was once in his power to have done it ; and had surrendered himself without any resistance. He desired the witnesses might be brought face to face with him ; but

30*

this common act of justice was denied, and their depositions were only read.　During the trial, he behaved with great temper, and all the abuse which the king's counsel made use of in pleading against him, did not provoke him to any indecent passion.

When sentence was given, his courage sunk a little, and he begged pardon of the three lords, who were his enemies, and entreated them to solicit the king in his favour, or at least to protect his wife and children.　But instead of interceding for him, Northumberland determined to free himself from all further fear, by the sacrifice of his ancient rival, and accordingly employed his emissaries to prejudice the king against his uncle, by pretending that, while in the tower, he had confessed a design to employ some persons to assassinate Northumberland, Northampton, and Pembroke.　This being believed by the king, he gave him up to his enemies

Stanhope, Partridge, Arundel, and Vane, the duke's friends and pretended accomplices, were next tried : the two first were not much pitied, for they had made an ill use of their interest with the duke while in power : the last two were much lamented. They were all condemned; Partridge and Vane were hanged, the other two were beheaded.

Six weeks after his trial, the unfortunate duke was brought to the scaffold, and as Mr. Fox, the author of this work, was present at his execution, we shall give his account of it in his own words.

" In the year of our Lord 1552, the two and twentieth of January, the duke of Somerset, uncle to king Edward, was brought out of the tower of London, and according to the manner delivered to the sheriffs of the city, and compassed about with a great number of armed men, both of the guard and others.　He was brought unto the scaffold on Tower-hill, where he, nothing changing either voice or countenance, but in a manner with the same gesture which he commonly used at home, kneeling upon both his knees, and lifting up his hands, commended himself unto God.

" After he had ended a few short prayers, standing up again, and turning himself toward the east side of the scaffold, nothing at all abashed (as it seemed to me, standing about the midst of the scaffold, and diligently marking all things) either with the sight of the axe, or yet of the executioner, or of present death ; but with the same alacrity and cheerfulness of mind and countenance as he was accustomed to show when he heard the causes and supplication of others, and especially the poor, (toward whom, as it were with a certain fatherly love to his children, he always showed himself most attentive) he uttered these words to the people :

" ' Dearly beloved friends, I am brought hither to suffer death, albeit that I never offended against the king, neither by word nor deed, and have been always as faithful and true unto this realm as any man. But forasmuch as I am by a law condemned to die, I do acknowledge myself as well as others to be subject thereunto. Wherefore, to testify my obedience which I owe unto the laws, I am come hither to suffer death ; whereunto I willingly offer myself, with most hearty thanks unto God, that hath given me this time of repentance, who might, through sudden death, have taken away my life, that neither I should have acknowledged him nor myself.

" ' Moreover, dearly beloved friends, there is yet somewhat that I must put you in mind of, as touching Christian religion ; which so long as I was in authority, I always diligently set forth and furthered to my power. Neither do I repent me of my doings, but rejoice therein, sith that now the state of Christian religion cometh most near unto the form and order of the primitive church. Which thing I esteem as a great benefit given of God both unto you and me ; most heartily exhorting you all, that this, which is most purely set forth unto you, you will with like thankfulness accept and embrace, and set out the same in your living. Which thing if you do not, without doubt greater mischief and calamity will follow.'

" When he had spoken these words, there was suddenly a terrible noise heard ; whereupon there came a great fear upon all men. This noise was as it had been the noise of some great storm or tempest, which to some seemed to be from above ; as if a great deal of gunpowder being inclosed in an armoury, and having caught fire, had violently broken out. But unto some it seemed as though it had been a great multitude of horsemen running together, or coming upon them. Such a noise then was in the ears of all, although they saw nothing. Whereby it happened that all the people being amazed without any evident cause they ran away, some into the ditches and puddles, and some into the houses thereabout; others fell down groveling unto the ground, with their pollaxes and halberds; and most of them cried out, 'Jesus save us! Jesus save us!' Those who remained in their places, for fear knew not where they were; and I myself, who was there among the rest, being also afraid in this hurly burly, stood still amazed. It happened here, as the evangelist wrote of Christ, when as the officers of the high priests and pharisees, coming with weapons to take him, being astonished, ran backwards and fell to the ground.

"In the meantime, while these things were thus in doing, the people by chance espied one sir Anthony Brown riding under the scaffold; which was the occasion of a new noise. For when they saw him coming, they conjectured that which was not true, but which they all sincerely wished for, that the king by that messenger had sent his uncle pardon: and therefore with great rejoicing and casting up their caps, they cried out, 'Pardon, pardon is come! God save the king.' Thus this good duke, although he was destitute of all men's help, yet he saw, before his departure, in how great love and favour he was with all men. And truly I do not think that in so great a slaughter of dukes as hath been in England within these few years, there were so many weeping eyes at one time; and not without cause. For all men saw in his fall the public ruin of England, except such as indeed did perceive nothing.

"But to return from whence we have strayed; the duke in the meantime standing still in the same place, modestly and with a grave countenance made a sign to the people with his hand, that they would keep themselves quiet. Which done and silence obtained, he spake unto them in this manner

"'Dearly beloved friends, there is no such matter here in hand as you vainly hope or believe. It seemeth thus good unto Almighty God, whose ordinance it is meet and necessary that we all be obedient unto. Wherefore I pray you all to be quiet, and to be contented with my death, which I am most willing to suffer; and let us now join in prayer unto the Lord for the preservation of the king's majesty, unto whom, hitherto, I have always showed myself a most faithful and true subject. I have always been most diligent about his majesty in his affairs both at home and abroad, and no less diligent in seeking the common good of the whole realm.' At which words all the people cried out, ' It is most true.'

"Then the duke proceeding, said, ' Unto whose majesty I wish continual health, with all felicity, and all prosperous success.' Whereunto the people again cried out ' Amen.'

"' Moreover, I do wish unto all his counsellors the grace and favour of God, whereby they may rule in all things uprightly with justice. Unto whom I exhort you all in the Lord to show yourselves obedient, as it is your bounden duty, under the pain of condemnation, and also most profitable for the preservation and safeguard of the king's majesty.

"' Moreover, as heretofore I have had often times affairs with divers men, and hard it is to please every man, therefore if there be any who hath been offended and injured by me, I most humbly require and ask him forgiveness; but especially Almighty God, whom throughout all my life I have most grievously offended: and all other whatsoever they be that have offended me, I do with my whole heart forgive them. Now I once again require you, dearly beloved in the Lord, that you will keep yourselves quiet and still, lest through your tumult you might trouble me. For albeit the spirit be willing and ready, the flesh is frail and wavering, and through your quietness I shall be much more composed. Moreover, I desire you all to bear me witness that I die here in the faith of Jesus Christ; desiring you to help me with your prayers, that I may persevere constantly in the same unto my end.'

"After this, turning himself again, he kneeled down. Then Dr. Cox, who was present to counsel and advise him, delivered a certain scroll into his hand, wherein was contained a brief confession unto God. Which being read, he stood up again upon his feet, without any trouble of mind, as it appeared, and first bade the sheriffs farewell, then the lieutenant of the tower, and others, taking them all by the hands which were upon the scaffold with him.

Then he gave money to the executioner; which done, he put off his gown, and kneeling down again in the straw, untied his shirt-strings. After that, the executioner coming to him turned down his collar about his neck, and all other things which hindered him. Then lifting up his eyes to heaven, and covering his face with his own handkerchief, he laid himself down along, showing no trouble or fear, neither did his countenance change.

"Thus this meek and gentle duke lying along, and looking for the stroke, because his doublet covered his neck, he was commanded to rise up and put it off; and then laying himself down again upon the block, and calling thrice upon the name of Jesus, saying, 'Lord Jesus, save me,' as he was the third time repeating the same, even as the name of Jesus was in uttering, in a moment he was bereft both of head and life, and slept in the Lord; being taken away from all dangers and evils of this life, and resting now in the peace of God; in the preferment of whose truth and gospel he always showed himself an excellent instrument and member and therefore hath received the reward of his labours."

Somerset was a man of extraordinary virtues, great candour, and eminent piety: he was always a promoter of justice, and a patron of the oppressed. He was a better soldier than a statesman, being too easy and open hearted for his situation. The people saw that the conspiracy, for which he and the other four suffered, was merely a pretence for their murder: the other accomplices were soon discharged, and Palmer, the chief witness, became Northumberland's particular confidant. The whole affair was looked on as a contrivance of the latter, by which he entirely lost the affections of the people. The chief objection to Somerset was, his having raised much of his estate out of the spoils of church lands, and his palace of Somerset-house in the Strand, out of the ruins of some churches and bishop's palaces.

The day after the duke of Somerset's execution, parliament assembled. The first act they passed was the established common prayer book, as it was then amended. Another law was passed, by which it was enacted that "No days were to be esteemed holy in their own nature,

but by reason of those holy duties which ought to be done
in them, for which they were dedicated to the service of
God.   Days were esteemed to be dedicated only to the
honour of God, even those in which the saints were commemorated ; Sundays, and the other holydays, were to be
religiously observed, and the bishops were to proceed to
censures against offenders.   The eves before them were
to be fasts, and abstinence from flesh was ordered both in
Lent, and on every Friday and Saturday."   An act likewise passed for the marriage of the clergy, in which it
was stated, " That, whereas, the former act about it was
thought only a permission of it, as some other unlawful
things were connived at ; upon which the wives and children
of the clergy were reproachfully used, and the word of
God was not heard with due reverence ; therefore their
marriages were declared good and valid."   The bishopric
of Westminister was reunited to London, only the colle-
giate church was still continued.

The convocation now confirmed the articles of religion
which had been prepared the former year, and thus was
the reformation of worship and doctrine brought to such a
degree of perfection, that since that time there has been
very little alteration made.   Another branch of it was still
unfinished, but was now under consultation, touching the
government of the church and the ecclesiastical courts.
This matter had been attempted several times during the
last and present reigns ; but the changes in the government had caused it to be laid aside.   It was now revived,
and eight eminent bishops, and others, were appointed to
draw up a plan, which was afterward to be submitted to
thirty-two commissioners.   It was generally believed that
Cranmer drew it entirely by himself, while the others only
corrected what he designed.   Haddon and Check translated it into Latin ; which they did with great ability.   The
work was divided into fifty-one titles ; and being laid before the commissioners, was by them to have been presented to the king for his confirmation ; but he died before
it was quite finished, nor was it ever afterward resumed.

About this time the dilapidated state of the church revenues engaged the attention of the council, but so many
persons of power and influence were interested to prevent
a remedy being afforded, that the affair was dropped.   In

every see as it became vacant, the best manors were laid
hold of by such hungry courtiers as could procure the
grant of them.   They seemed to think, that the bishops'
sees were so rich that they could never be made poor
enough ; but they were soon reduced to so low a condition
that it was hardly possible for a bishop to subsist in them.
If what had been thus taken from them had been converted
to good uses, such as the maintenance of the poor and inferior clergy, it would have been some excuse for the violence ; but the lands were laid hold of by laymen, who
made no compensation for the spoils thus gained by them.

The King's Sickness.

We now draw to the conclusion of the reign of this
youthful king; who, while he was a child in age, was a man
in wisdom.

He had contracted great colds by violent exercises,
which in January settled into so obstinate a cough, that all
the skill of physicians and the aid of medicine proved
ineffectual.   There was a suspicion over all Europe that
he was poisoned : but no certain grounds appear for justi
fying it.

During his sickness, Ridley preached before him, and
among other things spoke much on works of charity, and
the duty of men of high condition, to be eminent in good
works.   The king was much touched with this : and after
the sermon, he sent for the bishop, and treated him with
such respect, that he made him sit down and be covered :
he then told him what impression his exhortation had
made on him, and therefore he desired to be directed by
him how to do his duty in that matter.

Ridley took a little time to consider of it, and after
some consultation with the lord mayor and aldermen of
London, he brought the king a scheme of several foundations ; one for the sick and wounded, another for such as
were wilfully idle or were mad, and a third for orphans.
Edward, acting on this suggestion, endowed St. Bartholomew's hospital for the first, Bridewell for the second, and
Christ's hospital, near Newgate, for the third ; and he enlarged the grant which he had made the year before, for
St. Thomas' hospital, in Southwark.   The statutes and

warrants relating to these were not finished till the 26th
of June, though he gave orders to make all the haste that
was possible: and when he set his hand to them he blessed
God for having prolonged his life till he had finished his
designs concerning them. These houses have, by the
good government and the great charities of the city of
London, continued to be so useful, and grown to be so
well endowed, that now they may be reckoned among the
noblest in Europe.

The king bore his sickness with great submission to the
will of God; and seemed concerned in nothing so much
as the state that religion and the church would be in after
his death. The duke of Northumberland, who was at the
head of affairs, resolved to improve the fears the king was
in concerning religion, to the advantage of lady Jane
Grey, who was married to his son, lord Guilford Dudley.
Edward was easily persuaded by him to order the judges
to put some articles, which he had signed, for the succes
sion of the crown, in the common form of law. They answered, that the succession being settled by act of parliament, could not be taken away, except by parliament:
yet the king persisted in his orders.

The judges then declared before the council, that it had
been made treason by an act passed in this reign, to
change the succession; so that they could not meddle with
it. Montague was chief justice, and spake in the name
of the rest.

On this, Northumberland fell into a violent passion,
calling him traitor, for refusing to obey the king's commands. But the judges were not moved by his threats;
and they were again brought before the king, who sharply
rebuked them for their delays. They replied that all they
could do would be of no force without a parliament: yet
they were required to perform it in the best manner they
could.

At last Montague desired they might first have a pardon
for what they were to do, which being granted, all the
judges, except Cosnald and Hales, agreed to the patent,
and delivered their opinions, that the lord chancellor might
put the seal to the articles, drawn up by the king, and that
then they would be good in law. Cosnald was at last prevailed on to join in the same opinion, so that Hales, who

31

was a zealous protestant, was the only man who stood out to the last.

The privy councillors were next required to sign the paper. Cecil, in a relation he wrote of this transaction, says, that "Hearing some of the judges declare so positively that it was against law, he refused to set his hand to it as a privy councillor, but signed it only as a witness to the king's subscription."

Cranmer came not to the council when it was passed there, and refused to consent to it, when he was pressed to it; saying, "He would never have a hand in disinheriting his late master's daughters." The dying king at last by his importunity prevailed with him to do it; upon which the great seal was put to the patents.

The king's distemper continued to increase, so that the physicians despaired of his recovery. A confident woman undertook his cure, and he was put into her hands, but she left him worse than she found him; and this heightened the jealousy against the duke of Northumberland, who had introduced her, and dismissed the physicians. At last, to crown his designs, he got the king to write to his sisters to come and divert him in his sickness: and the exclusion had been conducted so secretly, that they, apprehending no danger, began their journey.

On the 6th of July the king felt the approach of death, and prepared himself for it in a most devout manner. He was often heard offering up prayers and ejaculations to God: particularly, a few moments before he died, he prayed earnestly that the Lord would take him out of this wretched life, and committed his spirit to him; he interceded very fervently for his subjects, that God would preserve England from popery, and maintain his true religion among them. The last words he uttered were these, "I am faint; Lord have mercy upon me, and take my spirit." Soon after that he breathed out his innocent soul in sir Henry Sidnov's arms.

PART VI.

Reign of Queen Mary, Subversion of the Protestant Religion, and awful Persecutions by the Papists

---

CHAPTER I.

Accession of Queen Mary to the Throne.

Dress of a Male Recanting Peni- | Dress of a Female Recanting Peni-
tant. | tant.

WE now call the attention of the British protestants to a period of their church history that cannot fail to awaken in their hearts that love for their ancestors, which at present, we fear, lies dormant in too many. A long career of ease appears to have obliterated from their minds the troubles of their generous forefathers, who, for them, bled in every vein—for them, were consigned to the devouring flames in every part of their country; preparing and establishing for their descendants, by the sacrifice of themselves, political and religious liberty. And, while we behold, with gratitude and admiration, the effects of their noble self-devotion, let us thence learn to appreciate those blessings which, by the continued providence of God, **we have so long enjoyed; and let us be confirmed more and** more in our determination to resist every attempt, whether by open force or secret fraud, to deprive us and our descendants of the privileges so dearly purchased.

It has been asserted by the Roman catholics, "That all those who suffered death, during the reign of queen Mary, had been adjudged guilty of high treason, in consequence of their rising in defence of lady Jane Grey's title to the crown." To disprove this, however, is no difficult matter, since every one conversant in English history, must know that those who are found guilty of high treason are to be hanged and quartered. But how can even a papist affirm, that ever a man in England was *burned* for high treason? We admit, that some few suffered death in the ordinary way of process at common law, for their adherence to lady Jane; but none of those were burned. Why, if traitors, were they taken before bishops, who have no power to judge in criminal cases? Even allowing the bishops to have had power to judge, yet their own bloody statute did not empower them to execute. The proceedings against the martyrs are still extant, and they are carried on directly according to the forms prescribed by their own statute. Not one of those who were burned in England, was ever accused of high treason, much less were they tried at common law. And this should teach the reader to value a history of transactions in his own country, particularly as it relates to the sufferings of the blessed martyrs in defence of the religion he professes, in order that he may be able to remove the veil which falsehood has cast over the face of truth. Having said thus much, by way of introduction, we shall proceed with the Acts and Monuments of the British Martyrs.

By the death of king Edward, the crown devolved, according to law, on his eldest sister Mary, who was within a half a day's journey to the court, when she had notice **given her by the earl of Arundel, of her brother's death, and of the patent for lady Jane's succession. Upon this she retired to Framlingham, in Suffolk, to be near the sea, that she might escape to Flanders, in case of necessity. Before she arrived there, she wrote, on the 9th of July, to the council, telling them, that "She understood, that her** brother was dead, by which she succeeded to the crown, but wondered that she heard not from them; she well understood what consultations they had engaged in, but she would pardon all such as would return to their duty, and proclaim her title to the crown."

Lady Jane Grey.

It was now found, that the king's death could be no longer kept a secret; accordingly some of the privy council went to lady Jane, and acknowledged her as their queen.* The news of the king's death afflicted her much, and her being raised to the throne, rather increased than lessened her trouble. She was a person of extraordinary abilities, acquirements, and virtues. She was mistress both of the Greek and Latin tongues, and delighted much in study. As she was not tainted with the levities which usually accompany her age and station, so she seemed to have attained to the practice of the highest fortitude; for in those sudden turns of her condition, as she was not exalted with the prospect of a crown, so she was little cast down when her palace was made her prison. The only passion she showed, was that of the noblest kind, in

* The lady Jane was daughter to the duke of Suffolk, and grand-daughter to Mary, sister to Henry VIII., who, on the death of her first husband, the king of France, married Charles Brandon, afterward created duke of Suffolk.

31*

the concern she expressed for her father and husband, who fell with her, and seemingly on her account; though, in reality, Northumberland's ambition and her father's weakness ruined her.

She rejected the crown when it was first offered her; she said she knew of right it belonged to the late king's sisters, and therefore could not with a good conscience assume it; but she was told, that both the judges and privy councillors had declared, that it fell to her according to law. This, joined with the importunities of her husband, her father, and father-in-law, made her submit. Upon this, twenty-one privy counsellors set their hands to a letter to Mary, telling her that queen Jane was now their sovereign, and that as the marriage between her father and mother had been declared null, so she could not succeed to the crown; they therefore required her to lay down her pretensions, and to submit to the settlement now made; and if she gave a ready obedience promised her much favour. The day after this they proclaimed Jane.

Northumberland's known enmity to the late duke of Somerset, and the suspicions of his being the author of Edward's untimely death, begot a great aversion in the people to him and his family, and disposed them to favour Mary; who, in the meantime, was very active in raising forces to support her claim. To attach the protestants to her cause, she promised not to make any change in the reformed worship, as established under her brother; and on this assurance a large body of the men of Suffolk joined her standard.

Northumberland was now perplexed between his wish to assume the command of an army raised to oppose Mary, and his fear of leaving London to the government of the council, of whose fidelity he entertained great doubts. He was, however, at length obliged to adopt the latter course, and before his departure from the metropolis he adjured the members of the council, and all persons in authority, to be steadfast in their attachment to the cause of queen Jane, on whose success, he assured them, depended the continuance of the protestant religion in England. They promised all he required, and he departed encouraged by their protestations and apparent zeal.

Mary's party in the meantime continued daily to augment. Hastings went over to her with 4000 men out of Buckinghamshire, and she was proclaimed queen in many places. At length the privy council began to see their danger, and to think how to avoid it: and beside fears for their personal safety, other motives operated with many of the members. To make their escape from the tower, where they were detained, ostensibly to give dignity to the court of queen Jane, but really as prisoners, they pretended it was necessary to give an audience to the foreign ambassadors, who would not meet them in the tower; and the earl of Pembroke's house was appointed for the audience.

When they met there they resolved to declare for queen Mary, and rid themselves of Northumberland's yoke, which they knew they must bear, if he were victorious. They sent for the lord mayor and alderman, and easily gained their concurrence; and Mary was proclaimed queen on the 19th of July. They then sent to the Tower, requiring the duke of Suffolk to quit the government of that place, and the lady Jane to lay down the title of queen. To this she submitted with much greatness of mind, and her father with abjectness.

The council next sent orders to Northumberland to dismiss his forces, and to obey the queen. When Northumberland heard this he disbanded his forces, went to the market place at Cambridge, where he then was, and proclaimed Mary as queen. The earl of Arundel was sent to apprehend him, and when Northumberland was brought before him, he, in the most servile manner, fell at his feet to beg his favour. He, with three of his sons and sir Thomas Palmer, his wicked tool in the destruction of the duke of Somerset, were all sent to the tower.

Every one now flocked to implore the queen's favour, and Ridley among the rest, but he was committed to the tower; the queen being resolved to put Bonner again in the see of London. Some of the judges, and several noblemen, were also sent thither, among the rest the duke of Suffolk; who was, however, three days after set at liberty. He was a weak man, could do little harm, and was consequently selected as the first person toward whom the queen should exert her clemency.

Mary came to London on the 3d of August, and on the

way was met by her sister, lady Elizabeth, with a thousand horse, whom she had raised to assist the queen. On arriving at the Tower, she liberated the duke of Norfolk, the dutchess of Somerset, and Gardiner; also the lord Courtney, son to the marquis of Exeter, who had been kept there ever since his father's attainder, and whom she now made earl of Devonshire.

Thus was seated on the throne of England the lady Mary, who, to a disagreeable person and weak mind, united bigotry, superstition, and cruelty. She seems to have inherited more of her mother's than her father's qualities. Henry was impatient, rough, and ungovernable; but Catharine, while she assumed the character of a saint, harboured inexorable rancour and hatred against the protestants. It was the same with her daughter Mary, as appears from a letter in her own hand-writing, now in the British Musuem. In this letter, which is addressed to bishop Gardiner, she declares her fixed intention of burning every protestant; and there is an insinuation, that as soon as circumstances would permit, she would restore back to the church the lands that had been taken from the convents. This was the greatest instance of her weakness that she could show: for in the first place the convents had been all demolished, except a few of their churches; and the rents were in the hands of the first nobility, who, rather than part with them, would have overturned the government both in church and state.

Mary was crowned at Westminister in the usual form; but dreadful were the consequences that followed. The narrowness of spirit that always distinguishes a weak mind from one that has been enlarged by education, pervaded all the actions of this princess. Unacquainted with the constitution of the country, and a slave to superstition, she thought to domineer over the rights of private judgment, and trample on the privileges of mankind.

The first exertion of her regal power was, to wreak her vengeance upon all those who had supported the title of lady Jane Grey.

The first of these was the duke of Northumberland, who was beheaded on Tower-hill, and who, in consequence of his crimes, arising from ambition, died unpitied: nay, he was even taunted on the scaffold by the spectators, who knew in what manner he had acted to the good duke of Somerset.

The other executions that followed were numerous indeed, but as they were all upon the statute of high treason, they cannot, with any degree of propriety, be applied to protestants, or, as they were then called, *heretics*. The parliament was pliant enough to comply with all the queen's requests, and an act passed to establish the popish religion. This was what the queen waited for, and power being now put into her hands, she was determined to exercise it in the most arbitrary manner. She was destitute of human compassion, and without the least reluctance could tyrannise over the consciences of men.

This leads us to the conclusion of the first year of her reign; and we consider it the more necessary to take notice of these transactions, although not, strictly speaking, *martyrdoms*, that our readers might be convinced of the great difference there is between dying for religion, and for high treason. It is history alone that can teach them such things, and it is reflection only that can make history useful. We frequently read without reflection, and study without consideration; but the following portions of our history, in particular, will furnish ample materials for serious thought to our readers, and we entreat their attention to them.

Martyrdoms in the Second year of Queen Mary's Reign.

The queen having satiated her malice upon those persons who had adhered to lady Jane Grey, she had next recourse to those old auxiliaries of popery, fire, fagot, and the stake, in order to convert her heretical subjects to the *true* catholic faith.

Martyrdom of the Rev. John Rogers.

Mr. John Rogers, the aged minister of St. Sepulchre's church, Snow hill, London, was the protomartyr: he was the first sacrifice, strictly speaking, offered up in this reign to popery, and led the way for those sufferers, whose blood has been the foundation, honour, and glory of the church of England.

This Mr. Rogers had been some time chaplain to the English factory at Antwerp. There he became acquainted with Mr. Tindal, and assisted him in his translation of the New Testament. There were several other worthy protestants there at that time, most of whom had been driven out of England, on account of the persecutions for the six articles, in the latter end of the reign of Henry VIII. Mr. Rogers, knowing that marriage was lawful, and even enjoined in scripture, entered into that state with a virtuous woman, and soon after set out for Saxony, in consequence of an invitation to that effect.

When Edward ascended the throne of England, Mr. Rogers returned to his native country, and was promoted by bishop Ridley to a prebendary of St. Paul's. He was also appointed reader of the divinity lecture in that cathedral, and vicar of St. Sepulchre's.

In this situation he continued some years: and as queen Mary was returning from the tower, where she had been imbibing Gardiner's pernicious counsels, Mr. Rogers was preaching at St. Paul's Cross. He inveighed much against popery, expatiated on the many virtues of the late king Edward, and exhorted the people to abide in the protestant religion.

For this sermon he was summoned before the council; but he vindicated himself so well, that he was dismissed.

This lenity shown by the council was rather displeasing to the queen; and Mr. Roger's zeal against popery being equal to his knowledge and integrity, he was considered as a person who would prevent the re-establishment of popery.

For this reason it was, that he was summoned a second time before the council; and although there were many papists among the members, yet such was the respect almost universally felt for Mr. Rogers, that he was again dismissed, but was commanded not to go out of his own house. This order he complied with, although he might have made his escape if he would. He knew he could have had a living in Germany, and he had a wife and ten children: but all these things did not move him; he did not court death, but met it with fortitude when it came.

He remained confined in his own house several weeks, till Bonner, bishop of London, procured an order to have him committed to Newgate, where he was lodged among thieves and murderers.

He was afterward brought a third time before the council, where Gardiner, bishop of Winchester, presided. It was not with any view of showing lenity to the prisoner; it was not with a view of convincing him of error, supposing him to be guilty of any; it was not to recall him to the Romish Church that he was brought there : no, his destruction was designed, and he was singled out to be an example to all those who should refuse to comply with Romish idolatry.

The questions asked him were of a very frivolous nature but still they were such, that answers to them served to criminate the man. It is a maxim in common law, that no man is to be his own accuser; by which is meant, that he is not to answer any questions which may bring the guilt home to him, unless at his option, leaving his enemies to prove the assertions.

On the other hand, it is laid down as a maxim by divines, and certainly it is a good one, that no man should tell a falsehood. Christ said, *" He that denies me before men, him will I also deny before my father, who is in heaven."* We know the weakness of human nature, but we ought to be much upon our guard against speaking any thing that is false. This shows us to be cowards : let us, like Christ Jesus, witness a true confession ; let us not shrink back at the thought of suffering for the truth, as it is in Jesus; but let us remember that the pleasures of sins are momentary; the punishment of them eternal.

Such sentiments as these took place in the mind of Mr. Rogers, when he was brought before the chancellor and council. He freely acknowledged, that he had been fully convinced, in his own mind, that the pope was Antichrist and that his religion was contrary to the gospel.

He made a most elaborate defence, which, however, did not avail him in the minds of his persecutors. He showed them that the statute upon which he was prosecuted had never legally passed, and even if it had, it was in all respects contrary to the word of God : for whatever emoluments might have been bestowed upon the clergy from time to time, they had no right to persecute those who differed from them in sentiment.

After he had been examined several times before a council, which was a mere mockery of justice, he was turned over to Bonner, bishop of London, who caused him to go through a second mock examination ; and, at last, declared him to be an obstinate heretic. A certificate of this was, in the ordinary course, sent into chancery, and a writ was issued for the burning of Mr. Rogers in Smithfield. This sentence did not in the least frighten our martyr, who, by faith in the blood of Christ, was ready to go through with his attachment to the truth, without paying any regard to the malice of his enemies.

On the 4th of February, 1555, Mr. Rogers was taken out of Newgate, to be led to the place of execution, when the sheriff asked him if he would recant his opinions? To this he answered, " That what he had preached he would seal with his blood." " Then," said the sheriff, " thou art a heretic." To which Mr. Rogers answered, " That will be known when we meet at the judgment seat of Christ."

As they were taking him to Smithfield, his wife and eleven children went to take their last farewell of a tender husband and an indulgent parent. The sheriffs, however, would not permit them to speak to him ; so unfeeling is bigotry, so merciless is superstition! When he was chained to the stake he declared that God would in his own good time vindicate the truth of what he had taught, and appear in favour of the protestant religion. Fire was then set to the pile, and he was consumed to ashes.

He was a very pious and humane man, and his being singled out as the first victim of superstitious cruelty, can only entitle him to a higher crown of glory in heaven.

Martyrdom of Laurence Saunders.

The next person who suffered in this reign was the reverend Mr. Laurence Saunders, of whose former life we have collected the following particulars : his father had a considerable estate in Oxfordshire, but dying young, left a large family of children. Laurence was sent to Eton school as one of the king's scholars.

From Eton he was, according to the rules of the foundation, sent to King's college in Cambridge, where he studied three years, and made great progress in the different sorts of learning then taught in the schools. At the end of the three years he left the university, and returning to his mother, prevailed upon her to place him with a merchant.

He was accordingly articled to sir William Chester, a rich merchant in London, who was afterward sheriff of that city. He had not been long in his employment, when he became weary of a life of trade. He sunk into a deep melancholy, and afterward went into a retired chamber, to mourn for his imprudence, and to beg of God that he would, in some manner or other, deliver him from a life so disgustful.

His master, who was a worthy man, took notice of this, and asked Saunders his reasons for being in that desponding condition? The young gentleman candidly told him; upon which he immediately gave him up his indentures, and sent him home to his relations.

This Saunders considered as a happy event, and that no time might be lost, he returned to his studies at Cambridge; and, what was very uncommon in that age, he learned the Greek and Hebrew languages. After this he devoted himself wholly to the study of the sacred scriptures, in order to qualify himself for preaching the gospel.

In study he was diligent, and practical in holiness of life: in doing good few equalled him, and he seemed to have nothing in view but the happiness of immortal souls.

In the beginning of king Edward's reign, when the true religion began to be countenanced, he entered into orders, and preached with great success. His first appointment was at Fotheringhem, where he read a divinity lecture; but that college having been dissolved, he was appointed a preacher in Lichfield. In that new station his conduct entitled him to great respect; for such was his sweetness of temper, his knowledge in his profession, his eloquent manner of addressing his hearers, the purity of his manners, and his affectionate addresses to the heart, that he was universally respected, and his ministry was very useful.

After being some months in Lichfield, he removed to the living of Church-Langton, in Leicestershire: there he resided with his people, and instructed many who before

32

were ignorant of the true principles of the Christian reli
gion.   He was the same to men's bodies as to their sou.s.
All that he received, beside the small pittance that supported his person, was given away to feed the hungry and
clothe the naked.   Here was the Christian minister indeed!
for no instructions will make a lasting impression on the
mind, while the example is contrary.

His next removal was to Allhallows, in Bread-street,
London ; and when he had taken possession of it, he went
down to the country, to part, in an affectionate manner,
with his friends.

While he was in the country king Edward died, and
Mary succeeding, published a proclamation, commanding all
her subjects to attend mass.   Many pious ministers refused to obey the royal proclamation, and none was more forward in doing so than Mr. Saunders.   He continued to
preach whenever he had an opportunity, and read the
prayer-book, with the scriptures, to the people, till he was
apprehended in the following manner :

Mr. Saunders was advised to leave the nation, as pious
Dr. Jewel and many others did ; but he would not, declaring to his friends, that he was willing to die for the name
of the Lord Jesus.   Accordingly, he left his people in
Leicestershire, and travelled toward London, on his arrival near which, he was met by sir John Mordant, a privy
counsellor to queen Mary, who asked him where he was
going? Mr. Saunders said, to his living in Bread-street, to
instruct his people.   Mordant desired him not to go : to
which Mr. Saunders answered, " How shall I then be
accountable to God? If any be sick and die before consolation, then what a load of guilt will be upon my conscience, as an unfaithful shepherd, an unjust steward ?"

Mordant asked him whether he did not frequently preach
in Bread-street ; and being answered in the affirmative,
he endeavoured to dissuade him from doing so any more.
Saunders, however, was resolute, and told him he would
continue to preach as long as he lived, and invited the
other to come and hear him the next day ; adding that he
would confirm him in the truth of those sentiments which
he taught.   Upon this they parted, and Mordant went and
gave information to bishop Bonner, that Saunders would
preach in his church the next Sunday.

In the meantime Saunders went to his lodgings, with a mind resolved to do his duty; when a person came to visit him, and took notice to him that he seemed to be in trouble. He said he was; adding, " I am, as it were, in prison, till I speak to my people." So earnest was his desire to discharge his duty, and so little did he regard the malice of his enemies.

The next Sunday he preached in his church, and made a most elaborate discourse against the errors of popery; he exhorted the people to remain steadfast in the truth; not to fear those who can only kill the body, but to fear Him who can throw both body and soul into hell. He was attended by a great concourse of people, which gave much offence to the clergy, particularly to bishop Bonner.

No notice, however, was taken of him in the forenoon, but in the afternoon, when he intended to have preached again, Bonner sent an officer to apprehend him; accordingly, he went with the officer, and sir John Mordec: appeared to give evidence against him. It was certainly unbecoming the character of a gentleman of rank, thus to become a common informer; but bigotry so infatuates the minds of its votaries, that they forget every other consideration in order to gratify their hatred against those who differ from them in opinion. Perhaps, however, sir John might be actuated by wordly motives; and, by thus ingratiating himself with the bishop, who then enjoyed great power, he might hope to obtain the favour of the queen.

Mr. Saunders was charged with treason and sedition, for having disobeyed the queen's proclamation; but Bonner had other objects in view than that of bringing this man to a trial at common law. Heresy was the main charge he wished to punish him on.

After much conversation on different points of religion, the bishop, desired him to write his sentiments concerning transubstantiation. To this request Mr. Saunders replied, " My lord, I know you want to ensnare me; you seek for my blood, and you shall have it. Perhaps the reflection of taking my life without cause may bring you to a sense of guilt, and make you a better man."

The bishop, on this, sent Mr. Saunders, under the care

of sir John Mordant, to the house of the chancellor, who happened not to be at home; so that he was obliged to wait for him four hours in the servants' hall. During the whole of this time, Mr. Saunders stood bareheaded, while Mordant kept walking backwards and forwards across the room.

At length the chancellor arrived, and sending for Mr. Saunders into his chamber, asked him how he could be so bold as to disobey the queen's proclamation. Saunders acknowledged that "He had preached contrary to the proclamation, and that he thought it his duty to do so, even although it should cost him his life. He added, that what he did arose from the dictates of his heart, which commanded him to preach the gospel, in season and out of season; and that he must be accountable at the judgment seat of Christ, if he neglected any part of his duty in teaching and comforting his people in their most holy faith, so as to meet them on the right hand of the judge."

The chancellor poured out much abuse on Mr. Saunders, telling him he was a hypocrite and a heretic, notwithstanding all his pretensions to a tender conscience. He accused him, further of having called the queen a bastard, or rather worse, namely, that she had been born in a state of incest.

It was well known that Henry's marriage with Catharine had been declared inconsistent with the canons of the church; and, therefore, had Mr. Saunders called her by such names, he might, according to law, have sheltered himself under an act of parliament. But the truth is he never traduced her character; but in speaking to Gardiner he made use of a most severe sarcasm, by telling him that "there need not to be much dispute concerning this matter with his lordship, who had actually signed the declaration concerning the illegitimacy of Mary's birth." This was bringing the argument home to him; but the severity of the satire augmented Gardiner's desire of revenge.

Saunders told the chancellor, "He had no objection to suffer for that God who had given him courage to declare his sentiments without fear, and would support him under all sorts of afflictions; and although he would never give intentional offence, yet he would not, by any means, injure his conscience, by giving up the truth as it was revealed in the word of God."

Gardiner upon this, remanded Mr. Saunders to prison; but first told him he was out of his mind, and a disturbed madman, without the use of sense or reason

He was confined in the Marshalsea prison, and strict orders were given to the keepers not to suffer any person to converse with him. His wife, however, came to the prison with her young child in her arms, and the keeper had so much compassion, that he took the child and carried it to its father.

Mr. Saunders seeing the child, rejoiced greatly, saying, it was a peculiar happiness for him to have such a boy. And to the bystanders, who admired the beauty of the child, he said, "What man, fearing God, would not lose his life, sooner than have it said that the mother of this child was a harlot?"

He said these words, in order to point out the woful effects of popish celibacy; for the priests being denied the privilege of marriage, seduced the wives and daughters of many of the laity, and filled the nation with bastards, who were left exposed to all sorts of hardships.

After all these afflictions and sufferings, Mr. Saunders was brought before the council, where the chancellor sat as president; and there he was asked a great number of questions concerning his opinions. These questions were proposed in so artful and ensnaring a manner, that the prisoner, by telling the truth, must criminate himself; and to have stood mute would have subjected him to the torture. Under such circumstances God gave him fortitude to assert the truth, by declaring his abhorrence of all the doctrines of popery.

The examination being ended, the officers led him out of the place, and then waited till some other prisoners were examined. While Mr. Saunders was standing among the officers, seeing a great number of people assembled, as is common on such occasions, he exhorted them to beware of falling off from Christ to Antichrist, as many were then returning to popery, because they had not fortitude to suffer.

The chancellor ordered him to be excommunicated, and committed him to the Compter. This was a great com-

32*

fort to him, because he was visited by many of his people, whom he exhorted to constancy; and when they were denied admittance, he spoke to them through the grate.

On the 4th of February the sheriff of London delivered him to the bishop, who degraded him; and Mr. Saunders said, "Thank God, I am now out of your church."

The day following he was given up to some of the queen's officers, who were appointed to convey him down to Coventry, there to be burned. The first night they lay at St. Albans, where Mr. Saunders took an opportunity of rebuking a person who had ridiculed the Christian faith.

After they arrived at Coventry, a poor shoemaker, who had formerly worked for Mr. Saunders, came to him, and said, "Oh! my good master, may God strengthen you." "Good shoemaker," answered Mr. Saunders, "I beg you will pray for me, for I am at present in a very weak condition; but I hope my gracious God, who hath appointed me to it, will give me strength."

The same night he spent in the common prison, praying for and exhorting all those who went to hear him.

The next day, which was the 8th of February, he was led to the place of execution, in the Park, without the gate of that city, going in an old gown and a shirt, barefooted, and often fell on the ground and prayed. When he approached the place of execution, the under-sheriff told him ne was a heretic, and that he had led the people away from the true religion; but yet, if he would recant, the queen would pardon him. To this Mr. Saunders answered, "That he had not filled the realm with heresy, for he had taught the people the pure truths of the gospel; and in all his sermons, while he exhorted the people firmly, desired his hearers to be obedient to the queen."

When brought to the stake he embraced it, and after being fastened to it, and the fagots lighted, he said, "Welcome the cross of Christ, welcome everlasting life;" soon after which he resigned his soul into the hands of him who gave it.

CHAPTER II.

Sufferings and Martyrdom of Bishop Hooper.

WE have seen in our account of the pious Mr. Saunders, that a man by nature weak and timorous, could bear, with an undaunted boldness, all those torments which were prepared for him by his enemies, and by the enemies of Christ Jesus; and we have seen that gracious Being, for whose name's sake he suffered, supporting him under all his afflictions.

We shall now bring forth another martyr, whose name will ever be esteemed for his sincere attachment to the protestant religion, and for the little regard he paid to ceremonies, about which there has been much unnecessary, and indeed angry contention.

The person to whom we allude was DR. JOHN HOOPER, a man of eminence in his profession. He was educated in Oxford, but in what college does not appear; probably it was in Queen's college, because he was a north countryman, that seminary of learning being appropriated for those of the northern counties.

He made a great progress in his studies, and was remarkable for early piety. He studied the sacred scriptures with the most unremitting assiduity, and was for some time an ornament to the university.

His spirit was fervent, and he hated every thing in religion that was not of an essential nature. When the six articles were published, Hooper did all he could to oppose them, as maintaining every thing in the popish system, except the supremacy. He preached frequently against them, which created him many enemies in Oxford; but Henry VIII. had such an opinion of him, that he would not suffer him to be molested. Soon after this he was obliged to leave the university, and assuming a lay character, became steward to sir Thomas Arundel, who at first treated him with great kindness, till having discovered his sentiments as to religion, he became his most implacable enemy.

Mr. Hooper having received intelligence that some mischief was intended against him, left the house of sir Thomas Arundel, and borrowing a horse from a friend, whose life he had saved, rode off toward the sea-side, intending to go to France, sending back the horse by a servant. He resided some time at Paris, in as private a manner as possible. Returning again to England he was informed against, and obliged to leave his native country a second time.

He went over again to France, but not being safe there, he travelled into Germany: from thence he went to Basil, where he married a pious woman, and afterward settled some time at Zurich, in Switzerland: there he applied closely to his studies, and made himself master of the Hebrew language.

At length when the true religion was set up after the death of king Henry VIII., among other English exiles that returned was Mr. Hooper. In the most grateful manner he returned thanks to all his friends abroad, who had shown him so much compassion; particularly to the learned Bullinger, who was a great friend to all those who were persecuted for the gospel. When he took an affectionate leave of Bullinger, he told him that he would write to him as often as he could find an opportunity, but added. "Probably I shall be burned to ashes, and then some friend will give you information. Another circumstance should not be omitted in this place, and that is, that when he was appointed bishop of Gloucester and Worcester, the herald who emblazoned his arms put the figure of a lamb in a fiery bush, with the rays of glory descending from heaven on the lamb, which had such an effect on Dr. Hooper, that he said he knew he should die for the truth; and this consideration inspired him with courage. But to return to our narrative.

When Dr. Hooper arrived in London, he was so much filled with zeal to promote the gospel, that he preached every day to crowded congregations. In his sermons he reproved sinners in general, but particularly directed his discourse against the peculiar vices of the times.

The abuses he complained of were owing to a variety of causes: the nobility had got the church lands, and the clergy were not only seditious in their conduct, but ignorant even to a proverb. This occasioned a scene of general immorality among all ranks and degrees of people, which furnished pious men with sufficient matter for reproof.

In his doctrine, Hooper was clear, plain, eloquent, and persuasive, and so much followed by all ranks of people, that the churches could not contain them.

Although no man could labour more indefatigably in the Lord's vineyard, yet Hooper had a most excellent constitution, which he supported by temperance, and was therefore enabled to do much good. In the whole of his conversation with those who waited on him in private, he spoke of the purity of the gospel, and of the great things of God, cautioning the people against returning to popery, if any change in the government should take place. This was the more necessary, as the people in general were but ill grounded, though Cranmer, Ridley, and many other pious men were using every means in their power to make them acquainted with the principles of the Christian religion. In this pious undertaking, no one was more forward than Dr. Hooper; at all times, " in season, and out of season," he was ready to discharge his duty as a faithful minister of the gospel.

After he had preached some time, with great success, in the city, he was sent for by Edward VI., who appointed him one of his chaplains, and soon after made him bishop of Gloucester, by letters-patent under the great seal; having at the same time the care of the bishopric of Worcester committed to him.

As Dr. Hooper had been some time abroad, he had contracted an aversion to the popish ceremonies, and before he went to his bishopric, he requested of the king that he might not be obliged to give countenance to them, which request the monarch complied with, though much against the inclinations of the other bishops. Dr. Hooper and his brethren of the reformed church had many disputes about the Romish tenets, which shows that there are some remains of corruption in the best of men. Some persons seek honours with unwearied zeal, and seem to take more pleasure in titles, than in considering that an elevated rank only increases the necessity of being more observant of our duty.

Dr. Hooper differed from these men, for instead of seeking preferments, he would never have accepted of any, had they not been pressed on him. Having the care of two dioceses, he held and guided them both together, as if they had been but one. His leisure time, which was but little, he spent in hearing causes, in private prayer, and reading the scriptures. He likewise visited the schools, and encouraged youth in the pursuit of learning. He had children of his own, whom he likewise instructed, and treated them with all the tenderness of a good parent, but without the indulgence of a weak one.

He kept open house, with provisions for the poor; which was a very pious and necessary action in those times, because many persons who had been driven out of the convents roved up and down the country starving. He relieved a certain number of these every day, and when they had satisfied their hunger he delivered a discourse to them on the principles of the Christian religion.

After this manner, bishop Hooper continued to discharge his duty as a faithful pastor, during the whole of king Edward's reign. But no sooner was Mary proclaimed, than a sergeant at arms was sent to arrest our bishop, in order to answer to two charges:

First, to Dr. Heath, who had been deprived of the diocess of Gloucester for his adherence to popery, but was now restored by the queen: secondly, to Dr. Bonner, bishop of London, for having given evidence to king Edward against the persecuting prelate.

Bishop Hooper was desired by some of his friends to make his escape, but his answer was, "I once fled for my life, but I am now determined, through the strength and grace of God, to witness the truth to the last."

Being brought before the queen and council, Gardiner, sitting as president, accused bishop Hooper of heresy, calling him by the most opprobrious names. This was in September, 1553, and although he satisfactorily answered the charges brought against him, he was committed to prison on the pretence of being indebted to the queen in several sums of money. On the 19th of March, 1554, when he was called again to appear before Gardiner, the chancellor, and several other bishops, would not suffer him to plead his cause, but deprived him of his bishopric.

Being asked whether he was a married man, he answered in the affirmative, and declared that he would not be unmarried, till death occasioned the separation; because he looked upon the marriage of the clergy, as necessary and legal.

The more they attempted to browbeat him, the more resolute he became, and the more pertinent in his answers. He produced the decrees of the council of Nice, which first ascertained the canon of scripture, where it was ordained to be lawful, as well as expedient, for the clergy to marry. These arguments were to little purpose with men who had their instructions from the queen, and were previously determined to punish him; the good bishop was therefore committed to the tower, but afterward removed to the Fleet.

As the determination for burning him was not agreed on, he was only considered as a debtor to the queen, for the rents of his bishopric, which was the reason of his being sent to the Fleet. This, however, was a most unjust charge; for the protestant religion had been established in the first year of the reign of her brother Edward, by act of parliament; so that Dr. Hooper's acceptance of bishopric was in all respects legal and constitutional.

As a debtor, he was to have the rules of the Fleet, which the warden granted him for five pounds sterling; but went immediately and informed Gardiner, who, notwithstanding he had paid the money, ordered him to be closely confined.

The following account of his cruel treatment while confined here, was written by himself, and affords a picture of popish barbarity, which cannot fail to make a due impression on our readers.

"The first of September, 1553, I was committed unto the Fleet, from Richmond, to have the liberty of the prison; and within six days after I paid five pounds sterling to the warden for fees, for my liberty; who immediately upon payment thereof complained unto the bishop of Winchester, upon which I was committed to close prison one quarter of a year in the tower-chamber of the Fleet, and used extremely ill. Then, by the means of a good gentlewoman, I had liberty to come down to dinner and supper, though not suffered to speak with any of my friends; but as soon as dinner and supper were done, to repair to my chamber again. Notwithstanding, while I came down thus to

dinner and supper, the warden and his wife picked quarre.s
with me, and complained untruly of me to their great
friend, the bishop of Winchester.

"After one quarter of a year, Babington the warden, and
his wife, fell out with me, respecting the wicked mass:
and thereupon the warden resorted to the bishop of Winchester, and obtained to put me into the wards, where I
have continued a long time, having nothing appointed to
me for my bed but a little pad of straw and a rotten
covering, with a tick and a few feathers therein, the chamber being vile and stinking, until by God's means good
people sent me bedding to lie on. On one side of the
prison is the sink and filth of the house, and on the other
the town ditch, so that the stench of the house has infected
me with sundry diseases.

"During which time I have been sick, and the doors,
bars, hasps, and chains being all closed upon me, I have
mourned, called and cried for help; but the warden, when
he hath known me many times ready to die, and when the
poor men of the wards have called to help me, hath com
manded the doors to be kept fast, and charged that none
of his men should come at me, saying, 'Let him alone, it
were a good riddance of him.'

"I paid always like a baron to the said warden, as well
in fees, as for my board, which was twenty shillings a
week, beside my man's table, until I was wrongfully deprived of my bishoprics, and since that time I have paid
him as the best gentleman doth in his house; yet hath he
used me worse and more vilely than the veriest slave that
ever came to the common side of the prison.

"The warden hath also imprisoned my man, William
Downton, and stripped him out of his clothes to search for
letters, and could find none but a little remembrance of
good people's names who had given me their alms to
relieve me in prison; and to undo them also, the warden
delivered the same bill unto the said Stephen Gardiner,
God's enemy and mine.

"I have suffered imprisonment almost eighteen months,
my goods, livings, friends, and comfort taken from me;
the queen owing me, by just account, fourscore pounds or
more. She hath put me in prison, and giveth nothing to
keep me, neither is there suffered any one to come at me,

whereby I might have relief. I am with a wicked man and woman, so that I see no remedy, saving God's help but I shall be cast away in prison before I come to judg ment. But I commit my just cause to God, whose will be done, whether it be by life or death."

After he had been eighteen months in prison, on the 22d of January, in 1555, the warden of the Fleet was ordered to bring him before the Chancellor Gardiner, who, with other bishops, were appointed to examine him a second time, at Gardiner's palace in Southwark.

When brought before these merciless persecutors, the chancellor made a long speech to him, desiring him to forsake the opinions he had embraced, and return to the bosom of the church; adding, that as the pope was the head of the church, so it was breaking through her unity to separate from her. He promised to procure him the pope's absolution if he would recant his opinions; but this was merely an ostentatious pretence to mercy; for Gardiner knew, that Hooper was too well grounded in his religious opinions, to comply with his request.

To this Dr. Hooper, answered, that as the pope's doctrine was contrary to the sacred scriptures, and as he could not be the head of the church, because there was no head of it but Christ, so he would live and die asserting the doctrines he had taught.

Gardiner replied, that the queen would never show any mercy to the enemies of the pope : whereupon Babington, the warden, was commanded to take him back to the Fleet. It was likewise ordered, that he should be shifted from his former chamber, which was done ; and he was searched, to find, if possible, whether he had any books concealed about him, but none were found.

On the 25th of January he was again brought before the chancellor to be examined, and was again asked whether or not he would recant ; but nothing could shake his constancy.

On Monday morning, February 4th, the bishop of London went to the prison to degrade him, which was done in the usual form, by putting the different robes upon him worn by priests and then taking them off. They did not put on him the bishop's robes, because they did not admit of the validity of his ordination. While they were stripping him of these

33

Romish rags, he told them he was glad to part with them, because his mind had been always against them, and considered them as no better than heathenish relics ; as in fact they were, for the same kind of robes were worn by the priests before the time of Constantine the Great.

A few hours after he was degraded, the keeper came to him and told him, he was to be sent down to Gloucester to suffer death. Upon this he lifted up his eyes and hands to heaven, praising God that he was to die among his people, as it would be the means of confirming them in the truth of what he had taught them. He immediately sent to his servant for his boots and cloak, that he might be in readiness to attend the officers whenever they should come for him.

About four in the morning he was taken out of prison by the sheriff, and conducted to the sign of the Angel, near St. Dunstans's church, Fleet-street. There he was received by the queen's officers, who had the warrant for his execution ; after which they permitted him to take some refreshment.

About break of day he cheerfully mounted on horseback without help, having a hood on his head under his hat, that he should not be known ; and thus equipped, with a serene and cheerful countenance, proceeded on the road for Gloucester, attended by his keepers. The guards asked him what houses he was accustomed to use on the road and when they were informed, in order to perplex him, they took him to others.

On the Thursday following they arrived at Cirencester, a town in his own diocess, and about eleven miles from Gloucester, where they dined at the house of a woman who had always hated the protestants, and traduced bishop Hooper's character as much as possible. This woman, seeing his constancy, was so affected, that she lamented his case with tears, and begged his pardon for the manner in which she had spoken of him.

Dinner being over, they proceeded to Gloucester, where they arrived about five in the afternoon. A great crowd of people were assembled about a mile without the town ; so that one of the guard, fearing a rescue, rode up to the mayor's house to demand aid and assistance. This being granted, the people dispersed.

Hooper was that night lodged in the house of one Ingram,

where he ate his supper with a good appetite, and slept very quietly, as those who were with him, for they continued in the chamber with him all the night. In the morning he arose up, and having prayed most fervently, was visited by sir Anthony Kingston, who was one of the persons appointed to see him executed. When sir Anthony came into the chamber he found him at his prayers, and waiting till he had done asked if he did not know him. To this bishop Hooper answered, that he did know him, and was glad to see him in good health. He added, that he was come there to end his life, and blessed God that it was to be in the midst of his own diocese. He said he loved life as well as it ought to be loved, but he was not to enjoy it at the expense of his future welfare. He was not to blaspheme his Saviour by denying his name, through which alone he looked for salvation; but prayed that he should be endowed with fortitude sufficient to bear all the torments his enemies could inflict upon him.

Sir Anthony Kingston had profited much from the preaching of Bishop Hooper, and taking his leave, told him with tears, that he was extremely sorry to lose so worthy a person. Dr. Hooper answered, that it was his duty to persevere in the truth, and not to be ashamed of the gospel, lest Christ should refuse to acknowledge him before his Father in heaven.

The same day, in the afternoon, a poor blind boy came to visit Bishop Hooper, and falling on his knees before him, said, "Ah, my lord, I am blind in my eyes, but your pious instructions have removed a spiritual blindness from my heart. May God support you under all your sufferings, and bring you even through flames, to heaven!"

Several other persons visited the bishop, among whom was a very wicked man, a bigoted papist, who had known him formerly. This man upbraided him with what he called his heresy; but Hooper bore all his insults with patience and meekness.

The time appointed for the execution of this pious bishop drawing nigh, he was delivered to the sheriffs of Gloucester, who, with the mayor and alderman, repaired to his lodgings, and at the first meeting, having saluted him, took him by the hand. The resigned martyr thanked the mayor with the rest of the officers, for taking a condemned man by the hand, and for all the friendship that had formerly subsisted between them, for he had long been acquainted with them. He begged of the sheriffs that they would make the fire as violent as possible, that his pains might be of the shorter duration; adding, that he might have had his life if he chose it, but could not consistently with that duty he owed to God, and his own conscience. He said, he knew the Bishop of Rome was Antichrist, and therefore he could not be obedient to him. He desired they would not deny his request, but let him suffer as soon as possible, without exercising any unnecessary cruelty, which was unbecoming the dignity of men of honour.

A consultation was held by the sheriffs, whether or not they should lodge him, the evening before his execution, in the common gaol over the north gate of the city; but the guards who had brought him from London, interceded so earnestly in his favour, that he was permitted to remain in his former lodgings; and he spent the evening in prayer, together with as much of the night as he could spare from his ordinary rest. The believer, who is to rest in Christ Jesus throughout the endless ages of eternity, may well enjoy an hour's sleep, before the commencement of even the most excruciating tortures.

When bishop Hooper arose in the morning, he desired that no person whatever should disturb him in his devotions, till the officers came to lead him out to execution.

About eight o'clock, the lord Chandois, attended by several other noblemen and gentlemen, came to conduct him to the place of execution; and at nine Dr. Hooper was ready. Being brought down from his chamber, when he saw the guards, he told the sheriffs he was no traitor, but one who was willing to die for the truth; and that, if they would have permitted him, he would have willingly gone unguarded to the stake, without troubling any officers. Afterward looking upon the multitude of people that were assembled, above seven thousand in number, he said: "Alas! why are so many people assembled? I dare not speak to them as formerly."

He was led forward between the two sheriffs, as a lamb to the slaughter, having on a gown which the man of the house, where he was confined, had lent him; and being much afflicted with an illness he had contracted in prison, he was obliged to walk with a staff in his hand. The sheriffs having commanded him not to speak one word, he was not seen to open his mouth; but beholding the people, who mourned bitterly, he sometimes lifted up his eyes toward heaven, and looked cheerfully upon such as he knew; and, indeed, his countenance was more cheerful than it had been for a long time before.

When he was brought to the stake, he embraced it, and looked smilingly at a place where he used formerly to preach. He then kneeled down to pray, and beckoned several times to one whom he knew very well, to come and hear him that he might give a faithful account of what he said, after his death, as he was not permitted to speak aloud. When he had been some time at prayer, a pardon was brought, and offered to him, on condition that he would recant; but neither promises of pardon, nor threatenings of punishment, had any effect on him; so immoveable was he in the faith, and so well established in the principles of the gospel.

Prayers being ended, he prepared himself for the stake, by taking off his landlord's gown, which he delivered to the sheriffs, requesting them to see it restored to the owner. He then took off the rest of his clothes, except his doublet and hose, in which he intended to be burned; but the sheriffs not permitting that, he patiently submitted. After this a pound of gunpowder was placed between his legs, and the same quantity under each arm; three chains were then fixed round him, one to his neck, another to his middle, and a third to his legs; and with these he was fastened to the stake.

This being done, fire was put to the fagots; but they being green, he suffered inexpressible torment. Soon after this, a load of dry fagots was brought, but still the wind blew away the flames; so that he begged for more, that he might be put out of his misery.

At length the fire took effect, and the martyr triumphantly ascended into heaven, after such a fiery trial as almost exceeds any thing we meet with in the primitive ages. His last words were, "Lord Jesus have mercy upon me; enable me to bear my sufferings, for thy name's sake, and receive my spirit."

Such was the end of one of the most eminent fathers of the church of England; and surely that religion which could support him under such dreadful tortures must be of God Fanaticism and superstition may give resolution; but it is only the divine influence of pure religion which can bestow calmness in the hour of death.

Sufferings and Martyrdom of Dr. Rowland Taylor.

Dr. Rowland Taylor was born in the town of Hadleigh, in Suffolk, which was one of the first places in England that received the gospel; and here he preached constantly during the reign of king Edward. Archbishop Cranmer, who was a good judge of merit, and loved to reward it in learned men, took him into his family, and presented him to the living of Hadleigh. Here he proved himself a most excellent preacher and a faithful pastor. He made himself acquainted with every individual in his parish; he taught them like the apostles and primitive Christians, who went from house to house. The love of Christ wrought so strongly on his mind, that every Sunday and holiday he preached in the most fervent manner to his people.

Nor did he restrict himself to preaching: his life was one continued comment on his doctrine: it was a life of holiness; he studied nothing so much as to do good; was a stranger to pride; and was clothed with humility. He was particularly attentive to the poor, and his charity was bounded only by his ability. While he rebuked sinners for their enormities, he was ready to relieve their wants. This was a godlike disposition, and the characteristic of a true Christian.

In the course of his ministerial labours he often met with opposition, and even with abuse; but he attended to the maxim laid down by the apostle, that we must go through evil, as well as through good report. He was a married man, but never set down to dinner with his family, without first inquiring whether the poor wanted any thing. To those who were distressed, he gave relief before he ate any thing himself. He familiarized himself with all ranks of men, in order that he might win them to the knowledge and practice of the truth. He was an indulgent, tender, affectionate husband, and brought up his children in the fear of God; well knowing, that to lay a good foundation is the only way to secure a beautiful superstructure.

In this excellent manner, Dr. Taylor continued to discharge his duty at Hadleigh, as long as king Edward lived; but no sooner was that pious monarch dead, than affairs took a different turn.

And here we may observe, that if a man be ever so pious, if he be ever so faithful in the discharge of his duty, yet he will meet with many enemies: this was the case with Dr. Taylor. In his parish, notwithstanding all his endeavours to suppress popery, yet some papists remained; and their hatred of his doctrine was extended to the preacher, and rendered them blind to his excellencies.

Two of these persons, named Clarke and Foster, hired a Romish priest to come to Hadleigh to say mass. For this purpose, they ordered an altar to be built with all convenient speed, and appointed that mass should be said on Palm Sunday. But the reformers met together in the evening, and pulled down the altar; it was, however, built up again, and a watch was appointed, lest it should be demolished a second time.

The day following, Clarke and Foster came, bringing along with them their popish priest, who was to perform the service of mass. The priest was dressed in his robes for the occasion, and had a guard with him, lest he should be interrupted by the populace.

When Dr. Taylor heard the bells ring, he went into the church to know the reason, but found the doors of the chancel barred against him. However, getting within the chancel, he saw the popish priest at the altar, attended by a great number of people, with their swords drawn. The doctor accused the priest with idolatry, but the priest retorted upon him, and called him traitor, for disobeying the queen's proclamation. Dr. Taylor said he was no traitor, but a minister of the gospel, commanded to teach the people; and then ordered the popish priest to retire, as one who came in there to poison the flock of Christ with his most abominable doctrines. Foster, who was principally concerned in this affair, called Dr. Taylor a traitor, and violently dragged him out of the church; while his wife, on her knees, begged that God would vindicate his innocence, and avenge the injuries so wrongfully inflicted on him.

Foster and Clarke next exhibited a charge of heresy

against Dr. Taylor, to the chancellor Gardiner, who sent a messenger, commanding Dr. Taylor to appear before him, in order to answer to the charge.

When Dr. Taylor's friends heard of this, they were much grieved, and fearing what would be the result, as justice was not to be expected from the furious bigots then in power, advised him to go abroad to save his life. But this he would by no means comply with; saying that it was more honourable to suffer for the cause of God, than to flee from the wrath of wicked men. "God," said he, "will either protect me from sufferings, or he will enable me to bear them." He added, "That he knew his dying for the truth would be of more service to the cause of Christ, than his flying away from the malice of his persecutors."

When his friends saw that nothing could prevail upon him, they took leave of him with tears; after which he set out for London, accompanied by a servant named John Hull, who had been a considerable time in his family. This faithful servant advised him to make his escape, but to no purpose; for Taylor said, that the good shepherd should never leave his sheep, till he was torn from them by force. In the same heavenly manner he exhorted John to be constant in the profession of Christianity, and not to return to popery. He said, that worldly wisdom was apt to take too deep a root in our hearts, and that it was, therefore, our duty to do all we could to triumph over the world, the flesh, and the devil; to be consistent in our attachment to the truth; to keep in view the glorious eternity provided for the faithful; to despise earthly enjoyments, while we strive to render ourselves worthy of heaven; to fear God more than men; to believe that he will sweeten all our sufferings, by the influences of his Holy Spirit; to think nothing too hard to endure, in order to obtain a blessed immortality; and, with a Christian courage, to trample on death, and triumph over the grave.

When Dr. Taylor was brought before the chancellor Gardiner, that prelate reviled him in the most shocking manner, calling him a traitor and heretic; all which our pious martyr patiently submitted to. In the opinion of Gardiner he might have been a heretic, but, according to law, he could not have been a traitor; for the statute of high treason and the statute of heresy enforced different punishments: for treason the offending party was to be hanged and quartered; for heresy he was to be burned alive. Had queen Mary proceeded against this man, and many others, on the statute of high-treason, they must have been acquitted, as the trial would then have been conducted according to the principles of common law. But this she had no intention to do; her design was to gratify the clergy, by causing all those who opposed their sentiments, to be put death in the most barbarous manner.

Dr. Taylor answered the chancellor with becoming firmness: he told him, that he was the persecutor of God's people, and that he, himself, had adhered to our Saviour and his word: he put bishop Gardiner in mind of the oath he had taken in the beginning of king Edward's reign, to maintain the protestant religion, and oppose the papal supremacy: but Gardiner answered that the oath had been extorted, so that he was not obliged to abide by it.

It is certain, that every oath extorted by the threatening of punishment, can have no moral force; and the man who has been weak enough to swear, may recede from the obligatory part as soon as he had an opportunity. But this was not the case with Gardiner; had he refused the oath, all the punishment inflicted upon him would have been the loss of his bishopric. And surely he who pays the least regard to the sacred Name invoked to witness his sincerity, will not choose to enjoy a temporal subsistence at the expense of a guilty conscience.

Dr. Taylor explained to the bishop the nature of an oath, and told him, that as he had not been forced to take one contrary to the dictates of conscience, so he was either prejudiced in what he did, or what was still worse, he trifled with a sacred obligation; that no man whatever could dispense with an oath, unless he knew it was his duty to do so, in consequence of its having been imposed on him by violence.

Gardiner who was self-convicted, turned the subject to the disputed points concerning the real presence, and some other things in popery.

With respect to the real presence in the sacrament, Dr. Taylor told him, that it had no foundation in scripture, but had been first taught about the tenth century. He

quoted the book of Bertram, which was written about that
time, wherein the real presence was denied, and transubstantiation considered as no better than a novel doctrine.
He made it appear, that Christ only commanded his followers to keep the feast of the Eucharist, in remembrance
of his last supper with them. That as Christ broke bread
and drank wine with his disciples in a friendly manner, before he was dragged to prison, to judgment, and to execution, consequently his followers should observe it as a feast
of unity to the end of the world.

Such were the sentiments of this pious man, concerning
a very disputed point. He was clear in his conceptions
concerning the scripture account of the last supper, for all
the primitive fathers have taught us to consider it in the
same light. When Christ said, " This is my body," he
could only mean the atonement that was to be made for sin,
and surely that could not be the bread he took in his hand.
The body of Christ, joined to his human soul, and both
united to the divine nature, are now in a state of glory in
heaven; and how then can the priest turn a morsel of
bread into the body of our Divine Redeemer? The bare
thought puts common sense to the blush. It is full of ab-
surdity, and can only impose on the grossest credulity, for
the purpose of increasing the influence of artful and designing priests.

Dr. Taylor, after being interrogated by the chancellor
for a considerable time, was at length committed to prison;
for bigotry knows no feeling; persecution no resting place.

While he was in prison, he spent the greatest part of
his time in prayer, in reading the sacred scriptures, and in
exhorting the poor prisoners confined with him to a sense
of their duty. This was the more necessary, as the people
at the time were extremely ignorant; light, indeed, was
beginning to break in upon them, but they knew not how
to walk. The prison in which Dr. Taylor was confined,
was that commonly called the King's Bench, and there he
met with that holy and pious man Mr. Bradford, whose
affinity in religious sentiments contributed to mitigate his
sufferings. If two virtuous or pious persons are of the
same opinion, and under the same circumstances, they
generally sympathize with each other. This was the case
with Dr. Taylor and Mr. Bradford; for no sooner did they

meet each other in prison; than they blessed God who had brought them together, to suffer for the truth of the gospel.

After Dr. Taylor had laid a considerable time in prison, he was cited to appear at Bow church in Cheapside, to answer to the dean of the arches concerning his marriage.

When be was brought before this officer, he defended marriage in such a masterly manner, that the dean would not venture to pronounce a divorce, but only deprived him of his benefice. He was then remanded to prison, and kept there above a year and a half; when he and several others were brought to be again examined before the chancellor.

Gardiner asked him whether he adhered to the form of religion, as established by king Edward VI.? Whether he approved of the English Book of Common Prayer? whether he were married? and many other questions. To all these Dr. Taylor gave clear and satisfactory answers, justifying his conduct; but these were not sufficient, seeing his death was resolved on.

Concerning marriage, Dr. Taylor proved, not only from the sacred scriptures, but likewise from the primitive writers, that the clergy were not prohibited from it. As he was a learned civilian and canonist, he proved from the Justinian institutions, that all oaths of celibacy were then condemned, and that the priests were exhorted to marry. Nay, so strict was the emperor in this particular, that if a man made over a legacy to his wife, on condition of her not marrying again, the will was to be void.

He added further, that it was contained in the pandects, that if a man had a female slave, and made her free, on condition she should never marry, the condition should not be binding, and she might marry, nor should her former master be permitted to reclaim her. It was the more proper to quote the pandects, because they were written in the sixth century, and although many abuses had then crept into the church, yet celibacy was not in the number.

The next time he was brought before the chancellor, was in company with Mr. Saunders, whose martyrdom we have already described, and Mr. Bradford. Dr. Taylor was charged with heresy by the chancellor and the other

bishops who were present.   He acknowledged that he abhorred all the popish doctrines of the church of Rome ,
that the pope was Antichrist : that to deny the clergy the
privilege of marriage was the doctrine of devils ; that there
were but two sacraments in the New Testament ; that the
mass was idolatry, the body of Christ being in heaven ;
and last of all, that he would abide by these sentiments to
the last, being convinced that they were consistent with
the doctrines laid down by Christ and his apostles.

One may easily imagine what would be the consequences of such a free and open declaration.   The papists
could not bear to hear their favourite notions thus called
in question, and even condemned as idolatry.

The chancellor therefore pronounced sentence on him,
and he was taken to a prison in Southwark, called the
Clink, where he remained till night, and then was sent to
the Compter in the Poultry.   Here he remained seven
days : when, on the 4th of February. 1555, Bonner, bishop
of London, with others, came to the said Compter to degrade him, bringing with them the popish habits.*

The last part of the ceremony of degradation is for the
bishop to strike the person degraded on the breast ; but
Bonner's chaplain advised him not to strike Dr. Taylor,
for he would surely strike again.   " Yes, that I will, by
St. Peter," said the doctor " for the cause is Christ's, and
I should not be a good soldier, if I did not fight my master's battles."

The bishop, therefore, contented himself with pronouncing
a curse upon Dr. Taylor ; to which the doctor answered,
" You may curse as long as you please, but I am confident
God will support me : I have the witness of a good conscience, that I am standing in defence of the truth ; whereas you dare not say that you are doing so : but I will pray
for you."

When he was brought up to his chamber, he told Mr.
Bradford that he had made the bishop of London afraid ;

* Superstition had risen to such a pitch in the reign of Henry I., that the
clergy were excirpted from corporeal punishments ; but his grandson
Henry II., in the constitutions of Clarendon, ordained that they should suffer the same punishments as the laity ; and therefore the clergy, that it
might not be said that a priest suffered death, always degraded him before
execution ; thus by a pitiful quibble maintaining the shadow of exemption, when they had lost the substance.

"for," said he, "his chaplain advised him not to strike me, lest I should strike him again, which I made him believe I would, although I never intended to do so."

To strike an enemy is strictly forbidden in the gospel; but ever had Dr. Taylor been so unguarded as to strike the bishop, it could only have been imputed to the ignorance which at that time prevailed, even over the minds of pious men.

The night after he was degraded, his wife, with his son Thomas, came to see him; and such was the good nature of the keeper, that he permitted them to go into his apartment and sup with him. Thus Dr. Taylor found a great difference between the keeper of the bishop's prison and the keeper of the Compter. The bishop's keepers were ever cruel, blasphemous, and tyrannical, like their master; but the keepers of the royal prisons, for the most part, showed as much favour as could be granted to those whom they had in custody. John Hull, the servant, came with the wife and son of Dr. Taylor; and at their first coming in, they all kneeled down and prayed.

After supper the doctor walked two or three times across the room, blessing God that he had singled him out to bear witness to the truth, as it is in Jesus: that he had been thought worthy to suffer for his name's sake: and then, turning to his son, he said, "My dear son, God Almighty bless you, and give you his Holy Spirit, to be a true servant of Christ; to hear his word, and constantly to stand by the truth all thy life long; and, my son, see that thou fear God always; flee from all sin and wicked living; be virtuous; attend closely to thy book, and pray to God sincerely. In all things that are lawful, see that thou be obedient to thy mother; love her and serve her; be ruled and directed by her now in thy youth, and follow her good counsel in all things. Beware of lewd company, of young men that fear not God, but indulge their vain appetites and lusts. Fly from whoredom, and abhor all filthy living; remembering that I, thy father, am to die in defence of holy marriage. Another day, when God shall bless thee, love and cherish the poor people, and count that thy chief riches is to be rich in alms: and when thy mother is far advanced in years, forsake her not, but provide for her according to thy abilities, and see that she want for nothing.

34

And God will bless thee, and give thee long life upon earth, and prosperity ; for which now, upon my knees, I pray, through the merits of Jesus Christ."

Then, turning to his wife, he said, " My dear wife, continue steadfast in the faith, fear, and love of God. Keep yourself undefiled by the popish idolatries and superstition. I have been unto you a faithful yoke-fellow ; and so have you been unto me ; for the which I pray God to reward you, and doubt not, my dear, but God will reward you. Now the time is come that I shall be taken from you, and you discharged of the wedlock bond toward me : therefore I will give you my counsel, that I think most expedient for you. You are yet a child-bearing woman, and, therefore, it will be most convenient for you to marry ; for, doubtless, you will not of yourself be able to support our dear children, nor be out of trouble, till you be married. Therefore, as soon as Providence shall point out some pious, honest man, who you think will support the poor children, be sure to marry him, and live in the fear of God ; but by all means avoid idolatry and superstition."

Having said these words, he fell down and prayed for his family ; and then he gave his wife an English Prayer Book, as set forth by king Edward VI. ; and to his son Thomas, he gave a Latin book, containing a collection of sentiments from the writings of the primitive fathers, relating to the courage and constancy of the ancient martyrs.

The reader who attends to the conduct of this dying martyr, will find that there is something in true religion far superior to deception. In the primitive times it was common for the martyrs, previous to their sufferings, to converse with their friends, and also to write epistles to the churches at a distance. Some of those epistles are still extant, and we know that they were frequently read in the churches afterward : but no eloquence can exceed that of Dr. Taylor, in taking leave of his wife and son. How sweetly do his expressions flow from the heart ! What a manly dignity under his sufferings does he display ! What resignation to the will of God, and what a firm reliance on divine Providence ! Here, indeed, grace triumphed over human nature, and the soul showed its native splendour, although confined within a mortal body.

The next morning, the 5th of February, so early as two o'clock, the sheriff of London, attended by his officers, came to the Compter, and took Dr. Taylor to the Woolpack, near Aldgate. His wife, having some suspicion that he was to be taken out that morning, waited all night in the church of St. Botolph, near Aldgate, having with her a poor orphan girl, whom the doctor had brought up from infancy, and one of her own children. When the sheriff and his company came opposite the church, the orphan girl cried out, "O, my dear father; mother, mother, here is my father led out." Then Mrs. Taylor cried out, "Rowland! Rowland! where art thou?" for the morning was extremely dark. To this Dr. Taylor answered, "Here I am, but I am confined.' The sheriff's officers wanted to hurry him away; but the sheriff, who had more humanity, ordered them to let him speak to his wife.

She then came to him, when, taking his wife and daughter, with the orphan girl, by the hands, he kneeled down and prayed with them; which, when the sheriff and the other persons present saw, they shed tears. Prayers being over, he rose up, and taking his wife by the hand, bid her have good comfort, for he had a clear conscience. "God,' said he, "will provide a father for my children, but let them be steadfast in the faith." To which his wife answered, "God be with you my dear Rowland, and I will, with his grace, meet you at Hadleigh."

He was then put into a chamber, with four of the yeoman of the guard, and the sheriff's officers. As soon as he entered the chamber he knelt down, and gave himself wholly to prayer. There the sheriff, seeing Mrs. Taylor, told her that she must not speak to her husband; but that she might go to his house, and he would provide for her, so that she should not want for any thing. To this she answered, "she would rather go to her mother's house," and two officers were sent to conduct her thither.

This part of the sheriff's conduct doubtless arose from principles of humanity; for what man can see a wife and children weeping over a father and husband, condemned to a cruel death, for a disputable offence, without shedding a tear of compassion?

Dr. Taylor remained at the Woolpack till eleven in the forenoon, when the sheriff of Essex came to receive him, and they prepared to set out on horseback. As they came out of the gate of the inn, John Hull, his old servant whom we have mentioned before, was there waiting, having with him Dr. Taylor's son Thomas; John lifted up the boy that he might see his father, and then set him on the horse before him. Dr. Taylor, taking off his hat, said, "Good people, this is my own son, begotten in lawful wedlock, and I bless God for lawful matrimony." He then lifted up his eyes toward heaven, and prayed for his son; laid his hand upon the boy's head, and blessed him. After this he delivered him to John Hull, whom he shook by the hand, and said, "Thou hast been the faithfullest servant ever man had."

When they arrived at Brentwood, they made a close hood for Dr. Taylor, having two holes for his eyes, and one for his mouth to breathe at. They did this, that no man should know him, or speak to him; which practice was frequently used in such cases. The evidence of their own consciences convinced them that they were leading innocent people to the slaughter. Guilt creates fear, and thus does Satan reward his vassals.

All the way Dr. Taylor was as joyful as if he had been going to take possession of an estate; and, indeed, how could it be otherwise? He knew he was suffering for the faith, and that the truth was able to support him; and he anticipated a glorious reward from Him for whose cause he suffered.

At Chelmsford they were met by the sheriff of Suffolk, who was to take him into that county to be executed. While they were at supper, the sheriff of Essex laboured earnestly with him to return to the popish religion. He told him, "That as he was a man of universal learning, so his death would be a great loss to the nation." The sheriff, whatever his own opinions were, said a great deal to Dr Taylor, and falling before him on his knees, with the tears running down his cheeks, earnestly begged of him to recant his opinions, and be reconciled to the church; promising that he and all his friends would procure his pardon.

Dr. Taylor then took the cup in his hand, and looking to the company, particularly to the sheriff of Essex, said, "I heartily thank you for your good will; I have hearkened to your words, and minded well your counsels; and, to be plain with you, I do perceive that I have been deceived myself, and am likely to deceive a great many in Hadleigh of their expectations." At these words the whole company clapped their hands with joy: " God bless you," said the sheriff of Essex, " keep to that, it is the most comfortable word we have heard from you. Why should you cast away yourself? Play a wise man's part, and then I am certain you will find favour." Upon this Dr. Taylor replied, " I am, as you see, a man of a very large body, which I thought should have lain in Hadleigh churchyard, and there are a great number of worms there who would have had the feasting, which no doubt they wished for many a day; but I know I am deceived," said he, " and the worms are so too, for my body is to be burned to ashes, and they will lose their feast."

When the sheriff and his companions heard him say this, they were amazed at his constancy; for the nearer his sufferings approached, the more he was strengthened to endure them. In this he imitated our blessed Redeemer, who, when he felt his father's wrath beginning to be inflicted upon him, he sweated as it were great drops of blood; but when led forth, and nailed to the cross, he looked round with complacency, and convinced the spectators that the glory of God shone through his human nature.

Such has been the case of the martyrs in all ages and nations. Human nature might, at first, shudder and shrink back at the thought of the sufferings they were exposed to; but their constancy increased as the fiery trial drew near.

When the procession arrived at Aldham Common, where Dr. Taylor was to be burnt, he lifted up his eyes to heaven, and thanked God that the last struggle was come, and he hoped he should be enabled to go through with it.

He tore the hood from his face, that he might be seen by the numerous spectators, many of whom had formerly been his parishoners. He then began to speak to the people who were praying for him; but the officers thrust sticks into his mouth, and threatened to cut his tongue out, unless he would promise to keep silence at the place of execution.

When he had prayed, he kissed the stake, and got into a
34*

barrel partly filled with pitch, which was placed for that purpose. Fire being set to the pitch, Dr. Taylor continued praying in the most devout manner, till one of the officers, more humane than the rest, knocked out his brains with a halberd, and thus put an end to his misery.

We have in this case an instance of popish superstition, in some respects more violent than any we have yet taken notice of. Dr. Taylor was not only a pious man, but he had been, for his knowledge of the canon and civil laws, long esteemed as the glory of Cambridge. He had, from his distinguished abilities and learning, confuted the chancellor in his arguments concerning the marriage of the clergy; and, indeed, in all other respects, he was so well acquainted with the ancient fathers, that he was with great propriety called "The Walking Library." But no mercy can be shown, where religious rancour takes place. There is something in such persecutions that shuts up the bowels of compassion, even toward the nearest relations. Civil persecutors may occasionally relax into compassion; but those who persecute from erroneous notions of religion, are strangers to every humane sensation; and pant for the blood of those who differ from them, " even as the hart doth for the water-brooks."

CHAPTER III.

Martyrdom of numerous Persons in various parts of England.

THE following persons were next called to seal their faith with their blood, the particulars of whose martyrdoms our limits will not permit us to give.

Thomas Tomkins, a weaver in the parish of St. Leonards, Shoreditch, and William Hunter, a silk-weaver in Coleman-street, London, were burnt; the former at Smithfield, and the latter at Brentwood, on the 16th of March, 1555.

On the 28th day of the same month, William Pigot and Stephen Knight were burnt; the former at Braintree, and the latter at Malden in Essex, and the day following, the Rev. John Lawrence was also burnt at Colchester.

On the 30th day of the same month, Dr. Farrar bishop of St. Davids, suffered at the market-place in Caermarthen, giving a striking evidence of his unshaken confidence in the Redeemer.

Rawlins White, a poor fisherman, also suffered martyrdom on the same day, his constancy and faith being thus described:

Upon the day appointed for terminating his life, which was March 30th, 1555, he was brought from prison, and in his way to the place appointed for the bloody scene, met his wife and children, wringing their hands, and most bitterly lamenting his approaching fate. This affecting sight drew tears from his eyes; but soon recollecting himself, and striking his breast with his hand, he said, " Ah ! flesh, stayest thou me, wouldst thou fain prevail ? Well, do what thou canst, by God's grace thou shalt not get the victory."

As soon as he arrived at the stake, he fell on his knees, and kissed the earth, saying, " Earth to earth and dust to dust ; thou art my mother, to thee I must return."

When he was fastened to the stake, and the straw, reeds, and wood were placed round him, a priest, appointed for the purpose, stood up and harangued the spectators, who were very numerous, it being market-day.

The priest, having finished his discourse, in which he inveighed against the opinion of the protestants concerning the sacrament of the altar, our martyr rebuked him, proved his doctrine to be false, and cited, as his authority, those words of our Lord, " Do this in remembrance of me."

The fire being kindled, he was soon surrounded by the flames, in the midst of which this good old man, (for he was sixty years of age) held up his hands till the sinews shrunk, crying earnestly, " O Lord, receive my soul ! O Lord, receive my spirit !" The flames were so vehement about his legs, that they were almost consumed, before the upper part of his body was injured by the fire ; notwithstanding which he bore his sufferings with the greatest composure and resignation, cheerfully resigning his soul into the hands of Him who gave it, in sure and certain hope of being rewarded for his constancy with a crown of eternal life.

Martyrdom of the Rev. George Marsh.

This eminent and pious divine was descended from poor but honest and religious parents, who educated him, from his earliest years, in the principles of the reformed religion; so that when he arrived at manhood, he was well versed in the doctrines of the pure gospel of Christ.

At his first entrance into the business of life he followed the occupation of farming, and by his honest endeavours maintained his family with decency and reputation for some years: but, on the decease of his wife, being disposed to study, he placed his children with his father, quitted his farm, and went to Cambridge, where he made such progress in literature, that he soon entered into holy orders.

He officiated as curate in several parishes in the county of Lancaster, kept a school at Dean, and was a zealous promoter of the true religion, as well as a vigorous opposer of the idolatries of the church of Rome, during the reign of Edward VI. But when popery again raised its destructive head, he, among many others, became the object of its persecution, as one that propagated doctrines contrary to the *infallible church*, and, therefore, liable to the severest censure and punishment.

Mr. Marsh, on hearing that search was made after him, absconded for some time, and in his retirement often deliberated with himself, whether he should go abroad to save his life, or surrender himself up, in order to ward off the mischief which threatened his mother and brother, who were suspected of having concealed him.

During this unsettled state of his mind, he consulted with his friends, and earnestly sought direction of God, that he might be guided in the way, which most conduced to His glory, and his own spiritual and eternal interest.

At length, thinking that flight would evince cowardice in the best of causes, he determined, by the grace of God, to abide by the consequence, and accordingly surrendered himself to the earl of Derby, at his seat at Latham, in the county of Lancaster.

When he was brought into the earl's presence, he was charged with propagating heresy, and sowing sedition among the people; but he denied the charge, and declared, that he preached no other doctrine than what was contained in the word of God, and that he always enforced allegiance to his sovereign according to the will of God.

Being asked to deliver a summary of his belief, he declared, that he believed in God the Father, Son, and Holy Ghost, according to the creeds of the Apostles, the council of Nice, and the saints Athanasius, Austin, and Ambrose.

A Romish priest, who was present, then proceeded to inquire his opinion concerning the favourite tenet of the church of Rome, relating to the sacrament. Marsh answered, in general, that he believed whosoever received the holy sacrament of the body and blood of Christ, according to his own appointment, did eat and drink his body and blood, with all the benefits arising from the same, because our Lord was ever present at his own ordinances.

This general reply not appearing satisfactory, the inquisitors descended to particulars, and demanded his opinion, whether or not the elements were changed into the very body and blood of Christ after consecration. Our martyr briefly observed, that what he believed he had already declared, and desired them not to propose to him such hard and unprofitable questions, in order to endanger his life, and, as it were, to suck from him his very blood.

Incensed at this reply, the earl told him, that instead of seeking his destruction, he meant to preserve his life in this world, and secure his happiness in that which is to come, by converting him from damnable errors and heresies, and bringing him over to the holy mother-church, out of the pale of which there was no salvation.

After many questions and exhortations, finding he still persevered in the faith which opposed that of the " infallible church," the earl gave him pen and ink, and ordered him to write down his belief concerning the sacrament of the altar; and on his writing the same words he had before delivered, he was commanded to be more particular, when he wrote only the following: "Further I know not."

This resolute behaviour exposed him to the keenest resentment of his popish persecutors, who committed him to prison, and suffered no one to come near him but the keeper, who brought him daily the scanty allowance of the place. Various attempts were made, during his confinement, to bring him to a recantation; but as he still remained fixed and determined in his faith, they administered to him the four following articles, and the earl declared, if he would not subscribe them, he should be imprisoned, and proceeded against with the utmost severity.

"1. Whether the mass now used in the church of England was according to Christ's institution; and with faith and reverence and devotion, to be heard and seen?"

"2. Whether Almighty God, by the words pronounced by the priest, did change the bread and wine, after the words of consecration, into the body and blood of Christ, whether it were received or reserved?"

"3. Whether the lay-people ought to receive it but under the form of bread only, and whether the one kind was sufficient for them?"

"4. Whether confession to the priest now used in England was godly and necessary?"

Having retired for some time to consider of these articles, he returned, and delivered his opinion of them as follows:

The first he absolutely denied.

The second he answered in the very words he had before written.

With respect to the third, he declared, that lay-people, according to the institution of Christ, ought to receive under both kinds, and that, therefore, to receive under one kind only was not sufficient.

To the last he observed, that though auricular confession was a good means to instruct ignorant people, it was not necessary to salvation, because not commanded by God.

To these answers he added, that his faith in Christ, founded on the infallible word of the only living and true God, he never would deny at the instance of any living creature, or through fear of any punishment whatsoever.

He was afterward committed to Lancaster gaol, laid in irons, and arraigned at the bar with the common felons, where the persecutors endeavoured to extort from him informations of several persons in that county, whom they suspected of maintaining heretical opinions; but nothing could prevail with him to utter a word that might endanger the lives or liberties of his faithful brethren in Christ

He was severely reprimanded for reading aloud to the people, who came in crowds every morning and evening under his prison window, the litany and prayers of the reformed church, together with select passages of holy writ in the English tongue, which they termed " preaching," and, therefore, deemed criminal.

After remaining some weeks in confinement at Lancaster he was removed to Chester, and placed in the bishop's custody, when his lordship frequently conferred with him, and used his utmost endeavours to bring him to an acknowledgment of the corporal presence in the sacrament of the altar, the mass, confession, and, in short, all the tenets and practices of the church of Rome.

When the bishop found he would not assent to a single point, he remanded him to prison ; and in a few days summoned him before him in the cathedral church of Chester, where, in the presence of the mayor, chancellor, and principal inhabitants of that city, both laity and clergy, he caused him to take a solemn oath, to answer truly to such articles as might be alleged against him.

After he was sworn, the chancellor accused him of having preached and published, most heretically and blasphemously, within the parishes of Dean, Eccles, Berry, and many other parishes within the bishop's diocess, directly against the pope's authority, the Catholic church of Rome, the mass, and the sacrament of the altar ; with many other articles.

To all these charges Mr. Marsh answered, that he had neither heretically nor blasphemously preached or published against any of the articles, but as occasion served ; and as his conscience obliged him to maintain the truth, as declared in God's word, and as all then present had acknowledged in the preceding reign.

Being examined as to every particular article, he modestly answered according to the doctrine publicly taught in the reign of Edward VI.

After a further confinement of three weeks in prison, Marsh was again brought into the cathedral, where the chancellor made a formal harangue on the bishop's care of his flock, " in order to prevent infection from scabby sheep," and the like ; which being ended, the former articles were propounded to him; to which he severally answered in the negative.

Being charged with having declared that the church and doctrine taught and set forth in king Edward's time was the true church, and that the church of Rome is not the true Catholic church; he acknowledged the declaration and ratified it by a repetition.

Several persons present taking occasion to ask him, as he denied the bishop of Rome's authority in England, whether Linus, Anacletus, and Clement, who were bishops of Rome, were not good men; he replied in the affirmative, but reminded them that they claimed no more authority in England, than the archbishop of Canterbury doth in Rome.

As this observation highly reflected on the validiity of the papal supremacy, the bishop was so incensed, that he gave Marsh very abusive language, calling him, "a most damnable, irreclaimable, unpardonable heretic.

In return for this, Mr. Marsh mildly expostulated with the bishop, telling him, if he could be persuaded, in his own conscience, that the articles proposed to him were founded on God's word, he would gladly yield in every point; declaring, that he held no heretical opinion, but utterly abhorred every kind of heresy; and then called all present to bear witness, that in the articles of religion he held no other opinion than what was by law established, and publicly taught in England, in the time of Edward VI. and in such religion and doctrine, by the grace of God he would live, and die.

He was then, for the last time, asked, whether he would stand to these opinions, being full of heresies, or forsake them, and return to the Catholic church; and on his heartily declaring he would continue steadfast and immoveable in the faith of God's word, nor ever return to any church that was not founded on scripture authority, the bishop began to read his sentence of condemnation, but was interrupted by the chancellor, in order to give him another opportunity of recanting.

He resolutely withstood the earnest entreaties of several people, who desired him to accept of the proffered mercy; nor could even the repeated exhortations of the bishop and chancellor prevail with this eminent servant of Christ, to deny his Lord and master, and submit **to the usurpation of** cruel, tyrannical men.

All endeavours proving ineffectual, t**he bishop proceeded** in passing sentence, which being ended, **Marsh was deli-** vered up to the sheriffs, who conveyed **him to North-Gate** prison, where he was confined in a **dungeon till the day** appointed for his execution.

On the 4th of April, 1555, this firm **believer was led** to the place appointed for his martyr**dom, amid a crowd** of lamenting spectators. It was ne**ar a village, called** Spittle-Boughton, at a small distance **from Chester. As** soon as he arrived at the place, the **chamberlain of that** city showed him a box, containing the **queen's pardon, on** condition that he would recant. Our **martyr coolly an-** swered, "that he would gladly accep**t the same, for he** loved the queen; but as it tended to pluck **him from God,** who was King of kings, and Lord of **lords, he could not** receive it on such terms."

Then turning to the spectators, he **told them the cause** of the cruel death which awaited him, **and exhorted them** to remain steadfast in the faith of Christ. **As soon as he** was chained to the stake, he again **addressed himself** earnestly in prayer to God; and the **fire being kindled, he** suffered for a considerable time, the **most exquisite torture,** his flesh being so broiled and puffed **up, that those who** stood before him could not see the chain **with which he was** fastened. At length, with the utmost **fortitude, he spread** forth his arms, and said, with a voice **to be universally** heard by the spectators, "Father of **Heaven, have mercy** upon me." Soon after which he yield**ed up his spirit into** the hands of Him who gave it.

Thomas Hawkes.

This person was the son of reputable and **pious parents,** who gave him a good education, and brought him up in he reformed religion. He strictly adhered to the religious principles which had been instilled into his youthful mind; so that finding the gospel, after the death of king Edward, began to decline, (especially among great families, in one of which, that of lord Oxford, he lived,) he returned home,

35

where he hoped quietly to enjoy the worship of God, according to the dictates of his own conscience.

In these expectations, however, he soon found himself disappointed. As there were now popish emissaries in every corner, lying in wait to give information of those who favoured the doctrines of the reformation, Hawkes was apprehended, and brought before the earl of Oxford, his former master. The earl referred him to bishop Bonner, to whom having written that he had refused to have his child baptized according to the order of the church now in use, he left him to his lordship's discretion.

When Hawkes was brought before the bishop, he was asked the cause of keeping the child unbaptized so long: to which he returned for answer that he was bound to do nothing contrary to the word of God.

The bishop then urged, that baptism being a sacrament contained in the word of God, and incumbent on every Christian, he was, consequently, criminal in denying, or not conforming to the same. To this he said, that he by no means denied God's institution, but men's invention therein; such as the use of oil, cream, spittle, salt, candle, &c.

After much debate on the subject, the bishop asked him if he would have his child baptized according to the service-book, set out in the reign of Edward VI. To which he replied, that it was the very thing he desired from his soul. This, however, was but mere equivocation to learn his sentiments; for it appeared, in the sequel, that Bonner's wish was to compel him to submit to the superstitions of the church of Rome; but this, with all his artifice, he was unable to effect.

The bishop, with several others, held various conferences with Hawkes, concerning his belief of the corporeal presence in the sacrament of the altar, the mass, the holy creed, holy water, and other ceremonies of the church of Rome: but these also he rejected as he had done that of baptism. At length Bonner, finding he could by no means prevail with him to recant his opinions and submit to the church of Rome, sent him prisoner to the Gatehouse, in Westminister, commanding the keeper to confine him closely, and not to permit any person to converse with him.

During his confinement, various methods were used to bring him over to recant, such as conversation, reading to him, taking him to hear sermons, and the like; but all proved ineffectual; his constant answer to all who spoke to him on that subject, being, "I am no changeling."

Bonner, incensed at his steadfastness, told him on his second examination, he should find him " no changeling" neither, and immediately went out and wrote the following paper:

" I, Thomas Hawkes, do here confess and declare, before my ordinary, Edmund, bishop of London, that the mass is abominable, detestable, and full of all superstition; and also concerning the sacrament of the body and blood of Christ, commonly called the sacrament of the altar, that Christ is no part thereof, but only in heaven. This I have believed, and this I do believe."

Bonner ordered Hawkes to subscribe to this paper; but he refused to set his name to what he had not written himself; upon which the haughty prelate struck him on the breast, declaring, at the same time, that " He would severely chastise all such proud and disobedient knaves."

A few days after this the bishop summoned him, with several others, to appear publicly in the consistory court at St. Paul's, where the several articles alleged against him, together with the bill of confession, were read to him, in all which he firmly continued.

They then strongly exhorted him to recant, that they might not be obliged to pass the awful sentence of death upon him. To which he cheerfully replied, that if he had a hundred bodies, he would suffer them all to be torn to pieces, rather than abjure the faith of Christ's gospel.

On his thus steadfastly persevering in the faith which he professed, the bishop read the sentence of condemnation against him, and five others; after which he was sent back to prison, where he remained till June following, when he was delivered into the hands of lord Rich, who caused him to be conveyed to Chelmsford, and from thence to Coxall, in Essex, where he was burned on the 10th of the same month.

Mr. Hawkes gave many pious exhortations to his friends

who came to visit him ; and several of them requesting, if it were possible, that he would show them some token, by which the possibility of burning without repining might appear, he promised " by the help of God, to show them that the most exquisite torments were to be endured in the glorious cause of Christ.   Accordingly, it was agreed between them, that if the rage of pain were tolerable, he should lift up his hands toward heaven, before he gave up the ghost.

A short time after this agreement, he was led to the place of execution, and after having fervently prayed to Almighty God, the flames were kindled around him, and he continued in them so long, that his speech was taken away by their violence ; his skin was contracted, and the spectators thought he was dead, when, on a sudden, and contrary to all expectation, this eminent and zealous servant of God, mindful of the promise he had made to his friends, held his hands flaming over his head, and, as if in an ecstacy of joy, clapped them thrice together.

The astonished multitude testified their approbation of his faith and patience, and his friends, to whom he made the promise, were exceedingly confirmed in their most holy faith, by being eye-witnesses to the power of divine strength, which is able to support the servants of God, under every trial that may befall them, for the sake of the truth, as it is in our Blessed Redeemer.

CHAPTER IV.

Margaret Polley, first Female Martyr in England.

SUCH was the fury of bigoted zeal during the reign of Mary, that even the more tender sex did not escape the resentment of the Romish persecutors.   These monsters in human form, embraced every opportunity of exercising their cruelty, tyranny, and usurpation ; nor could youth, age, or sex, impress on their minds the least feelings of humanity.

Information being given against Margaret Polley, to Maurice, bishop of Rochester, she was brought before him, and was examined as to her belief on the contested points of religion. Her doctrines being contrary to those taught by the church of Rome, and refusing to recant, the bishop pronounced sentence of condemnation against her; after which she was carried back to prison, where she remained for upward of a month.

She was a woman in the prime of life, pious, charitable, humane, learned in the scriptures, and beloved by all who were acquainted with her.

During her imprisonment she was repeatedly exhorted to recant; but she refused all offers of life on such terms, choosing glory, honour, and immortality hereafter, rather than a few short years in this vale of grief, and even those purchased at the expense of truth and conscience.

When the day appointed for her execution arrived, which was in July, 1555, she was conducted from the prison at Rochester to Tunbridge, where she was burned, sealing the truth of what she had testified with her blood, and showing that the God of all grace, out of the weakest vessel can give strength, and cause the meanest instrument to magnify the glories of his redeeming love.

Christopher Wade.

On the same day that Margaret Polley suffered, one Christopher Wade, a weaver of Dartford, in Kent, who had likewise been condemned by the bishop of Rochester, shared the same fate, and at the same place; but they were executed separately, he first submitting to the dreadful sentence.

Other Martyrs.

About the same time, John Bland, John Frankesh, Nicholas Sheterden, and Humphrey Middleton, were all burnt together at Canterbury. The first two were ministers and preachers of the gospel, the one being rector of Adesham, and the other vicar of Rolvindon, in Kent. They all resigned themselves to their fate with Christian fortitude, fervently praying to God to receive them into his heavenly kingdom.

35*

Martyrdom of John Denley, John Newman, and Patrick Packingham

So perpetually were the popish emissaries in search of their prey, in all parts of the kingdom, that it was almost impossible long to escape them. As Mr. Denley and Mr. Newman were travelling together in Essex, they were met by Mr. Tyrrel, justice of the peace for the county, who, suspecting them of heresy, caused them to be apprehended, and searched; and, at the same time, took from Mr. Denley a confession of his faith in writing, concerning the sacrament of the altar, together with certain notes collected from the holy scriptures.

The justice immediately sent them to London, and with them a letter to be presented to the council, together with the papers he found on the former.

On their being brought before the council, they were admonished to yield obedience to the queen's laws; but this advice proving ineffectual, their examination was referred to Bonner, bishop of London.

On the 28th of June, 1555, Denley and Newman, together with Patrick Packingham, who had been apprehended two days before, were brought before Bonner, at his palace in London.

On the 5th of July the bishop proceeded, in the usual form, against these three persons, in his consistory court at St. Paul's. After the various articles and their answers had been read, they were exhorted to recant, and both promises and threats were used by Bonner, in order to prevail with them; but on their remaining steadfast in their faith, they were all condemned as heretics, and delivered into the custody of the sheriffs of London, who conducted them to Newgate, where they were kept till writs were issued for their execution.

Denley was ordered to be burned at Uxbridge, where, being conveyed on the day appointed, he was chained to the stake, and expired amid the flames, singing a Psalm to the praise of his Redeemer. A popish priest who was present, was so incensed at his singing, that he ordered one of the attendants to throw a fagot at him, which was accordingly done, and he received a violent fracture in his skull, which, with the fire, soon deprived him both of speech and life.

A few days after, Packingham suffered at the same place; but Newman was executed at Saffron-Walden, in Essex. They both died with great fortitude and resignation, cheerfully resigning their souls into the hands of him who gave them, in full expectation of receiving crowns of glory in the heavenly mansions.

CHAPTER V.

The Life and Martyrdom of Hugh Latimer, Bishop of Worcester; and Nicholas Ridley, Bishop of London.

HUGH LATIMER was born of humble parents at Thirkeston, in Leicestershire, about the year 1475, who gave him a good education and sent him to Cambridge, where he showed himself a zealous papist, and inveighed much against the reformers, who, at that time, began to make some figure in England. But, conversing frequently with Thomas Bilney, the most considerable person at Cambridge, of those who favoured the reformation, he saw the errors of popery, and became a zealous protestant.

Latimer, being thus converted, laboured both publicly and privately, to promote the reformed opinions, and pressed the necessity of a holy life, in opposition to those outward performances, which were then thought the essentials of religion. This rendered him obnoxious at Cambridge, then the seat of bigotry and superstition. However the unaffected piety of Mr. Bilney, and the eloquence of Latimer, wrought greatly upon the junior students, and increased the credit of the protestants so much, that the papist clergy became greatly alarmed, and, according to their usual practice, called aloud for the secular arm.

Under this arm Bilney suffered at Norwich: but his sufferings, far from shaking the reformation at Cambridge, inspired the leaders of it with new courage. Latimer began to exert himself more than he had yet done; and succeeded to that credit with his party, which Bilney had so long supported. Among other instances of his zeal and resolution in this cause, he gave one which was very remarkable: he had the courage to write to Henry VIII, against a proclamation, then just published, forbidding the use of the bible in English, and other books on religious subjects. He had preached before his majesty once or twice at Windsor; and had been taken notice of by him in a more affable manner, than that monarch usually indulged toward his subjects. But whatever hopes of preferment his sovereign's favour might have raised in him, he chose to put all to the hazard rather than omit what he thought his duty. His letter is the picture of a sincere heart, and concludes in these terms; " Accept, gracious sovereign, without displeasure, what I have written : I thought it my duty to mention these things to your majesty. No personal quarrel, as God shall judge me, have I with any man : I wanted only to induce your majesty to consider well what kind of persons you have about you, and the ends for which they counsel. Indeed, great prince, many of them, or they are much slandered, have very private ends. God grant your majesty may see through all the designs of evil men, and be in all things equal to the high office, with which you are intrusted. Wherefore, gracious king, remember yourself; have pity upon your own soul, and think that the day is at hand, when you shall give account of your office and the blood which hath been shed by your sword : in the which day, that your grace may stand steadfastly and not be ashamed, but be clear and ready in your reckoning, and have your pardon sealed with the blood of our Saviour Christ, which alone serveth at that day, is my daily prayer to him, who suffered death for our sins. The spirit of God preserve you."

Lord Cromwell, who was now in power, being a favourer of the reformation, obtained a benefice in Wiltshire for Latimer, who immediately went thither and resided, discharging his duty in a conscientious manner, though much persecuted by the Romish clergy ; who at length obtained an archiepiscopal citation for his appearance in London. His friends would have had him quit England ; but their persuasions were in vain.

He set out for London in the depth of winter, and under a severe fit of the stone and cholic ; but he was most distressed at the thoughts of leaving his parish exposed to the popish clergy. On his arrival at London, he found a court of bishops and canonists ready to receive him ; where, instead of being examined, as he expected, about his sermons, a paper was put in his hands, which he was ordered to subscribe, declaring his belief in the efficacy of masses for the souls in purgatory, of prayers to dead saints, of pilgrimages to their sepulchres, the pope's power to forgive sins, the doctrine of merit, the seven sacraments, and the worship of images; which, when he refused to sign, the archbishop ordered him to consider what he did. "We intend not," said he, "Mr. Latimer, to be hard upon you; we dismiss you for the present; take a copy of the articles: examine them carefully, and God grant that at our next meeting we may find each other in better temper."

At several succeeding meetings the same scene was acted over again. He was inflexible, and they continued to distress him. Three times every week they sent for him with a view either to draw something from him by captious questions, or to tease him at length into compliance. Tired out with this usage, when he was again summoned, instead of going, he sent a letter to the archbishop, in which, he told him, "That the treatment he had lately met with had brought him into such a disorder as rendered him unfit to attend that day; that in the meantime he could not help taking this opportunity to expostulate with his grace for detaining him so long from his duty; that it seemed to him most unaccountable, that they, who never preached themselves, should hinder others; that as for their examination of him, he really could not imagine what they aimed at; they pretended one thing in the beginning, and another in the progress; that if his sermons gave offence, although he persuaded himself they were neither contrary to the truth, nor to any canon of the church, he was ready to answer whatever might be thought exceptionable in them; that he wished a little more regard might be had to the judgment of the people: and that a distinction might be made between the ordinances of God and man; that if some abuses in religion did prevail, he thought preaching was the best means to discountenance them; that he wished all pastors might be obliged to perform their duty; but that, however, liberty might be given to those who were willing; that as to the articles proposed to him, he begged to be excused subscribing to them; while he lived, he never would abet superstition; and that, lastly, he hoped the archbishop would excuse what he had written ; he knew his duty to his superiors, and would practise it ; but in that case he thought a stronger obligation lay upon him."

The bishops, however, continued their persecutions, but their schemes were frustrated in an unexpected manner. Latimer being raised to the see of Worcester, in the year 1533, by the favour of Anne Boleyn, to whom he was recommended by lord Cromwell, he had now a more extensive field to promote the principles of the reformation, in which he laboured with the utmost assiduity. All the historians of those times mention him as a person remarkably zealous in the discharge of his new office. In visiting, he was frequent and observant ; in ordaining, strict and wary ; in preaching, indefatigable ; and in reproving and exhorting, severe and persuasive.

In 1536 he received a summons to attend the parliament and convocation, which gave him a further opportunity of promoting the work of reformation, whereon his heart was so much set. Many alterations were made in religious matters, and the Bible was translated into English, and recommended to a general perusal, in October, 1537.

Latimer, highly satisfied with the prospect of the times, now repaired to his diocess, having made no longer stay in London than was absolutely necessary. He had no talents, and he pretended to have none, for state affairs. His whole ambition was to discharge the pastoral functions of a bishop; neither aiming to display the abilities of a statesman, nor of a courtier. How very unqualified he was to support the latter of these characters, the following story will prove : It was the custom in those days for the bishops to make presents to the king on New-Year's day, and many of them presented very liberally, proportioning their gifts to their hopes and expectations. Among the rest, Latimer, being then in town, waited upon the king, with his offering ; but instead of a purse of gold, which was the common oblation, he presented a New Testament, with a leaf doubled down in a very conspicuous manner, at this passage, " Whoremongers and adulterers God will judge."

In 1539 he was summoned again to attend the parliament : Gardiner, bishop of Winchester, was his great enemy ; and, upon a particular occasion, when the bishops were with the king, kneeled down and solemnly accused bishop Latimer of a seditious sermon preached at court. Being called upon by the king, with some sternness, to vindicate himself, Latimer was so far from palliating what he had said, that he nobly justified it; and turning to the king, with that noble unconcern which a good conscience inspires, " I never thought myself worthy," said he, " nor did I ever sue to be a preacher before your grace; but I was called to it, and would be willing, if you mislike it, to give place to my betters; for I grant there may be many more worthy of the room than I am. And if it be your grace's pleasure to allow them for preachers, I can be content to bear their books after them. But if your grace allow me for a preacher, I would desire you to give me leave to discharge my conscience, and to frame my doctrine according to my audience. I had been a very dolt, indeed, to have preached so at the borders of your realm, as I preach before your grace." The boldness of his answer baffled his accuser's malice; the severity of the king's countenance changed into a gracious smile, and the bishop was dismissed with that obliging freedom, which this monarch never used but to those he esteemed.

However, as Latimer could not give his vote for the six papistical articles, drawn up by the duke of Norfolk, he thought it wrong to hold any office in a church where such terms of communion were required, and therefore resigned his bishopric, and retired into the country, where he proposed to live a sequestered life. But in the midst of his security, an unhappy accident carried him again into the tempestuous atmosphere of the court: he received a bruise by the fall of a tree, and the contusion was so dangerous, that he was obliged to seek for better assistance than could be afforded him by the surgeons of the part of the country where he resided. With this view he repaired to London, where he had the misfortune to see the fall of his patron, lord Cromwell: a loss which he was soon made sensible of. For Gardiner's emissaries quickly found him out in his concealment, and a pretended charge of having spoken against the six articles, being alleged against him, he was sent to the tower; where, without any judicial examination, he suffered imprisonment for the remaining six years of king Henry's reign.

On the death of Henry the protestant interest revived

under Edward, and Latimer was set at liberty. An address was made to the protector, to restore him to his diocess: the protector was willing to gratify the parliament, and proposed the resumption of his bishopric to Mr. Latimer; who, thinking himself unequal to the weight of it, refused to resume it, choosing rather to accept an invitation from archbishop Cranmer, to take up his residence with him at Lambeth; where his chief employment was to hear the complaints and redress the grievances of the poor people; and his character for services of this kind, was so universally known, that strangers from every part of England resorted to him.

In these employments he spent two years, during which time he assisted the archbishop in composing the homilies, which were set forth by authority, in the reign of Edward; he was also appointed to preach the Lent sermons before his majesty, which office he performed during the first three years of his reign.

Upon the revolution, which happened at court, after the death of the duke of Somerset, he retired into the country and preached in those places, where he thought his labours might be most serviceable.

He was thus employed during the remainder of that reign, and continued the same course, for a short time, in the beginning of the next; but when the reintroduction of popery was resolved on, the first step toward it was the prohibition of all preaching, and licensing only such as were known to be popishly inclined. The bishop of Winchester, who was now prime minister, having proscribed Mr. Latimer, sent a message to cite him before the council. He had notice of this design some hours before the messenger's arrival, but he made no use of the intelligence. The messenger found him equipped for his journey, at which expressing his surprise, Mr. Latimer told him that he was as ready to attend him to London, thus called upon to answer for his faith, as he ever was to take any journey in his life; and that he doubted not but that God, who had already enabled him to preach the word before two princes, would enable him to witness the same before a third. The messenger acquainted him that he had no orders to seize his person, delivered the letter and departed. However, opening the letter and finding it a citation from the council, he resolved to obey it, and set out immediately. As he passed through Smithfield, he said cheerfully, "This place of burning hath long groaned for me." The next morning he waited upon the council, who sent him to the tower, from whence, after some time, he was removed to Oxford.

NICHOLAS RIDLEY, bishop of London, received the earliest part of his education at Newcastle-upon-Tyne, from whence he was removed to the university of Cambridge, where his learning and abilities so recommended him, that he was made master of Pembroke-hall, in that university. After being some years in this office, he left Cambridge, and travelled for his advancement in knowledge. On his return to England he was made chaplain to Henry VIII. and bishop of Rochester, from which he was translated to the see of London by Edward VI.

In private life he was pious, humane, and affable: in public he was learned, sound, and eloquent; diligent in his duty, and very popular as a preacher.

He had been educated in the Roman Catholic religion, but was brought over to the reformed faith by reading Bertram's book on the Sacrament; and he was confirmed in the same by frequent conferences with Cranmer and Peter Martyr, so that he became a zealous promoter of the reformed doctrines and discipline during the reign of king Edward.

On the accession of queen Mary he shared the same fate with many others who professed the truth of the gospel Being accused of heresy, he was removed from his bishopric and sent prisoner to the tower of London, and afterward to Bocardo prison, in Oxford; from whence he was committed to the custody of Mr. Irish, mayor of that city, in whose house he remained till the day of his execution.

On the 30th of September, 1555, these two eminent prelates were cited to appear in the divinity school at Oxford, which they accordingly did.

Dr. Ridley was first examined, and severely reprimanded by the bishop of Lincoln, because, when he heard the "cardinal's grace" and the "pope's holiness" mentioned in the commission, he kept on his cap. The words of the bishop were to this effect: "Mr. Ridley, if you will not be uncovered, in respect to the pope and the cardinal his legate, by whose authority we sit in commission, your cap shall be taken off."

Examination of Ridley and Latimer.

The bishop of Lincoln then made a formal harangue, in which he entreated Ridley to return to the holy mother-church, and insisted on the antiquity and authority of the see of Rome, and of the pope, as the immediate successor of St. Peter.

Dr. Ridley, in return, strenuously opposed the arguments of the bishop, and vindicated the doctrines of the reformation.

After much debate the five following articles were proposed to him, and his immediate and explicit answers required.

1. That he had frequently affirmed, and openly maintained and defended, that the true natural body of Christ, after consecration of the priest, is not really present in the sacrament of the altar.

2. That he had often publicly affirmed and defended, that in the sacrament of the altar remaineth still the substance of bread and wine.

3. That he had often openly affirmed, and obstinately maintained, that in the mass is no propitiatory sacrifice for the quick and the dead.

4. That the aforesaid assertions have been solemnly condemned by the scholastical censure of this school, as heretical, and contrary to the Catholic faith, by the prolocutor of the convocation-house, and sundry learned men of both universities.

5. That all and singular the premises are true, and notoriously known, by all near at hand, and in distant places.

To the first article Dr. Ridley replied, " That he believed Christ's body to be in the sacrament, really, by grace and spirit effectually, but not so as to include a lively and moveable body under the forms of bread and wine." To the second he answered in the affirmative. Part of the fourth he acknowledged, and part he denied. To the fifth he answered, " That the premises were so far true, as his replies had set forth. Whether all men spake evil of them he knew not, because he came not so much abroad to hear what every man reported."

He was then ordered to appear the following day in St. Mary's church, in Oxford, to give his final answer; after which he was committed to the custody of the mayor.

When Latimer was brought into court, the bishop of Lincoln warmly exhorted him to return to the unity of the church, from which he had revolted.

The same articles which were proposed to Dr. Ridley were read to Latimer, and he was required to give a full and satisfactory answer to each of them.

His replies not being satisfactory to the court, he was dismissed, but ordered to appear in St. Mary's church at the same time with Dr. Ridley.

On the day appointed, the commissioners met, when Dr. Ridley being first brought before them, the bishop of Lincoln stood up, and began to repeat the proceedings of the former meeting, assuring him that he had full liberty to make what alterations he pleased in his answers to the articles proposed to him, and to deliver the same to the court in writing.

After some debate, Dr. Ridley took out a paper, and began to read; but the bishop interrupted him, and ordered the beadle to take it from him. The doctor desired permission to read on, declaring the contents were only his answers to the articles proposed ; but the bishop having privately reviewed it, would not permit it to be read in open court.

When the articles were again administered, he referred the notary to his writing, who set them down according to the same.

The bishop of Gloucester, affecting much concern for Dr. Ridley, persuaded him not to indulge an obstinate temper, but recant his erroneous opinions, and return to the unity of the holy catholic church.

Dr. Ridley coolly replied, he was fully persuaded that the religion he professed was founded on God's most holy and infallible church ; and, therefore, he could not abandon or deny the same, consistently with his regard for the honour of God, and the salvation of his soul. He desired to declare his reasons, why he could not admit of the popish supremacy, but his request was denied.

The bishop finding him inflexible in the faith, according to the doctrines of the reformation, thus addressed him : " Dr. Ridley, it is with the utmost concern that I observe your stubbornness and obstinacy, in persisting in damnable errors and heresies ; but unless you recant, I must proceed to the other part of my commission, though very much against my will and desire." Ridley not making any reply, sentence of condemnation was read ; after which he was carried back to confinement.

When Latimer was brought before the court, the bishop of Lincoln informed him, that though they had already taken his answers to certain articles alleged against him, yet they had given him time to consider on the same, and would permit him to make what alterations he should deem fit, hoping, by such means, to reclaim him from his errors, and bring him over to the faith of the holy Catholic church.

The articles were again read to him, but he deviated not, in a single point, from the answers he had already given.

Being again warned to recant, and revoke his errors, he refused, declaring that he never would deny God's truth, which he was ready to seal with his blood. Sentence of condemnation was then pronounced against him, and he was committed to the custody of the mayor.

Burning of Ridley and Latimer

"On the north side of the town, in a ditch over against Baliol-college, the place of execution was appointed: and for fear of any tumult that might arise to hinder the burning, the lord Williams was commanded by the queen's letters, and the householders of the city to be there assistant sufficiently appointed; and when every thing was in readiness, the prisoners were brought forth by the mayor and bailiffs.

"Dr. Ridley had on a black gown furred and faced with foins, such as he used to wear when he was a bishop; a tippet of velvet, furred, likewise about his neck, a velvet night-cap upon his head, with a corner cap, and slippers on his feet. He walked to the stake between the mayor and an alderman, &c.

"After him came Mr. Latimer, in a poor Bristol frieze frock much worn, with his buttoned cap and kerchief on his head, all ready to the fire, a new long shroud hanging down to the feet: which at the first sight excited sorrow in the spectators, beholding, on the one side, the honour they once had, and, on the other, the calamity into which they had fallen.

"Dr. Ridley looking back, saw Mr. Latimer coming after. Unto whom he said, 'Oh, are you the ... ?' 'Yea,' said Mr. Latimer, 'have after, as fast ... ' he followed at a distance, till they came to the stake. Dr. Ridley first entering the place, earnestly held up both his hands, and looked toward heaven: then shortly after seeing Mr. Latimer with a cheerful look, he ran to him, and embraced him, saying, 'Be of good heart, brother, for God will either assuage the fury of the flame, or else strengthen us to abide it.'

"He then went to the stake, and kneeling down, prayed with great fervour, while Mr. Latimer following, kneeled also, and prayed as earnestly as he. After this they arose and conversed together, and while thus employed, Dr. Smith began his sermon to them upon this text of St. Paul, in the 13th chapter of the epistle to the Corinthians: 'If I yield my body to the fire to be burnt, and have not charity, I shall gain nothing thereby.' Wherein he alleged, that the goodness of the cause, and not the order of death, maketh the holiness of the person: which he confirmed by the examples of Judas, and of a woman in Oxford who of late hanged herself, for that they and such like as he recited, might then be adjudged righteous, which desperately seperated their lives from their bodies, as he feared those men that stood before him would do. But he cried still to the people to beware of them, for they were heretics and died out of the church. He ended with a very short exhortation to them to recant and come home again to the church, and save their lives and souls, which else were condemned. His sermon scarcely lasted a quarter of an hour.

"At its conclusion, Dr. Ridley said to Mr. Latimer, 'Will you answer the sermon, or shall I?' Mr. Latimer said, 'Begin you first, I pray you?'—'I will,' said Dr. Ridley.

"He then, with Mr. Latimer, kneeled to lord Williams, the vice-chancellor of Oxford, and the other commissioners appointed for that purpose, who sat upon a form thereby, and said, 'I beseech you, my lord, even for Christ's sake, that I may speak but two or three words:' and while my lord bent his head to the mayor and vice-chancellor, to know whether he might have leave to speak, the bailiffs, and Dr. Marshal, the vice-chancellor ran hastily unto him, and with their hands stopping his mouth, said, 'Mr. Ridley, if you will revoke your erroneous opinions, you shall not only have liberty so to do, but also your life.'—'Not otherwise?' said Dr. Ridley.—' No,' answered Dr. Marshal; ' therefore if you will not do so, you must suffer for your deserts.'—' Well,' said the martyr, ' so long as the breath is in my body, I will never deny my Lord Christ, and his known truth: God's will be done in me:' with that he rose and said, ' I commit our cause to Almighty God who will indifferently judge all.'

" To which Mr. Latimer added his old saying, ' Well, there is nothing hid but it shall be opened ;' and said he could answer Smith well enough, if he might be suffered. They were then commanded to prepare immediately for the stake.

" They, according, with all meekness obeyed. Dr. Ridley gave his gown and tippet to his brother-in-law Mr. Shipside, who all the time of his imprisonment, although he was not suffered to come to him, lay there at his own charges to provide him necessaries, which from time to time he sent him by the sergeant who kept him. Some other of his apparel he also gave away, the remainder the bailiffs took.

" Mr. Latimer quietly suffered his keeper to pull off his hose, and his other apparel, which was very simple ; and being stripped to his shroud, he seemed as comely a person as one could well see.

"Then Dr. Ridley standing as yet in his trousers, said to his brother, 'It were best for me to go in my trousers still.' ' No,' said Mr. Latimer, ' it will put you to more pain : and it will do a poor man good.' Whereunto Dr. Ridley said, ' Be it in the name of God, and so unlaced himself. Then being in his shirt, he stood upon the aforesaid stone, and held up his hand and said, ' O heavenly Father, I give unto thee most hearty thanks, that thou hast called me to be a professor of thee, even unto death ; I beseech thee **Lord God, have mercy on this realm of England, and deliver it from all her enemies.**

" **The smith then took a chain of iron, and brought it about their middles : and as he was knocking in the staple, Dr. Ridley took the chain in his hand, and looking aside to the smith, said ' Good fellow, knock it in hard, for the flesh will have it's course.' Then Mr. Shipside brought him a bag of gunpowder, and tied it about his neck. Dr. Ridley asked him what it was, he answered gunpowder,**

' Then' said he, 'I will take it to be sent of God, therefore I will receive it. And have you any,' said he, 'for my brother ?' (meaning Mr. Latimer.) ' Yea, sir, that I have, said he. ' Then give it unto him,' said he, ' in time, lest you come too late.' So his brother went and carried it to Mr. Latimer.

" They then brought a lighted fagot, and laid it at Dr. Ridley's feet ; upon which Mr. Latimer said, ' Be of good comfort, Mr. Ridley, and play the man, we shall this day light such a candle by God's grace in England, as I trust never shall be put out.' When Dr. Ridley saw the fire flaming up toward him, he cried with an amazing loud voice : ' Into thy hands, O Lord, I commend my spirit ; Lord, receive my spirit ;' and continued often to repeat, ' Lord, Lord, receive my spirit.' Mr. Latimer, on the other side, cried as vehemently, ' O father of heaven, receive my soul. After which he soon died, seemingly with very little pain.

" But Dr. Ridley, from the ill-making of the fire, the fagots being green, and piled too high, so that the flames being kept down by the green wood, burned fiercely beneath, was put to such exquisite pain, that he desired them for God's sake, to let the fire come unto him ; which his brother-in-law hearing, but not very well understanding, to rid him out of his pain, heaped fagots upon him, so that he quite covered him, which made the fire so vehement beneath, that it burned all his nether parts before it touched the upper, and made him struggle under the fagots, and often desire them to let the fire come to him, saying, ' I cannot burn.' Yet, in all his torment he forgot not to call upon God, still having in his mouth, ' Lord have mercy upon me,' intermingling his cry, ' Let the fire come unto me, I cannot burn.' In which pains he laboured till one of the bystanders, with his bill, pulled the fagots from above, and where he saw the fire flame up, he wrestled himself to that side. And when the fire touched the gunpowder, he was seen to stir no more, but burned on the other side, falling down at Mr. Latimer's feet ; his body being divided.

" The dreadful sight filled almost every eye with tears. Some took it grievously to see their deaths whose lives they had held so dear. Some pitied their persons, who thought their souls had no need thereof. But the sorrow of his brother, whose extreme anxiety had led him to attempt to put a speedy end to his sufferings, but who, from error and confusion, had so unhappily prolonged them, surpassed that of all; and so violent was his grief, that the spectators pitied him almost as much as they did the martyr."

Thus did these two pious divines and steadfast believers, testify, with their blood, the truth of the everlasting gospel, upon which depends all the sinner's hopes of salvation ; to suffer for which was the joy, the glory of many eminent Christians, who, having followed their dear Lord and Master, through much tribulation in this vale of tears, will be glorified for ever with him, in the kingdom of his father and our father, of his God and our God.

CHAPTER VI.

History and Martyrdom of Mr. John Philpot.

Mr. Philpot was of a family highly respectable, (his father being a knight,) and was born in Hampshire. He was brought up at New College, Oxford, where he studied civil law and other branches of a liberal education, particularly the learned languages, and became a great proficient in the Hebrew. He was accomplished, courageous, and zealous ; ever careful to adorn his doctrine by his practice ; and his learning is fully evinced by what he has left ou record.

Desirous to travel, he went over to Italy, and journeying from Venice to Padua, he was in danger, through a Franciscan friar, who accompanied him, and at Padua, sought to accuse him of heresy. At length he returned to England, strengthened in his faith, by beholding the absurdities and iniquities of Antichrist in his strong hold, and finding that the time permitted more boldness unto him, it being the reign of Edward, he had several conflicts with bishop Gardiner in the city of Winchester.

After that, he was made archdeacon of Winchester, under Dr. Poinet, who then succeeded Gardiner in that bishopric, and here he continued during the reign of Edward, to the great profit of those whom his office placed under his care. When that pious prince was taken away, and Mary succeeded, her study was wholly to alter the state of religion in England : and she caused a convocation of the prelates and other retainers of her faith, to be assembled for the accomplishment of her desire.

In this convocation, Mr. Philpot, with a few others, sustained the cause of the gospel against the adversary, for which, notwithstanding the liberty the house had promised, he was called to account before the chancellor, by whom he was first examined. From thence again he was removed to bishop Bonner, and other commissioners, with whom he had divers conflicts, the last of which we shall give verbatim according to his own statement.

Conference between Bishop Bonner, Mr. Philpot, and other Prisoners.

Two days after, an hour before it was light, the bishop sent for me again by the keeper.

Keeper. Mr. Philpot arise, you must come to my lord.

Philpot. I wonder what my lord meaneth, that he sendeth for me thus early ; I fear he will use some violence toward me, wherefore I pray you make him this answer : That if he do send for me by an order of law, I will come and answer ; otherwise, since I am not of his diocess, neither is he my ordinary, I will not, without I be violently constrained, come unto him.   •

With that, one of them took me by force by the arm, and led me up into the bishop's gallery.

Bonner. What, thou art a foolish knave indeed ; thou wilt not come without thou be fetched.

Philpot. I am brought indeed, my lord, by violence unto you, and your cruelty is such, that I am afraid to come before you ; I would your lordship would gently proceed against me by the law.

Bonner. I am blamed by the bishops that I have not despatched thee ere this ; and am commanded to take a further order with thee, and in good faith, if thou wilt not relent, I will make no further delay. Marry, if thou wilt yet be conformable, I will forgive thee all that is past, and thou shalt have no hurt for any thing that is already spoken or done.

Philpot. My lord, I have answered you already in this behalf, what I will do.

Bonner. Hadst thou not a pig brought thee the other day with a knife in it? Wherefore was it but to kill thyself? or, as it is told me, (marry I am counselled to take heed of thee) to kill me? But I fear thee not; I think I am able to tread thee under my feet, do the best thou canst.

Philpot. My lord, I cannot deny but that there was a knife in the pig's belly that was brought me. But who put it in, or for what purpose, I know not, unless it were because he that sent the meat, thought I was without a knife. But other things your lordship needeth not to fear; for I was never without a knife since I came to prison. And touching your own person, you shall live long if you should live till I go about to kill you; and I confess, by violence your lordship is able to overcome me.

Bonner. I charge thee to answer to mine articles. Hold him a book. Thou shalt swear to answer truly to all such articles as I shall demand of thee.

Philpot. I refuse to swear in these causes before your lordship, because you are not mine ordinary.

Bonner. I am thine ordinary, and here do pronounce, by sentence peremptory, I am thine ordinary, and that thou art of my diocess: (and here he ordered others to be called in to bear him witness.) And I make thee (taking one of his servants by the arm) to be my notary. And now hearken to my articles, to which, when he had read them, he admonished me to make answer, and said to the keeper, Fetch me his fellows, and I shall make them to be witnesses against him.

In the meanwhile came in one of the sheriffs of London, whom the bishop placed by him, saying, Mr. Sheriff, I would you should understand how I do proceed against this man. Mr. Sheriff, you shall hear what articles this man doth mantain; he then read a rabblement of feigned articles: That I should deny baptism to be necessary to them that were born of Christian parents, that I denied fasting and prayer, and all other good deeds; that I maintained only bare faith to be sufficient to salvation, whatsoever a man did beside, and I maintained God to be the author of all sin and wickedness.

Philpot. Ah, my lord, have you nothing of truth to charge me withal, but you must be fain to imagine these blasphemous lies against me? You might as well have said I had killed your father. The scriptures say, "That God will destroy all men that speak lies." And is not your lordship ashamed to say before this gentleman, (who is unknown to me,) that I maintain what you have rehearsed? which if I did I were well worthy to be counted a heretic, and to be burnt.

Bonner. Wilt thou answer to them?

Philpot. I will first know you to be my ordinary, and that you may lawfully charge me with such things.

Bonner. Well, then I will make thy fellows to be witnesses against thee: where are they? are they come?

Keeper. They are here, my lord.

Bonner. Come hither, sirs; (hold them a book) you shall swear by the contents of that book, that you shall say the truth of all such articles as shall be demanded of you concerning this man here present, and take you heed of him that he doth not deceive you, as I am afraid he doth, and strengtheneth you in your errors.

Prisoners. My lord, we will not swear, except we know whereto; we can accuse him of no evil; we have been but a while acquainted with him.

Philpot. I wonder your lordship, knowing the law, will go about, contrary to the same; for your lordship doth take them to be heretics, and by the law a heretic cannot be a witness.

Bonner. Yes, one heretic against another may be well enough. And, Mr. Sheriff, I will make one of them to be a witness against another.

Prisoners. No, my lord.

Bonner. No! will you not? I will make you swear, whether you will or no. I think they be anabaptists, Mr. Sheriff, they think it not lawful to swear before a judge.

Philpot. We think it lawful to swear for a man judicially called, as we are not now, but in a blind corner.

Bonner. Why then, seeing you will not swear against your fellow, you shall swear for yourselves, and I do here in the presence of Mr. Sheriff, object the same articles unto you, as I have done unto him, and require you, under pain of excommunication, to answer particularly unto every one of them when you shall be examined, as you shall be soon, by my register and some of my chaplains.

Prisoners. My lord, we will not accuse ourselves. If any man can lay anything against us, we are here ready to answer thereto: otherwise we pray your lordship not to burden us; for some of us are here before you, we know no just cause why.

Bonner. Mr. Sheriff, I will trouble you no longer with these froward men. And so he rose up, and was going away, talking with Mr. Sheriff.

Philpot. Mr. Sheriff, I pray you record how my lord proceedeth against us in corners, without all order of law, having no just cause to lay against us. And after this, we were all commanded to be put in the stocks, where I sat from morning until night; and the keeper at night upon favour let me out.

The Sunday after, the bishop came into the coal-house at night, with the keeper, and viewed the house, saying, that he was never there before: whereby a man may guess how he kept God's commandment in visiting the prisoners. Between eight and nine, he sent for me, saying:

Bonner. Sir, I have great displeasure of the queen and council for keeping you so long, and letting you have so much liberty; and besides that, you strengthen the other prisoners in their errors, as I have laid wait for your doings, and am certified of you well enough; I will sequester you therefore from them, and you shall hurt them no more as you have done, and I will out of hand despatch you as I am commanded, unless you will be a conformable man.

Philpot. My lord, you have my body in your custody, you may transport it whither you please; I am content. And I wish you would make as quick expedition in my judgment as you say; I long for it: and as for conformity, I am ready to yield to all truth, if any can bring better than I.

Bonner. Why, will you believe no man but yourself, whatsoever they say?

Philpot. My belief must not hang upon men's sayings, without sure authority of God's word, which if they can

37

show me, I will be pliant to the same ; otherwise I cannot go from my certain faith to that which is uncertain.

Bonner. Have you then the truth only ?

Philpot. My lord, I will speak my mind freely unto you and upon no malice that I bear to you, before God. You have not the truth, neither are you of the church of God ; but you persecute both the truth and the true church of God, for which cause you cannot prosper long. You see God doth not prosper your doings according to your expectations : he hath of late showed his just judgment against one of your greatest doers, who, by reports, died miserably. I envy not the authority you are in. You that have learning, should know best how to rule. And seeing God hath restored you to your dignity and living again, use the same to God's glory, and to the setting forth of his true religion ; otherwise it will not continue, do what you can. With this saying he paused, and at length said :

Bonner. That good man was punished for such as thou art. Where is the keeper ? Come, let him have him to the place that is provided for him. Go your way before.

He then followed me, calling the keeper aside, commanding him to keep all men from me, and narrowly to search me, commanding two of his men to accompany the keeper to see me placed.

I afterward passed through St. Paul's, up to Lollards' Tower, and after that turned along the west side of St. Paul's through the wall, and passing through six or seven doors, came to my lodging through many straits ; where I called to remembrance, that strait is the way to heaven. And it is in a tower, right on the other side of Lollards' Tower, as high almost as the battlements of St. Paul's, eight feet in breadth, and thirteen in length, and almost over the prison where I was before, having a window opening toward the east, by which I could look over the tops of a great many houses, but saw no man passing into them.

And as I came to my place, the keeper took off my gown, searched me very narrowly, and took away a pen-case, ink-horn, girdle, and knife, but (as God would have it) I had an inkling a little before I was called, of my removal, and thereupon made an errand to the stool, where, full sore against my will, I cast away many a friendly letter: but that which I had written of my last examination before, I thrust into my hose, thinking the next day to have made an end thereof, and with walking it was fallen down to my leg, which he by feeling soon found out, and asked what that was. I said, they were certain letters: and with that he was very busy to have them out. Let me alone, said I, I will take them out: with that I put my hand, having two other letters therein, and brought up the same writing into my breeches, and there left it, giving him the other two that were not of any importance: which to make a show that they had been weighty, I began to tear as well as I could, till they snatched them from me; and so deluded him of his purpose.

Then he went away, and as he was going, one of them that came with him, said that I did not deliver the writing I had in my house, but two other letters I had in my hand before. Did he not? says he, I will go and search him better: which I hearing, conveyed my examination I had written, into another place near my bed, and took all my letters I had in my purse, and was tearing of them when he came again, and as he came threw the same out of the window, saying, That I heard what he said. By this, I prevented his searching any further.

This zealous servant of God still continued to be held in suspense, and underwent seven more examinations, being combated with all the learning and sophistry of the various heads of the corrupted church; but armed with truth, he bravely stood the test, and proved himself to be *founded on a rock.*

To relate the whole of the examinations, would only be a tedious repetition of the insolence of Bonner, of the pride and arrogance of the other bishops, and of points of dispute, already discussed. We, therefore, proceed to his fourteenth and final examination.

Bishop Bonner having wearied himself with repeated conferences with our Christian champion; by turns insulting, threatening, and exhorting him, with equally hopeless effect, at length resolved to terminate the contest. Accordingly, on the 13th of December, he ordered him to be brought before him and others, in the consistory of St. Paul's, and thus addressed him:

"Mr. Philpot, among other things that were laid and

objected against you, these three you were principally charged with.

" The first is, that you being fallen from the unity of Christ's Catholic church, do refuse to be reconciled thereunto.

" The second is, That you have blasphemously spoken against the sacrifice of the mass, calling it idolatry.

" And the third is, That you have spoken against the sacrament of the altar, denying the real presence of Christ's body and blood to be in the same.

"And according to the will and pleasure of the synod legislative, you have been often by me invited and required to go from your said errors and heresies, and to return to the unity of the Catholic church, which, if you will now willingly do, you shall be mercifully and gladly received, charitably used, and have all the favour I can show you And now, to tell you true, it is assigned and appointed me to give sentence against you, if you stand herein and will not return. Wherefore if you so refuse, I do ask of you whether you have any cause that you can show why I now should not give sentence against you.

Philpot. Under protestation, not to go from my appeal that I have made, and also not to consent to you as my competent judge, I say, respecting your first objection concerning the Catholic church, I neither was nor am out of the same. And as to the sacrifice of the mass, and the sacrament of the altar, I never spoke against the same. And as concerning the pleasure of the synod, I say, that these twenty years I have been brought up in the faith of the true Catholic church, which is contrary to your church, whereunto you would have me to come : and in that time I have been many times sworn, both in the reign of Henry VIII. and of Edward VI. his son, against the usurped power of the bishop of Rome, which oath I think I am bound in my conscience to keep, because I must perform unto the Lord mine oath. But if you, or any of the synod, can, by God's word, persuade me that my oath was unlawful, and that I am bound by God's law to come to your church, faith, and religion, I will gladly yield unto you, otherwise not.

      then, not able with all his learned doctors to accomplish this offered condition, had recourse, as usual, to promises and threats; to which Mr. Philpot answered:

"You, and all other of your sort, are hypocrites, and I wish all the world knew your hypocrisy, your tyranny, ignorance, and idolatry."

Upon these words the bishop dismissed him, commanding that on Monday, the 16th of the same month he should again be brought thither, there to have the definitive sentence of condemnation pronounced against him, if he then remained resolved.

The day being come, Mr. Philpot was presented before the bishops of London, Bath, Worcester, and Lichfield; when the former thus began:

Bonner. My lords, Stokesly, my predecessor, when he went to give sentence against a heretic, used to make this prayer:

Deus qui errantibus, ut in viam possint redire, justitiæ veritatisque tuæ lumen ostendis, de cunctis qui Christiana professione censentur, et illa respuere quæ huic inimica sint nomini, et ea quæ sint apta sectari per Christum Dominum nostrum. Amen. Which I will follow. And so he read it with a loud voice in Latin.

Philpot. I wish you would speak in English, that all men might understand you; for St. Paul willeth, that all things spoken in the congregation to edify, should be spoken in a tongue that all men might understand.

Whereupon the bishop read it in English.

"O God, who showest the light of thy truth and righteousness to those that stray, that they may return into thy way, give to all who profess themselves Christians, to refuse those things which are foes to thy name, and to follow those things which are fit, by Christ our Lord. Amen." And when he came to these words, "To refuse those things which are foes to thy name," Mr. Philpot said,

"Then they all must turn away from you; for you are enemies to that name."

Bonner. Whom do you mean?

Philpot. You, and all of your generation and sect. And I am sorry to see you sit in the place that you now sit in, pretending to execute justice, and to do nothing less but deceive all in this realm. And then turning himself unto the people, he said, "O all you gentlemen, beware

37*

of these men, and their doings, which are contrary to the primitive church. And I would know of you, my lord, by what authority you proceed against me."

Bonner. Because I am bishop of London.

Philpot. Well, then you are not my bishop, nor have I offended in your diocess ; and, moreover, I have appealed from you, and, therefore, by your own law you ought not to proceed against me, especially being brought hither from another place by violence.

Bonner. Why, who sent you hither to me ?

Philpot. Dr. Story and Dr. Cook, with other commissioners of the king and queen : and, my lord, is it not enough for you to worry your own sheep, but you must also meddle with other men's ?

The bishop then delivered two books to Mr. Philpot, one of the civil, and the other of the canon law, from which he would have proved that he had authority to proceed against him. Mr. Philpot perusing them, and seeing the slender proof that was there alleged, said to the bishop : " I perceive your law and divinity are all one ; for you have knowledge in neither of them ; and I wish you knew your own ignorance : but you dance in a net and think that no man doth see you." Hereupon they had much talk. At last Bonner said unto him :

" Philpot, as concerning your objections against my jurisdiction, you shall understand that both the civil and canon laws make against you ; and as for your appeal, it is not allowed in this case : for it is written in the law, There is no appeal from a judge executing the sentence of the law."

Philpot. My lord, it appeareth by your interpretation of the law, that you do not understand it : for if you did, you would not bring in that text.

Hereupon the bishop recited a law of the Romans, That it was not lawful for a Jew to keep a Christian in captivity and to use him as a slave, laying to Philpot's charge that he did not understand the law, but did like a Jew. Whereunto Philpot answered :

" No, I am no Jew, but you, my lord, are a Jew. For you profess Christ, and maintain Antichrist ; you profess the gospel, and maintain superstition, and you are able to charge me with nothing."

Bonner and another bishop. With what can you charge us?

Philpot. You are enemies to all truth, and all your doings are full of idolatry, saving the article of the Trinity.

While they were thus debating, there came thither sir William Garret, mayor of London, sir Martin Bowes, and Thomas Leigh, sheriff of the same city, and sat down with the bishops in the consistory.

They were no sooner seated than Bonner again addressed Mr. Philpot, with the prayer, and again repeated the charge against him; after which he addressed him in a formal exhortation, which he had no sooner ended than Mr. Philpot turned himself to the lord mayor, and said:

Philpot. I am glad, my lord, now to stand before that authority, that hath defended the gospel and the truth of God's word: but I am sorry to see that that authority, which representeth the king and queen's persons, should now be changed, and be at the command of Antichrist; and I am glad that God hath given me power to stand here this day, to declare and defend my faith, which is founded on Christ. Therefore, turning to the bishops, as touching your first objection, I say, that I am of the Catholic church; whereof I never was out, and that your church is the church of Rome, and so the Babylonical, and not the Catholic church; of that church I am not. As touching your second objection, which is, that I spoke against the sacrifice of the mass; I do say, that I have not spoken against the true sacrifice, but I have spoken against your private masses that you use in corners which is blasphemy to the true sacrifice; for your daily sacrifice is reiterated blasphemy against Christ's death, and is a lie of your own invention; and that abominable sacrifice, which you set upon the altar, and use in your own private masses, instead of the living sacrifice, is idolatry. Thirdly, where you lay to my charge, that I deny the body and blood of Christ to be in the sacrament of the altar, I cannot tell what altar you mean, whether it be the altar of the cross, or the altar of stone: and if you call it the sacrament of the altar in respect of the altar of stone, then I defy your Christ, for it is a false one. And as touching your transubstantiation, I utterly deny it, for it was first brought up by a pope. Now as concerning your offer made from the synod, which is gathered together in Antichrist's name ; prove to me that you be of the Catholic church, which you never can, and I will follow you, and do as you would have me.   But you are idolaters and traitors ; for in your pulpits ye rail against good things, as king Henry and Edward his son, who have stood the usurped power of the pope of Rome :   against whom I have also taken an oath, which if you can show me by God's law that I have taken unjustly, I will then yield unto you : but I pray God turn the king and queen's heart from your synagogue and church.

Coventry.   In our Catholic church are the apostles, evangelists, and martyrs ; but before Martin Luther there was no apostle, evangelist, or martyr of your church.

Philpot.   Will you know the cause why? Christ did prophesy that in the latter days there should come false prophets and hypocrites, as you are.

Coventry.   Your church of Geneva, which you call the Catholic church, is that which Christ prophesied of.

Philpot.   I allow the church of Geneva, and the doctrine of the same, for it is Catholic and apostolic, and doth follow the doctrine which the apostles preached.

Bonner.   My lord, this man had a roasted pig brought unto him, and this knife was put secretly between the skin and flesh thereof.   And also this powder, under pretence that it was good and comfortable for him to eat and drink ; which powder was only to make ink to write withal.   For when his keeper perceived it, he took it and brought it unto me : which when I saw I thought it had been gunpowder, and thereupon put fire to it, but it would not burn Then I took it for poison, and so gave it to a dog, but it was not so.   I then took a little water, and made as good ink as ever I did write withal.   Therefore, my lord, you may understand what a naughty fellow this is.

Philpot.   Ah, my lord, have you nothing else to charge me withal, but these trifles, seeing I stand upon life and death.   Doth the knife in the pig prove the church of Rome to be the Catholic church?

Then the bishop brought forth a certain instrument, containing articles and questions, agreed upon both in Oxford and Cambridge.   Also he exhibited two books in print; the one was the catechism composed in king

Edward's days, in the year 1552, the other concerning the
report of the disputation in the convocation house, mention
whereof is above expressed. Moreover, he brought forth
two letters, and laid them to Mr. Philpot's charge; the one
was addressed to him by a friend, complaining of the
bishop's ill usage of a young man named Bartlet Green;
the other was a consolatory letter from Lady Vane. Beside these, was introduced a memorial drawn up by Mr.
Philpot, to the queen and parliament, stating the iregula-
rity of his being brought to bishop Bonner, he not being of
his diocess; also complaining of the severity of his treatment.

These books letters, supplications, &c. having been
read, the bishop demanded of him, if the book entitled,
" The true report of the disputation, &c," were of his
penning, or not? To this Mr. Philpot answered in the affirmative.

The bishops growing weary, and not being able to convince and overcome him, began with flattering speech to
persuade him: promising, if he would revoke his opinions,
and return to their Romish church, he would not only be
pardoned that which was past, but they would, also, receive him again as a true member thereof. But when
Bonner found that it would take no effect, he demanded of
Mr. Philpot, whether he had any just cause to allege why
he should not condemn him as a heretic. " Well," quoth
Mr. Philpot, " your idolatrous sacrament, which you have
found out, you would fain defend, but you cannot, nor
ever shall."

In the end the bishop, seeing his steadfastness in the
truth, openly pronounced the sentence of condemnation
against him. In the reading whereof, when he came to
these words, " and you, an obstinate, pernicious, and impenitent heretic," &c. Mr. Philpot said, " I thank God
that I am a heretic out of your cursed church; I am no
heretic before God. But God bless you, and give you
grace to repent your wicked doings."

When Bonner was about the midst of the sentence, the
bishop of Bath pulled him by the sleeve, and said, " My
ord, my lord, know of him first whether he will recant or
not." " O, let him alone:" said he; and so read forth the
sentence.

When he had concluded, he delivered him to the sheriffs; and so two officers brought him through the bishop's house into Paternoster-row, where his servant met him, and when he saw him, he said, " Ah, dear master !"

" Content thyself," said Mr. Philpot, " I shall do well enough; for thou shalt see me again."

The officers then took him to Newgate, where they delivered him to the keeper. Then his man strove to go in after his master, and one of the officers said unto him, " Hence, fellow what wouldst thou have?" And he said, " I would speak with my master." Mr. Philpot then turned about, and said to him, " To-morrow thou shalt speak with me."

When the keeper understood it to be his servant, he gave him leave to go in with him. And Mr. Philpot and his man were turned into a chamber on the right hand, and there remained a short time, when the chief keeper came unto him; who said, " Ah, hast thou not done well to bring thyself hither?" " Well," said Mr. Philpot, " I must be content, for it is God's appointment; and I shall desire you to let me have your gentle favour, for you and I have been of old acquaintance.

" If you will recant," said the keeper, " I will show you any pleasure I can."—" Nay," said Mr. Philpot, " I will never recant that which I have spoken, while I have life, for it is most certain truth, and in witness thereof, I will seal it with my blood." Then the keeper said, " This is the saying of the whole pack of you heretics." Whereupon he commanded him to be set upon the block, and as many irons to be put upon his legs as he could bear.

Upon Tuesday, the 17th of December, while he was at supper, there came a messenger from the sheriffs, and bade Mr. Philpot make ready, for the next day he should suffer, and be burned at a stake. Mr. Philpot answered, " I am ready; God grant me strength and a joyful resurrection." And so he went into his chamber, and poured out his spirit unto the Lord God, giving him most hearty thanks, that he had made him worthy to suffer for his truth.

In the morning the sheriffs came according to order, about eight o'clock, and calling for him, he most joyfully came down to them. And there his man met him, and said, " Ah, dear master, farewell." His master answered,

" Serve God, and he will help thee." And so he went with the sheriffs to the place of execution; and when he was entering into Smithfield, the way was foul, and two officers took him up to bear him to the stake. Then he said merrily, " What, will you make me a pope? I am content to go to my journey's end on foot." But on entering into Smithfield, he kneeled down, and said, " I will pay my vows in thee, O Smithfield."

On arriving at the place of suffering, he kissed the stake, and said, " Shall I disdain to suffer at this stake, seeing my Redeemer did not refuse to suffer the most vile death upon the cross for me?" And then with an obedient heart he repeated the 106th, 107th, and 108th Psalms: and when he had made an end of all his prayers, he said to the officers, " What have you done for me?" And when they severally declared what they had done, he gave money to them.

They then bound him to the stake, and lighted the fire, when the blessed martyr soon resigned his soul into the hands of him who gave it.

CHAPTER VII.

Martyrdom of Thomas Cranmer, Archbishop of Canterbury, who was burnt at Oxford, March 21st, 1556.

THIS eminent prelate was born at Aslacton, in Nottinghamshire, on the 2d of July, 1489. His family was ancient, and came in with William the Conqueror. He was early deprived of his father, and, after a common school education, was sent by his mother to Cambridge, at the age of fourteen, according to the custom of those times.

Having completed his studies at the university, he took the usual degrees, and was chosen fellow of Jesus college. In 1521 he married, by which he forfeited his fellowship : but his wife dying within a year after his marriage, he was re-elected. This favour he gratefully acknowledged, and declined an offer of a more valuable fellowship in cardinal Wolsey's new seminary at Oxford, rather than relinquish friends who had treated him with such respect.

In 1523 he commenced doctor of divinity ; and being

in great esteem for theological learning, he was chosen
divinity lecturer in his own college, and appointed, by the
university, one of the examiners in that science. In this
office he inculcated the study of the scriptures, then
greatly neglected, as being indispensable for the professors
of that divine knowledge.

The plague breaking out at Cambridge, Mr. Cranmer,
with some of his pupils, removed to Waltham-abbey, where,
meeting with Gardiner and Fox, one the secretary, the
other almoner of Henry VIII. that monarch's intended
divorce of Catharine, the common subject of discourse in
those days, was mentioned: when Cranmer advising an
application to the universities, for their opinion in the case,
they introduced him to the king, who was so pleased with
him, that he ordered him to write his thoughts on the subject, made him his chaplain, and admitted him into that
favour and esteem, which he never afterward forfeited.

In 1530 he was sent by the king to dispute on the subject of the divorce, at Paris, Rome, and other foreign parts.
At Rome he delivered his book, which he had written in
defence of the divorce, to the pope, and offered to justify
it in a public disputation: but after various appointments
none appeared to oppose him; while, in private conferences,
he forced them to confess that the marriage was contrary
to the law of God. The pope constituted him penitentiary-
general of England, and dismissed him.

During the time he was abroad, archbishop Warham
died: Henry, convinced of Cranmer's merit, determined
that he should succeed him: and commanded him to return
for that purpose. He was desirous, by all means, to decline
this high station, for he had a true and primitive sense of
the office, but a spirit so different from that of the churchmen of his times, stimulated the king's resolution; and the
more reluctance Cranmer showed, the greater resolution
Henry exerted. He was consecrated on March 30th, 1533,
to the office; and though he received the usual bulls from
the pope, he protested, at his consecration, against the
oath of allegiance, &c. to him.

The first service he did the king in his archiepiscopal
character, was pronouncing the sentence of his divorce
from Catharine: and the next was joining his hand with
Anne Boleyn, the consequence of which marriage was the

birth of the glorious Elizabeth, to whom he stood god-father.

As the queen was greatly interested in the reformation, the friends to that good work began to conceive high hopes; and, indeed, it went on with desirable success. But the fickle disposition of the king, and the fatal end of the unhappy Anne, for awhile alarmed their fears; though, by God''s providence, without any ill effects. The pope's supremacy was universally exploded; monasteries, &c. destroyed, upon the fullest detection of the most abominable vices existing in them; that valuable book of the "Erudition of a Christian Man," was set forth by our great archbishop, with public authority; and the sacred scriptures, at length, to the infinite joy of Cranmer, and of lord Cromwell, his constant friend and associate, were not only translated, but introduced into every parish. The translation was received with inexpressible joy: every one that was able, purchased it, and the poor flocked greedily to hear it read, some persons in years learned to read on purpose that they might peruse it, and even little children crowded with eagerness to hear it!

A short time after this, he gave a shining proof of his disinterested constancy, by his opposition to Henry's "Six Articles," described in a former part of this volume. However, he weathered the storm, and published, with an incomparable preface, written by himself, the larger Bible; six of which, even Bonner, then newly consecrated bishop of London, caused to be fixed, for the perusal of the people, in his cathedral of St. Paul's.

The enemies of the reformation, however, were restless, and Henry, alas! was no protestant in his heart. Cromwell fell a sacrifice to them; and they aimed their malignant shafts at Cranmer. Gardiner, in particular, was indefatigable: he caused him to be accused in parliament, and several lords of the privy council moved the king to commit the archbishop to the tower. The king perceived their malice; and one evening, on pretence of diverting himself on the water, ordered his barge to be rowed to Lambeth. The archbishop, being informed of it, came down to pay his respects, and was ordered, by the king, to come into the barge, and sit close by him. Henry made him acquainted with the accusations which were laid against
38

him; and spoke of his opposition to the six articles; the archbishop acknowledged himself to be of the same opinion, with respect to them.   The king then, putting on an air of pleasantry, asked him, if his bed chamber could stand the test of these articles?   The archbishop confessed that he was married in Germany, before his promotion; but assured the king, that, on the passing of that act, he had parted with his wife, and sent her abroad to her friends. His majesty was so charmed with his openness and integrity that he discovered the whole plot that was laid against him; and gave him a ring of great value to produce upon any future emergency.

A few days after this, Cranmer's enemies summoned him to appear before the council.   He accordingly attended, when they suffered him to wait in the lobby, among the servants, treated him on his admission with haughty contempt, and would have sent him to the Tower.   But he produced the ring, which changed their tone; and, while his enemies received a severe reprimand from Henry, Cranmer himself gained the highest degree of favour.

On this occasion he showed that lenity and mildness for which he was always so much distinguished: he never persecuted any of his enemies; but, on the contrary, freely forgave even the inveterate Gardiner, on his writing a supplicatory letter to him.   The same lenity he showed toward Dr. Thornton, the suffragan of Dover, and Dr. Barber, who, though entertained in his family, intrusted with his secrets, and indebted to him for many favours, had ungratefully conspired with Gardiner to take away his life.

When Cranmer first discovered their treachery, he took them aside into his study, and telling them, that he had been falsely accused by some in whom he had always reposed the greatest confidence, desired them to advise him how he should behave himself toward them?   They replied, that "such abandoned villains ought to be prosecuted with the greatest rigour: nay, deserved to die without mercy."   At this the archbishop, lifting up his hands to heaven, cried out, "Merciful God! whom may a man trust?"   And then taking out of his bosom the letters by which he had discovered their treachery, asked them, if they knew those papers?   When they saw their own letters produced against them, they were in the utmost confusion;

and falling down upon their knees, humbly sued for forgiveness. The archbishop told them, "that he forgave them, and would pray for them; but that they must not expect him ever to trust them for the future."

In 1547, Henry died, and left his crown to his only son, Edward, who was godson to Cranmer, and had imbibed all the spirit of a reformer. This excellent young prince, influenced no less by his own inclinations than by the advice of Cranmer, and the other friends of the reformation, was diligent in every endeavour to promote it. Homilies and a catechism were composed by the archbishop; Erasmus' notes on the New Testament were translated and fixed in churches; the sacrament was administered in both kinds, and the liturgy was read in the vulgar tongue. Ridley, the archbishop's great friend, and one of the brightest lights of the English reformation, was equally zealous in the good cause; and in concert with him the archbishop drew up the forty-two articles of religion, which were revised by other bishops and divines: as, through him, he had perfectly conquered all his scruples respecting the doctrine of the corporeal presence, and published a much esteemed treatise, entitled, "A Defence of the True and Catholic Doctrine of the Sacrament of the Body and Blood of our Lord Jesus Christ."

But this happy scene of prosperity was not to continue: God was pleased to deprive the nation of Edward, in 1553, designing, in his wise providence, to perfect the new-born church of his son Jesus Christ in England by the blood of martyrs, as at the beginning he perfected the church in general.

Anxious for the success of the reformation, and wrought upon by the artifices of the Duke of Northumberland, Edward had been persuaded to exclude his sisters, and to bequeath the crown to that duke's amiable and every way deserving daughter-in-law, the Lady Jane Grey. The archbishop did his utmost to oppose this alteration in the succession, but was over-ruled; the will was made, and subscribed by the council and the judges. The archbishop was sent for, last of all, and required to subscribe; but he answered that he could not do so without perjury; having sworn to the entail of the crown on the two princesses Mary and Elizabeth. To this the king replied,

" that the judges, who, being best skilled in the constitution, ought to be regarded on this point, had assured him, that notwithstanding that entail, he might lawfully bequeath the crown to Lady Jane." The archbishop desired to discourse with them himself about it; and they all agreeing that he might lawfully subscribe the king's will, he was at .ast prevailed with to resign his own private scruples to their authority, and.set his hand to it.

Having done this, he thought himself obliged in conscience to join the lady Jane: but her short-lived power soon expired; when Mary and persecution mounted the throne, and Cranmer could expect nothing less than what ensued—attainder, imprisonment, deprivation, and death.

He was condemned for treason, and, with pretended clemency, pardoned; but, to gratify Gardiner's malice, and her own implacable resentment against him for her mother's divorce, Mary gave orders to proceed against him for heresy. His friends, who foresaw the storm, had advised him to consult his safety by retiring beyond sea; but he chose rather to continue steady to the cause, which he had hitherto so nobly supported; and preferred the probability of sealing his testimony with his blood, to an ignominious flight.

The tower was crowded with prisoners; insomuch that Cranmer, Ridley, Latimer, and Bradford, were all put into one chamber; which they were so far from thinking an inconvenience, that, on the contrary, they blessed God for the opportunity of conversing together: reading and comparing the scriptures, confirming themselves in the true faith, and mutually exhorting each other to constancy in professing it, and patience in suffering for it.

In April, 1554, the archbishop, with bishops Ridley and Latimer, was removed from the tower to Windsor, and from thence to Oxford, to dispute with some select persons of both universities. But how vain are disputations, where the fate of men is fixed, and every word is misconstrued! And such was the case here; for, on April the 20th, Cranmer was brought to St. Mary's, before the queen's commissioners, and refusing to subscribe to the popish articles, he was pronounced a heretic, and sentence of condemnation was passed upon him. Upon which he told them, that he appealed from their unjust sentence to first of the Almighty; and that he trusted to be received into his presence in heaven for maintaining the truth, as set forth in his most holy gospel.

After this his servants were dismissed from their attendance, and himself closely confined in Bocardo, the prison of the city of Oxford. But this sentence being void in law, as the pope's authority was wanting, a new commission was sent from Rome in 1555; and in St. Mary's church, at the high altar, the court sat and tried the already condemned Cranmer. He was here well nigh too strong for his judges; and if reason and truth could have prevailed, there would have been no doubt who should have been acquitted, and who condemned.

The February following, a new commission was given to bishop Bonner and bishop Thirlby, for the degradation of the archbishop. When they came down to Oxford he was brought before them; and after they had read their commission from the pope, (for not appearing before whom in person, as they had cited him, he was declared contumacious, though they themselves had kept him a close prisoner) Bonner, in a scurrilous oration, insulted over him in the most unchristian manner, for which he was often rebuked by bishop Thirlby, who wept, and declared it the most sorrowful scene he had ever beheld in his whole life. In the commission it was declared, that the cause had been impartially heard at Rome, the witnesses on both sides examined, and the archbishop's counsel allowed to make the best defence for him they could.

At the reading this, the archbishop could not help crying out, "Good God! what lies are these; that I, being continually in prison, and not suffered to have counsel or advocate at home, should produce witnesses, and appoint my counsel at Rome! God must needs punish this shameless and open lying!"

When Bonner had finished his invective, they proceeded to degrade him; and that they might make him as ridiculous as they could, the episcopal habit which they put on him was made of canvas and old rags. Bonner, in the mean time, by way of triumph and mockery, calling him "Mr. Canterbury," and the like.

He bore all this treatment with his wonted fortitude and patience; told them, "the degradation gave him no con
38*

cern, for he had long despised those ornaments;" but when they came to take away his crosier, he held it fast, and delivered his appeal to Thirlby saying, "I appeal to the next general council."

When they had stripped him of all his habits, they put on him a poor yeoman-beadle's gown, thread-bare and ill-shaped, and a townsman's cap; and in this manner delivered him to the secular power to be carried back to prison, where he was kept entirely destitute of money, and totally secluded from his friends. Nay, such was the fury of his enemies, that a gentleman was taken into custody by Bonner, and narrowly escaped a trial, for giving the poor archbishop money to buy him a dinner.

Cranmer had now been imprisoned almost three years, and death should have soon followed his sentence and degradation; but his cruel enemies reserved him for greater misery and insult. Every engine that could be thought of was employed to shake his constancy; but he held fast to the profession of his faith. Nay, even when he saw the barbarous martyrdom of his dear companions Ridley and Latimer, he was so far from shrinking, that he not only prayed to God to strengthen them, but also, by their example, to animate him to a patient expectation and endurance of the same fiery trial.

The papists, after trying various severe ways to bring Cranmer over, without effect, at length determined to try what gentle methods would do. They accordingly removed him from prison to the lodgings of the dean of Christ-church, where they urged every persuasive and affecting argument to make him deviate from his faith; and, indeed, too much melted his gentle nature, by the false sunshine of pretended civility and respect.

The unfortunate prelate, however, withstood every temptation, at which his enemies were so irritated, that they removed him from the dean's lodgings to the most loathsome part of the prison in which he had been confined, and then treated him with unparalleled severity. This was more than the infirmities of so old a man could support: the frailty of human nature prevailed; and he was induced to sign the following recantation, drawn from him by the malices and artifices of his enemies.

"I, THOMAS CRANMER, late archbishop of Canterbury,

do renounce and abhor, and detest, all manner of heresies and errors of Luther and Zuinglius, and all other teachings which are contrary to sound and true doctrine. And I believe most constantly in my heart, and with my mouth I confess one holy and Catholic church visible, without which there is no salvation; and thereof I acknowledge the bishop of Rome to be supreme head in earth, whom I acknowledge to be the highest bishop and pope, and Christ's vicar, unto whom all Christian people ought to be subject.

" And as concerning the sacraments, I believe and worship in the sacrament of the altar the very body and blood of Christ, being contained most truly under the forms of bread and wine; the bread through the mighty power of God being turned into the body of our Saviour Jesus Christ, and the wine into his blood.

"And in the other six sacraments, also, like as in this, I believe and hold as the universal church holdeth, and the church of Rome judgeth and determineth.

" Furthermore, I believe that there is a place of purgatory, where souls departed be punished for a time, for whom the church doth godly and wholesomely pray, like as it doth honour saints and make prayers to them.

" Finally, in all things I profess, that I do not otherwise believe, than the Catholic church and church of Rome holdeth and teacheth. I am sorry that ever I held or thought otherwise. And I beseech Almighty God, that of his mercy he will vouchsafe to forgive me, whatsoever I have offended against God or his church, and also I desire and beseech all Christian people to pray for me.

" And all such as have been deceived either by mine example or doctrine, I require them, by the blood of Jesus Christ, that they will return to the unity of the church, that we may be all of one mind, without schism or division.

" And to conclude, as I submit myself to the Catholic church of Christ, and to the supreme head thereof, so I submit myself unto the most excellent majesties of Philip and Mary, king and queen of this realm of England, &c. and to all other their laws and ordinances, being ready always as a faithful subject ever to obey them. And God is my witness, that I have not done this for favour or fear of any person, but willingly and of mine own conscience, as to the instruction of others "

This recantation was immediately printed, and distributed throughout the country, and to establish its authenticity, first was added the name of Thomas Cranmer, with a solemn subscription, then followed the witnesses of his recantation, Henry Sydal and friar John do Villa Garcirna. All this time Cranmer had no certain assurance of his life, although it was promised to him by the doctors : but after they had gained their purpose, the rest they committed to chance, as usual with men of their religion. The queen, having now found a time to revenge her old grudge against him, received his recantation very gladly, but would not alter her intention of putting him to death, taking secret counsel how to despatch him out of the way. She appointed Dr. Cole to prepare a funeral sermon for Cranmer's burning, against the 21st of March ensuing.

Soon after, lord Williams, of Tame, lord Shandois, sir Thomas Bridges, and sir John Brown, were sent for, and commanded in the queen's name to be at Oxford on the same day, with their servants and retinue, lest Cranmer's death should raise there any tumult.

Dr. Cole the day before the execution took place, came into the prison to Dr. Cranmer, to try whether he abode in the Catholic faith, to whom Cranmer answered, that by God's grace he would be daily more confirmed in the Catholic faith ; Cole departing for that time, the next day following repaired to the archbishop again, giving no signification as yet of his death that was prepared. And therefore in the morning, which was the 21st day of March, appointed for Cranmer's execution, Cole coming to him, asked him if he had any money, to whom, when he had answered that he had none, he delivered fifteen crowns to give to the poor, to whom he would : and so exhorting him as much as he could to constancy in faith, departed thence about his business, as to his sermon appertained.

By this, and other like arguments, the archbishop began more and more to surmise what they were about. Then because the day was not far spent, and the lords and knights that were looked for were not yet come, there came to him the Spanish friar, witness of his recantation, bringing articles, which Cranmer should openly profess in his recantation before the people, earnestly desiring him that he would write the said instrument and articles with his own hand, and sign it with his name : which, when he had done, the said friar desired that he would write another copy thereof, which should remain with him, and that he did also. But yet the archbishop, being not ignorant whereunto their secret devices tended, and thinking that the time was at hand in which he could no longer dissemble the profession of his faith with Christ's people, he put his prayer and his exhortation, written in another paper, secretly into his bosom, which he intended to recite to the people before he should make the last profession of his faith, fearing lest, if they heard the confession of his faith first, they would not afterward have suffered him to exhort the people.

Soon after lord Williams, sir Thomas Bridges, sir John Brown, and the other justices, came to Oxford with a great train of waiting-men. The multitude also gathered on every side, as is wont in such a matter, and great expectations were excited, for first of all, they that were of the pope's side were in great hope that day to hear something of Cranmer that should establish the vanity of their opinion ; the other part, who were endued with a better mind, could not think that he who, by continued study and labour for so many years, had set forth the doctrine of the gospel, either would or could, in the last act of his life, forsake the good part.

During this great expectation, the procession at length came forth in the following order : The mayor went before, next him the aldermen in their place and degree ; after them was Cranmer brought between two friars, which mumbling to and fro certain psalms in the streets, answered one another until they came to the church door, and there they began the song of Simeon, " *Nunc dimittis ;*" and entering into the church, the psalm-singing friars brought him to his standing, and there left him. There was a stage set over against the pulpit, of a mean height from the ground, where Cranmer had his standing, waiting until Dr. Cole made ready for his sermon.

The lamentable case and sight of that man was a sorrowful spectacle to all Christian eyes that beheld him. He that lately was archbishop, metropolitan, and primate of all England, and the king's privy counsellor, being now in a bare and ragged gown, and ill-favouredly clothed, with

an old square cap, exposed to the contempt of all men, did
admonish men not only of his own calamity, but also of
their state and fortune. For who would not pity his case,
and might not fear his own chance, to see such a prelate,
so grave a counsellor, and of so long continued honour,
after so many dignities, in his old years to be deprived of
his estate, adjudged to die, and in so painful a death to end
his life, and now presently from such fresh ornaments, to
descend to such vile and ragged apparel ?

In this habit, when he had stood a good space upon the
stage, turning to a pillar near adjoining thereunto, he lifted
up his hands to heaven, and prayed unto God once or
twice, till at length Dr. Cole coming into the pulpit, and
beginning his sermon, entered first into mention of Tobias
and Zachary ; whom after he had praised in the beginning
of his sermon for their perseverance in the true worshipping of God, he then divided his whole sermon into three
parts, according to the solemn custom of the schools,
intending to speak first of the mercy of God : secondly, of
his justice to be showed : and last of all, how the prince's
secrets are not to be opened. And proceeding a little from
the beginning, he took occasion by and by to turn his tale
to Cranmer, and with many hot words reproved him, that
he, being one endued with the favour and feeling of wholesome and Catholic doctrine, fell into a contrary opinion of
pernicious error ; which he had not only defended by his
writings and all his power, but also allured other men to do
the like, with great liberality of gifts, as it were appointing
rewards for error ; and after he had allured them, by all
means did cherish them.

It were too long to repeat all things, that in long order
were pronounced. The sum of his tripartite declamation
was, that he said God's mercy was so tempered with his
justice, that he did not altogether require punishment according to the merits of offenders, nor yet suffered the
same to go unpunished, yea, though they had repented.
As in David, who when he was bidden to choose of three
kinds of punishment which he would, and he had chosen
pestilence for three days, the Lord forgave him half the
time, but did not release all : and that the same thing
came to pass in him also, to whom although pardon and
reconciliation was due according to the canons, seeing he

repented of his errors, yet there were causes why the queen and the council at this time judged him to death; of which, lest he should marvel too much, he should hear some.

First, that being a traitor, he had dissolved the lawful matrimony between the king and queen, her father and mother; beside the driving out of the pope's authority, while he was metropolitan. Secondly, That he had been a heretic, from whom, as from an author and only fountain, all heretical doctrine and schismatical opinion, that so many years have prevailed in England, did first rise and spring; of which he had not been a secret favourer only, but also a most earnest defender, even to the end of his life, sowing them abroad by writings and arguments, privately and openly, not without great ruin to the catholic church. And further it seemed meet, according to the law of equality, that as the death of the late duke of Northumberland *made even* with Thomas More, chancellor, that died for the church; so there should be one that should *make even* with Fisher, of Rochester: and because that Ridley, Hooper, and Farrar were not able to make even with that man, it seemed that Cranmer should be joined to them to fill up their part of the equality.*

Beside these, there were *other just* and *weighty* causes, which appeared to the queen and council, which were not meet at that time to be opened to the common people.

After this, turning his tale to the hearers, he bid all men beware by this man's example, that among men nothing is so high that can promise itself safety on the earth, and that God's vengeance is equally stretched against all men, and spareth none; therefore they should beware, and learn to fear their prince. And seeing the queen's majesty would not spare so notable a man as this, much less in the like cause would she spare other men, that no man should think to make thereby any defence of his error, either in riches or any kind of authority. They had now an example to teach them all, by whose calamity every man might consider his own fortune; who, from the top of dignity, none being more honourable than he in the whole realm, and

* This *arithmetical reason* for burning a man, is certainly the very acme of Romish logic. If all accounts were to be thus settled, what would be the balance due from popery.

next the king, was fallen into such great misery, that the poorest wretch would not change condition with him; and had become so surrounded with misery on all sides, that neither was left in him any hope of better fortune, nor place for worse.

The latter part of his sermon he converted to the archbishop, whom he comforted and encouraged to take his death well, by many places of scripture, bidding him not to mistrust, but he should incontinently receive what the thief did, to whom Christ said, " This day thou shalt be with me in paradise :" and out of St. Paul he armed him against the terror of fire by this, " The Lord is faithful, which will not suffer you to be tempted above your strength :" by the example of the three children, to whom God made the flame to seem like a pleasant dew; adding also the rejoicing of St. Andrew on his cross, the patience of St. Laurence in the fire, assuring him, that God, if he called on him, either would abate the fury of the flame, or give him strength to abide it.

He glorified God much in his (Cranmer's) conversion, because it appeared to be only His (the Almighty's) work ; declaring what travail and conference had been with him to convert him, and all prevailed not, till that it pleased God of his mercy to reclaim him, and call him home. In discoursing of which place, he much commended Cranmer, saying, that all the time he flowed in riches and honour, he was unworthy of his life ; and now that he might not live, he was unworthy of death. But lest he should carry with him no comfort, he promised, in the name of all the priests that were present, that immediately after his death there should be dirges, masses, and funerals, executed for him in all the churches of Oxford, for the succour of his soul.

All this time with what grief of mind Cranmer stood hearing this sermon, the outward shows of countenance did better express, than any man can declare ; now lifting up his hands and eyes unto heaven, and then again for shame letting them down to the earth. They that were present testified that they never saw in any child more tears than came from him at that time, during the whole sermon ; but especially when he recited his prayer before the people.

After Cole had ended his sermon, he called back the people to prayers that were ready to depart. " Brethren," said he, "lest any man should doubt of this man's earnest conversion and repentance, you shall hear him speak before you; and therefore I pray you, Mr. Cranmer, to perform that now, which you promised not long ago; namely, that you would openly express the true and undoubted profession of your faith, that you may take away all suspicion from men, and that all men may understand that you are a catholic indeed." "I will do it," said the archbishop, "and that with a good will;" who, rising up and putting off his cap, spoke thus unto the people:

"Good Christian people, my dearly beloved brethren and sisters in Christ, I beseech you most heartily to pray for me to Almighty God, that he will forgive me all my sins and offences, which be many without number, and great above measure. But yet one thing grieveth my conscience more than all the rest, whereof, God willing, I intend to speak more hereafter. But how great and how many soever my sins be, I beseech you to pray to God of his mercy to pardon and forgive them all." And here kneeling down, he said the following prayer:

"O Father of heaven, O Son of God, Redeemer of the world, O Holy Ghost, three persons and and one God, have mercy upon me, most wretched caitiff and miserable sinner. I have offended both against heaven and earth, more than my tongue can express. Whither then may I go, or whither shall I flee? To heaven I may be ashamed to lift up mine eyes, and in earth I find no place of refuge or succour. To thee, therefore, O Lord, do I humble myself; saying O Lord my God, my sins be great, but yet have mercy upon me, for thy great mercy. The great mystery that God became man, was not wrought for little or few offences. Thou didst not give thy Son, O heavenly Father, unto death for small sins only, but for all the greatest sins of the world, so that the sinner return to thee with his whole heart, as I do at this present. Wherefore have mercy on me, O God, whose property is always to have mercy; have mercy upon me, O Lord, for thy great mercy. I crave nothing for mine own merits, but for thy name's sake, that it may be hallowed thereby, and for thy Son Jesus Christ's sake. And now, therefore, O Father of heaven, hallowed be thy name," &c. And then rising, he said:

39

"Every man, good people, desireth at the time of his death to give some good exhortation, that others may remember the same before their death, and be the better thereby: so I beseech God grant me grace, that I may speak something at this my departing, whereby God may be glorified, and you edified.

"First it is a heavy cause to see that so many folk so much doat upon the love of this false world, and be so careful for it, that of the love of God, or the world to come they seem to care very little or nothing. Therefore, this shall be my first exhortation: That you set not your minds overmuch upon this deceitful world, but upon God, and upon the world to come, and to learn to know what this lesson meaneth which St. John teacheth, 'That the love of this world is hatred against God.'

"The second exhortation is, That next under God you obey your king and queen willingly and gladly, without murmuring or grudging; not for fear of them only, but much more now for the fear of God; knowing that they be God's ministers, appointed by God to rule and govern you: and, therefore, whosoever resisteth them resisteth the ordinance of God.

"The third exhortation is, That you love altogether like brethren and sisters. For, alas! pity it is to see what contention and hatred one Christian man beareth to another, not taking each other as brother and sister, but rather as strangers and mortal enemies. But I pray you learn and bear well away this one lesson, To do good unto all men, as much as in you lieth, and to hurt no man, no more than you would hurt your own natural loving brother or sister. For this you may be sure of, that whosoever hateth any person, and goeth about maliciously to hinder or hurt him, surely and without all doubt, God is not with that man, although he think himself ever so much in God's favour.

"The fourth exhortation shall be to them that have great substance and riches of this world; That they will well consider and weigh three sayings of the Scripture: one is of our Saviour himself, who saith, 'It is hard for a rich man to enter into the kingdom of heaven.' A sore saying, and yet spoken by him who knoweth the truth.

"The second is of St. John, whose saying is this, 'He that hath the substance of this world, and seeth his brother in necessity, and shutteth up his mercy from him, how can he say that he loveth God ?'

"The third is of St. James, who speaketh to the covetous rich man, after this manner, ' Weep you and howl for the misery that shall come upon you: your riches do rot, your clothes be moth-eaten, your gold and silver doth canker and rust, and their rust shall bear witness against you, and consume you like fire: you gather a hoard or treasure of God's indignation against the last day.' Let them that be rich ponder well these three sentences: for if they ever had occasion to show their charity, they have it now at this present, the poor people being so many, and victuals so dear.

" And now forasmuch as I am come to the last end of my life, whereupon hangeth all my life past, and all my life to come, either to live with my master Christ for ever in joy, or else to be in pain for ever with wicked devils in hell, and I see before mine eyes presently either heaven ready to receive me, or else hell ready to swallow me up: I shall therefore declare unto you my very faith how I believe without any colour of dissimulation: for now is no time to dissemble, whatsoever I have said or written in times past.

" First, I believe in God the Father Almighty, maker of heaven and earth, &c. And I believe every article of the Catholic faith, every word and sentence taught by our Saviour Jesus Christ, his apostles and prophets, in the New and Old Testament.

" And now I come to the great thing which so much troubleth my conscience, more than any thing that ever I did or said in my whole life, and that is the setting abroad of a writing contrary to the truth; which now here I renounce and refuse, as things written with my hand contrary to the truth which I thought in my heart, and written for fear of death, and to save my life, if it might be; and that is, all such bills and papers which I have written or signed with my hand since my degradation, wherein I have written many things untrue. And forasmuch as my hand hath offended, writing contrary to my heart, therefore my hand shall first be punished; for when I come to the fire, it shall be first burned.

" And as for the pope, I refuse him, as Christ's enemy and Antichrist, with all his false doctrine.

" And as for the sacrament, I believe as I have taught in my book against the bishop of Winchester, which, my book, teacheth so true a doctrine of the sacrament, that it shall stand at the last day before the judgment of God, where the papistical doctrine contrary thereto shall be ashamed to show her face."

Here the bystanders were all astonished, and looked upon one another, whose expectation he had so notably deceived. Some began to admonish him of his recantation, and to accuse him of falsehood.

Briefly, it was strange to see the doctors beguiled of so great a hope. I think there was never cruelty more notably or better in time deluded and deceived. For it is not to be doubted, but they looked for a glorious victory, and a perpetual triumph by this man's retraction.

As soon as they heard these things, they began to rage, fret, and fume ; and so much the more, because they could not revenge their grief : for they could now no longer threaten or hurt him. For the most miserable man in the world can die but once ; and whereas of necessity he must needs die that day, though the papists had been ever so well pleased, being ever so much offended with him, yet could he not be twice killed by them. And so when they could do nothing else unto him, yet lest they should say nothing, they ceased not to object unto him his falsehood and dissimulation.

Unto which accusation he answered, "Ah, my masters do you not take it so ? Always since I lived hitherto, I have been a hater of falsehood, and a lover of simplicity, and never before this time have I dissembled ;" and in saying this, all the tears that remained in his body appeared in his eyes. And when he began to speak more of the sacrament and of the papacy, some of them began to cry out, yelp, and bawl, and especially Cole cried out upon him, " Stop the heretic's mouth and take him away." And then Cranmer being pulled down from the stage, was led to the fire, accompanied with those friars, vexing, troubling, and threatening him most cruelly. " What madness," say they, " hath brought thee again into this error, by which thou wilt draw innumerable souls with thee into hell ?" To whom he answered nothing, but directed all his talk to the people, saving that to one troubling him in the way, he spake, and exhorted him to get home to his study, and apply to his book diligently; saying, if he did diligently call upon God, by reading more he should get knowledge.

But when he came to the place where the holy bishops and martyrs of God, bishop Latimer and bishop Ridley, were burnt before him, for the confession of the truth, kneeling down he prayed to God, and not long tarrying in his prayers, putting off his garment to his shirt, he prepared himself for death. His shirt was made long down to his feet. His feet were bare; likewise his head, when both his caps were off, was so bare that one hair could not be seen upon it. His beard was so long and thick, that it covered his face with marvellous gravity; and his reverend countenance moved the hearts both of his friends and enemies.

Burning of Cranmer.

The Spanish friars, John and Richard, of whom mention was made before, now began to exhort him, and play their parts with him afresh, but with vain and lost labour. Cranmer, with steadfast purpose abiding in the profession of his doctrine, gave his hand to certain old men, and others that stood by, bidding them farewell. An iron chair was now tied about him, and they commanded the fire to be set upon him. When the wood was kindled, and the fire began to burn near him, he stretched forth his right hand, which had signed his recantation, into the flames, and there held it so steadfast that all the people might see it burnt to a coal before his body was touched. In short, he was so patient and constant in the midst of these extreme tortures, that he seemed to move no more than the stake to which he was bound; his eyes were lifted up to heaven, and he often repeated, "this unworthy right hand," so long as his voice would suffer him; and as often using the words of the blessed martyr St. Stephen, "Lord Jesus, receive my spirit," till the fury of the flames putting him to silence, he gave up the ghost.

Thus died Thomas Cranmer, in the 67th year of his age. He was a man of great candour, and a firm friend, which appeared signally in the misfortunes of Anne Boleyn, Cromwell, and the duke of Somerset. In his writings he rather excelled in great industry and good judgment, than in quickness of apprehension, or a closeness of style. He employed his revenues on pious and charitable uses; and in his table he was truly hospitable, for he entertained great numbers of his poor neighbours often at it. The gentleness and humility of his deportment were very remarkable. His last fall was the greatest blemish of his life, yet that was expiated by a sincere repentance; and while we drop a tear over this melancholy instance of human frailty, we must acknowledge with praise the interposition of Divine Providence in his return to the truth. And it seemed necessary that the reformation of the church, being the restoring of the primitive and apostolical doctrine, should have been chiefly carried on by a man thus eminent for primitive and apostolical virtues.

CHAPTER VIII.

*Martyrdom of various Persons after the death of Arch-
bishop Cranmer.*

---

*Martyrdoms of Richard and Thomas Spurg, John
Cavill, and George Ambrose, Laymen; and of
Robert Drake and William Tims, Ministers.*

THESE six pious Christians resided in the county of Essex. Being accused of heresy, they were apprehended, and sent by lord Rich, at different times, to bishop Gardiner, who, after a short examination, sent the first four to the Marshalsea prison in the Borough, and the latter two to the King's Bench, where they continued during a whole year, till the death of Gardiner.

When Dr. Heath, archbishop of York, succeeded to the chancellorship, four of these, Richard and Thomas Spurg, John Cavill, and George Ambrose, weary of their tedious confinement, presented a petition to the lord chancellor, requesting his interest for their enlargement. A short time after the delivery of the petition, sir Richard Read, one of the officers of the court of Chancery, was sent to examine them.

RICHARD SPURG, the first who passed examination, being asked the cause of his imprisonment, replied, that he, with several others, being complained of by the minister of Bocking, for not coming to their parish church, to the lord Rich, was thereupon sent up to London by his lordship, to be examined by the late chancellor. He acknowledged that he had not been at church since the English service was changed into Latin, except on Christmas day was twelvemonth, because he disliked the same, and the mass also, as not agreeable to God's holy word. He then desired that he might be no further examined concerning this matter until it pleased the chancellor to inquire his faith concerning the same, which he was ready to testify.

THOMAS SPURG, on his examination, answered to the

same effect with the other, confessing that he absented himself from church, because the word of God was not there truly taught, nor the sacraments of Christ duly administered, as prescribed by the same word. Being further examined, touching his faith in the sacrament of the altar, he said that if he stood accused in that particular, ho would answer as God had given him knowledge, which he should do at another opportunity.

JOHN CAVILL likewise agreed in the chief particulars with his brethren: but further said, the cause of his absenting himself from church was, that the minister thero had advanced two doctrines contrary to each other; for first, in a sermon which he delivered when the queen came to the crown, he exhorted the people to believe the gospel, declaring it to be truth, and that, if they believed it not, they would be damned; and secondly, in a future discourse, he declared that the New Testament was false in forty places; which contrariety gave Cavill much disgust, and was, among other things, the cause of his absenting himself from church.

GEORGE AMBROSE answered to the same effect, adding, that after he had read the late bishop of Winchester's book, entitled *De verâ Obedientia*, with Bonner's preface annexed, both inveighing against the authority of the bishop of Rome, he esteemed their principles more lightly than he had done before.

ROBERT DRAKE was minister of Thundersly, in Essex, to which living he had been presented by lord Rich in the reign of Edward VI. when he was ordained priest by Dr. Ridley, then bishop of London, according to the reformed English service for ordination. On the accession of queen Mary to the throne of England, he was sent for by Gardiner, who demanded of him whether he would conform to the laws of the realm then in force? He answered, that he would abide by those laws that were agreeable to the law of God; upon which he was immediately committed to prison.

WILLIAM TIMS was a deacon and curate of Hockley, in Essex, in the reign of Edward VI. but being deprived of his living soon after the death of that monarch, he absconded, and privately preached in a neighbouring wood, whither many of his flock attended to hear the word of

God. In consequence of these proceedings, he was apprehended by one of the constables, and sent up to the bishop of London, by whom he was referred to Gardiner, who committed him to the King's Bench prison.

A short time after his confinement, he, with the others beforementioned, was ordered to appear before the bishop of London, who questioned him concerning his faith in the sacrament of the altar. Mr. Tims answered, that the body of Christ was not in the sacrament of the altar, really and corporeally, after the words of consecration spoken by the priest; and that he had been of that opinion, ever since it had pleased God to call him to the true gospel of his grace.

On the 28th of March, 1556, these persons were all brought into the consistory court before the bishop of London, in order to be examined, for the last time; when he assured them, that if they did not submit to the church of Rome, they should be condemned for heresy.

The bishop began his examination with Tims, whom he called the ringleader of the others: he told him, that he had taught them heresies, and endeavoured, as far as in him lay, to render them as abominable as himself; with many other accusations equally false and opprobious. He was then asked by the bishop what he had to say in his own vindication, in order to prevent him from proceeding against him as his ordinary. To which he replied as follows:

" My lord, I am astonished that you should begin your charge with a falsehood; you aver that I am the ringleader of the company now brought before you, and have taught them principles contrary to the Romish church, since we have been in confinement; but the injustice of this declaration will soon appear, if you will inquire of these my brethren, whether, when at liberty, and out of prison, they dissented not from popish principles as much as they do at present; such inquiry, I presume, will render it evident, that they learned not their religion in prison.

For my own part, I declare I never knew them, till such time as I became their fellow-prisoner; how then could I be their ringleader and teacher? With respect to the charge alleged against me, whatever opinion you maintain concerning me, I am well assured I hold no other reli-

gion than what Christ preached, the apostles witnessed,
the primitive church received, and of late the apostolical
and evangelical preachers of this realm have faithfully
taught, and for which you have cruelly caused them to be
burnt, and now seek to treat us with the like inhuman
severity.   I acknowledge you to be my ordinary."

The bishop demanded if he would submit himself to the
holy mother-church, promising that, if he did, he should be
kindly received ; and threatening, at the same time, that,
if he did not, judgment should be pronounced against him
as a heretic.

In answer to this, Tims told his lordship, he was well
persuaded that he was within the pale of the Catholic
church ; and reminded him, that he had most solemnly
abjured that very church to which he since professed such
strenuous allegiance ; and that, contrary to his oath, he
again admitted, in this realm, the authority of the pope,
and was, therefore, perjured and forsworn in the highest
degree. He also recalled to his memory, that he had spoken
with great force and perspicuity against the usurped power
of the pope, though he afterward sentenced persons to be
burnt, because they would not acknowledge the pope to be
the supreme head of the church.

On this, Bonner sternly demanded, what *he* had written
against the church of Rome ?

Mr. Tims pertinently answered, " My lord, the late
bishop of Winchester wrote a very learned treatise, entitled
De vera Obedientia, which contains many solid arguments
against the papal supremacy : to this book *you* wrote a
preface, strongly, inveighing against the bishop of Rome,
reproving his tyranny and usurpation, and showing that his
power was ill-founded, and contrary both to the will of God
and the real interest of mankind."

The bishop, struck with the poignancy of this reproof,
evasively told him, that the bishop of Winchester wrote a
book against the supremacy of the pope's holiness, and he
wrote a preface to the same book, tending to the same
purpose : but that the cause of this arose not from their
disregard to his holiness, but because it was then deemed
treason, by the laws of the realm, to maintain the pope's
authority in England.

He also observed, that at such a time it was dangerous

to profess to favour the church of Rome, and therefore fear compelled them to comply with the prevailing opinions of the times: for if any person had conscientiously acknowledged the pope's authority in those days, he would have been put to death; but that since the queen's happy accession to the throne, they might boldly speak the dictates of their consciences; and further reminded him, that as my lord of Winchester was not ashamed to recant his errors at St. Paul's cross, and that he himself had done the same, every inferior clergyman should follow the example of his superiors.

Mr. Tims, still persisting in the vindication of his own conduct, and reprehension of that of the bishop, again replied, " My lord, that which you have written against the supremacy of the pope may be well proved from scripture to be true; that which you now do is contrary to the word of God, as I can sufficiently prove."

Bonner, after much further conversation, proceeded according to the form of law, causing his articles, with the respective answers to each, to be publicly read in court.

Mr. Tims acknowledged only two sacraments, baptism and the Lord's supper: commended the bishop of Winchester's book *De verâ Obedientia*, and the bishop of London's preface to the same. He declared that the mass was blasphemy of Christ's passion and death; that Christ is not corporeally but spiritually present in the sacrament, and that, as they used it, it was an abominable idol.

The bishop, finding Mr. Tims so inflexible in his adherence to the faith he professed, that every attempt to draw him from it was vain and fruitless, read his definitive sentence, and he was delivered over to the secular power. Bonner then used the same measures with the others as he had with Tims; but they all refused consenting to the church of Rome, but said they were willing to adhere to the true Catholic church, and continue in the same.

Bonner then read their several definitive sentences, after which he committed them to the custody of the sheriffs of London, by whom they were conducted to Newgate.

On the 14th of April, 1556, they were all led to Smithfield, where they were chained to the same stake, and burnt in one fire.

Martyrdoms of Hugh Laverock, a decrepid old man and John Apprice, a blind man.

The former of these martyrs was by trade a painter, and lived in the parish of Barking, in Essex.   At the time of his apprehension he was in the 68th year of his age, and very helpless from the natural infirmities of life. Being accused of heresy by some of the popish emissaries in his neighbourhood, he, with his fellow-sufferer, was taken before Bonner to be examined with respect to his faith.   The bishop laid before them the same articles as have been mentioned in former instances ; and they returned answers to the same effect as those of other advocates for the truth of the gospel.

On the 9th of May, 1556, they were both brought into the consistory court, where their articles and answers were publicly read ; after which the bishop endeavoured to persuade them to recant their opinions concerning the sacrament of the altar.

Hugh Laverock declared, that by the grace of God he would continue in the profession he had already made, for he could not find the least authority in the word of God for approving the doctrine of the corporeal presence in the sacrament.

The bishop then addressed himself to John Apprice, and demanded what he had to say in his defence ?   The honest blind man answered the haughty prelate, " that the doctrine he set forth and taught was so conformable to the world, that it could not be agreeable to the scripture of God ; and that he was no member of the Catholic church of Christ, seeing he made laws to kill men, and made the queen his executioner."

The first examination being over, they were dismissed, but ordered to appear the next day at the bishop's palace at Fulham.   Being accordingly conducted there, the bishop, after some discourse with them, and finding them steadfast, pronounced the definitive sentence ; when, being delivered over to the secular power, they were committed to Newgate.   On the 15th of May, they were conveyed to Stratford-le-Bow, the place appointed for their execution.   As soon as they arrived at the stake, Laverock threw away his crutch, and thus addressed his fellow-sufferer :

"Be of good comfort, brother, for my lord of London is our good physician : he will cure us both shortly, thee of thy blindness, and me of my lameness."

These two undaunted believers in Christ were both chained to one stake. They endured their sufferings with great fortitude, and cheerfully yielded up their lives in testimony of the truth of their blessed Redeemer.

Martyrdom of Thomas Drowry, a blind boy, and Thomas Croker.

We have just before related the sufferings of two men, the one blind and the other lame ; and we have now another instance of natural blindness conjoined with mental illumination, leading the possessor to a glorious death, and a never-ending felicity in heaven.

Thomas Drowry, a blind boy, was brought before Dr. Williams, chancellor of Gloucester, and examined as to his belief in regard to the real presence in the sacrament of the altar. His answers were such as to draw down upon him the anger of the haughty prelate, and he was condemned to be executed for heresy. Refusing all persuasions to recant, he was burnt at Gloucester, on the 15th of May, 1556, together with Thomas Croker, a bricklayer, condemned also for his testimony to the truth.

CHAPTER IX.

Proclamation of Queen Mary.

WHEN this horrid persecution had continued for two years, and many hundreds had fallen victims to the rage of those popish monsters, the blood-thirsty cravings of Queen Mary were not yet satisfied ; as will appear by the following proclamation, dated February, 1557 :

"Philip and Mary, by the grace of God, king and queen of England, &c. To the right reverend father in God, our right trusty and well-beloved counsellor Thomas, bishop of Ely, and to our right trusty and well-beloved William Windsore, knight, lord Windsore ; Edward North,

40

knight, lord North; and to our trusty and well-beloved counsellor J. Bourn, knight, one of our chief secretaries, J. Mordaunt, knight, Francis Englefield, knight, master of our wards and liveries, Edward Walgrave, knight, master of our great wardrobe, Nicholas Hare, knight, master of the rolls, Thomas Pope, knight, Roger Cholmley, knight, Richard Rede, knight, Rowland Hill, knight, William Rastal, sergeant at law, Henry Cole, clerk, dean of Paul's, William Roper, and Ralph Cholmey, esquires, William Cook, Thomas Martin, John Story, and John Vaughen, doctors of the law, greeting.

" Forasmuch as divers devilish and slanderous persons have not only invented, bruited, and set forth divers false rumours, tales, and seditious slanders against us, but also have sown divers heresies, and heretical opinions, and set forth divers seditious books within this our realm of England, meaning thereby to stir up division, strife, contention, and sedition, not only among our loving subjects, but also between us and our said subjects, with divers other outrageous misdemeanors, enormities, contempts, and offences, daily committed and done, to the disquieting of us and our people : we, minding the due punishment of such offenders, and the repressing of such like offences, enormities, and misbehaviours from henceforth, having special trust and confidence in your fidelities, wisdoms, and discretions, have authorized, appointed, and assigned you to be our commissioners ; and by these presents do give full power and authority unto you, and three of you, to inquire, as well by the oaths of twelve good and lawful men, as by witnesses, and all other means and politic ways you can devise, of all and singular heretical opinions, lollardies, heretical and seditious books, concealments, contempts, conspiracies, and all false rumours, tales, seditious and slanderous words or sayings, raised, published, bruited, invented, or set forth against us, or either of us, or against the quiet governance and rule of our people and subjects, by books, lies, tales, or otherwise, in any county, key, nowing, or other place or places, within this our realm of England, or elsewhere, in any place, or places, beyond the seas, and of the bringers in, utterers, buyers, sellers, readers, keepers, or conveyers of any such letter, book, rumour and tale ; and of all and every their coadjutors, counsellors, comforters, procurers, abettors and maintainers, giving unto you, and three of you, full power and authority, by virtue hereof, to search out, and take into your hands and possessions, all manner of heretical and seditious books, letters, and writings, wheresoever they, or any of them, shall be found, as well in printers, houses and shops as elsewhere, willing you, and every of you, to search for the same in all places, according to your discretions.

" And also to inquire, hear, and determine, all and singular enormities, disturbances, misbehaviours, and negligences committed in any church, chapel, or other hallowed place within this realm ; and also, for and concerning the taking away, or withholding any lands, tenements, goods, ornaments, stocks of money, or other things belonging to every of the same churches, and chapels, and all accounts and reckonings concerning the same.

" And also to inquire and search out all such persons as obstinately do refuse to receive the blessed sacrament of the altar, to hear mass, or to come to their parish churches, or other convenient places appointed for divine service ; and all such as refuse to go on procession, to take holy bread or holy water, or otherwise do misuse themselves in any church, or other hallowed places, wheresoever any of the same offences have been, or hereafter shall be committed, within this our said realm.

" Nevertheless, our will and pleasure is, that when, and as often as any person, or persons, hereafter being called and convened before you, do obstinately persist, or stand in any manner of heresy, or heretical opinion, that then ye, or three of you, do immediately take order, that the same person, or persons, so standing, or persisting, be delivered and committed to his ordinary, there to be used according to the spiritual and ecclesiastical laws.

" And also we give unto you, or three of you, full power and authority, to inquire and search out all vagabonds, and masterless men, barretours, quarrellers, and suspected persons, abiding within our city of London, and ten miles compass of the same, and all assaults and affrays done and committed within the same city and compass.

" And further, to search out all wastes, decays, and ruins of churches chancels, chapels, parsonages, and vicarages, in the diocess of the same, being within this realm, giving you, and every of you, full power and authority, by virtue hereof, to hear and determine the same, and all other offences and matters above specified and rehearsed, according to your wisdoms, consciences, and discretions, willing and commanding you, or three of you, from time to time, to use and devise all such politic ways and means, for the trial and searching out of the premises, as by you, or three of you, shall be thought most expedient and necessary : and upon inquiry, and due proof had, known, perceived, and tried out, by the confession of the parties, or by sufficient witnesses before you, or three of you, concerning the premises, or any part thereof, or by any other ways or means requisite, to give and award such punishment to the offenders, by fine, imprisonment, or otherwise ; and to take such order for redress and reformation of the premises, as to your wisdoms, or three of you, shall be thought meet and convenient.

" Further willing and commanding you, and every three of you, in case you shall find any person, or persons, obstinate or disobedient, either in their appearance before you, or three of you, at your calling or assignment, or else in not accomplishing, or not obeying your decrees, orders, and commandments, in any thing or things, touching the premises, or any part thereof, to commit the same person, or persons so offending to ward, there to remain, till by you, or three of you, he be discharged or delivered, &c."

Martyrdom of three Women and an Infant, in Guernsey.

Of all the singular and tragical histories in this book, nothing can be more barbarous, if any thing can equal, the inhumanity of this execution upon three women and an infant, whose names were Catherine Cawches, the mother; Guillemine Gilbert, and Perotine Massey, her daughters ; and an infant, the son of Perotine.

These victims of popish cruelty owed their suffering to the following circumstances. A woman, named Gosset, having stolen a cup, took it to Mrs. Massey, who lived with her mother and sister, and requested of her to lend ner six-pence upon it. The latter, suspecting the theft, at first refused ; but thinking she would return it to the owner, whom she knew, in order to prevent Gosset's taking it elsewhere, gave her the sixpence, and made known the affair to the owner, who charging the offender with her crime, she confessed, and the cup was, accordingly, restored. On a pretended suspicion, however, that Mrs. Massey, with her mother and sister, was a sharer in the crime, they were imprisoned and brought to trial, when it appeared that they were perfectly innocent. It was found, however, that they did not attend the *church*, and on further investigation, they were discovered to be, in the judgment of the papists, heretics; and they were condemned to be burnt.

The day being **come when** these innocents should suffer, July 18, 1556, in the place where they stood to consummate their martyrdom were three stakes set up, to which they were bound. They were first strangled, but the rope breaking before they were dead, they fell into the fire. Perotine, who was then in a very advanced stage of pregnancy, fell on her side, and her womb bursting asunder, by the vehemency of the flame, the infant, being a male, fell into the fire, and being immediately taken out by one W. House, was laid upon the grass. The child was carried to the provost, and from him to the bailiff, who gave order that it should be carried back again and cast into the fire. And so the infant, baptized in his own blood, to fill up the number of God's innocent saints, was both born and died a martyr, leaving behind a spectacle wherein the whole world may see the Herodian cruelty of this graceless generation of popish tormentors, to their perpetual shame and infamy.

Martyrdoms of William Bongeor, Thomas Benhote, William Purchase, Agnes Silverside, Helen Ewring, Elizabeth Folk, William Munt, John Johnson, Alice Munt, and Rose Allen, at Colchester.

Previous to the event which we are now about to record, twenty-two persons were brought from Colchester to London, and there discharged on signing a confession. Among these were William Munt, Alice his wife, and Rose Allen, her daughter. After their return they absented themselves from the popish church, and refused to join in their idolatrous ceremonies. This so incensed the priest of the town, that he addressed petitions to lord Darcy and bishop Bonner, which caused so strong a persecution to be raised against these poor people, as compelled them for a time to withdraw from its rage; after a short time, however, lulled into security by its apparent cessation, they returned to their house, where they had not long been, when Edmund Tyrrel, a descendant of the person who murdered king Edward V., in the Tower of London, assisted by a great number of other attendants, came to the door, and told Mr. Munt that he and his wife must go with him to Colchester castle.

This sudden surprise greatly affected Mrs. Munt, who was much indisposed in consequence of the cruel treatment she had before received from the popish party; but after she had a little recovered herself, she desired of Tyrrel to permit her daughter to fetch her something to drink. This being granted, Tyrrel took the opportunity of advising the daughter to admonish her father and mother to behave more like good Christians, and members of the catholic church; to which she replied, "Sir, they have a better instructer than me, for the Holy Ghost doth teach them, I hope, which I trust will not suffer them to err."

Tyrrel. Why, art thou still in that mind, thou naughty

housewife? marry, it is time to look upon such heretics indeed.

Rose. Sir, with what you call heresy, do I worship my Lord God; I tell you truth.

Tyrrel. Then I perceive you will burn, gossip, with the rest, for company's sake.

Rose. No sir, not for company's sake, but for Christ's sake, if so I be compelled, and I hope in his mercy, if he call me to it, he will enable me to bear it.

Then Tyrell, turning to his company, said, " Sirs, this gossip will burn: what do you think of her?"—" Why, truly, sir," said one, " prove her, and you shall see what she will do by and by."

Tyrrel, then taking the candle from her, held her wrist, and the lighted candle under her hand, burning it across the back, till the sinews cracked; during which barbarous operation he said often to her, " Why, wilt thou not cry?" To which she answered, that " She thanked God she had no cause, but rather to rejoice. But, he had more cause to weep than she, if he considered the matter well." At last he thrust her violently from him, with much scurrilous language; of which she took no other notice than by inquiring, " Sir, have you done what you will do?" To which he replied, " Yea, and if you think not well of it, then mend it."

Rose. " Mend it ? nay, the Lord mend you, and give you repentance, if it be his will ; and now, if you think it good, begin at the feet, and burn the head also : for he that set you on work, shall pay you your wages one day, I warrant you :" and so went and carried her mother drink as she was commanded.

Tyrrel then seized William Munt, his wife, and Rose Allen, and conducted them to Colchester castle, together with John Johnson, whom they took in their way, on an information against him for heresy.

They also the same morning apprehended six others, namely, William Bongeor, Thomas Benhote, William Purchase, Agnes Silverside, Helen Ewring, and Elizabeth Folk ; but not choosing to place these with the rest, they sent them prisoners to Mote-hill.

After they had been confined a few days, they were all brought together before several justices of the peace, priests and officers, (among whom were Kingston, the commissary, and Boswell, the bishop of London's secretary,) with many others, in order to be examined relative to their faith.

They were questioned separately as to their religious tenets, and their belief in the real presence in the sacrament of the altar, auricular confession, &c. So little satisfaction did their answers give to their popish persecutors, that sentence of condemnation was read against them, and they were all delivered over to the secular power.

Bishop Bonner having an account transmitted to him of the condemnation of these ten innocent persons, sent down a warrant for their being burned, and fixed the day for the 2d of August. As the prisoners were confined in different places, it was resolved by the officer that part of them should be executed in the former, and the rest in the latter part of that day. Accordingly William Bongeor, William Purchase, Thomas Benhote, Agnes Silverside, Helen Ewring, and Elizabeth Folk, were brought early in the morning to the place appointed for them to suffer. When our martyrs arrived at the spot, they humbly addressed themselves to Almighty God, though they were interrupted by their popish enemies. Having concluded their prayers, they arose, were fastened to the stakes, and all burnt in one fire. They died with amazing fortitude and resignation, triumphing in the midst of the flames, and exulting in hopes of the future glory that awaited them after their departure from a sinful world.

In like manner, in the afternoon, William and Alice Munt, Rose Allen, and John Johnson, were brought to the place where their fellow-martyrs had suffered in the morning. As soon as they arrived at the fatal spot, they all kneeled down, and, for some time, prayed with the greatest fervency. After prayers they arose, and cheerfully submitted to be fastened to the stakes, and with their latest breath testified their faith in Christ crucified

Martyrdoms of Cuthbert Simson, Hugh Fox, and John Davenish.

Cuthbert Simson tortured.

Cuthbert Simson, deacon of a small congregation in London, was committed prisoner to the tower, where he was examined by the recorder of London and one Mr. Cholmley, who commanded him to declare what persons he had summoned to come to the English service; but he told them he would not comply with their request.

They then ordered him to be put to the rack, on which he lay, in great agonies, upwards of three hours. While he was in the most excruciating torment, they asked him the same question as they had done before, and he made them the same answer. He was then released from the rack, and conducted to the room appointed for his confinement.

On the Sunday following he was again brought to the room in which he had been racked, when the recorder of London and the lieutenant of the tower once more desired him to confess; but he still refused, saying, he was determined not to satisfy them.

They then tied his two fore-fingers together, with a small arrow between them : this done, they drew the arrow backward and forward so quick, that the blood followed, and the arrow broke; after which they racked him twice more, and then again conducted him to his dungeon.

About ten days after this the lieutenant again asked him if he would confess what had been repeatedly asked by himself and the recorder; to which Mr. Simson answered, that he would say no more than he had said.

On the 19th of March he was taken before the bishop of London for examination. While in the consistory court, bishop Bonner took particular notice of him to the people. " Ye see," said he, " this man, what a personable man he is ; and I tell you, that if he were not a heretic, he is a man of the greatest patience that ever came before me. He hath been twice racked in one day in the tower, and also in my house he hath felt much sorrow, and yet I never saw his patience broken."

On the 28th of March, 1558, he, together with Hugh Fox and John Devenish, who had also been condemned for heresy, was conducted by the sheriffs, and their officers, to Smithfield, where they were all fastened to one stake, and burnt in the same fire. They behaved with truly Christian fortitude to the last, praising and glorifying God, that he had enabled them to go through the horrid punishment allotted them, for no other reason than their strict adherence to the truth of his most holy gospel.

William Fetty scourged to Death.

If dying innocently in the cause of religion constitute a martyr, no one can be better entitled to a place in our catalogue than this youth, who was unmercifully scourged to death, at the instigation of the relentless Bonner.

Among those who were imprisoned for the profession of Christ's gospel, and yet delivered by the providence of God, was John Fetty, the father of this lad. He had been accused by his own wife, to the minister of the parish, of absenting himself from church; for which he was apprehended by one of the officers employed for that purpose. Immediately after his apprehension his wife grew delirious, in consequence of which, though they were regardless of him, pity toward her wrought upon the magistrates, so that, for the support of her and her children, they discharged him, with an order that he should continue in his own house. Notwithstanding the ingratitude of his wife, he provided for her in such a manner, that within three weeks, she had, in some measure, recovered her senses. But such was the disposition of this woman, that, notwithstanding this instance of his conjugal affection, she laid a second information against him; upon which he was apprehended, and carried before sir John Mordaunt, one of the queen's commissioners, by whom he was sent to Lollard's tower, where he was put into the stocks, and had a dish of water set by him, with a stone in it, to point out to him, that it was the chief sustenance he might expect to receive.

After he had been in prison for fifteen days, William

to the frivolous ceremonies and pompous nothingness of the Popish worship.

WE have now arrived at the close of the darkest reign that disgraces the pages of English history, and with it ends the account of Christian Martyrdom, as originally compiled by Mr. Fox. Since his death, which happened April 18, 1587, much interesting matter has been added to the original work; and this will be found in a condensed form, in the Appendix. The selections which we have made have necessarily been limited to the most important and the most interesting, as even the names of those who suffered by imprisonment, torture, banishment, and death, would make a volume. The work, as originally published, consisted of three large quarto volumes—it could hardly be expected, therefore, that we should compress *all* of this vast fund of matter into the limits of an humble duodecimo. To the world we now intrust the book, with all its imperfections on its head, confident that it will be found no unacceptable present to those readers who are unable to afford the expense of the larger work.

The bishop was so enraged at this, that he called him a vile heretic, and said, " I will burn thee, or I will spend all that I possess." However, in a little time his passion cooled, and thinking of the consequences that might arise from scourging the child, he ordered them both to be discharged.

The father immediately went home with his son; but the poor boy, from an extraordinary effusion of blood, and a mortification which ensued, died a few days after, to the great grief of his persecuted and indulgent parent.

The old man remained without further persecution during the remainder of his life, often praising God for delivering him out of the hands of his enemies, and expressing the deep sense he had of the divine protection.

Martyrdom of John Cornford, Christopher Browne, John Herst, Alice Snoth, and Catharine Knight, (alias Tinley.)

These five persons were the last who suffered in queen Mary's reign for the testimony of that word for which so many had died before, and gave up their lives meekly and patiently, suffering the violent malice of the papists.

Notwithstanding the sickness of queen Mary, whereof

Lady Elizabeth, who until now had resided at court, and been treated with the utmost confidence and friendship, was suddenly sent to her own house at Ashbridge, with strict orders not to leave it without the queen's permission. Here, however, she did not long remain, before she was arrested on the pretended suspicion of her being concerned with sir Thomas Wyat in an attempt to cast off the papal yoke. As she was already aware that it was the intention of Mary to insnare her, if possible, she was put little at ease at this measure; and though extremely ill at the time she received the summons to appear before the queen, she readily complied, and expressed a wish to be brought immediately to trial, that she might be able to confound her accusers. This, however, was refused her, and for two weeks after being brought to court, she was kept in close confinement, and suffered to see nor hold communication with none but her keepers.

She was then sent to the tower, where she was kept a close prisoner, and not permitted to hold intercourse with any but such as the queen had placed about her, and who often treated her with great indignity. To add still more to the unpleasantness of her situation, Gardiner, bishop of Winchester, and others of the catholic clergy, visited her for the purpose of entrapping her with their conversation; that they might be able to bring against her the charge of heresy. But, aware of their nefarious designs, she withstood their subtlety in so artful a manner as to avoid the snare thus laid for her.

After remaining for several months at the tower, the agent of the queen could not manage to substantiate against her either the charge of high treason or any other; she was next removed to Woodstock, where she was carefully watched, and for the greater portion of the time confined to her room. Here also she remained several months longer; during which time she was repeatedly promised a pardon and her liberty, if she would acknowledge herself guilty of high treason, and throw herself upon the queen's mercy. This, however, she constantly refused to do, declaring herself wholly innocent of any connexion with Wyat, and of any thought or intention of injuring the queen.

Finding, finally, that neither threats or promises could prevail on her to acknowledge herself guilty of a crime of which she was innocent, she was kept a close prisoner for ten months.

There can be no doubt that it was the intention of Mary to have put her sister Elizabeth to death, either secretly or otherwise, and was only deterred from her purpose by Philip her husband, to whom Elizabeth herself acknowledged she owed her safety; but whether principle or state policy moved him to such a measure, it is not for us to determine.

EVENTS IN THE REIGN OF ELIZABETH.

The Spanish Armada.

On the accession of Elizabeth to the throne, the persecution not only ceased, but the protestant religion was again established throughout the kingdom; such a measure, as may well be supposed, excited the envy of the papal powers of Europe, who seemed determined to unite their efforts to re-establish the dominion of the pope, which could only be affected by first overthrowing the civil power. Measures were accordingly concerted for affecting this object, the most formidable of which was the noted Spanish Armada, fitted out by Philip, king of Spain.

This mighty fleet, which was three years in fitting out, and the expenses of which drained the coffers of its projector, occasioned great consternation and alarm in England at first, but being delayed one year longer than was intended, preparations were made to repel the intended invasion, which, with adverse winds, and other providential occurrences, served to show the ambitious Philip how vain and futile are the efforts of kings when heaven interposes in behalf of those whom they doom to destruction.

This formidable fleet was first separated and dispersed by a violent storm as it approached the coast of England; and before they could again unite their strength, the greater portion was captured by the British fleet fitted out for the purpose; and of all this terrible Armada, only a few small vessels ever returned to bear the melancholy news of the fatal disaster to the country from which they had sailed.

It may not be improper here to subjoin a list of the different articles taken on board the Spanish ships, designed for the tormenting of the protestants, had their scheme taken effect.

1. The common soldiers' pikes, eighteen feet long, pointed with long sharp spikes, and shod with iron, which were designed to keep off the horse, to facilitate the landing of the infantry.

2. A great number of lances used by the Spanish officers. These were formerly gilt, but the gold is almost worn off by cleaning.

3. The Spanish rancents, made in different forms, which were intended either to kill the men on horseback, or pull them off their horses.

4. A very singular piece of arms, being a pistol in a shield, so contrived as to fire the pistol, and cover the body at the same time with the shield. It is to be fired by a match-lock, and the sight of the enemy is to be taken through a little grate in the shield, which is pistol proof.

5. The banner, with a crucifix upon it, which was to have been carried before the Spanish general. On it is engraved the pope's benediction before the Spanish fleet sailed; for the pope came to the water-side, and, on seeing the fleet, blessed it, and styled it INVINCIBLE.

6. The Spanish cravats, as they are called. These are engines of torture, made of iron, and put on board to lock together the feet, arms, and heads of Englishmen.

7. Spanish bilboes made of iron likewise, to yoke the English prisoners two and two.

8. Spanish-shot, which are of four sorts: pike-shot, star-shot, chain-shot, and link-shot, all admirably contrived, as well for the destruction of the masts and rigging of ships, as for sweeping the decks of their men.

9. Spanish spades poisoned at the points, so that if a man received the slightest wound with one of them, certain death was the consequence.

10. A Spanish poll-axe, used in boarding of ships.

11. Thumb screws, of which there were several chests full on board the Spanish fleet. The use they were intended for is said to have been to extort confession from the English where their money was hid.

12. The Spanish morning star: a destructive engine resembling the figure of a star, of which there were many thousands on board, and all of them with poisoned points; and were designed to strike at the enemy as they came on board, in case of a close attack.

13. The Spanish general's halberd, covered with velvet. All the nails of this weapon are double gilt with gold; and on its top is the pope's head, curiously engraved.

14. A Spanish battle-axe, so contrived as to strike four holes in a man's head at once; and has beside a pistol in its handle, with a match-lock.

15. The Spanish general's shield, carried before him as an ensign of honour. On it are depicted, in most curious workmanship, the labours of Hercules, and other expressive allegories.

When the Spanish prisoners were asked by some of the English what their intentions were, had their expedition succeeded, they replied, "To extirpate the whole from the island, at least all heretics, (as they called theprotestants,) and to send their souls to hell." Strange infatuation! Ridiculous bigotry! How infernally prejudiced must the minds of those men be, who would wish to destroy their fellow-creatures, not only in this world, but, if it were possible, in that which is to come, merely because they refused to believe on certain subjects as the Spaniards themselves did.

EVENTS IN THE REIGN OF JAMES I.

The Gunpowder Plot

The papists were so irritated at the failure of the Spanish Armada, that they were determined, if possible, to project a scheme at home that might answer the purposes, in some degree, of their blood-thirsty allies. The vigorous administration of Elizabeth, however, prevented their carrying any of their iniquitous designs into execution, although they made many attempts with that view. The commencement of the reign of her successor was destined to be the era of a plot, the infernal barbarity of which transcends every thing related in ancient or modern history.

In order to crush popery in the most effectual manner in this kingdom, James, soon after his accession, took measures for eclipsing the power of the Roman catholics, by enforcing those laws which had been made against them by his predecessors. This enraged the papists to such a degree, that a conspiracy was formed to blow up the king, the royal family, and both houses of parliament, while in full session, and thus to involve the nation in utter and inevitable ruin.

The infernal cabal who formed the resolution of putting in practice this horrid scheme, consisted of the following persons: Henry Garnet, an Englishman, who, about the year 1586, had been sent over as superior of the English Jesuits; Catesby, an English gentleman; Tesmond, a Jesuit; Thomas Wright; two gentlemen of the name of Winter; Thomas Percy, a near relation of the earl of Northumberland; Guido Fawkes, a bold and enterprising soldier of fortune; sir Edward Digby; John Grant, Esq.; Francis Tresham, Esq.; and Robert Keyes and Thomas Bates, gentlemen.

Most of these were men both of birth and fortune: and Catesby, who had a large estate, had expended two thousand pounds in voyages to Spain, in order to introduce an army of Spaniards into England, for overturning the protestant government, and restoring the Roman catholic religion; but, being disappointed in his project of an invasion, he took an opportunity of disclosing to Percy, who was his intimate friend, and who had hinted a design of assassinating the king, a nobler and more extensive plan of treason, such as would include a sure execution of vengeance, and at one blow consign over to destruction all their enemies.

Percy assented to the project proposed by Catesby, and they resolved to impart the matter to a few more, and, by degrees, to all the rest of their cabal, every man being bound by an oath not to disclose the least syllable of the matter, or to withdraw from the association, without the consent of all persons concerned.

These consultations were held in the spring and summer of the year 1604, and it was toward the close of that year that they began their operations; the manner of which, and the discovery, we shall relate with as much brevity as is consistent with perspicuity.

It had been agreed that a few of the conspirators should run a mine below the hall in which the parliament was to assemble, and that they should choose the moment when the king should deliver his speech to both houses, for springing the mine, and thus, by one blow, cut off the king, the royal family, lords, commons, and all the other enemies of the catholic religion, in the very spot where that religion had been most oppressed. For this purpose, Percy undertook to hire a house adjoining to the upper house of parliament, with all diligence. This was accordingly done, and the conspirators, expecting the parliament would meet on the 17th of February, began, on the 11th of December, to dig in the cellar, through the wall of partition, which was three yards thick. There were seven in number joined in this labour; they went in by night, and never after appeared in sight, for having supplied themselves with provisions, they had no occasion to go out. In case of discovery, they had provided themselves with powder, shot, and fire-arms, and had formed a resolution to die rather than be taken.

On Candlemas-day, 1605, they had dug so far through the wall as to be able to hear a noise on the other side; upon which unexpected event, fearing a discovery, Guido Fawkes, who personated Percy's footman, was despatched to know the occasion, and returned with the favourable report, that the place from whence the noise came was a large cellar, under the upper house of parliament, full of coal, which was then on sale, and the cellar offered to be let.

On this information, Percy immediately hired the cellar, and bought the remainder of the coals; he then sent for thirty barrels of gunpowder from Holland, and conveyed them privately by night to this cellar, where they were covered with stones, iron bars, a thousand billets, and five hundred fagots; all which they did at their leisure, the parliament being prorogued to the 5th of November.

This being done, the conspirators next consulted how they should secure the duke of York, afterward Charles I., who was too young to be expected in the parliament house, and his sister the princess Elizabeth, educated at lord Harrington's, in Warwickshire. It was resolved that Percy and an other should enter into the duke's chamber, and a dozen more, properly disposed at several doors, with two or three on horse-back at the court-gate to receive him, should carry him safe away as soon as the parliament-house was blown up; or, if that could not be effected, that they should kill him, and declare the princess Elizabeth queen, having secured her, under pretence of a hunting-match, that day.

Several of the conspirators proposed obtaining foreign aid previous to the execution of their designs; but this was over-ruled, and it was agreed only to apply to France, Spain, and other powers, for assistance after the plot had taken effect; they also resolved to proclaim Elizabeth queen, and to spread a report that the puritans were the perpetrators of so inhuman an action.

All matters being now prepared by the conspirators, they, with the utmost impatience, expected the 5th of November. But all their counsels were blasted by a happy and providential circumstance. One of the conspirators, having a desire to save William Parker, lord Monteagle, sent him the following letter:

"My Lord,

"Out of the love I bear to some of your friends, I have a care for your preservation; therefore I advise you, as you tender your life, to devise you some excuse to shift off your attendance at this parliament; for God and man have concurred to punish the wickedness of this time: and think not slightly of this advertisement, but retire yourself into the country, where you may expect the event with safety; for though there be no appearance of any stir, yet I say they shall receive a terrible blow, this parliament, and yet they shall not see who hurts them. This counsel is not to be contemned, because it may do you good, and can do you no harm; for the danger is past so soon, or as quickly, as you burn this letter; and I hope God will give you the grace to make good use of it, to whose holy protection I commend you."

Lord Monteagle was, for some time, at a loss what judgment to form of this letter, and unresolved whether he should slight the advertisement or not; and fancying it a trick of his enemies to frighten him into an absence from parliament, would have determined on the former, had his own safety been only in question: but apprehending the king's life might be in danger, he took the letter at midnight to the earl of Salisbury, who was equally uncertain about the meaning of it; and though he was inclined to think it merely a waggish contrivance to alarm Monteagle, yet he thought proper to consult about it with the earl of Suffolk, lord chamberlain. The expression, "That the blow should come, without knowing who hurt them," made them imagine that it would not be more proper than the time of parliament, nor by any other way like to be attempted than by gunpowder, while the king was sitting in that assembly: the lord chamberlain thought this the more probable, because there was a great cellar under the parliament chamber (as already mentioned) never used for any thing but wood or coal, belonging to Whinyard, the keeper of the palace; and having communicated the letter to the earls of Nottingham, Worcester, and Northampton, they proceeded no further till the king came from Royston, on the 1st of November.

His majesty being shown the letter by the earls, who, at the same time, acquainted him with their suspicions, was of opinion that either nothing should be done, or else enough to prevent the danger; and that a search should be made on the day preceding that designed for the execution of the diabolical enterprise.

Accordingly, on Monday, the 4th of November, in the afternoon, the lord chamberlain, whose office it was to see all things put in readiness for the king's coming, accompanied by Monteagle, went to visit all places about the parliament house, and taking a slight occasion to see the cellar, observed only piles of billets and faggots, but in greater number than he thought Whinyard could want for his own use. On his asking who owned the wood, and being told it belonged to one Mr. Percy, he began to have some suspicions, knowing him to be a rigid papist, and so settled there, that he had no occasion for such a quantity of fuel; and Monteagle confirmed him therein, by observing that Percy had made him great professions of friendship.

Though there were no other materials visible, yet Suffolk thought it was necessary to make a farther search; and, upon his return to the king, a resolution was taken that it should be made, in such a manner as should be effectual, without discountenancing any body, or giving any alarm.

Sir Thomas Knevet, steward of Westminster, was accordingly ordered, under the pretext of something for stole or tap stry hangings in that place, and to set houses thereabout, to remove the wood, and see if any thing was concealed underneath. This gentleman going at midnight, with several attendants, to the cellar, met Fawkes, just coming out of it, booted and spurred, with a tinder-box and three matches in his pockets, and seizing him without any ceremony, or asking him any questions, as soon as the removal of the wood discovered the barrels of gunpowder, he caused him to be bound, and properly secured.

Fawkes, who was a hardened and intrepid villain, made no hesitation

of avowing the design, and that it was to have been executed on the morrow. He made the same acknowledgment at his examination before a committee of the council; and though he did not deny having some associates in this conspiracy, yet no threats of torture could make him discover any of them, he declaring that "He was ready to die, and had rather suffer ten thousand deaths, than willingly accuse his master, or any other"

By repeated examinations, however, and assurances of his master's being apprehended, he at length acknowledged, "That while he was abroad, Percy had kept the keys of the cellar, had been in since the powder had been laid there, and, in effect, that he was one of the principal actors in the intended tragedy."

In the meantime it was found out, that Percy had come post out of the north on Saturday night, the 2d of November, and had dined on Monday at Sion House, with the earl of Northumberland; that Fawkes had met him on the road; and that, after the lord chamberlain had been that evening in the cellar, he went, about six o'clock, to his master, who had fled immediately, apprehending the plot was discovered.

The news of the discovery immediately spreading, the conspirators fled different ways, but chiefly into Warwickshire, where sir Everard Digby had appointed a hunting-match, near Dunchurch, to get a number of recusants together, sufficient to seize the princess Elizabeth; but this design was prevented by her taking refuge in Coventry; and their whole party, making about one hundred, retired to Holbeach, the seat of sir Stephen Littleton, on the borders of Staffordshire, having broken open stables, and taken horses from different people in the adjoining countries.

Sir Richard Walsh, high sheriff of Worcestershire, pursued them to Holbeach, where he invested them, and summoned them to surrender. In preparing for their defence, they put some moist powder before a fire to dry, and a spark from the coals setting it on fire, some of the conspirators were so burned in their faces, thighs, and arms, that they were scarcely able to handle their weapons. Their case was desperate, and no means of escape appearing, unless by forcing their way through the assailants, they made a furious sally for that purpose. Catesby, who first proposed the manner of the plot, and Percy were both killed. Thomas Winter, Grant, Digby, Rookwood, and Bates, were taken and carried to London, where the first made a full discovery of the conspiracy. Tresham, lurking about the city, and frequently shifting his quarters, was apprehended soon after, and, having confessed the whole matter, died of the strangury, in the tower. The earl of Northumberland, suspected on account of his being related to Thomas Percy, was, by way of precaution, committed to the custody of the archbishop of Canterbury, at Lambeth; and was afterward fined thirty thousand pounds, and sent to the tower, for admitting Percy into the band of gentlemen pensioners, without tendering him the oath of supremacy.

Some escaped to Calais, and arriving there with others who fled to avoid a prosecution, which they apprehended on this occasion, were kindly received by the governor; but one of them declaring before him, that he was not so much concerned at his exile, as that the powder-plot did not take effect, the governor was so much incensed at his glorying in such an execrable piece of iniquity, that, in a sudden impulse of indignation, he endeavoured to throw him into the sea.

On the 27th of January, 1606, eight of the conspirators were tried and convicted; among whom was sir Everard Digby, the only one that pleaded guilty to the indictment, though all the rest had confessed their guilt before. Digby was executed on the 30th of the same month, with Robert Winter, Grant, and Bates, at the west end of St. Paul's churchyard; Thomas Winter, Keyes, Rookwood, and Fawkes, were executed the following day in Old Palace-yard.

Garnet was tried on the 28th of March, "For his knowledge and concealment of the conspiracy; for administering an oath of secrecy to the conspirators; for persuading them of the lawfulness of the treason, and for praying for the success of the great action in hand at the beginning of the parliament." Being found guilty, he received sentence of death, but was not executed till the 3d of May, when, confessing his own guilt, and the iniquity of the enterprise, he exhorted all Roman catholics to abstain from the like treasonable practices in future. Gerard and Hull, two Jesuits, got abroad, and Littleton, with several others, was executed in the country.

Lord Monteagle had a grant of two hundred pounds a year in land, and a pension of five hundred pounds for life, as a reward for discovering the letter which gave the first hint of the conspiracy; and the anniversary of this providential deliverance was ordered to be forever commemorated by prayer and thanksgiving.

In this affair providence manifestly interposed in behalf of the protestants, and saved them from that destruction which must have taken place, had the scheme succeeded according to the wishes of a bigoted and bloodthirsty faction.

EVENTS IN THE REIGN OF CHARLES I.

Massacre of Protestants in Ireland.

Soon after the commencement of the reformation in England, a spirit of inquiry was awakened in Ireland, and many distinguished prelates began openly to expose the usurpations and blasphemous practices of the Roman church; among whom was George Broom, archbishop of Dublin, who is justly termed the great Irish reformer.

Our prescribed limits will not suffer us to trace this devoted and holy man through his long and painful struggle with a blinded and bigoted populace, but shall only observe that the seeds of reformation sown by him, in due time not only led to the wide dissemination of gospel truth, but to corresponding scenes of bloodshed and persecution.

We shall lay before our readers only a short detail of the enormities committed by the catholics subsequent to the year 1642, which it will be recollected was after the commencement of the reign of Charles I

The following is an account of some of their enormities.

In the castle of Lisgool upward of one hundred and fifty men, women, and children, were all burnt together; and at the castle of Moneah no less than one hundred were put to the sword. Great numbers were also murdered at the castle of Tullah, which was delivered up to M'Guire, on condition of having fair quarter; but no sooner had that base villain got possession of the place, than he ordered his followers to murder the people, which was immediately done with the greatest cruelty.

Many others were put to deaths of the most horrid nature, and such as could have been invented only by demons instead of men. Some of them were laid with the centre of their backs on the axletree of a carriage, with their legs resting on the ground on one side, and their arms and head on the other. In this position one of the savages scourged the wretched objects on the thighs, legs, &c., while another set on furious dogs, who tore to pieces the arms and upper parts of the body; and in this dreadful manner were they deprived of their existence.

Great numbers were fastened to horses' tails, and the beasts being set on full gallop by their riders, the wretched victims were dragged along till they expired. Others were hung on lofty gibbets, and a fire being kindled under them, they finished their lives, partly by hanging, and partly by suffocation.

Nor did the more tender sex escape the least particle of cruelty that could be projected by their inhuman and furious persecutors. Many women, of all ages, were put to deaths of the most cruel nature. Some, in particular, were fastened with their backs to strong posts, and being stripped to the waist, the inhuman monsters cut off their right breasts with shears, which, of course, put them to the most exquisite torments; and in this position they were left till, from the loss of blood, they expired.

Such was the savage barbarity of these barbarians, that even unborn infants were dragged from their wombs to become victims to their rage. Many unhappy mothers were hung naked on the branches of trees, and their bodies being cut open, the innocent offspring was taken from them, and thrown to dogs and swine. And, to increase the horrid scene, they would oblige the husband to be a spectator before he suffered himself.

At the town of Lissenskeath they hanged above one hundred Scottish protestants, showing them no more mercy than they did to the English.

M'Guire, going to the castle of that town, desired to speak with the governor, when, being admitted, he immediately burnt the records of the county, which were kept there. He then demanded one thousand pound, of the governor, which having received, he immediately compelled him to hear mass, and to swear that he would ever continue so to do. And to complete his horrid barbarities, he ordered the wife and children of the governor to be hung up before his face; besides massacreing at least one hundred of the inhabitants.

Upward of one thousand men, women, and children, were driven, in different companies, to Portadown bridge, which was broken in the middle, and there compelled to throw themselves into the water; and such as attempted to reach the shore were knocked on the head.

In the same part of the country, at least four thousand persons were drowned in different places. The inhuman papists, after first stripping them, drove them like beasts to the spot fixed for their destruction; and if any, through fatigue or natural infirmities, were slack in their pace, they pricked them with their swords and pikes; and to strike a further terror on the multitude, they murdered some by the way. Many of these poor creatures, when in the water, endeavours of to save themselves by swimming to the shore; but two merciless persecutors prevented their endeavours taking effect, by shooting them in the water.

In one place one hundred and forty English, after being driven for many miles stark naked, and in the most severe weather, were all murdered on the same spot, some being hanged, others burnt, some shot, and many of them buried alive; and so cruel were their tormentors, that they would not suffer them to pray before they robbed them of their miserable existence.

Other companies they took under pretence of safe-conduct, who, from that consideration, proceeded cheerfully on their journey; but when the treacherous papists had got them to a convenient spot, they butchered them all in the most cruel manner.

One hundred and fifteen men, women, and children were conducted, by order of sir Phelim O'Neal, to Portendown bridge, where they were all forced into the river, and drowned. One woman, named Campbell, finding no probability of escaping, suddenly clasped one of the chief of the papists in her arms, and held him so fast, that they were both drowned together.

In Killoman they massacred forty-eight families, among whom twenty-two were burnt together in one house. The rest were either hanged, shot, or drowned.

In Killmore the inhabitants, which consisted of about two hundred families, all fell victims to their rage. Some of the protestants were set in the stocks till they confessed where their money was; after which they were put to death. The whole country was one common scene of butchery, and many thousands perished, in a short time, by sword, famine, fire, water, and all other the most cruel deaths that rage and malice could invent.

These inhuman villains showed so much favour to some as to despatch them immediately; but they would by no means suffer them to pray. Others they imprisoned in filthy dungeons, putting heavy bolts on their legs, and keeping them there till they were starved to death.

At Cashel some were barbarously mangled, and left on the highways to perish, others were hanged, and some were buried in the ground upright, with their heads above the earth, the papists, to increase their misery, treating them with derision during their sufferings.

In the county of Antrim they murdered 954 protestants in one morning; and afterward about 1200 more in that country.

At a town called Lisnegary, they forced 24 protestants into a house, and then setting fire to it, burned them together, counterfeiting their outcries in derision to others. Among other acts of cruelty, they took two children belonging to an Englishwoman, and dashed out their brains before her face; after which they threw the mother into a river, and she was drowned.

In Kilkenny all the protestants, without exception, were put to death; and some of them in so cruel a manner, as, perhaps, was never before thought of. They beat an Englishwoman with such barbarity, that she had scarce a whole bone left; after which they threw her into a ditch; but not satisfied with this, they took her child, a girl about six years of age, and after ripping open its body, threw it to its mother, there to languish till it perished. They forced one man to go to mass, after which they ripped open his body, and in that manner left him. They sawed another asunder, cut the throat of his wife, and after having dashed out the brains of their child, an infant, threw it to the swine, who greedily devoured it. After committing these and many other horrid cruelties, they took the heads of seven protestants, and among them that of a pious minister, all which they fixed up at the market cross. They put a gag into the minister's mouth, then slit his cheeks to his ears, and laying a leaf of a bible before it, bid him preach, for his mouth was wide enough.

One of these miserable miscreants would come into a house with his hands imbrued in blood, and boast that it was English blood, and that his sword had pricked the white skins of the protestants, even to the hilt. When any one of them had killed a protestant, others would come and receive a gratification in cutting and mangling the body; after which they left it to be devoured by dogs; and when they had slain a number of them, they would boast that the devil was beholden to them for sending so many souls to hell!

But it is no wonder they should thus treat the innocent Christians, when they hesitated not to commit blasphemy against God and his most holy word. In one place they burnt two protestant bibles, and then said they had burnt hell-fire. In the church at Powers-court, they burnt the pulpit, pews, chests, and bibles belonging to it. They took other bibles, and, after wetting them with dirty water, dashed them in the faces of the protestants, saying, " We know you have a good lesson ; here is an excellent one for you ; come to-morrow, and you shall have as good a sermon as this."

In Munster they put to death several ministers in the most shocking manner. One, in particular, they stripped stark naked, and driving him before them, pricked him with swords and pikes till he fell down, and expired.

In some places they plucked out the eyes, and cut off the hands of the protestants, and in that condition turned them into the fields, there to linger out the remainder of their miserable existence. They obliged many young men to force their aged parents to a river, where they were drowned; wives to assist in hanging their husbands; and mothers to cut the throats of their children.

At a place called Glaslow, a popish priest, with some others, prevailed on forty protestants to be reconciled to the church of Rome, under the vain hope of saving their lives. They had no sooner done this, than the deceivers told them they were in a good faith, and that they would prevent their falling from it and turning heretics, by sending them out of the world; which they did by immediately cutting their throats.

In the county of Tipperary a great number of protestants, men, women, and children, fell into the hands of the papists, who, after stripping them naked, murdered them with stones, pole-axes, swords, and other weapons.

In the county of Mayo, about sixty protestants, fifteen of whom were ministers, were, upon covenant, to be safely conducted to Galway, by one Edmund Burke and his soldiers: but that inhuman monster by the way drew his sword, as an intimation of his design to the rest, who immediately followed his example, and murdered the whole, some of whom they stabbed, others were run through the body with pikes, and several were drowned.

In Queen's county great numbers of protestants were put to the most shocking deaths. Fifty or sixty were confined together in one house, which being set on fire, they all perished in the flames. Many were stripped naked, and being fastened to horses by ropes placed round their middles, were dragged through bogs till they expired. Some were hung by the feet to tenter-hooks driven into poles, and in that wretched posture left till they perished. Others were fastened to the trunk of a tree, with a branch at the top. Over this branch hung one arm, which principally supported the weight of the body ; and one of the legs was turned up, and fastened to the trunk, while the other hung straight. In this dreadful and uneasy posture did they remain, as long as life would permit, pleasing spectacles to their blood-thirsty persecutors.

At Clownes seventeen men were buried alive; and an Englishman, his wife, five children, and a servant maid, were all hung together, and afterward thrown into a ditch. Several were hung on windmills, and before they were half dead, the barbarians cut them in pieces with their swords. Others, both men, women, and children, they cut and hacked in various parts of their bodies, and left them wallowing in their blood, to perish where they fell. One poor woman they hung on a gibbet, with her child, an infant about a year old, the latter of whom was hung by the neck with the hair of its mother's head, and in that manner finished its short but miserable existence.

In the country of Tyrone no less than three hundred protestants were drowned in one day, and many others hanged, burned, and otherwise put to death. Dr. Maxwell, rector of Tyrone, lived at this time near Armagh, and suffered greatly from these merciless savages. This clergyman, in his examination, taken upon oath before the king's commissioners, declared that the Irish papists owned to him, that they had destroyed in one place, at Glynwood, 12,000 protestants, in their flight from the county of Armagh.

As the river Bann was not fordable, and the bridge broken down, the Irish forced thither, at different times, a great number of unarmed, defenceless protestants, and with pikes and swords violently thrust above

1000 into the river, where they miserably perished. Nor did the cathedral of Armagh escape the fury of these barbarians, it being set on fire by their leaders, and burnt to the ground. And to extirpate, if possible, the very race of protestants, who lived in or near Armagh, the Irish first burnt all their houses, and then gathered together many hundreds of those innocent people, young and old, on pretence of allowing them a guard and safe conduct to Coleraine; when they treacherously fell on them by the way, and inhumanly murdered them.

The like horrid barbarities with those we have particularized, were practised on the wretched protestants in almost all parts of the kingdom; and, when an estimate was afterward made of the number massacred by papists, it amounted to 150,000.

These desperate wretches, flushed and grown insolent with success, soon got possession of the castle of Newry, where the king's stores and ammunition were lodged; and, with as little difficulty, made themselves masters of Dundalk. They afterward took the town of Ardee, where they murdered all the protestants, and then proceeded to Drogheda. The garrison of Drogheda was in no condition to sustain a siege; notwithstanding which, as often as the Irish renewed their attacks, they were vigorously repulsed, by a very unequal number of the king's forces, and a few faithful protestant citizens, under sir Henry Tichborne, the governor, assisted by the lord viscount Moore. The siege of Drogheda began on the 30th of November, 1541, and held till the 4th of March, 1642, when sir Phelim O'Neal, and the Irish miscreants under him, were forced to retire.

In the meantime 10,000 troops were sent from Scotland to the relief of the remaining protestants in Ireland, which being properly divided into various parts of the kingdom, happily suppressed the power of the Irish savages and the protestants, for several years, lived in tranquility.

EVENTS IN THE REIGN OF CHARLES II.

Burning of the City of London.

Stimulated by revenge, and prompted by superstition, the papists unceasingly turned their thoughts to obtain their long-wished-for purpose, the overthrow of the protestant religion, and the destruction of its adherents.

Having failed in several efforts, they thought of a scheme for destroying the capital of the kingdom, which they flattered themselves might greatly facilitate their intentions: but although, unhappily, their diabolical scheme in some measure took place, yet it was not productive of the consequences they hoped and wished for. A great part of the city was, indeed, destroyed; the melancholy particulars of which we shall copy from the London Gazette, published at the time:

"*Whitehall, September* 8, 1666.

"On the second instant, at 1 o'clock in the morning, there happened to break out a sad and deplorable fire, at a baker's, in Pudding-lane, near Fish-street, which falling out at that hour of the night, and in a quarter of the town so close built with wooden pitched houses, spread itself so far before day, and with such distraction to the inhabitants and neighbours, that care was not taken for the timely preventing the further diffusion of it, by pulling down houses, as ought to have been; so that this lamentable fire, in a short time, became too big to be mastered by any engines, or working near it. It fell out most unhappily too, that a violent easterly wind fomented it, and kept it burning all that day, and the night following, spreading itself up to Gracechurch-street, and downward from Cannon-street to the water-side, as far as the Three Cranes in the Vintry.

"The people, in all parts about it, were distracted by the vastness of it, and their particular care to carry away their goods. Many attempts were made to prevent the spreading of it, by pulling down houses, and making great intervals, but all in vain, the fire seizing upon the timber and rubbish, and so continuing itself, even through those spaces, and raging in a bright flame all Monday and Tuesday, notwithstanding his majesty's own, and his royal highness' indefatigable and personal pains to apply all possible remedies to prevent it, calling upon, and helping the people with their regiments, and a great number of nobility and gentry unweariedly assisting therein, for which they were requited with a thousand blessings from the poor distressed people.

"By the favour of God, the wind slackened a little on Tuesday night, and the flames meeting with brick buildings at the Temple, by little and little it was observed to lose its force on that side, so that on Wednesday morning we began to hope well, and his royal highness never despairing, or slackening his personal care, wrought so well that day, assisted in some parts by the lords of the council before and behind it, that a stop was put to it at the Temple church; near Holborn bridge; Pie-corner; Aldersgate; Cripple-gate; near the lower end of Coleman street; at the end of Basinghall-street, by the Postern; at the upper end of Bishops gate-street, and Leadenhall-street; at the standard in Cornhill; at the church in Fenchurch street; near Clothworkers'-hall in Mincing lane; at the middle of Mark-lane, and at the Tower-dock.

"On Thursday, by the blessing of God, it was wholly beat down and extinguished; but so as that evening it unhappily burst out again afresh at the Temple, by the falling of some sparks (as is supposed) upon a pile of wooden buildings; but his royal highness, who watched there that whole night in person, by the great labours and diligence used, and especially by applying powder to blow up the houses about it, before day most happily mastered it.

"His majesty then sat hourly in council, and ever since hath continued making rounds about the city, in all parts of it where the danger and mischief was the greatest, till this morning that he hath sent his grace the duke of Albemarle, whom he hath sent for to assist him on this great occasion, to put his happy and successful hand to the finishing this memorable deliverance."

During the progress of this dreadful conflagration, orders were given for pulling down various houses in the Tower of London, in order to preserve the grand magazine of gunpowder in that fortress, to the preservation of which, however, the violent easterly wind contributed more than the precaution.

Many thousands of citizens, who, by this calamity, were deprived of their habitations, retired to the fields, destitute of all necessaries, and exposed to the inclemency of the weather, till a sufficient number of tents or huts could be erected for their reception. In order to mitigate the distresses of the people, a great quantity of naval bread was distributed among them, and a proclamation issued commanding the magistrates of the city to encourage the bringing in of all kinds of provisions.

By the certificate of James Moore and Ralph Gatrix, the surveyors appointed to examine the ruins, it appeared that this dreadful fire overran 436 acres of ground within the walls, and almost 100 out houses, 89 parish churches, beside chapels; and that only 11 parish churches within the walls were left standing.

To this account of its devastations may also be added the destruction of St. Paul's cathedral, Guildhall, the Royal Exchange, Custom-house, and Blackwell hall; many hospitals and libraries, 52 halls of the city companies, and a great number of other stately edifices; together with those of the city gates, and the prisons of Newgate, the Fleet, the Poultry and Wood-street Compters; the loss of which, by the best calculation, amounted to upwards of ten millions sterling. Yet, notwithstanding all this destruction, only six persons lost their lives.

Various were the conjectures of the people on the cause of this singular calamity; at first some imagined it to be casual, but, from a train of circumstances, it afterward appeared to have been done from the malice and horrid contrivances of the papists. Several suspected persons were taken into custody ; but, although there were very strong presumptions, no posi tive proof being produced against them, they were discharged.

Life and Death of Sir Edmundbury Godfrey.

This great and good man was descended from an ancient and respecta ble family in the county of Kent, who gave him an education suitable to his birth and quality. He received the first rudiments of learning at West minster school, and finished his studies at the university of Oxford. In order to improve himself still more, he travelled into foreign countries, and, during his residence there, was as careful to avoid immorality as he was to escape from the delusion of the false worship practised there. From the sound principles of religion and virtue which he had imbibed from his parents and instructors, he was sufficiently armed against both ; and returned home rather informed than corrupted.

On his return to England, he entered himself a member of Gray's Inn, where, by diligent application, he soon acquired a competent knowledge of the laws of his country. His intention was, to have obtained a situation at the bar ; but having a natural defect in his hearing, he thought it would be an impediment to his progress; and, therefore, after continuing some years at that Inn, he left it, and retired to his friends in the country.

Being naturally of an active disposition, he soon became weary of soli tude, and determined to undertake some enterprise, in which his time might be usefully employed. He accordingly left the country, and came to London, where he entered into partnership with a person who kept a wood-wharf near Dowgate.

After prosecuting this business for awhile, with profit to himself as wel as to the community in general, his integrity was noticed by some persons of distinction, who recommended him to the king ; by whom he was ap pointed a magistrate for the city of Westminster, in which capacity he served until his death.

As a city magistrate, perhaps no man was ever more distinguished for industry, integrity, and every other virtue, that could render him worthy of esteem ; for in addition to his other acts of benevolence and charity, he remained in London during the awful visitation of the plague in 1777, and, at the eminent hazard of his own life, was found constantly at his post, as the guardian both of the living and the dead. There are many instances still on record of his heroic conduct during that awful period, which serve to elevate his name among the noblest benefactors of mankind.

From a strict attention to business, and the natural fatigue consequent thereupon, sir Edmundbury Godfrey, in the year 1678, became so reduced by bodily illness, that his life was apparently in danger. He was therefore advised by his physicians to go to Montpelier, in France, the air of that country being esteemed an almost certain restorative to decayed constitutions. He accordingly took their advice, and after residing there a few months, returned to England greatly benefited by his excursion.

But the pains he thus took to preserve that life, which had hitherto been so remarkably beneficial to great numbers of his fellow creatures, were at last by a most horrid plot which was discovered soon after his return, and which exposed him to an untimely and cruel death.

This horrid conspiracy was formed by the papists, and is distinguished in the annals of England by the name of the POPISH PLOT. It was said that the design of the conspiracy was to kill the king, to subvert the government, to extirpate the protestant religion, and to establish popery. The authors and promoters of the plot were said to be the pope and cardinals, the Romish, French, Spanish and English Jesuits, the seminary priests in England, who at this time came over in great numbers, and several popish lords, and others of that party. The duke of York himself was deeply suspected of being concerned in it, except that part of killing the king; and that point excepted, the king himself was supposed to have favoured the conspiracy. The article of taking off the king appeared to be only the project of a part of the conspirators, to make way for the duke of York to ascend the throne, who was more forward, active, and less fearful than the king, and consequently more likely to bring the grand design of the conspiracy, the changing of the government and religion, to a speedier conclusion.

The chief discoverer of this conspiracy was one Titus Oates, who had formerly been a clergyman of the church of England, but had now reconciled himself to the church of Rome, or at least pretended so to do, and entered into the number of the English seminarists at St. Omer's. He also went into Spain, and was admitted to the counsels of the Jesuits. By these means he became acquainted with all the secret designs that were carrying on, in order to establish popery in this nation; and then returning to England, he digested the several matters he had heard into a narrative, and by the means of Dr. Tonge, a city divine, got a copy of it delivered to the king, who referred him to the lord treasurer Danby.

These two informers, finding the king did not take much notice of their discovery, resolved to communicate it to the parliament; previous to which Oates went and made oath of the truth of the narrative before sir Edmundbury Godfrey, leaving one copy of it with him, and reserving another for himself.

The affair having now taken wind, it was resolved to bring it before the council, who accordingly sat twice in a day for a considerable period to examine into it; and Tonge and Oates had lodgings assigned them in Whitehall, with a handsome allowance to each for their maintenance, and a guard for the security of their persons.

On their informations several persons were apprehended, particularly one Wakeman, the queen's physician, and Coleman, the duke of York's secretary. In the latter's house were found several letters which seemed to concur with Oates' testimony, and gave great weight to what he advanced. This, with the murder of sir Edmundbury Godfrey soon after, who had taken Oates' oath to his narrative, confirmed the people in their belief of the plot.

Sir Edmundbury Godfrey had been remarkably active in his office against the papists, to whom his murder was immediately ascribed; and the truth was confirmed by the evidence of Bedloe and Prance, the latter of whom deposed, that, "After sir Edmundbury had several days been dogged by the papists, they at last accomplished their wicked design, on Saturday, October 12, 1678, and under pretence of a quarrel, which they knew his care for the public peace would oblige him to prevent, about 9 o'clock at night, as he was going home, got him into the Water-Gate at Somerset-House. When he was thus trepanned in, and got out of hearing from the street, toward the lower end of the yard, Green, one of the assassins, threw a twisted handkerchief round his neck, and drew him behind the rails, when three or four more of them immediately falling on him, there they throttled him; and lest that should not be enough, punched and kicked him on the breast, as sufficiently appeared, when his body was found, by the marks upon it; and lest he should not be yet dead enough, another of them, Girald, or Fitzgerald, would have run him through, but was hindered by the rest, lest the blood should have discovered them. But Green, to make sure work, wrung his neck round, as it was found afterward on the inspection of the surgeons.

"For the disposal of the body, they all carried it up into a little chamber of Hill's, another of the murderers, who had been, or was, Dr. Godwin's man, where it lay till Monday night, when they removed it into another room, and thence back again till Wednesday, when they carried him out in a sedan about 12 o'clock, and afterward upon a horse, with Hill behind him, to support him, till they got to Primrose-Hill, or, as it is called by some, Green-Bury-Hill, near a public house, called the White House, and there threw him into a ditch, with his gloves and cane on a bank near him, and his own sword run through him; on purpose to persuade the world he had killed himself. Very cunningly making choice of a place to lay him where they might both think he would be some time concealed, and near where he had been seen walking the same day." The body was accordingly found there several days afterward.

Thus died that good man, and wise magistrate, sir Edmundbury Godfrey, who fell a martyr to the diabolical machinations of some wicked and blood-thirsty papists. His body was interred with great solemnity in the church of St. Martin-in-the-Fields; and he was attended to the grave by an incredible number of lamenting spectators.

This horrid conspiracy engaged the whole attention of the parliament, who addressed the king to remove all popish recusants out of the cities of London and Westminster, and from within ten miles of them: and in another address they besought his majesty to take care of his royal person; that he would command the lord-mayor and lieutenancy of London to appoint proper guards of the trained bands during the sitting of parliament; and that the lords-lieutenants of the counties of Middlesex and Surry should appoint sufficient guards in Middlesex, Westminster, and Southwark.

The houses attended to no other business but this plot; and so warmly did they enter into the matter, that several days they sat from morning till night examining Oates, and other witnesses. At length, on the 31st of October, 1678, they unanimously resolved, "That the lords and commons are of opinion, that there hath been, and still is, a damnable and hellish plot, contrived and carried on by popish recusants, for assassinating and murdering the king, for subverting the government, and rooting out and destroying the protestant religion."

These opinions were further confirmed by a circumstance which happened soon after; for, about the beginning of May, 1679, the citizens discovered a plot, formed by the Jesuits and other papists, for destroying the city of London a second time by fire. One Elizabeth Oxley, a servant in Petter-lane, having set fire to her master's house, was apprehended and committed to prison, when she confessed the fact, and declared that she had been hired to do it by one Stubbs, a papist, who was to give her five pounds as a reward.

Stubbs being immediately secured, confessed that he had persuaded her to it; but that he himself had been prevailed on by one father Gifford, his confessor, who, he said, assured him that instead of its being a sin, it would be a great service to the "Holy Catholic Church," to burn and destroy all the houses of heretics; saying, that he had conversed many times on that affair with Gifford, and two Irishmen. And the maid and Stubbs jointly declared that the papists intended to rise in London, in expectation of being assisted by a powerful army from France.

Soon after this, a prosecution being commenced against several of the Jesuits who were concerned in the plot, five of them were convicted and executed; and several lords being also impeached of the same, were committed prisoners to the tower.

The parliament meeting on the 21st of October, the lord Stafford, who was one of those impeached of being concerned in the popish plot, was brought to his trial; and being convicted of high-treason, received sentence to be hanged and quartered. The king, however, as is usual in such cases, remitted this sentence, and left Stafford to be beheaded; but the zeal of the two sheriffs of London started a doubt as to the king's power of mitigating the sentence in any part. They proposed queries on this point to both houses; the peers deemed them superfluous; and the commons, apprehensive lest an examination into these queries might produce the opportunity of Stafford's escape, expressed themselves satisfied with the manner of execution, by severing his head from his body.

The Meal-tub Plot.

In a very short time after the before-mentioned conspiracies, a sham plot was discovered to have been formed by the papists, in order to throw off the odium they had justly acquired, and to place it on the presbyterians.

One Dangerfield, a fellow who had suffered almost every punishmen the law could inflict on the most abandoned, was tutored for the purpose.

The catholic party released him out of Newgate, where he was impri soned for debt, and set him to work. He pretended to have been privy to a design for destroying the king and the royal family, and converting the government into a commonwealth. The king and his brother countenanced the tale, and rewarded him for his discovery, with a sum of money; but certain papers which he produced in evidence of his assertions appearing upon his examination to be forged by himself, he was pu under an arrest. All his haunts were ordered to be searched; and in t house of one Mrs. Collier, a midwife, a Roman catholic, and an intimat acquaintance of his, was found the model of the pretended plot, written very fair, neatly made up in a book, tied with a riband, and concealed in a meal-tub, from whence it acquired the name of the MEAL-TUB PLOT.

Dangerfield, finding himself thus detected, applied to the lord-mayor made an ample confession of the imposition, and discovered his em ployers.

The detection of this contrivance so irritated the populace in genera against the papists, that it added much to the whimsical solemnity of burning the effigy of the pope; for, on the 17th of November, the anniversary of queen Elizabeth's accession to the throne, the ceremony was performed with the most singular pomp and magnificence; and every mark was shown by the people, that could demonstrate their abhorrence of popery.

Thus were all these diabolical schemes, projected by the papists to injure the protestants, happily rendered abortive; but we must not quit this subject, without taking notice, that, on the accession of James II. to the English throne, the famous Titus Oates, who was so materially concerned in the discovery of the popish plot, was tried for perjury on two indictments; and being found guilty, was sentenced to be fined one thousand marks for each; to be whipped on two different days, from Aldgate to Newgate, and from Newgate to Tyburn; to be imprisoned during life, and to stand on the pillory five times every year. He made the most solemn appeals to heaven, and the strongest protestations of the veracity of his testimony. The whipping was so severe, that he swooned several times, and it was evidently the design of the court to have put him to death by that punishment. He was, however, enabled, by the care of his friends, to recover; and he lived till William III. came to the throne, when he was released from his confinement, and had a pension allowed him of 100l. per annum.

EVENTS IN THE REIGN OF JAMES II.

Account of the Insurrection, Defeat, and Execution of the Duke of Monmouth, the Earl of Argyle, and their followers.

THE duke of York having ascended the throne by the title of James II., soon began to manifest his tyrannical intentions against religion and liberty. He seemed inclined to place himself and his government entirely in the hands of the Jesuits; and such was his zeal for the Roman catholic religion, that pope Innocent XI., to whom he had sent lord Castlemaine as ambassador, cautioned him not to be too hasty. While James was indulging himself in the prospect of subverting the established religion, the duke of Monmouth, who, on the death of lord Russel, had gone over to Flanders, trusting to the regard he had always enjoyed among the protestants, formed the design of bringing about a revolution. To the immediate execution of this rash and unhappy enterprise, which his own judgment led him to wish deferred, he was chiefly instigated by the active spirit of the earl of Argyle. Having prepared a squadron of six vessels, badly manned, and very ill supplied, they divided, and with three each, sailed for the places of their destination: Monmouth landed at Lyme, in Dorsetshire, on the 11th of June 1685, with 150 men, and marching thence to Taunton, his army increased to 6000; beside which, he was obliged to dismiss great numbers for want of arms.

In the meanwhile, the earl of Argyle had landed in Argyleshire, where he found the militia prepared to oppose him. But being immediately joined by his brave vassals and partisans, he penetrated into the western counties, hoping to be joined by the disaffected covenanters. But his little squadron being captured, and his brave followers having lost their baggage in a morass in Renfrewshire, were necessitated to disperse for immediate preservation. The unfortunate nobleman assumed a disguise, but he was taken by two peasants, and conducted to Edinburgh, where he was executed, without a trial, on an unjust sentence which had been formerly pronounced on him.

The news of the defeat of this nobleman no sooner reached the duke of Monmouth than he sunk into despondency. He now saw the temerity of his undertaking, and endeavoured to provide for his safety and that of his army. He therefore retreated to Bridgewater, the royal army being in his rear. Here he ascended a tower, from whence viewing the army of lord Feversham, his hopes again revived, while he meditated an attack. He made the most skilful arrangements, but committing an important post to lord Grey, that dastardly soldier betrayed him, and, notwithstanding the courage of his troops, who repulsed the forces of the king, and drove them from the field, a want of ammunition prevented them from pursuing their advantages, the royal troops rallied, dispersed their adversaries, and slew about 1500 of them in the battle and pursuit.

Monmouth, seeing the conflict hopeless, galloped off the field, and continued his flight until his horse sunk under him, when the unfortunate prince wandered on foot for a few miles, and then sunk down, overcome with hunger and fatigue. He was shortly afterward discovered, lying in a ditch, almost senseless. He burst into tears when seized by his enemies, and being still anxious to preserve his life, for the sake of his wife and children, wrote very submissively to James, conjuring him to spare the issue of a brother who had always shown himself firmly attached to his interest. The king finding him thus depressed, admitted him into his presence, with the hope of extorting from him a discovery of his accomplices. Monmouth, however, scorned to purchase life at the price of so much infamy. Finding that all efforts to excite the compassion of James were fruitless, he prepared himself for death, and on the 15th of July was brought to the scaffold. Previously to his death, he said that he repented of his sins, and was more particularly concerned for the blood that had been spilt on his account. He conjured the executioner to spare him the second blow; but the man, whose heart was unfit for his office, struck him feebly, on which the duke, gently turning himself round, cast a look of tender reproach upon him, and then again meekly submitted his head to the axe; the executioner struck him again and again to no purpose, and then threw aside the axe, declaring that he was incapable of completing the bloody task. The sheriff, however, obliged him to renew the attempt, and by two blows more the head was severed from the body.

After the defeat of the duke of Monmouth, thirty prisoners were immediately tried and executed. Most of the others, terrified with this example, pleaded guilty; and no less than two hundred and ninety-two received sentence at Dorchester. Of these, eighty were executed. In Exeter two hundred and forty three were tried, of whom a great number were condemned and executed. Beside those who were butchered by the military commanders, two hundred and fifty-one are computed to have fallen by the hand of justice. The whole country was strewed with the heads and limbs of traitors. Every village, almost, beheld the dead carcase of a wretched inhabitant. And all the rigours of justice, unabated by any appearance of clemency, were fully displayed to the people by the inhuman Jefferys, the then chief justice.

Of all the executions during this dismal period, the most remarkable were those of Mrs. Gaunt and Lady Lisle, who had been accused of harbouring traitors. Mrs. Gaunt was an anabaptist noted for her beneficence, which she extended to persons of all professions and persuasions. One of the rebels, knowing her humane disposition, had recourse to, and was concealed by her. Hearing of the proclamation, which offered an indemnity and rewards to such as discovered criminals, he betrayed his benefactress, and bore evidence against her. He received a pardon, as a recompense for his treachery; she was burned alive for her charity, on the 23d of October, 1685.

Lady Lisle was widow of one of the regicides, who had enjoyed great favour and authority under Cromwell, who, having fled, after the restoration, to Lauzanne, in Switzerland, was there assassinated by three Irish ruffians, who hoped to make their fortune by this piece of service. His widow was now prosecuted for harbouring two rebels the day after the battle of Sedgemoor; and Jefferys pushed on the trial with unrelenting violence. In vain did the aged prisoner plead that these criminals had been put into no proclamation; had been convicted by no verdict; that it appeared not that she was acquainted with the guilt of the persons, or had heard of their joining the rebellion of Monmouth; that though she might be obnoxious on account of her family, it was well known that her heart was ever loyal, and that no person in England had shed more tears for the tragical event, in which her husband had unfortunately borne too great a share; and that the same principles which she herself had embraced, she had instilled into her son, and had sent him to fight against those rebels whom she was now accused of harbouring. Though these arguments did not move Jefferys, they had influence on the jury. Twice they seemed inclined to bring in a favourable verdict: they were as often sent back with menaces and reproaches, and at last were constrained to give sentence against the prisoner. And notwithstanding all applications for pardon, she was shortly after executed at Winchester.

EVENTS IN THE REIGN OF WILLIAM III.

Siege of Londonderry.

After James II. had abandoned England, he maintained a contest for some time in Ireland, where he did all in his power to carry on that persecution which he had been happily prevented from persevering in, in England: accordingly, in a parliament held at Dublin, in 1689, great numbers of the protestant nobility, clergy, and gentry of Ireland, were attainted of high treason. The government of the kingdom was, at that time, invested in the earl of Tyrconnel, a bigoted papist, and an inveterate enemy to the protestants. By his orders they were again persecuted in various parts of the kingdom. And had it not been for the resolution and bravery of the garrisons in Londonderry, and Inniskillen, there had not one place remained for refuge to the distressed protestants in the whole kingdom; but all must have been given up to James, and to the popish party that governed him.

The remarkable siege of Londonderry was opened on the 18th of April, 1689, by 20,000 papists, the flower of the Irish army. The city was not properly circumstanced to sustain a siege, the defenders consisting of a body of undisciplined protestants, who had fled thither for shelter, and half a regiment of lord Mountjoy's soldiers, with the inhabitants, making in all only 7361 fighting men.

The besieged hoped, at first, that their stores of corn, and other necessaries, would be sufficient; but by the continuance of the siege their wants increased; and these at last became so heavy, that for a considerable time before the siege was raised, a pint of coarse barley, a small quantity of greens, a few spoonsful of starch, with a very moderate portion of horse-flesh, were reckoned a week's provision for a soldier. At length to such extremities were they reduced, they ate dogs, cats, and mice; and it is remarkable, that when their long-expected succours arrived from England, they were upon the point of being reduced to this alternative, either to preserve their existence by eating each other, or attempting to fight their way through the Irish, which must have infallibly produced their destruction. These succours were brought by the ship Mountjoy, of Derry, and the Phœnix, of Coleraine, at which time they had only nine lean horses left, with a pint of meal to each man. By hunger, and the fatigues of war, their 7361 fighting men were reduced to 4300, one fourth part of whom were rendered unserviceable.

As the calamities of the besieged were very great, so likewise were the terrors and sufferings of their protestant friends and relations; all of whom were forcibly driven from the country 30 miles round, and inhumanly reduced to the sad necessity of continuing some days and nights, without food or covering, before the walls of the town; and were thus exposed to the continual fire both of the Irish army from without, and the shot of their friends from within. But the succours from England happily arriving, put an end to their affliction; and the siege was raised on the 31st of July, having been continued upward of three months.

The day before the siege of Londonderry was raised, the Inniskilleners engaged a body of 6000 Irish Roman catholics, at Crown Castle, of whom near 5000 were slain. This, with the defeat at Londonderry, so much dispirited the papists, that they gave up all further attempts at that time to persecute the protestants.

In the year following, 1690, the Irish who had taken up arms in favour of James II., were totally defeated by William III.; and that monarch, before he left the country, reduced them to a state of subjection, in which they long continued, at least so far as to refrain from open violence, although they were still insidiously engaged in increasing their power and influence.

EVENTS IN FRANCE.

Persecutions of the Protestants in the south of France, in the years 1814 and 1820.

The persecution of this protestant part of France had continued with very little intermission from the revocation of the edict of Nantes, by Louis XIV., till a very short period previous to the commencement of the late French revolution. In the year 1785, M. Rebaut, St. Etienne and the celebrated La Fayette were among the first persons who interested themselves with the court of Louis XVI., in removing the scourge of persecution from this injured people, the inhabitants of the south of France.

Such was the opposition on the part of the catholics and the courtiers, that it was not till the end of the year 1790, that the protestants were freed from their alarms. Previously to this, the catholics at Nismes in particular, had taken up arms: Nismes then presented a frightful spectacle; armed men ran through the city, fired from the corners of the streets, and attacked all they met with swords and forks. The citizens that fled were arrested by the catholics upon the roads, and obliged to give proofs of their religion before their lives were granted. The atrocities provoking the troops to unite in defence of the people, a terrible vengeance was retaliated upon the catholic party that had used arms, which, with other circumstances, especially the toleration exercised by Napoleon Buonaparte, kept them down completely till the year 1814, when the unexpected return of the ancient government rallied them all once more round the old banners.

This was known at Nismes on the 13th of April, 1814. In a quarter of an hour, the white cockade was seen in every direction, the white flag floated on all the public buildings, on the splendid monuments of antiquity, and even on the tower of Magne, beyond the city walls. The protestants were among the first to unite in the general joy, and to send in their adhesion to the senate and the legislative body; and several of the protestant departments sent addresses to the throne; but unfortunately, the boldness and fury of the sixteenth century rapidly succeeded the intelligence and philanthropy of the nineteenth. A line of distinction was traced between men of different religious opinions: the difference of religion was now to govern every thing else; and even catholic domestics who had served protestants with zeal and affection, began to neglect their duties, or to perform them ungraciously. The bigots of Nismes even succeeded in procuring an address to be presented to the king, stating that there ought to be in France but one God, one King, and one Faith. In this they were imitated by the catholics of several towns.

Napoleon's return from the Isle of Elba.

Soon after this event, the duke d'Angoleme was at Nismes, and remained there some time; but even his influence was insufficient to bring about a reconciliation between the catholics and the protestants of that city. During the hundred days between Napoleon's return from the Isle of Elba and his final downfall, not a single life was lost in Nismes, not a single house was pillaged: only four of the most notorious disturbers of the peace were punished, or rather prevented from doing mischief; and even this was not an act of the protestants, but the *arrete* of the catholic prefect, announced every where with the utmost publicity.

The Catholic arms of Beaucaire.

In May 1815, a federative association similar to those of Lyons, Grenoble, Paris, Avignon, and Montpelier, was desired by many persons at

Nismes; but this federation terminated here after an ephemeral existence of fourteen days. In the meanwhile a large party of catholic zealots were in arms at Beaucaire, who soon pushed their patrols so near the walls of Nismes 'as to alarm the inhabitants.' These catholics applied to the English of Marseilles for assistance, and obtained the grant of 1000 muskets, 10,000 cartouches, &c. General Gilly, however, was soon sent against these partisans, who prevented them from coming to extremes by granting them an armistice; and yet when Louis XVIII. had returned to Paris after the expiration of Napoleon's reign of a hundred days, and peace and party spirit seemed to have been subdued, even at Nismes, bands from Beaucaire joined Trestaillon in that city, to glut the vengeance they had so long premeditated. General Gilly had left the department several days: the troops of the line left behind had taken the white cockade, and waited further orders, while the royal commissioners had only to proclaim the cessation of hostilities, and the co uple e establishment of the king's authority. No commissioners appeared, no despatches arrived to calm and regulate the public mind; but toward evening the advanced guard of the banditti, to the amount of several hundreds, entered the city, undesired, but unopposed. As they marched, without order or discipline, armed with muskets, sabres, forks, pistols, and pruning hooks, intoxicated with wine, and stained with the blood of the protestants whom they had murdered on their route, they presented a most hideous and appalling spectacle. In the open place in the front of the barracks, this banditti was joined by the city armed mob, headed by Jacques Dupont, commonly called Trestaillon. To save the effusion of blood, the garrison consented to capitulate, and marched out and defenceless; but when about fifty had passed, the rabble commenced a fire on their unprotected victims; nearly all were killed or wounded, and but very few could re-enter the yard before the garrison gates were again closed. These were forced in an instant, and all were massacred who could not climb over roofs or leap into the adjoining gardens. In a word, death met them in every place and in every shape, and this catholic massacre rivalled in cruelty the crimes of the September massacre of Paris, and the Jacobinical butcheries of Lyons and Avignon. It was marked, not only by the fervour of the Revolution, but by the artillery of the legion, and will long remain a blot upon the history of the second restoration.

Nismes now exhibited a most awful scene of outrage and carnage. Though many of the protestants had fled, the barbarities committed were too numerous for us to record; and many of the actions of this band of assassins were too gross for rehearsal in our pages.

Interference of Government against the Protestants.

M. Bernis, extraordinary royal Commissioner, in consequence of these abuses, issued a proclamation which reflects disgrace on the authority from which it emanated "Considering," it said, "that the residence of citizens in places foreign to their domicile can only be prejudicial to the commerce they have left, and to those to which they have repaired, it is ordered that those inhabitants who have quitted their residence since the commencement of July, return home by the 28th at the latest, otherwise they shall be deemed accomplices of the evil-disposed persons who disturb the public tranquillity, and their property shall be placed under provisional sequestration.

The fugitives had sufficient inducements to return to their hearths, without fear of sequestration. They were more anxious to embrace their fathers, mothers, wives, and children, and to resume their ordinary occupations, than M. Bernis could be to ensure their return. But this denouncing men as criminals who fled for safety from the sabres of assassins, was adding oil to the fire of persecution. On this occasion it was remarked that "The system of specious and deceptive proclamations was perfectly understood, and had long been practised in Languedoc; it was now too late to persecute the protestants simply for their religion. Even in the good times of Louis XIV. there was public opinion enough to make that arch tyrant have recourse to the meanest stratagems."

Royal Decree in favour of the Persecuted.

At length the decree of Louis XVIII., which annulled all the extraordinary powers conferred either by the king, the princes, or subordinate agents, was received at Nismes, and the laws were now to be administered by the regular organs, and a new prefect arrived to carry them into effect; but in spite of proclamations, the work of destruction, stopped for a moment, was not abandoned, but soon renewed with fresh vigour and effect. If murder some time after became less frequent for a few days, pillage and forced contributions were actively enforced. Desolation reigned in the sanctuary, and in the city. Those protestants who remained were deprived of all their civil and religious rights. The protestant deacons who had the charge of the poor were all scattered. Of five pastors only two remained; one of these was obliged to change his residence, and could only venture to administer the consolations of religion, or perform the functions of his ministry, under cover of the night. Hundreds were dragged to prison without even so much as a *written order*; and an Official Newspaper, bearing the title of the *Journal du Gard*, represented the suffering protestants as "Crocodiles, only weeping from rage and regret that they had no more victims to devour; as persons who had surpassed Danton, Marat, and Robespierre in doing mischief: and as having prostituted their daughters to the garrison to gain it over to Napoleon." An extract from this article, stamped with the crown and the arms of the Bourbons, was hawked about the streets, and the vender was adorned with the medal of the police.

Monstrous outrage upon Females.

At Nismes there is a large basin near the fountain, where numbers of women wash their clothes, and beat them with heavy pieces of wood in the shape of battledoors. This spot became the scene of the most shameful and indecent practices. The catholic rabble turned the women's petticoats over their heads, and so fastened them as to continue their exposure, and their subjection to a newly-invented species of chastisement for nails being placed in the wood of the *battoirs* in the form of *fleur-de-lis*, they beat them till the blood streamed from their bodies, and their cries rent the air. The surgeons who attended on those women who were dead, can attest, by the marks of their wounds, the agonies which they must have endured, which, however horrible, is most strictly true.

Outrages committed in the Villages, &c.

We now quit Nismes to take a view of the conduct of the persecutors in the surrounding country. At the village of Milhaud, near Nismes, the inhabitants were frequently forced to pay large sums to avoid being pillaged. In the canton of Vauvert, where there was a consistorial church, 80,000 franks were extorted. In the communes of Beauvoisin and Generac similar excesses were committed by a handful of licentious men, under the eye of the catholic mayor, and to the cries of "Vive le Roi." St. Gilles was the scene of the most unblushing villany. The protestants, the most wealthy of the inhabitants, were disarmed, while their houses were pillaged. It would be wearisome to read the lists of the crimes that occurred during many months. In fact, to continue the relation of the scenes that took place in the different departments of the south of France, would be little better than a repetition of those we have already described, excepting a change of names. These shameful persecutions continued till after the dissolution of the Chamber of Deputies at the close of the year 1816. No excuse can be made for the government, by saying it was not in their power to prevent these excesses, as it is evident that where a government possesses absolute power, such events could not have been prolonged for many months, and even for years, over a vast extent of country, had it not been for the systematic and powerful support of the higher departments of the state.

Interference of the British Government.

To the credit of England, the reports of these cruel persecutions carried on against the protestants in France, produced such a sensation on the part of government as determined them to interfere; and now the persecutors of the protestants made this spontaneous act of humanity and religion the pretext for charging the sufferers with a treasonable correspondence with England; but in this state of their proceedings, to their great dismay, a letter appeared, sent some time before to England by the duke of Wellington, stating "That much information existed on the events of the south."

The ministers of the reformed churches in London, anxious not to be misled, requested one of their brethren to visit the scenes of persecution, and examine with impartiality the nature and extent of the evils they were desirous to relieve. The Rev. Clement Perrot undertook this difficult task, and fulfilled their wishes with a zeal, prudence, and devotedness, above all praise. His return furnished abundant and incontestible proof of a shameful persecution, materials for an appeal to the British parliament, and a printed report which was circulated through the continent, and which first conveyed correct information to the inhabitants of France.

Foreign interference was now found eminently useful; and the declarations of tolerance which it elicited from the French government, as well as the more cautious march of the catholic persecutors, operated as decisive and involuntary acknowledgments of the importance of that interference which some persons at first censured and despised: but though the stern voice of public opinion in England and elsewhere produced a reluctant suspension of massacre and pillage, the murderers and plunderers were still left unpunished, and even caressed and rewarded for their crimes; and while protestants in France suffered the most cruel and degrading pains and penalties for alleged trifling crimes, *catholics*, covered with blood, and guilty of numerous and horrid murders, were acquitted.

Perhaps the virtuous indignation expressed by some of the more enlightened catholics against these abominable proceedings, had no small share in restraining them. Many innocent protestants had been condemned to the galleys, and otherwise punished for supposed crimes, upon the oaths of wretches the most unprincipled and abandoned.

It was not, however, until the injured protestants resorted to arms that a final period was put to the barbarities of the popish miscreants. This attitude apprized these butchers that they could no longer murder with impunity. Every thing now was changed. Those who for four years had filled the breasts of others with terror, now trembled at the effects of the storm which they themselves had raised. The demands of the protestants were moderate. They asked not for revenge, nor indemnification for past losses; they merely stipulated for present safety, and security for the future. Their demands, modest as they were, obtained from the government the adoption of such measures only as secured them for the present. Many of the friends of the protestant cause were fearful that fresh disorders would soon arise, but happily, since the year 1820, no fresh complaints have issued from the south of France on the score of religion

TABLE OF CONTENTS.

CHAPTER IV.

PART II.

CHAPTER I.

CHAPTER II.

CHAPTER III.

CHAPTER IV.

CHAPTER V.

CHAPTER VI.

PART III.

CHAPTER I.

CHAPTER IV.

CHAPTER V.

PART V.

CHAPTER I.

CHAPTER II.

CHAPTER III.

CHAPTER IV.

CHAPTER IX.

LIST OF ENGRAVINGS

THE FARM AND THE FIRESIDE;

OR,

THE ROMANCE OF AGRICULTURE,

BEING

HALF HOURS OF LIFE IN THE COUNTRY, FOR RAINY DAYS AND WINTER EVENINGS.

BY REV. JOHN L. BLAKE, D.D.

AUTHOR OF FARMER'S EVERY-DAY BOOK; THE FARMER AT HOME; AND A
GENERAL BIOGRAPHICAL DICTIONARY.

COMMENDATIONS OF THE PERIODICAL PRESS.

From the Ohio Farmer.

DR. BLAKE is justly regarded as one of the best agricultural writers in the country, and the work before us is one of the most interesting productions of his pen. Its peculiar merit, as a work for the fireside, consists in the variety of its topics, its plain and simple, yet attractive style, its fine engravings, and the interesting romance which the author has thrown around Rural and Agricultural Life. In this respect, "The Farm and the Fireside" is a work well adapted to the youthful mind. We hope it may be extensively read, as it cannot fail to improve the taste and promote inquiry in the most useful and practical of all departments of science

From the New-York Evangelist.

The aim of the author has been to throw over labor, home and agricultural life, their true dignity and charm; to introduce the farmer to the delights and privileges of his lot; to embellish the cares of toil with those kindly sentiments so naturally associated with the country and its employments. It is a pleasant book—one that will enliven the fireside, elevate and purify the thoughts, and, at the same time, impart a great deal of valuable agricultural knowledge. We know not how the natural trains of thought of the farmer could be more aptly met, or more safely and agreeably led, than they are by these brief and varied discussions. The range is as wide as life itself—morals, religion, business, recreation, education, home, wife and daughters—every relation and duty is touched upon, genially and instinctively.

From the New-York Tribune.

We have here another highly instructive and entertaining volume from an author, who had laid the community under large obligations by the enterprise and tact with which he has so frequently catered to the popular taste for descriptions of rural life. Its contents are of a very miscellaneous character, embracing sketches of natural history, accounts of successful farming operations, anecdotes of distinguished characters, singular personal reminiscences, pithy moral reflections, and numerous picturesof household life in the country. No family can add this volume to their collection of books without increasing their sources of pleasure and profit.

From the Northern Christian Advocate.

The venerable author of this work is entitled to the warmest thanks of the public for his numerous and valuable contributions to our literature. He is truly an American classic. We have been conversant with his writings for the last twenty years, and have always found them both useful and entertaining in a high degree. His writings on Agriculture contain much real science, with numerous illustrative incidents, anecdotes, and aphorisms, all in the most lively and pleasing manner. By this means the dry details of farming business are made to possess all the interest of romance. The style is clear, easy, and dignified; the matter instructive, philosophical, and persuasive. This work is an eloquent plea for the noble and independent pursuit of Agriculture.

From the National Magazine.

We return our thanks for the new volume of Dr. Blake, " The Farm and the Fireside, or the Romance of Agriculture, being Half Hours and

Sketches of Life in the Country," a charming title, certainly, and one that smacks of the man as well as of the country. Eschewing the dryness of scientific forms and erudite details, the author presents detached, but most entertaining, and often very suggestive articles on a great variety of topics—from the "Wild Goose" to "Conscience in the Cow,"—from the "Value of Lawyers in a Community" to the "Objections to early Marriages." The book is, in fine, quite unique, and just such a one as the farmer would like to pore over at his fireside on long winter evenings.

From the New-York Recorder.

"The Farm and the Fireside," is a most interesting and valuable work, being a series of Sketches relating to Agriculture and the numerous kindred arts and sciences, interspersed with miscellaneous moral instruction, adapted to the life of the farmer.

From the Germantown Telegraph.

We have looked through this work and read some of the "Sketches," and feel a degree of satisfaction in saying that it possesses decided merit, and will commend itself, wherever known, as a volume of much social interest and entertainment. The sketches comprise "Country Life" generally—some of them are just sufficiently touched with romance to give them additional zest; while others are purely practical, and relate to the farmer's pursuit. We regard it as a valuable book, and are sorry our limits will not admit of bestowing upon it such a notice as it really deserves.

From Harper's New Monthly Magazine.

This work is a collection of miscellaneous sketches on the Romance of Agriculture and Rural Life. Matters of fact, however, are not excluded from the volume, which is well adapted for reading in the snatches of leisure enjoyed at the farmer's fireside.

From the True Democrat.

Dr. Blake's publications are all of a high order, and are doing a most important work towards refining the taste, improving the intellect, and rendering attractive the various branches of Agricultural science. Indeed we know no author who has so successfully blended the romantic, the rural and beautiful with the poetical, the useful, and true, as has Dr. Blake. This is a peculiar feature of all his works. His style is plain, simple, and perspicuous; and, with unusual tact and judgment, he so manages to insinuate himself upon you, that you are at once amused, delighted, and instructed with the subject he is discussing. In this respect he relieves the study of agricultural science from the abstruseness of technical science, and thus renders himself easily comprehended by all classes of readers.

From the New-York Evening Post.

The author's object is to improve the soil through the mind—not so much to place in the hands of farmers the best methods of raising large crops—for these he refers them to Leibig's Agricultural Chemistry, and to treatises of the like description—but to make them feel how useful, agreeable, and ennobling, is the profession of agriculture, and, above all, how profitable the business must become when skilfully and economically carried on. These money-making considerations are, we suspect, the best moral guano that can be applied to the farmer's spiritual soil. The author writes well of the countryman's independence, the good effect of fresh salubrious air upon his health, and the moral influence of his every-day intimacy with nature upon his mind.

"The Farm and the Fireside" is a kind of Bucolical annual—to be read in seasons of leisure—intended for the Phyllises and Chloes, as well as for the Strephons and Lindors. Dr. Blake has enriched it with curious anecdotes of domestic animals, and of the best way of raising and selling them. He describes model-farms, and the large incomes made from them. He expatiates on the advantages of matrimony in rural life, expounds the true theory of choosing a helpmate, discusses the advantages of Sunday-Schools, and recommends neatness of attire and punctuality in bathing. In short, this volume is as diversified in its aspect as the small garden of a judicious cultivator, where, in a limited space, useful cabbages, potatoes, and all the solid esculent greens, grow side by side with choice fruits and pleasant flowers.

JENKINS'

UNITED STATES EXPLORING EXPEDITIONS.

VOYAGE OF THE U. S. EXPLORING SQUADRON under the command of Captain Wilkes, together with explorations and discoveries by D'Urville, Ross, and other navigators and travellers; and an account of the Expedition to the Dead Sea under Lieutenant Lynch. By John S. Jenkins Published by James M. Alden, Auburn, N. Y.

This valuable work has already passed through three large editions. It is beautifully illustrated, and forms a handsome octavo volume of 517 pages. Price, in cloth $2.25; in sheep, $2.50.

The following are some of the numerous flattering encomiums which the work has received from the public press :—

The voyages of D'Urville, Ross and others, the results of which are here described, have been productive of great good, in the extension of geographical and scientific knowledge; and it is every way desirable to possess full information concerning them. The necessary expensiveness of the original works will, no doubt, confine them for the most part, to public libraries, or to the shelves of the wealthy; but, in this volume, we are happy to say, all that is of general interest and adapted to popular reading may be found. Mr. Jenkins has modestly bestowed much labor on his book, and is an adept in the very difficult art of condensation. He has not merely abridged his materials, nor is his work a mere selection from other authors, but bears every mark of being a faithful digest from authentic sources. He is master of a terse style by which he is enabled to avoid all diffuseness and unnecessary circumlocution, and makes his statements with directness and precision. In the present day, when most men must depend on summaries, like the present, for a great part of their knowledge on a large class of subjects, it is a matter of satisfaction to light upon a book, which communicates so much in a cheap and compendious form. We have examined it with some care, and are persuaded that the author has executed his task with discretion and fidelity. Our interest in reading it has increased to the end, and we shut the volume with a sense of *gratification* in having easily acquired much valuable information, and with regret that we have reached the close.—*Old Colony Memorial.*

Now these Exploring Expeditions gave a vast amount of new information, and Mr. Jenkins has sought to present it in an attractive and condensed form. For an accurate knowledge of the places and localities described—of the Pacific and the Jordan—it will be found serviceable. Indeed, Mr. J. has not strictly followed his authors. He has gone outside of them, and obtained information gathered since their works were published—an anachronism for which the reader will not scold him.

To show the extent of Mr. Jenkins' labor, we may mention that the important results and actual information obtained by Lieut. Lynch, in his Dead Sea Expedition, are compressed in some forty-five pages. Yet nothing material is omitted! This is real service rendered. For Lieut. Lynch was verbose to a fault—right in his spirit; bold as an adventurer; truthful; but no writer.

We do not see why such books could not be introduced into our schools, so that while scholars are taught to read, they may be taught, also, living information. What lad is not interested in the Jordan and the Dead Sea? What scholar not anxious to know more about the Pacific and its wonders?—These are living topics. The one is hallowed by every association of the Past, and the other made alive by every interest of the Present. If boys in our schools—the more advanced, certainly—could have put in their hands books more to interest and instruct—could not the intelligent teacher do more towards making them good readers and well-informed men?—"*The Daily True Democrat,*" *Cleveland.*

The account of the United States Exploring Expedition, as detailed by Lieut. Wilkes, though highly interesting, is much too prolix for common readers.—Five octavo volumes require more patience and perseverance than ordinarily fall to the lot of individuals. There are also many young people who have not time to read, nor money to purchase extensive works, but who could profit much by a cheap, judicious synoptical class of publications. This is precisely the course adopted in schools—first rudiments, and then more expansive views in ample volumes. Mr. Jenkins has not barely abridged the works referred to in the title page; he has written, or rather compiled, a new work, making use of the authors referred to, and introducing considerable valuable matter from other sources. The reader may purchase here, for two dollars, all that is of consequence in volumes costing elsewhere from five to ten times that sum.—*Northern Christian Advocate.*

We are indebted to the publisher for a copy of the above work, which gives, in an attractive and condensed form, an account of the expeditions to the Pacific and the South Seas, together with a variety of interesting information in relation to the localities described in its pages. * * * It is a volume of over 500 pages, handsomely executed, and will no doubt meet a quick demand.—*Rochester Democrat*

One of the most valuable and attractive books of the present year. * * * No library can be complete without it.—*American Citizen.*

The comprehensive octavo of Mr. Jenkins will not take the place of its original sources, in the libraries of men of wealth, and of public institutions; yet its sale will by no means be confined to people of very limited means. The mass of book-buyers will prefer it, not only because they will avoid seven-eighths of an expense otherwise incurred, but also thus save an equal proportion of time. The book is not a mere abridgment, nor a selection from the larger works of Wilkes, Lynch, etc.; nor are its gleanings alone from their fields. We are given to understand that every line of the work is from the pen of Mr. Jenkins; and, in his preface, he tells us that a large proportion of his facts is derived from other works than any of the above-mentioned. Some twenty books of travel and history are cited as authorities, besides a "number of others referred to in the notes."

The volume is truly much in little——a summary and closely detailed review of all late explorations in and around the Pacific. In five hundred pages we have the results of many thousand. Some idea of its compression of volumes into a small space may be gained from the fact, that Lieut. Lynch's Expedition to the Dead Sea is thrown into fifty-five pages, in which the "important results and actual information" are given. At this day, when a golden key is not the only one that unlocks the treasures of learning; when all information must be laid before "the people" in an accessible shape; and when, in the bustle of the age, men can only read as they run; we cannot but regard Mr. Jenkins's book, so cheap and compendious, as a precious windfall to the multitude. And we may remark here, that some of our country friends—especially the "poor scholars" who live at a distance from public libraries——would be greatly favored by cheap editions of such works as Ticknor's Spanish Literature, Prescott's works, etc. It would not interfere with the sales of the fine edition, and would rather be an additional source of profit to the authors and copyright-holders.

So far as we have examined it, the volume before us is executed very understandingly. The style is close and perspicuous, and the screws are applied to difficult remark without the sacrifice of picturesque elegance of narration.—*Literary World.*

———

This is a handsome octavo volume of 517 pages, containing, as its title intimates, a compilation of scenes, incidents, adventures, etc., in, and descriptions of, various countries visited by celebrated navigators and travellers. It is divided into two parts. Part one comprises accounts of expeditions to the Pacific and the South Seas; Part two embraces a narrative of the voyage of Lieutenant Lynch to the Dead Sea, together with scenes and incidents in the Holy Land, from the writings of various travellers.

The work contains copious and interesting descriptions of the most important places and localities visited by the several travellers, from whose writings the book has been prepared. The information it contains is arranged in an attractive form, well suited to popular reading, and the work, as a whole, is admirably adapted to impart valuable knowledge.—*Boston Daily Journal.*

BOOKS RECENTLY PUBLISHED BY JAMES M. ALDEN.

We took it up, therefore, expecting to find it a mere compilation, or perhaps, an abridgment from the U. S. Exploring Expeditions of Wilkes and Lynch, with some added references to D'Urville and Ross. Had it been no more than this, it would have been a valuable thing for ordinary readers, since there are few who will buy the weighty volumes of Wilkes, and fewer still who will read them through. Most people, in this age, have too much to do to read quartos. They are obliged to wait till some one shall kindly condense them, and give us the *multum in parvo*.

The author of this volume is just the person for such a work. He understands the public taste, and adapts his labors to the million. In this case, however, he has in the first part travelled far beyond the record of Capt. Wilkes, whose narrative has been merely the thread on which he has strung the facts procured from many other sources. For instance, he has gleaned up everything of interest with regard to the South Sea Islands, from the days of Capt. Cook downward, and interwoven it with the visit of the Exploring Expedition to those Seas. We have, therefore, collected before us, at a view, all that ordinary readers wish. So it is with respect to the South American cities at which the Expedition stopped.

In the second part, Lynch's Expedition to the Dead Sea has been used in the same way, while everything else of interest with regard to that portion of the world, has been gathered from other sources. We have, therefore, in a narrow compass all the really valuable information to be obtained on this subject.—*Albany State Register.*

To the thousands of people in this land who are unable to purchase the several works herein consulted and abbreviated, the labors of Mr Jenkins will be very acceptable. He has done his work well—has made one good book out of a dozen others. —*Western Literary Messenger.*

This volume is an octavo of over 500 pages, printed in beautiful style, and embellished with the finest engravings on wood. It is verily a world in a nutshell—fifty dollars' worth of books in one volume. All that is of real interest and value in the large and expensive works of the United States Exploring Expedition, and Lynch's Expedition to the Dead Sea, together with the results of twenty other books of voyages, travels and history, pertaining to the Pacific, South America, California and New Holland, are here compressed into one volume. We have read some passages with much gratification; and promise ourselves great enjoyment in a more careful perusal. Although every page, every paragraph, teems with information, yet the author has found space for many entertaining anecdotes and pictures of scenery and customs. It is a book which may be read with great interest and profit at every fireside.—*Auburn Daily Advertiser.*

A book like this would possess more worth in the estimation of a reflecting mind, than five hundred of the ordinary light publications of the day.—*Havana Republican.*

LIFE OF JAMES K. POLK.

BY JOHN S. JENKINS,

AUTHOR OF THE "HISTORY OF THE WAR WITH MEXICO," ETC., ETC.

With a fine Portrait, on Steel. One volume, 12mo. 400pp. Price
$1 25, bound in sheep, or embossed muslin.

A succinct biography of the late President, tracing his personal career, from the early struggle that characterized its commencement, through a series of well-earned triumphs, which ended only with the highest reward of patriotic ambition that elevated him to the Presidency of the Republic. The interest inspired by a name intimately associated with a vast enlargement of the national limits, and with a policy whose results promise to transcend in magnitude and impor tance all previous events in our history, renders a faithful account of Mr. Polk's administration highly desirable. The work before us is written with a spirit and enthusiasm that evince a warm admiration for its subject, and will especially commend it to the partizans of Mr. Polk and the policy of his administration.—*Journal of Commerce.*

The author of this work is well known by his pains-taking, and accu-rate biographies of several of our prominent statesmen, and for a well-digested volume on the "War with Mexico." The present work seems to be prepared with the same care and attention, and presents the prominent events of Mr. Polk's life, and the great events of his administration, with clearness and force.—*Buffalo Courier.*

We have perused this volume with more than ordinary interest. The biographer, in the work before us, has done full justice to his illus-trious subject. The prominent acts of his administration are discussed and warmly approved. The work also embraces his annual and veto messages. Altogether, it is a book we should like to see in the hands of every democrat; for not one can rise from its perusal without an increased admiration of the *man*, whom he assisted to elevate to the highest position in our government.—*Geneva Gazette.*

A most valuable and opportune addition to the political history of the country has just been published, under the title of "The Life of James Knox Polk." The author, J. S. Jenkins, Esq., has brought to the task a discriminating industry which has enabled him to compile, in an intelligible manner, all that is valuable and instructive in the stirring political history of the times through which Mr. Polk passed in his ca-reer to the Presidency. To the mere politician this work is an indis-pensable adjunct, while at the same time it is such a history as the American citizen of whatever party can peruse with interest and ad-vantage. The book is dedicated to the Hon. W. L. Marcy, and cannot fail to have an extensive circulation.—*Brooklyn Daily Eagle.*

This is a handsome octavo volume of 895 pages. The work will undoubtedly excite a lively interest in the mind of every American reader. * * * The author of the work has ably discharged his duties as a biographer of Mr. Polk, and the smooth and easy style of the composition will so effectually secure the attention of the reader, that not a sentence will be lost in the perusal of the entire book.—*Auburn Daily Advertiser*

H. W. PARKER'S POEMS.

Some of the best fugitive literature of the day * * * has come from a writer who has just now published a volume of prose and poetry, Mr. H. W. Parker. * * * We have looked it through, and find a degree of excellence in its workmanship, with evidences of pure and strong natural genius which warrant us in commending a sight of it to all watchers of new stars.—*Home Journal.*

There is true poetry in the author's soul, as evinced alike in his metred and prose poems.—*New York Commercial Advertiser.*

The volume before us is an agreeable addition to our light literature. * * * The principal poems in it are fluently written, and are evidently the product of a warm heart, and a lively, playful fancy.—*Literary World.*

Seldom have we read a book whose contents exhibit more freshness, life, and sparkling originality, than the poems now before us. The author shows himself, in his acute taste, glow of feeling, and fervid imagination, the true poet.—*Protestant Churchman.*

Mr. Parker is the most promising young writer we have had for some time. He has the true stuff in him, and has not only the gift of poetry, but the gift of thought and common sense.—*Boston Post.*

A volume of first fruits by a new poet, indicating a pure and elegant mind, a vein of sweet meditative pathos, a lively turn for the humorous, and an eye observant of the picturesque and beautiful in the manifold phases of nature. * * * With a brilliant promise of future excellence, he has not yet attained the full possession of his powers.—*New York Tribune.*

We encounter in its pages many gems of thought and felicities of expression, which prove the writer to possess a poetical capacity of no ordinary character. * * * We shall watch Mr. Parker's literary career with interest. We think we discern in him the evidence of true genius.—*Knickerbocker Magazine.*

There are many good and pleasant things between these covers—a great variety of subjects boldly and ingeniously treated.—*New York Christian Enquirer.*

LIFE

OF

JOHN CALDWELL CALHOUN,

12mo. 457 pp.

WITH A FINE PORTRAIT.

PRICE $1 25, IN SHEEP OR EMBOSSED MUSLIN.

It is dedicated to the people of South Carolina; is written with marked ability, and with a high appreciation of the political principles and character of Mr. Calhoun.—*Charleston Mercury.*

A most valuable accession to the biographical literature of the country.—*New York Daily Globe.*

Mr. Jenkins has performed an acceptable service in preparing such a work as is well calculated to satisfy the present interest in the life and character of the great Carolinian.—*New York Journal of Commerce.*

The book is written in a style that will be admired by the reader and is another evidence that the author's mind has been highly cultivated, and is producing fruits that will speak well, in all future time, for his qualifications as an author.—*Auburn Daily Advertiser.*

It is a volume that can be read with pleasure and profit by all who wish to be well-informed concerning events that have recently occurred. It is neatly printed, and is embellished with a portrait of the man whose life it records. We commend it as a candid and reliable biography, well worthy of being read by all who seek information on which to base their judgment of the man and the administration to which it relates.—*Niagara Democrat.*

The author is a deservedly popular one, having given to the country several excellent and unprejudiced biographies of different distinguished statesmen, including Gen. Jackson, Silas Wright, and John C. Calhoun— all of which have had an extensive sale; and we are certain that the work before us will meet with the same favor.—*Cold Water (Mich.) Sentinel.*

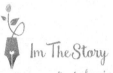

CPSIA information can be obtained
at www.ICGtesting.com
Printed in the USA
BVHW081606120819
555665BV00013B/960/P

9 780371 003794